Tell It Slant

Tell It Slant

Writing and Shaping Creative Nonfiction

Brenda Miller

Western
Washington
University

Suzanne Paola

Western
Washington
University

McGraw
Hill

Boston   Burr Ridge, IL   Dubuque, IA   Madison, WI   New York
San Francisco   St. Louis   Bangkok   Bogotá   Caracas   Kuala Lumpur
Lisbon   London   Madrid   Mexico City   Milan   Montreal   New Delhi
Santiago   Seoul   Singapore   Sydney   Taipei   Toronto

The McGraw-Hill Companies

Higher Education

TELL IT SLANT
Published by McGraw-Hill, an imprint of The McGraw-Hill Companies, Inc. 1221 Avenue of the Americas, New York, NY 10020. Copyright © 2004 by the McGraw-Hill Companies, Inc. All rights reserved. No part of this publication may be reproduced or distributed in any form or by any means, or stored in a database or retrieval system, without the prior written permission of The McGraw-Hill Companies, Inc., including but not limited to, in any network or other electronic storage or transmission, or broadcast for distance learning. Some ancillaries, including electronic and print components, may not be available to customers outside the United States.

This book is printed on acid-free paper.

2 3 4 5 6 7 8 9 0 DOC/DOC 0 9 8 7 6 5 4

ISBN: 0-07-251278-4

Publisher: Steve Debow
Sponsoring editor: Lisa Moore
Development editor: Anne Stameshkin
Marketing manager: David S. Patterson
Production editor: Jennifer Chambliss
Production supervisor: Randy Hurst
Design manager: Cassandra Chu
Interior design: Jeanne Calabrese
Cover design: Bill Stanton
Art editor: Cristin Yancey
Photo research coordinator: Alexandra Ambrose
Photo researcher: LouAnn Wilson
Compositor: Graphic Arts Center—Indianapolis
Text and paper: Printed in 10/12 Garamond on 45# New Era Matte
Printer: RR Donnelley—Crawfordsville, IN
Cover image: ©Fredrik Broden/nonstock

Library of Congress Cataloging-in-Publication Data

Miller, Brenda, creative writer.
    Tell it slant : writing and shaping creative nonfiction / Brenda Miller and Suzanne Paola. — 1st ed.
        p. cm.
    Includes bibliographical references (p.) and index.
    ISBN 0-07-251278-4
    1. English language—Rhetoric. 2. Creative writing. 3. Report writing.
I. Paola, Suzanne. II. Title

PE1408.M548 2003
808'.042—dc21

2003051377

www.mhhe.com

To Savannah and Madrona

Contents

PART IV Anthology

Preface
How To Use This Book

Breath Control: The Fine Art of Creative Nonfiction

Have you ever seen hand-blown glass? We—Suzanne and Brenda—live in an area renowned for its glassblowing. Most stores here carry samples of this art, ranging from simple drinking cups to lavish branching chandeliers. These artworks shimmer, alive with light and color, beautiful in themselves. They reflect the environment in which they're placed, holding a piece of the world up to an exquisite and clarifying mirror.

The essence of fine glassblowing is breath control. Learning breath control may seem counterintuitive; we all breathe, don't we? Yet breath control for the purpose of blowing art glass is treacherously hard and it takes a lifetime to master. A whiff too much or too little and the piece loses its symmetry, color, or clarity. Glassblowers begin as apprentices, working with simple pieces until artistic vision and breath control together can create more intricate structures.

Developing our skills in the language arts can feel much the same. We all come into this business knowing language, our basic tool—there's no tuba with an intricate set of keys or paint powders to mix to get started. Many beginning writers feel that, having such a fundamental part of the business down, they must be home free. But learning to use language for artistic purposes is a lot like learning breath control. The skills are so delicate and nuanced, the muscles to develop them so myriad and refined, that a lifetime is not enough to master them all.

Tell It Slant's Organization

We see the chapters in this book as presenting a series of introductions, lessons, sometimes provocations, in the art of writing creative nonfiction—ways of learning breath control. We move from the basics of good writing to the particular challenges of creative nonfiction in Part I, then go on to help you unearth your own subjects for writing in Part II. In Part III, we turn our attention to craft—delineating certain forms that have served creative nonfiction well, and ending with discussions of the writing process itself: How to get words on paper and how to revise.

A Variety of Ways In

We recognize that every user will have his or her own approach to this book. That's why we've broken it down into a series of sections that will make sense to different users in different ways. There's a wealth of information here and on the accompanying website, more than a few months' worth. Some users may want to read the last chapter first, needing that reminder of the writing process or giving themselves the courage to get themselves to the writing desk. After all, none of us learns exactly the same way or has the same goals: Some of us want to make vases; others, drinking cups.

Chapter Structure and Features

Our desire is to present the most comprehensive information about creative nonfiction possible, in an accessible form, with a sense of how these techniques have played a role in the lives of working writers. We also want all of the concepts we present to be immediately translatable into actual writing ideas. **Each chapter begins with a brief personal essay by one of the authors,** to give readers a sense of how we have negotiated the territory covered in the chapter. We're teaching what has worked for us—sharing ideas that we still use. And because we recognize the limits of what we know, we've gotten tips from many of the best nonfiction writers working today—Bernard Cooper, Philip Gerard, Robin Hemley, to name a few—to expand our expertise in particular areas of creative nonfiction.

At the end of each chapter come our "Try Its"—writing prompts generated by the material covered in the chapter. We offer these both as methods of learning new techniques—stretching those muscles so skills such as writing in scene and dialogue become second nature—and as possible beginnings for new essays. We know that some writers come to a book like this with a writing project in mind; they will find in these pages ways to enhance the stories they wish to tell. Using themes such as history and techniques such as characterization and research will help the story emerge from that quiet place where it lies hidden. For other writers, less sure of a writing direction, we offer myriad ideas for creating essays: sensory memories, family biography, the arts, and so on. The list of possibilities is endless.

The Anthology

We also include an anthology section, essays we've selected to illustrate the writing principles explored in the chapters. We refer to the anthology frequently in the book, and hope that you will use it to expand your understanding of the concepts we explore. We believe the best way to understand braiding is to read a braided essay, and the best way to comprehend strong dialogue is to read it in an actual piece. The anthology is illustrative and not exhaustive, and we hope you'll go on to become steady readers—both using our "Suggestions for Further Reading" and your own bookstore browsing to discover your personal storehouse of inspiration.

The Website

For additional essays, visit *www.mhhe.com/tellitslant,* our website built to accompany *Tell It Slant.* **The username for this site is "miller1" and the password is "slant04."** In addition to hosting essays, the site serves as an extension of the book, focusing on more specific areas of creative nonfiction, such as "Writing the Spiritual Autobiography," and "Using Mixed-Media and Hypertext."

As writers move along in their artistic development, gaining confidence and skills, they may want to look ahead at the literary markets, the worlds beyond apprenticeship. For these writers, we've included several online sections: On the topic of publication, on career opportunities, and the book-length project. We also anticipate the time that student writers no longer have the support of automatic peer groups in the online section "The Writing Group." This section gives detailed tips, including lists of questions for in-class workshops, and provides plans for forming your own writing group when the classroom has run its course.

The site also includes writing prompts, links to sites about authors in the anthology and about creative nonfiction, and—for instructors—an Instructor's Manual that includes sample syllabi and ideas for teaching each chapter and essay.

Acknowledgments

From Suzanne:

First and foremost, my thanks are due to Brenda Miller, who has, over the course of this project, been tireless and endlessly patient, a teacher as much as a partner to me, and as much an inspiration as a writer of creative nonfiction as for her seemingly endless knowledge of the field.

I would also like to thank Bruce and Jin, who have gotten me through many long days and nights with coffee, humor, hugs, and well-timed games of Candyland. Long may you both reign in King Kandy's castle!

From Brenda:

My warmest thanks to my friend and coauthor, Suzanne Paola, who ushered me into the realm of collaboration with strong faith and good humor—a woman who knows there's good cause for celebration at every step of the way and who ensured that our work was fueled with laughter, chocolate, and multiple rewards, culinary and otherwise.

Thanks also to my fellow writers, Less Esbenshade and Beth Judy, who helped this book along at its conception, and to my students at Western Washington University, who always show me what is possible.

Both of us owe an enormous debt of gratitude to a team of experts at McGraw-Hill: development editor, Anne Stameshkin, who has shepherded the project from a rough idea to completion, and served as guide, midwife, and handholder; Sarah Touborg, who initially took the project on and gave us much-needed feedback and encouragement; executive editor, Lisa Moore, who inherited the book; Jennifer Chambliss, our amazingly efficient production editor; Marty Granahan, who took on the daunting task of obtaining permissions; Mary Stoughton, our painstaking copyeditor, who saved us from ourselves many times over; and the wonderful, innovative design and production staff: production supervisor, Randy Hurst; design manager, Cassandra Chu; photo researcher, LouAnn Wilson; photo research coordinator, Alex Ambrose; art editor, Cristin Yancey; and media producer, Todd Vaccaro. We'd also like to thank marketing manager, David Patterson.

Many thanks to the following reviewers, who helped shape *Tell It Slant* with their excellent feedback and suggestions:

Susan Atefat-Peckham, Hope College
Mark Baechtel, Grinnell College
Alan Boye, Lyndon State College
John Calderazzo, Colorado State University
Cass Dalglish, Augsburg College
Julie Danho, Ohio State University
Bill Doyle, Florida Gulf Coast University
John Doyle, West Virginia University
Phil Druker, University of Idaho
Leslie Heywood, Binghamton University (SUNY)
Rod Kessler, Salem State College
Deirdre McNamer, University of Montana

Naeem Murr, Lynchburg College
Frances Paden, Northwestern University
Alison Russell, Xavier University
Ira Sukrungruang, Ohio State University
Michelle Tokarczyk, Goucher College
Kim Townshend, Amherst College
Leslie Ullman, University of Texas—El Paso
Connie Voisine, New Mexico State University
Carolyn Kott Washburne, University of Wisconsin—Milwaukee
Jane Armstrong Woodman, Northern Arizona University

For helping when we needed it, providing insights for us to use on a number of aspects of writing and researching creative nonfiction, we'd like to give thanks to the following generous individuals: Al Cordle, Bernard Cooper, Phil Gerard, Robin Hemley, Paul Piper, and Kathryn Trueblood. And a final, big thank you to our agent, Jill Grinberg.

In Conclusion

We believe strongly that deep within each of you is a work of art that only you can breathe into being. We can coach you, help you develop the muscles you need, and work with you to spin your material around to see every side of it. We trust that you'll find between the lines the prompts that spur only you—the book that begins where ours ends. Breathe deeply! Now let's begin.

Introduction

Where to Begin

The word is the making of the world.—**Wallace Stevens**

Here's how it happens: I'm at a party, or sitting quietly in my seat on an airplane, or milling around at a family reunion, and someone finally asks me the question: "So, you're a writer. What do you write?" It's a deceptively simple question that seems to demand a simple response.

But in the split second before I can answer, I go through all the possible replies in my head. Well, I could say, "I write essays." But "essays" sounds too much like academic papers and articles. I could say, simply, "nonfiction," but then they might think I write celebrity biographies, or cookbooks, or historical treatises on World War II. I could try to take the easy way out and say I write autobiography or memoir, but people would raise their eyebrows and say, "Memoir? Aren't you too young to write your memoirs?" And besides, not all of what I write is memoir; in fact, many of my pieces are not based on private memory at all.

All this is too much for casual party chat: I need a term that, once deployed, will answer all their questions for good. But I know that if I answer with the correct phrase—"creative nonfiction"—I'm in for a long night. My interrogator will warm up to the debate, throwing out the opening volley: "Creative nonfiction? Isn't that an oxymoron?" His forehead crinkles, and his eyes search mine, trying to understand what exactly I'm talking about.

I want to tell him that I love writing creative nonfiction precisely because of this ambiguity. I love the way writing creative nonfiction allows me to straddle a kind of borderland, one that allows me to discover new aspects of myself and the world, to forge surprising metaphors, to create artistic order out of life's chaos. I'm never bored when I write in this genre, always jazzed by the new ways I can stretch my writing muscles. But I rarely trust that my listener will understand. So, more often than not, I smile and say, "Maybe I'll show you sometime." Then I execute a pirouette and turn his attention toward the view out the window or the lovely fruit punch in its cut-glass bowl. I direct his attention to the myriad things of this world, and maybe that's the correct answer after all.

—**Brenda**

Tell all the Truth but tell it Slant
Success in Circuit lies . . .

What did Emily Dickinson mean by these lines? She meant, we think, that truth takes on many guises; that the truth of art can be very different from the truth of day-to-day life. Her poems and letters, after all, reveal her deft observation of the outer world, but this world is "slanted" through her distinctive vision. We chose her poem as both title and epigraph for this book because it so aptly describes the task of the creative nonfiction writer: To tell the truth, yes, but to become more than a mere transcriber of life's factual experiences.

Every few years, National Public Radio checks in on a man who feels compelled to record every minute of his day into a diary. The task, as you can imagine, is gargantuan and ultimately imprisons him: He becomes a slave to this recording act and can no longer function in the world. The transcription he leaves may be a comprehensive and "truthful" one, but it remains completely unreadable. Who, after all, cares to read reams and reams of such notes? What value do they hold apart from the author? If, in nonfiction, we place a premium on "fact," then this man's diary would be the ultimate masterpiece. But in literature and art, we applaud style, meaning, and effect over the bare facts.

We go to literature, and perhaps especially creative nonfiction literature, to learn not about the author, but about ourselves; we want to be *moved* in some way, and that emotional resonance happens only through skillful use of artistic techniques. As Salman Rushdie puts it: "Literature is where I go to explore the highest and lowest places in human society and in the human spirit, where I hope to find not absolute truth but the truth of the tale, of the imagination and of the heart."

Simply by choosing to write in this genre and to present your work as "nonfiction," you make an artistic statement. You're saying that the work is rooted in the real world; though the essay might contain some elements of fabrication, it's directly connected to you as the author behind the text. There's a truth to it that you want to claim as your own, a bond of trust between reader and writer. If you present a piece as fiction, you're saying that the work is rooted in the world of the imagination; although the story may contain autobiographical elements, the reader cannot assume that it has a direct bearing on the truth of the writer's life or experience. At some point, all writers need to decide how they want to place themselves in relation to the reader; the choice of genre establishes that relationship and the rules of engagement.

How do you begin to find your own voice in creative nonfiction? And where will you choose to focus your attention? Your own nonfiction writing may spring from the news stories unfolding around you, your own memories, the work you do in a science lab, or your observations of the October leaves whirling at your feet. It's at once exciting and confusing to work in a genre that opens up so many possibilities.

The more you read and study, the more you'll discover that creative nonfiction assumes a particular, creating *self* behind the nonfiction prose. When you set about writing creative nonfiction about any subject, you bring to this endeavor a strong voice and a singular vision. This voice must be loud enough, and interesting enough, to be heard among the noise coming at us in everyday life. If you succeed, you'll find yourself in a close, if not intimate, relationship with the reader, a relationship that demands honesty and a willingness to risk a kind of exposure you may never chance in face-to-face encounters.

This is not to say that creative nonfiction must be "self-centered"; on the contrary, creative nonfiction often focuses on material outside the life of the author, and it certainly need not use the personal "I." It's the "creative" part of the term "creative nonfiction" that means a single, active imagination is behind the slice of reality the author will inhabit. As the essayist Scott Russell Sanders puts it: "Feeling overwhelmed by data, random information, the flotsam and jetsam of mass culture, we relish the spectacle of a single consciousness making sense of a portion of the chaos. . . . The essay is a haven for the private, idiosyncratic voice in an era of anonymous babble."

This "idiosyncratic voice" uses all the literary devices available to fiction writers and poets—vivid images, scenes, metaphors, dialogue, satisfying rhythms of language—while still remaining true to experience and the world. Or as novelist and essayist Cynthia Ozick puts it: "Like a poem, a genuine essay is made out of language and character and mood and temperament and pluck and chance."

Creative nonfiction can focus on either private experience or public domain, but in either case, the inner self provides the vision and the shaping influence to infuse the work with this sense of "pluck and chance." In many cases, the essayist may find herself thinking out loud on the page: The essay becomes, then, a continual process of unexpected discovery. The creative nonfiction writer continually chooses to question and expand his or her own limited perceptions. In some forms of creative nonfiction, the self will be sublimated in service to a larger purpose, but behind the story the individual imagination still pulses, gives the text its heart blood, its language, its life.

Robert L. Root Jr. and Michael Steinberg in their book *The Fourth Genre: Contemporary Writers of/on Creative Nonfiction*, use the term "creative nonfiction" to distinguish it from the enormous amount of general writing that can be classified as nonfiction—cookbooks, after all, are nonfiction, but they have little in common with the kind of work contained in the anthology at the end of this book. Twenty years ago, the term didn't exist, and most of what we call creative nonfiction now would have been considered either personal essay or new journalism—useful categories, but not exactly right for the new growth flowering under the heading of creative nonfiction.

Nonfiction has traditionally been considered the most summarizing of literary forms, the one that gives newspaper-style capsules of events; this new, creative nonfiction will flourish in real time then, luxuriating in details, helping readers hear the crunch of those October leaves under their feet. Lee Gutkind, who edits the journal *Creative Nonfiction*, says that creative nonfiction "heightens the whole concept and idea of essay writing." He has come up with the "the five Rs" of creative nonfiction: "Real Life, Reflection, Research, Reading, and 'Riting." That second "R," Reflection, means that, in contrast to traditional objective journalism, creative nonfiction allows for and encourages "a writer's feelings and responses . . . as long as what [writers] think is written to embrace the reader in a variety of ways."

Imagination, coupled with facts, forms this hybrid genre that is both so exciting and so challenging to write.

As in any creative enterprise, the most difficult challenge to writing creative nonfiction lies in knowing where to begin. One might think that creative nonfiction would provide an easy out for this question. After all, someone might chide, all the material is at your fingertips! It's "nonfiction" after all—the world is yours for the taking! But the minute creative nonfiction writers put pen to paper, they realize a truth both invigorating and disheartening: We're not the rote recorder of life's experience; we're artists, creating artifice, and as such we have difficult choices to make every step of the way. If we work in an area such as science writing or new journalism, the challenges seem especially clear: How do we sift facts or tell others' stories, honestly, through the lenses of our own imagination?

Memoir may seem more straightforward, but as William Zinsser articulates in his introduction to *Inventing the Truth: The Art and Craft of Memoir,* "Good memoirs are a careful act of construction. We like to think that an interesting life will simply fall into place on the page. It won't. . . . Memoir writers must manufacture a text, imposing narrative order on a jumble of half-remembered events."

The essential questions remain. How do I find a way into this material? How do I situate this stuff in a way that's both interesting and aesthetically pleasing?

We've designed the first section of this book to help you gain access to the basic writing *tools* any writer has at his or her disposal, your writing "palette," if you will. We then provide a discussion of the particular challenges you'll face when you begin to write creative nonfiction. In the next section, we guide you in finding your particular stories or provide suggestions for turning your gaze onto the world in a way that will allow you to find material outside of the self. We begin with memory and move steadily outward to family, environment, history, the arts, and the world. In this way, we hope you'll begin to consider both your individual life and our collective lives as material for creative nonfiction. People will want to read your work not because they wish to lend a sympathetic ear to a stranger, but because of the way your truth-filled stories illuminate their own lives and perceptions of the world.

As you work your way through the book, allow these frameworks to become portals into your own storehouse of material. What is important to *you,* to your wild and unpredictable self? What incitement will loosen your tongue?

PART I

The Foundations of Creative Nonfiction

CHAPTER ONE
The Basics of Good Writing in Any Form

CHAPTER TWO
The Particular Challenges of Creative Nonfiction

The Basics of Good Writing in Any Form

I was delighted to find that nonfiction prose can also carry meaning in its structures and, like poetry, can tolerate all sorts of figurative language, as well as alliteration and even rhyme. The range of rhythms in prose is larger and grander than it is in poetry, and it can handle discursive ideas and plain information as well as character and story. It can do everything. I felt as though I had switched from a single reed instrument to a full orchestra.—**Annie Dillard**

People need maps to your dreams.—**Allen Gurganus**

▌ **Scene versus Exposition**
▌ **Specificity and Detail**
▌ **What You Don't Know You Know**
▌ **Developing Character**
▌ **Dialogue**
▌ **Point of View**
▌ **Image and Metaphor**
▌ **The Rhythm of Your Sentences**
▌ **Try It**

It's about two-thirds of the way through the quarter in an introductory nonfiction class. My students have plumbed their lives in ways they never thought possible: as environmental records, as living history, as a movement through various forms—scientific, spiritual, cultural, aesthetic—of inquiry. They come through the door of my classroom with varying degrees of eagerness and pull out their notebooks, pens cocked, waiting. They're used to coming in and interrogating themselves in different ways: Who are they really? How have they lived? Today, however, I know I'm going to make them groan. Instead of prompts like writing about the explosion of Mount St. Helens or the World Trade Organization riots in Seattle, I have them pull out a piece of their own prose and count the number of words in each sentence for three paragraphs. I also have them jot down comments on the kinds of sentences they use: simple declarative (basic subject-verb), complex, fragmented, etc. They do the assignment, because it would be even more boring to sit and do nothing, I suppose. Suddenly a little exclamation breaks out from a corner of the room.

"Ohmigod!" says one young woman. "All of my sentences are eleven words long!"

This young woman has been concerned about what feels to her like a flatness or lifelessness to her prose. Here, in one rather mechanical but not painful exercise, she's put her finger on the reason—or one of the reasons. On further analysis, she discovers that she has a penchant for writing one simple declarative sentence after another: "I drive to the forest in April. My car is almost ready for a new clutch. The forests are quiet at that time of year." The metronomic beat of the same sentence structure, the same sentence length, has robbed her otherwise sparkling essays of their life.

For the sake of comparison, listen to the difference created in those three sample sentences by a little more rhetorical inventiveness: "In April, a quiet time of year, I drive to the forest. My car almost ready for a new clutch." This small revision finds a kind of poetry in these simple ideas. —**Suzanne**

Scene versus Exposition

Generally speaking, scene is the building block of creative nonfiction. There are exceptions to this statement—more academic or technically oriented writing, the essay of ideas perhaps—but overall, the widespread notion that nonfiction consists of the writer's thoughts presented in an expository or summarizing way has done little but produce quantities of unreadable nonfiction. Scene is based on action unreeling before us, as it would in a film, and it will draw on the same techniques as fiction—dialogue, description, point of view, specificity, concrete detail. Scene also encompasses the lyricism and imagery of great poetry. We have, as the Dillard quote at the beginning of this chapter indicates, access to the full orchestra. We need to learn to play every instrument with brio.

Let's begin by defining our terms. *Expository* writing, as the term implies, exposes the author's thoughts or experiences for the reader; it summarizes, generally with little or no sensory detail. Expository writing compresses time: *For five years I lived in Alaska.* It presents a compact summation of an experience with no effort to re-create the experience for the person reading.

Scene, however, does the same thing in nonfiction that it does in fiction; it uses detail and sensory information to re-create experience, generally with location, action, a sense of movement through time, and possible dialogue. Scene is cinematic. Here's a possible reworking of the sentence, using scene: *For the five years I lived in Alaska, I awoke each morning to the freezing seat of the outhouse, the sting of hot strong coffee drunk without precious sugar or milk, the ringing "G'day!" of my Australian neighbor.*

This version of this sentence clearly presents the reader with a more experiential version of that time in Alaska, with details that provide a snapshot of the place. The slowness of time passing is stressed by the harsh dailiness of the coffee and outhouse; we get a sense of scarcity of supply; the neighbor even has a bit of swift characterization. Of course, for an essay in which Alaska is totally unimportant, the expository summation might be better. But if you find yourself writing nonfiction with very little scene, you're likely to produce flat writing that readers have to struggle to enter.

Here's an example of scene from an essay in our anthology section, Richard Selzer's "The Knife." The essay moves fluidly between scene and exposition; Selzer forces us to *live* the awesome power and responsibility of the surgeon before allowing himself the luxury of meditating about it.

> There is a hush in the room. Speech stops. The hands of the others, assistants and nurses, are still. Only the voice of the patient's respiration remains. It is the rhythm of a quiet sea, the sound of waiting. Then you speak, slowly, the terse entries of a Himalayan climber reporting back.
>
> "The stomach is okay. Greater curvature clean. No sign of ulcer. Pylorus, duodenum fine. Now comes the gall-bladder. No stones. Right kidney, left, all right. Liver . . . uh-oh."

Your speech lowers to a whisper, falters, stops for a long, long moment, then picks up again at the end of a sigh that comes through your mask like a last exhalation.

"Three big hard ones in the left lobe, one on the right. Metastatic deposits. Bad, bad. Where's the primary? Got to be coming from somewhere."

The arm shifts direction and the fingers drop lower and lower into the pelvis—the body impaled now upon the arm of the surgeon to the hilt of the elbow.

"Here it is."

Like fine fiction, this passage contains a clear setting—the hospital room, characterized appropriately enough by sound rather than appearance: the silence of life and death. There's action mimicking real time, containing the element of surprise. We learn, along with the surgeon, about the patient's metastasized cancer. There's dialogue, as the surgeon narrates to himself, to his surgical assistants, seemingly to the fates, his discovery of the patient's mortality. And like fine poetry, this piece of writing also organizes itself through imagery: the "quiet sea" of the passive patient's breathing versus the labored voice—like a Himalayan climber's—of the surgeon emphasizes the loss of control. The simile of the surgeon's breath coming "like a last exhalation" is ironic, since he has discovered not his own demise ahead, but that of the person on the table.

Selzer's passage would be easy to change to an expository sentence: *Often in surgery I found an unexpected cancer.* But the author's final purpose, which is an extended meditation on the relationship of human and tool, soul and body, would fall flat. The reader, lacking any feel for the grandeur and potential tragedy of exploring the body, would dismiss expository statements like "The surgeon struggles not to feel. It is suffocating to press the feeling out" as merely odd or grandiose.

Several other moves are worth noting in this passage. One is that, like the earlier sample Alaska sentence, Selzer's surgical description is *representative scene.* In other words, he doesn't pretend that this operation occurs at one specific time and place, but it represents a typical surgical procedure, one among many. Another technique to note is his use of the second person for a speaker that is presumably himself (Richard Selzer is a surgeon). Second person—the *you* rather than the *I*—is a point-of-view choice, discussed in more detail later in this chapter.

For a specific, not representative, scene, look at Jo Ann Beard's "The Fourth State of Matter" in our anthology section. The scenes comprising the essay all occur at very specific moments in time. Here's Beard at work, with her physicist colleagues.

> They're speaking in physics so I'm left out of the conversation. Chris apologetically erases one of the pictures I've drawn on the blackboard and replaces it with a curving blue arrow surrounded by radiating chalk waves of green.
>
> "If it's plasma, make it in red," I suggest helpfully. We're all smoking illegally, in the journal office with the door closed and the window open. We're having a plasma party.
>
> "We aren't discussing *plas*ma," Bob says condescendingly. He's smoking a horrendously smelly pipe. The longer he stays in here the more it feels like I'm breathing small daggers in through my nose. He and I don't get along; each of us thinks the other needs to be taken down a peg. Once we had a hissing match in the hallway which ended with him suggesting that I could be fired, which drove me to tell him he was *already* fired, and both of us stomped into our offices and slammed our doors.
>
> "I had to fire Bob," I tell Chris later.
>
> "I heard," he says noncommittally. Bob is his best friend.

This is a very pinpointed event, not representative, but presumably unlike any other moment in Beard's life. Notice how much suggestive detail she packs into a short space. These characters break rules, argue, exist in complex relationship to one another. Her relationship with Bob is established in this scene—a relationship that seems suffused with a genuine but relatively harmless tension, given their ability to issue dire threats to each other without consequences. The dialogue sounds real and secures the characters, capturing the nuanced pretense of Bob's stressing the "plas" part of the "plasma." Chris, the man in the middle, seems to have heard this kind of bickering from them before.

We all tend to use too little scene in creative nonfiction. We especially forget the possibilities of representative scene. Even when we're reporting a typical rather than a specific event, use of scenic elements, as in Selzer's surgery, conveys a sense of character and situation far more effectively than summary does.

Specificity and Detail

Scene forces us to use specificity and detail, elements that get lost in the quick wash of exposition. A priest we know once said that human beings are body-spirit people, and body comes first. Even in discussing the largest ideas, our brains engage with the small workings of the senses first. And the specificity of a piece of nonfiction is generally where the sensory details lie: the aroma of honeysuckle, the weak film of moonlight. While it's possible to go overboard with detail, in drafting it's generally best to keep going back and sharpening as much as possible: You leaned not just against a tree, but against a weeping silver birch; the voice at the other end of the phone sounded like the Tin Man in *The Wizard of Oz.* Your instructor or writing group can tell you when you've gone too far. When you write scene, your job is to mimic the event, create an experiential re-creation of it for the reader.

Look at the examples given earlier, and think about how much the details add to those scenes: the hushed silence of the hospital room and three hard tumors on the right lobe of the liver in Selzer. In Beard, we see the bickering but ultimate acceptance by this close group of co-workers of one another. We sense the author's ambivalent position in the group—shut out of their "talking physics," scribbling on the blackboard—but also her authority within the group. We sense, in the hyperbolic description of Bob's pipe smoke ("like daggers"), a bit of foreshadowing of the coming event.

William Strunk Jr., in *The Elements of Style,* talks about the one point of accord among good writers being the need for detail that is "specific, definite and concrete." We use "concrete" detail to refer to detail that appeals to the senses; other writers call such details "proofs." If Selzer told us that sometimes he found cancer during surgery, we might abstractly believe him, but it's hard to associate that fact with real life and death. What convinces us in this passage is the specifics: three hard tumors on the liver, the surgeon's voice mumbling, "Bad, bad."

The opposite of writing that relies on concrete detail is abstract language—the larger concepts we use that exist on a purely mental level, with no appeal to the senses: *liberty, justice, contentment,* and so on. These terms may contain the implication of sensory detail (you may flash on "warmth" when you hear "contentment," but that's a personal reaction that wouldn't make sense to, say, a penguin), but they are in themselves broad categories only. Of course, within the details you use emerges a wealth of abstract information. Beard could have summarized her relationships with her co-workers; Selzer could have presented a few expository sentences about soul and body, surgeon as God. We want experiences, not lectures. We want to enter into events and uncover their meanings for ourselves.

Paying attention to concrete detail and the input of our own senses also helps save us from the literary pitfall of cliché. A cliché is an expression or concept that's been overused; frequently, clichés are dead metaphors—metaphors so overused that we no longer pay attention to the comparisons they contain. (Do you actually think of a yellow metal when you hear "good as gold"? Do you even realize that this phrase comes from a time when the gold our country held validated our money?) If Beard had described Bob's pipe tobacco as smelling like "dirty socks," or "killing" her nose, she would have been indulging in cliché. Instead, she used the information her senses gave her to create a fresh image.

What You Don't Know You Know

To understand the most effective way to tell your story in print, think of how you tell your stories orally. Remember, there isn't any magic to words that appear on paper—they don't gain a special authority or sacred interest. Writing is like oral communication, only heightened and sharpened; basically it must obey the same rules.

In addition to creative writing, we teach literature classes—classes that require papers. Every quarter, some students miss the due dates on their papers, and never once have we gotten a phone call saying, "Sorry, I'm running late, I'm not turning this paper in." Naturally not: such an approach wouldn't incline us to clemency. What we hear from late students goes more like this (representative scene): a phone call, a breathy voice saying, "I'm so sorry, the clutch on my car has been acting up and when I called my mechanic, he said, 'Better not drive it, it could fall apart anytime,' so I haven't been able to get to the library, and on top of that my migraine's been acting up, and it feels like there's a bomb going off in my head. . . ."

This is persuasive communication. It contains action, suspense, dialogue, and concrete detail appealing to the senses. Even if you've never turned a paper in late, think of how you would communicate a bad day to a friend you met in the evening. If you stop at saying "I had a bad day," you're either unusually tight-lipped or you're not that concerned about your audience. Most of us dive right in to communicating in scene: "Well, first my alarm didn't go off, and my econ prof gave me that *look* where her eyes get all scrunched up, and my car was making that *wonk wonk* sound," etc. Although we authors fall into this lack-of-detail trap ourselves (and force ourselves to climb out of it, again and again), it amuses us that our students commit errors in writing personal essays they would never dream of falling into in conversation or excuse-making.

Chances are, you know more than you need to know to write effective scene, but you've been stifled, often by misguided advice from academic writing classes, about using your natural expressiveness in your nonfiction. Next time you work on a piece of creative nonfiction, hear yourself talking through the story to friends in a crowded coffee shop or club. There's plenty to divert their attention: music, people-watching, smoke (perhaps), and noise. What details do you use to hold their attention? Do you imitate the look on someone's face, the sound of a voice? Do you screech to demonstrate the squealing brakes? Your reading audience will be equally distractible. Think about how to render these attention-grabbing devices in your prose. You may want to consult Chapter 3, "The Body of Memory," to look at the sensory prompts given there.

Developing Character

Character development, like learning to write effective dialogue, is part of writing scene. It's another particularly easy-to-miss demand of good creative nonfiction. After all, *we* know what our parents, our children, our lovers look like. Unconsciously, we tend to assume that everyone else does as well; fiction writers will know that they have to tell us how that man in the bar holds his cigarette, what his gravelly voice sounds like. Suzanne had the experience of writing a long essay about a grandfather—an essay carefully polished, revised, and finally submitted for publication. Back it came with a letter from the editor (Lee Gutkind, a fine writer of creative nonfiction himself), saying something like "But I have no idea what your grandfather looks like, how he talks, anything." What a ridiculous, obvious mistake! But what an easy mistake to make.

Suzanne has by marriage a very funny grandmother. She wasn't intentionally funny, but nonetheless the mere mention of her name tends to bring down the room when the family's together. As courteous people, the family bears in mind that we need to break through our uncontrollable giggling and clue other listeners in to the source of our amusement: "Well, she came from a tiny town in south Georgia and talked about nothing all day long but her *ar-ther-itis* and her gall bladder that was *leakin'*, plus she lied compulsively and pursed her mouth in this funny way when she did. . . ." After a few minutes of this, our listeners understand why we find her so endlessly amusing. This kind of filling in, also natural in conversation, is the essence of character development.

Nothing demonstrates the power of fine characterization like studying writers who, in a few strokes, can help us apprehend someone sensually (through sight, sound, or feel) as well as give us a sense of their essence. The following are examples of quick, effective character development from essays in our anthology section or on the website:

> My best friend there shoed horses. He had ribs like barrel staves, his sweat was miniature glass pears. (Albert Goldbarth, "After Yitzl")

In the case of my father and myself, I had the fullness of his face and his desire to write, which had been abandoned when he came to America with a family to raise. . . . He was a middle-aged man who was sobbing and sweaty and his body was heavy and so soft I imagined his ribs giving way like a snowman's on the first warm winter day. I could hear his heart and it sounded as if it was working harder than it could take. (Lawrence Sutin, "A Postcard Memoir")

Mayme would step onto the platform wearing a dark purple coat, her black braids wound tightly around her head. Her skin was too soft and wrinkly. When you kissed her cheek, it wobbled, and you wished you didn't have to do that. (Judith Kitchen, "Things of This Life")

Occasionally we visited my grandparents in New York; they lived in a Brooklyn brownstone, descendents of Russian immigrants, and they murmured to each other in Yiddish in their tiny kitchen. They reflexively touched the mezuzah as they came and went from their house. When I watched my grandmother cooking knishes or stuffed cabbage, I imagined her in *babushka* and shawl. (Brenda Miller, "Basha Leah")

Details that give a sense of the essence of an individual—in all his or her typicality (commonness with their type; Russian immigrant women typically would cook cabbage and speak Yiddish) and individual, specific glory (sweat like miniature glass pears)—are hard to define, but blazingly effective when you come upon them. When you write about someone close to you, think how you would characterize that person in a stroke or two for someone else.

Dialogue

It can be difficult to allow ourselves to use direct dialogue in creative nonfiction. After all, memory is faulty. We can't recall conversations word-for-word, so why try? The answer is that we need to try, because insofar as nonfiction attempts to be an honest record of the observant mind's reflective movements, dialogue matters. We recall voices, not summaries; we observe scenes in our head, not expository paragraphs. In Chapter 2, "The Particular Challenges of Creative Nonfiction," we'll refer again to the dialogue question. For now, let's assume that as long as you somehow cue the reader in to your own degree of certainty or uncertainty about the dialogue you're using, you can and should use this tool of exciting prose. And that, of course, means learning some basic rules.

Dialogue generally moves action forward: Selzer quotes himself finding the metastasized cancer, and Beard gives a sense of the soon-to-be-crucial dynamics of her office. Dialogue must characterize and capture the voice of the speaker, however, not simply give information. In fiction writing, the latter is called "information dumping," and it occurs when you have people say things like, "Well, Carmen, I remember you told me you were taking the cross-town bus that day only because your white 1999 Volvo had developed a gasket problem." Information dumping is less of a problem in nonfiction because this genre is reality based (and people really *do not* talk that way), but if you cue your readers that you're re-creating a conversation, it may be tempting to lard the dialogue with information you can't figure out how to get in any other way. Don't do it.

Everyone has a natural cadence and a dialect to his or her speech. We nearly always speak in simple sentences, not compound-complex ones. We might say, "When the rain comes, the grass grows," which has one short dependent clause beginning with the word "when." We aren't likely to say, "Whenever it happens the rain comes, provided the proper fertilizer's been applied, grass grows, unless it's been masticated by cows grazing thereon"—a simple sentence or *main clause* ("the grass grows") festooned with wordy subordinate clauses. We frequently speak in sentence fragments or ungrammatical snippets—for example, the how-are-you question "Getting along?" instead of the grammatically correct "How are you getting along?" One exception to these rules of natural speech might be a person who *is* pompous and wordy. Perhaps you're writing dialogue to capture the voice of a stuffy English professor you know. In that case, go to town. Just bear in mind that what bores you will bore others fairly quickly. In the case of people who are boorish, dull, or otherwise hard to listen to, give readers a sample of the voice and they'll fill in the rest. A little goes a long way.

One final caveat: Beware of elaborate tag lines—lines that identify the speaker ("he said," "she argued," etc.). In a dialogue between two people, tag lines are often unnecessary after the first two. When you must use them, stick as much as possible to "said" and "asked," two fairly invisible words in the context of dialogue. It's an easy mistake to make—and a difficult one to overlook as a reader—to have all of your characters "retort," "storm," "muse," etc. And make sure the words themselves contain tone as much as possible (tone can also be conveyed in a character's gesture, as in Beard's colleagues casually breaking the rules by smoking in their office). Don't follow each speech tag with an adverb, like "angrily," "sadly," and so on. If you feel the need to use those words, ask yourself why the dialogue itself doesn't seem to contain those feelings.

Point of View

Every story is told by a storyteller (even in a piece with multiple speakers, one speaker dominates at a time), and every storyteller must be situated somehow within the frame of the work. This situating is called *point of view*, and we express it through choice of pronouns. To put it simply, the tale can be told by an "I" (first-person point of view), a "you" (second person), or a "he" or "she" (third person). Though at first blush it may seem like all nonfiction must use the first person—however much we may braid, dance around, or lyrically occlude our work, we're speaking as ourselves, aren't we?—but in fact, skillful writers do use second and third person to wonderful effect in nonfiction. And the more the genre stretches its limbs, takes risks, and remakes its rules, the more such untraditional devices appear and the more aware we become as writers of what they can do.

Of the three point-of-view choices, second person is the rarest, in nonfiction as well as in fiction and poetry. It's not hard to figure out why: Second person calls attention to itself and tends to invite reader resistance. Imagine recasting the *For five years I lived in Alaska* sentence as *For five years you lived in Alaska*. That's exactly what a shift to second person would do; it places the reader directly in the author's shoes, without narrative mediation. Clumsily used, second person screams out for the reader to say, "No I didn't," with an inner shrug of indignation, and stop reading. Skillfully used, however, that blurring of the line between reader and author can be very powerful.

Here's a sentence from Beard's "The Fourth State of Matter" again, a classic first-person approach.

> It's November 1, 1991, the last day of the first part of my life.

Compare that with a short passage from Richard Selzer, who uses second person liberally throughout his essay. Watch the careful way he slips from first to second person, as if inviting the reader to experience the fearfulness of a surgeon's power:

> I must confess that the priestliness of my profession has ever been impressed on me. In the beginning there are vows. . . . And if the surgeon is like a poet, then the scars you have made on countless bodies are like verses into the fashioning of which you have poured your soul.

Selzer continues to switch point of view, at one point making an even riskier switch into the viewpoint of the patient:

> And what of that other, the patient, you, who are brought to the operating room on a stretcher, having been washed and purged and dressed in a white gown? Fluid drips from a bottle into your arm, diluting you, leaching your body of its personal brine.

The reader here experiences both the surgeon's awe at the stakes of the surgical vocation and the patient's radical loss of self—a double whammy and a virtuoso move on the author's part. If you imagine re-casting the above passages with more traditional choices (*The scars I have made, the patient is brought to the operating room*), you can see how much Selzer would lose. The reader here must be entangled very personally in this struggle against disease.

Judith Kitchen's "Things of This Life," included on our website, uses third person to create a sense of freshness and excitement in a childhood memoir.

> Consider the child idly browsing in the curio shop. She's been on vaca-tion in the Adirondacks, and her family has (over the past week) canoed the width of the lake and up a small, meandering river. . . . So why, as she sifts through boxes of fake arrowheads made into key chains, passes down the long rows of rubber tomahawks, dyed rabbits' feet, salt shak-ers with the words "Indian Lake" painted in gold, beaded moccasins made of what could only in the imagination be called leather, is she hap-pier than any time during the past week?

Kitchen, later in the essay, tells us: "Now consider the woman who was that child." It seems at first an odd choice, to write about the self as if it were someone completely apart, a stranger. But as Kitchen unfolds her sense of her life as "alien," a space she's inhabiting that raises ques-tions she still can't answer ("How can she go on, wanting like this, for the rest of her life?"), the strategy becomes a coherent part of the ar-chitecture of the essay. Imagine the paragraphs it would take to ex-plain such an alienation from the self—a sense of distance from one's own desires—and the relative powerlessness such an explanation would have. Annie Dillard writes in our introductory quote that she "delighted" to learn that nonfiction, like poetry, can carry meaning in its structures. Kitchen has wisely chosen a structure to convey her feel-ing—a feeling open only to the clumsiest articulation.

Image and Metaphor

Janet Burroway, in her text *Writing Fiction,* describes metaphor as the foundation stone "from which literature derives." Image, defined as any literary element creating a sense impression in the mind, and metaphor, the use of comparison, form the heart of any literary work. Notice how, trying to impress this importance on you, we strain to make strong metaphor. Metaphors are the foundation stones of a building—the pumping hearts of literary writing. The ability to make metaphor is the most basic constituent of human thought and language. Yet too often we leave direct consideration of these devices to the poet.

In a certain sense, each of us sees the world in a way that's irre-producible. Our viewpoint is like our dreaming, and the images and metaphors we choose provide maps to our dreams, as Allen Gurganus reminds us in one of the epigraphs to this chapter. Do you see the snow-sleeked mountain as a cream-covered candy on the horizon? One of our students does. She dreams very differently from another woman we know, for whom it's always been the moon peeking in the window.

While essays can be organized many ways—through topic, through chronology or passage of time—organization through image and metaphor (a subject also covered in Chapter 10, "The Lyric Es-say") has become much more common. Clustering thoughts through images and loose associations (and metaphors are, at the most basic level, associations) seems fundamental to the way the human mind works. You may mentally jump from a look at a leaky faucet to a memory of watching the 1970s TV show *Charlie's Angels* because of the name of the actress Farrah Fawcett, gliding effortlessly from that thought to a sense memory of the powdered hot chocolate with marshmallows your mother made for you on weeknights while you watched TV. As we grow more aware of and sophisticated about the way human consciousness operates, it makes sense that our literature will come closer to these basic thought rhythms.

Two examples of this sort of organization, found on the website or in our anthology section, are Carol Guess's "Red" and Virginia Woolf's "The Death of the Moth." In "Red," a lyric essay and coming-out story, the transformation of the speaker, who begins as a debu-tante, is mirrored by the transformation of the color. The color red recurs as an image that becomes a powerful metaphor for the speaker's journey. Red is the color of lipstick, nail polish, a satin bra, a date's car, the menstrual bleeding the debutantes starve away. Fi-nally, in a brilliant metaphoric turn, the color evolves into the break-ing through of decades of repressed anger. The evolution of this image—its recurrence and transmutation—*is* the essay. Notice how a rich and skillfully used strain of imagery carries with it a sense of nar-rative, a substory playing off of and enhancing the story told by the speaker.

In Woolf's "The Death of the Moth," the seemingly mundane ex-perience of watching a moth die at the author's window becomes a metaphor for the pain and striving of life arrayed against the power, "massed outside indifferent, impersonal," that nullifies our strongest efforts. The moth's struggle becomes a reflection of the writer's struggle—her laborious scratching at the window of meaning, which time and the movement of the universe both seem to conspire against.

You can often find clues to your own imagistic or metaphoric organizations when you recall the sensory association a thought or experience calls to mind. If the summer your best friend was killed in a diving accident always comes back to you with a whiff of honeysuckle, stay with that image and explore it in writing for a while. Does it lead to concepts of sweetness, youth, temptation, or quick-blooming? If you let yourself write about the image alone for a while—not rushing to get to the subject your mind may insist is "the real story"—a more complex, truer series of themes will probably emerge.

The Rhythm of Your Sentences

It's a well-known fact that sentences must contain some variation. You must have become acquainted with this fact already. It's clear if you read a certain kind of prose. A work must use different kinds of sentence structures. Different kinds of sentence structures help alleviate that numbed feeling. It's a feeling you don't want your readers to have.

The preceding paragraph contains six sentences, each composed of a simple sentence of about ten words beginning with a subject and its verb. Unlike the sentence you're currently reading, none begins with a clause. None is short. None, unlike the twenty-three-word sentence introducing this second paragraph, engages us for very long. Read both of these paragraphs together. Do you sense a difference? Do you, as we do, begin to go blank by the middle of the first paragraph and finally feel some relief at the second one?

Notice that the second paragraph in this section, while clarifying many of the ideas that the first paragraph contains, varies sentence structure and length. It also varies mood: One sentence uses the vocative or command mood ("Read both of these paragraphs together"), and two are cast in the interrogative mood—they ask questions. Clauses like "Unlike this sentence" and "as we do" appear at the beginning, middle, and end of sentences to break up that repetitive simple structure.

There's a reason children and parents howl at each other, "Stop *saying* that!" Nothing's more boring than a voice repeating "Clean your room!" over and over again. Or the acquaintance who says "like" again and again, or the child banging out Chopsticks on the piano for the hundredth time. Nothing drives us quite as numbly mad as repetition does. Sentence structure is the poetic line, the bass and rhythm, of your prose. Riff, experiment, break it up.

Try It

Scene versus Exposition

1.   Go through a piece of your writing and find a passage of summary that could, or maybe even should, be in scene. Don't fret right now about whether scene is absolutely necessary here. The point is to develop the skill of automatically asking yourself whether that option will help you. Answering those basic questions of fiction (who, what, when, where, why), rewrite the passage as a scene.

In fiction, of course, you have the privilege of filling in rooms, dialogue, and so on, with invention. Sometimes we stymie ourselves by imagining we must remember *everything* or we can't describe *anything*. So work with what you remember. You may forget the look of a room but remember the sound or smell of it (think of Selzer's defining silence in that hospital room). Or create a bridge, such as writing a few sentences about how this is what a dialogue sounds like in your memory as you try to re-create it, giving yourself permission to fill in what you don't remember word for word. Remember that almost any reconstruction device is fine, as long as you let readers in on what you're doing.

2.   To get a feel for writing scene, re-create an event that took place in the past week—one with characters you can delineate and dialogue you can remember. It doesn't have to be important—it will probably help if it isn't. The point is simply to write two or three pages in which a location is established through description, people are characterized and talk, and something happens. You can describe an exchange with an auto mechanic, getting in the grease-and-oil smell of the shop, the mechanic's voice and way of talking, the "action" of learning about a car's mechanical problems. Or you can use a doctor's appointment, a phone call to a parent, a conversation with a friend, anything at all. Just make sure that, however trivial it is, the scene contains some sort of action. Look to the work of master scene-writers like Jo Ann Beard, whose "The Fourth State of Matter" is included in our anthology section, for guidance.

3.   Finally, when you feel confident of your basic skills, remember a scene out of your own life that was of the utmost importance. This will be different for everybody. It could be something as obviously important as the birth of a child or an argument leading to the end of a marriage; or its importance could be subtle but real to you—a conversation leading to a new closeness or a new distance between you and someone critical in your life. The point is that you must have a strong sense memory of this scene, one you can play back in your head over and over again—and it must matter to you.

Write the scene with as much fidelity as possible. Have the people in it enter and leave; describe what you saw, heard, and felt. If you still remember exactly how your mother asked, "Where were you last night?" describe the question in all the sensory detail you can muster, along with the wrench in your gut that came with it. Don't question right now why what matters, matters. Trust your intuition, and tap into all of the passion you have invested in this scene.

Now question yourself: Why was a certain gesture or inflection so important? Why did you spend most of this conversation staring at a loudly ticking clock on the wall? Why did you notice the caramel color of your drink? The chances are that like Selzer and Beard, your emotional story is locked in the details you remember of your life. When you begin to question the scene in this way, scrutinizing every detail, you'll probably discover an essay waiting to be written about this crucial moment. Using those crucial scenic elements, go back into the essay again, writing with an awareness of the deeper story your memory is playing back for you—an event in which time stood still, perhaps.

Developing Character

4. Go through the characterizations culled from the anthology section. *See* these people in your mind—imagine what they look like, how their voices sound, how they move through their homes. Then use a pen or highlighter to underline the details that really convey character to you: What if Mayme wore a pink coat and had a bun instead of braids? Who would she be then? What if the horseshoer had a thin body and sweat that dripped like a drizzle of rainwater? As you imagine how changes would alter the characterizations, try to articulate to yourself what qualities—frivolity, solemnity, vulnerability—those details seem to convey.

5. Write a portrait or character sketch. Sketches were a popular nineteenth-century nonfictional form—"Sketches by Boz," brief, vivid verbal portraits, became one of the first publications by the novelist Charles Dickens. A master of quick characterization, Dickens apprenticed his art in early sketchwork. Think of someone close to you and try to convey his or her essence, through clothing, sound, dialogue, gestures, and so on, in two or three paragraphs. Don't aim to write scene; this portrait doesn't need to contain action, merely characterization. You want to provide a verbal snapshot, a refined written version of the oral snapshot of the grandmother given above.

When you're reasonably finished, trade your piece with a writing partner. Read each other's sketches and then elaborate on the person described, giving an overall, abstract sense of that individual's personality. How close did you come? Discuss with your partner the ways this sketch could be refined—important details that may have been omitted or others that could be misleading. Is this character sketch on its way to becoming an essay? Articulate to yourself why this character matters, why she's different or he's intriguingly typical. Work on an essay in which you introduce your readers to someone you're convinced they'll be happy to know.

Dialogue

6.   As you did earlier, look at how dialogue functions in effective nonfiction. Choose one of these essays that uses dialogue effectively (or another essay of your own choosing): E. B. White's "Afternoon of an American Boy," or Andre Dubus's "Love in the Morning," Carol Guess's "Red" (on the website), or Richard Bausch's "So Long Ago" (in the anthology section). Highlight the dialogue and focus on that for a minute, as you did earlier with characterization. What do simple things like speech cadences and word choices tell you about these characters? How would the characterizations change if you changed the dialogue or eliminated it?

7.   Write a page or two of actual dialogue. Practice by using your notebook to record snippets of speech: exchanges with classmates, friends, spouses, or parents. Pay attention to syntax. How much is grammatically correct or incorrect? How much slang or dialect appears in different speakers' voices? When you feel ready, write a page or two of typical dialogue—you can record it and write it down, or try to re-create it—with someone fairly close to you. Do the same partner swap with this dialogue that you did with characterization, and see how much of the person you're describing comes through in his or her voice.

Point of View

8.   The only way to fully understand point of view is to experiment with it. Pull out an earlier essay of yours, or write a simple paragraph about some subject you've thought about as a likely one. Then recast the point of view, from first to second or third. Force yourself to keep going through at least one paragraph; don't look at the clunkiness of a sentence like *For five years you lived in Alaska* and give up. Push through, and open yourself up to moments when the point of view works, when you feel interesting possibilities arise (you can also refer to the "Try It" section of Chapter 10, "Lyric Essay"). Be sensitive to the nuances of placing the reader so squarely in your shoes in second person, of distancing yourself from your own life, as you must with third person. Examine the essay possibilities that arise out of each change—the alienation of third person, the direct implication of the reader in second person.

9.   Traditionally, *shifting* point of view—moving from the narrative position of one character to another within a piece—has been a problem area for fiction writers. Unintentional shifting is a common error for young writers; masterful shifts can make a story, as in Flannery O'Connor's famous shift to the

Misfit's point of view at the end of "A Good Man Is Hard to Find." As non-fiction expands its reach, we see point of view shifting in this genre as well. In addition to the Selzer example, look again at "The Fourth State of Matter," which briefly, on page 242, switches to the viewpoint of a disturbed student watching, among other people, the author. You might want to preface your own experiments with a class or writer's group discussion of how to switch like this ethically and appropriately; when you find a comfortable way (perhaps, as above, by signaling somehow your movement into imagination), see whether such a switch can enrich a piece of your own writing.

Image and Metaphor

10. It's important to understand just what a metaphoric organization feels like and how it works. Choose "Red" (on the website) or "The Death of the Moth" (in the anthology section) and follow the movement of the imagery. What are all the permutations of the color red, and what are their associations? What kind of closure does the ending bring to this color motif? How does the metaphor of the moth as a "tiny bead of pure life" evolve in the Woolf essay? How do the movements of the author's pencil enrich and complete the metaphor? You should become aware of the sense of a narrative conveyed by the imagery in a work.

The Rhythm of Your Sentences

11. There's no getting around it. Diagramming sentences and counting words pale in entertainment value compared with the preceding. But sooner or later you need to think about the basics of how you approach a sentence. Do a quick diagnostic of two to three paragraphs of your own prose (less might not be representative enough). How long do your sentences tend to be? How do you structure them? Do you vary mood, or speech acts, such as questioning, stating, and commanding, or do you simply use a declarative or simple statement? Challenge yourself to approach a piece of prose in a way you haven't in the past—more short sentences or sentence fragments, perhaps, or more shifts in mood. See how this change alters your work, and opens up the possibilities of the essay.

We've been explaining all of the building stones of creative nonfiction. Now is the time for you to pull them all together and look holistically at your own work. If you're reading this book as part of a class, you may want to dig out some nonfiction you've written. Try to think about how you approach it. Do you tend to write in scene? In concrete or abstract language? Are your characters developed by description? Do you use dialogue? If not, why not? What point of view do you tend to use? How much of the time do you use image and metaphor, and when you do so, are you aware of how your imagery evolves, how it seems to tell a story of its own? What kind of sentence rhythm characterizes your writing?

Once you have a sense of who you are as a writer, it makes sense to ask questions about the choices you're making. Be on the lookout for the techniques you haven't let yourself try, because you weren't aware of them or because they seemed off limits somehow. Now is the time to allow yourself to approach the technical aspects of your writing in a new way—to sound all the instruments of the orchestra.

Suggestions for Further Reading

In Our Anthology

Bausch, Richard, "So Long Ago"

Beard, Jo Ann, "The Fourth State of Matter"

Goldbarth, Albert, "After Yitzl"

Selzer, Richard, "The Knife"

Woolf, Virginia, "The Death of the Moth"

On Our Website

Dubus, Andre, "Love in the Morning"

Guess, Carol, "Red"

Kitchen, Judith, "Things of This Life"

Miller, Brenda, "Basha Leah"

Elsewhere

Bell, Madison Smartt, *Narrative Design: Working with Imagination, Craft, and Form*

Burroway, Janet, *Writing Fiction* (6th edition)

Goldberg, Natalie, *Writing Down the Bones: Freeing the Writer Within*

Gutkind, Lee, *The Art of Creative Nonfiction: Writing and Selling the Literature of Reality*

Lamott, Anne, *Bird by Bird: Some Instructions on Writing and Life*

Strunk, William Jr., and E. B. White, *The Elements of Style*

Zinsser, William, *On Writing Well: The Classic Guide to Writing Nonfiction*

Goldstein, Norm, *The Associated Press Stylebook and Briefing on Media Law*

Chapter Two

The Particular Challenges of Creative Nonfiction

Of course a picture can lie, but only if you yourself are not honest or if you don't have enough control over your subject. Then it is the camera working, not you.—**André Kertész, photographer**

- ■ **The "I" and the Eye: Framing Experience**
- ■ **The Autobiographical Act**
- ■ **The Persona of the First-Person Narrator**
- ■ **The Pact with the Reader: Creating Trust**
- ■ **The Permutations of "Truth": Fact versus Fiction**
- ■ **Cueing the Reader**
- ■ **Some Pitfalls to Avoid: "Revenge Prose" and "The Therapist's Couch"**
- ■ **Try It**

I'm writing an essay about my grandmother. I'm not sure why I'm writing this. There are just certain scenes and images that haunt me and I have to get them down on paper: my grandmother immobilized in a hospital bed, the ties of her hospital gown undone around her collarbone; my mother crying quietly in a restaurant as she tells me she can't bring herself to care for her mother in her home. As I write, I have to make several questionable choices: Do I really remember massaging my grandmother's back that day in the hospital? Now that I've written it, the scene's taken on the stamp of truth, seems to have replaced any "real" memories I might have of that day. And do I relate the scene of my mother's shame; is it really my story to tell? Can I imagine a scene between my mother and my grandmother, the difficulty of touch between them?

In the end, several months later, I decide to leave in the massage scene—it has an emotional truth to it, a resonance that indicates to me the memory is valid, not only for the essay but for myself. But I delete the scene with my mother in the restaurant; although the facts of this moment are more readily verifiable, I've decided that it oversteps some boundary I've set up for myself. That part is not my story to tell—I don't have the authority or the permission—and it feels too risky. I also, therefore, need to cut the scene where I imagine my mother and grandmother together in our family home. This is a difficult cut—I love the writing in that section—but it needs to go because the scene no longer fits in with the trajectory of the essay.

Yet I know that none of this writing has been wasted. Through writing the scenes I eventually eliminated, I came to understand what was important for this particular essay: to focus my attention on the metaphors of touch, the difficulties of such simple gestures within the family. I also learned how I draw the theoretical lines for myself, how I choose to go about negotiating the ethical land mines of creative nonfiction. —**Brenda**

Creative nonfiction is a tricky business. On the one hand there is the challenge—and the thrill—of turning real life into art. But on the other hand, we have to deal with all the issues that come attached to that "real life." When a fiction writer wants her character to remember the first time she ate ice cream, she can enter the problem imaginatively: place the character at Coney Island with a melting chocolate cone or at a birthday party with a neat scoop on a slice of cake. Can you do the same thing if you're writing from your own memory, even if you don't exactly remember the scene? A fiction writer can create the set number of characters necessary for the action; can you do the same thing with the characters you encounter in your own life and research? A fiction writer who needs dialogue writes it. As a nonfiction writer, can you make up dialogue you don't remember verbatim? If you're writing essays based on research, how much of your imagination can you use? Does "nonfiction" mean "no fiction"?

Even truth-gathering of the most mundane sort seems to require the finesse of fiction in order to get it right. No matter how meticulous your research or your notes, at some point you'll need to rely on memory and imagination to go beyond what lies at your fingertips in the form of fact. Even eyewitness accounts are notoriously unreliable for establishing the truth of a situation. Try this: Have the members of the group—a class or writing group—close their eyes and try to recall details of the room they're in. Few will agree on even the basic facts: the number of windows, the color of the carpet, how the drapes hang. Whether we work with our own stories or others', personal issues or science, imaginative memory must come into the equation. It would be a dry story indeed if the physicist you wrote about never appeared as a character, never worked in an office the reader can see, or never used the particular gesture of pushing her hair behind her ears.

The self inhabits the prose of creative nonfiction, whether or not you write directly about your own experiences. It is this "I" that picks and chooses among the facts. This "I" re-creates those essential scenes and makes crucial decisions about what to include and what to exclude. The "I" decides on the opening line that will set up the voice of the piece, the essential themes and metaphors. The "I" gives the essay its *personality,* both literally and figuratively. The essential question then is: How do you create a piece inhabited by the self without becoming self-centered? And how do you negotiate all the ethical and technical obstacles that come with writing from real life?

The "I" and the Eye: Framing Experience

A useful way of looking at how creative nonfiction employs the "I" is to align the genre with photography. Both photography and creative nonfiction operate under the "sign of the real" (a phrase coined by literary theorist Hayden White); both operate *as though* the medium itself were transparent. In other words, when you look at a photograph, you're lulled into the illusion that you see the world as it is—looking through a window, as it were—but in reality you're being shown a highly manipulated version of that world. The same is true with creative nonfiction: Since it operates under "the sign of the real," it can be easy to mistake the essay as presenting life itself, without adulteration.

But both photography and creative nonfiction actually function just as subjectively as fiction and painting, since the personal "eye" is the mechanism for observation, and the inner "I" is the medium through which these observations are filtered. As Joan Didion puts it:

"No matter how dutifully we record what we see around us, the common denominator of all we see is always, transparently, shamelessly, the implacable 'I.'" Direct representation without a mediating "I" is impossible. The photograph (or the essay) automatically translates the world into artifice. Simply the basic act of framing, as photography theorist Siegfried Kracauer argues, interprets the world: The photo is a "fragment of infinity" and so can never represent reality as experienced in its entire context. There's always a little "blood" on the frame, residue from this act of fragmentation.

The same holds true for the essayist. The minute you begin to impose form on experience—no matter how dutifully you try to remain faithful to history or the world—you're immediately faced with a technical dilemma: How do you effectively frame this experience? What gets left outside the confines of this frame? Are some frames more "truthful" than others? And the way you decide to frame the world directly reflects the "I" and the "eye" that perform this act of construction.

Joan Didion, for instance, in her essay "Goodbye to All That" (see the anthology section) chooses to frame her essay through a nostalgic retrospective that reconstructs threshold moments of her time in New York. She re-creates the point of view of a young woman new to the city, giving us many sensory details, and ends her first section with the memorable lines: "I would stay in New York, I told him, just six months, and I could see the Brooklyn Bridge from my window. As it turned out the bridge was the Triborough, and I stayed eight years."

Didion's essay may *appear* to be simply a faithful reconstruction of New York—a snapshot or a photograph—but in reality she has skillfully framed the experience through her particular voice and vision. Other writers may not have even noticed the bridges, choosing to focus instead on the hot dog vendors in the streets, or the lights of Times Square. Other writers may have chosen a less nostalgic voice, opting for a hard-edged realist vision of the city as it exists today. But for Didion, the bridges, and their mistaken names, represent her coming of age, the transition from bumbling innocence to a more sophisticated maturity. Bridges provide a metaphor for this process and so become an essential image for her essay. They're not a passing detail, available to anyone, but the result of a particular "I" and "eye" observing the world and framing it for significance. Her point of view, her language, her details, her scenes, and her structure for this essay all reflect this framing "I." No one else could have written "Goodbye to All That."

Wallace Stegner, in his book *Where the Bluebird Sings to the Lemonade Springs*, posits that our task as writers is

> to write a story, though ignorant or baffled. You take something that is important to you, something you have brooded about. You try to see it

as clearly as you can, and to fix it in a transferable equivalent. All you want in the finished print is the clean statement of the lens, *which is yourself,* on the subject that has been absorbing your attention (emphasis ours).

This rhetoric of photography lends itself to the language of creative nonfiction, since in both processes we link inner and outer worlds through our artistic intuition. A good photograph will mirror the inner vision of the photographer, just as a good essay will reflect the unique sensibility of the writer, whether or not that writer focuses on material interior to the self.

The Autobiographical Act

If you write from personal experience, your "I" will carry out what critic Elizabeth Bruss has termed an "autobiographical act." This term emphasizes that writing autobiographically can be, essentially, a *performance:* As you write autobiography, in a sense, you re-create your own past and your sense of self, and you do so in front of a live audience, over and over again. As one of the forefathers of the personal essay, Michel de Montaigne, put it in the sixteenth century: "I have no more made my book than my book has made me." The act of writing becomes an act of re-creation, perhaps more so than in other genres because you also, in a sense, alter or re-create the presence behind that prose at the same time.

While this process can be exhilarating, it can also frighten us: What if our writings take over our "real" memories? Will we become subservient to this created version of ourselves, with no solid center, no undeniable truths? Perhaps. As we will explore in chapter 3, memory is itself a myth and performs these kinds of narrative acts all the time. We seek to make sense of the world and we do this through story. We seek to impose form on something that remains essentially inchoate. Writing from memory and from personal experience takes this natural process one step further and problematizes it, since you have now chosen to make public what is more often a highly private, almost invisible, act.

Theorist Philippe LeJeune, in *On Autobiography,* delineates between two types of autobiographical acts: the "utterance" and the "enunciation." An *utterance* appears more as a bald statement of "what happened"—a description of events that have already occurred. The *enunciation* reveals the writer caught in the act of making these events unfold before our eyes, and making sense of them, forging connections and metaphors. Both readers and writers of creative nonfiction find themselves enthralled by the dual nature of this genre. We get two for the price of one: information, or story, and a glimpse into how the "I" continually re-creates itself, and situates itself, in the service of art.

The Persona of the First-Person Narrator

Just as the details of the world and experience may be framed, or constructed, by a mediating "I," so too is that "I" a fabrication for the purposes of the essay. We aren't the same on the page as we are in real life, and we must be aware that the "I" is just as much a tool—or a point of view, or a character—that we manipulate for particular effects. The "I" on the page is really a fictional construction, reflecting certain parts of us, and leaving others out, or exaggerating certain aspects for the purposes of the essay.

For instance, if you pull out any of the essays in the anthology section, you'll encounter narrators who have taken on certain voices for the purposes of the essay at hand. Or they've exaggerated their interests and obsessions in order to carry the essay through to completion. Bernard Cooper, for example, isn't *always* obsessed with the sound of sighs (see "The Fine Art of Sighing"), just as David James Duncan often has other things on his mind besides the baseball sent to his brother the day after the brother died (see "The Mickey Mantle Koan"). But for the time span of the essay, they create themselves as characters with these obsessions, which focus the piece and provide its reason for existing at all.

You'll also find, as you write creative nonfiction, that a distinction evolves between the "I" who exists as a character in your own narrative and the "I" who narrates that story for us from a more literary perspective. In your own writing, you'll find that the narrating "I" who unfolds on the page bears a resemblance to the person you know as yourself, but you must be willing to manipulate this sense of yourself for the purpose of your essay. For instance, the "I" who speaks on the page may seem more confident and carry more authority than you feel in real life. Or this "I" may take on different voices for different occasions—sometimes highly literary, other times more colloquial. In any case, this narrating "I" will be the guiding force that establishes the essay's literary merit.

Memoirist Vivian Gornick, in her book *The Situation and the Story,* writes about finding her voice in creative nonfiction: "I began to read the greats in essay writing—and it wasn't their confessing voices I was responding to, it was their truth-speaking personae," she writes. "I have created a persona who can find the story riding the tide that I, in my unmediated state, am otherwise going to drown in." The narrating "I," the persona you create, is the one who has the wherewithal to rescue experience from chaos and turn it into art.

The Pact with the Reader: Creating Trust

As you create this persona, you also establish a relationship between yourself and the reader. In creative nonfiction—more so, perhaps, than in any other genre—readers assume a real person behind the artifice, an author who *speaks* directly to them. Just as in spoken conversations, it's a symbiotic relationship: The reader completes this act of communication by paying attention to the author's story, and the author must establish right away a reason for the reader to be attentive. For this relationship to work, however, it's up to the author to establish a certain level of trust.

Simply presenting your work as an essay rather than a piece of fiction sets up a certain assumption: That is, readers will be engaged in a true story, one rooted in the world as we know it. Because of this assumption, readers need to know they are in good hands, in the presence of, in Vivian Gornick's words, a "truth-speaking" guide who will lead them somewhere worthwhile. Readers need to know that they won't be deceived along the way, led to believe something that turns out to be patently untrue. LeJeune calls this the "pact with the reader." The essayist pledges, in some way, both to be as honest as possible with the reader *and* to make this conversation worthwhile. Without this pact, true communication becomes impossible.

Creative nonfiction assumes an audience that listens and that will eventually reciprocate. As Patricia Hampl puts it: "You tell me your story, I'll tell you mine." Without this understanding, we become more like the people you occasionally see in the park: men and women talking to themselves, rehashing past wrongs, their arms gesticulating wildly in the air. We don't really *listen* to such a narrator; in fact, our impulse is to turn away and walk in the opposite direction.

So *how* does a writer establish this kind of pact with the reader? Essayist Phillip Lopate, in his introduction to *The Art of the Personal Essay,* writes that "part of our trust in good personal essayists issues, paradoxically, from their exposure of their own betrayals, uncertainties, and self-mistrust." When we reveal our own foibles, readers can relax and know that they engage in a conversation with someone as human as they are.

Good writers can also establish this pact through their skillful manipulation of the techniques that make for vivid writing (see chapter 1). If we know that we're in the hands of a literary artist, one who won't let us down with clichés or a weak infrastructure, then we're usually willing to go wherever he or she leads. We assume that the writer has shaped the material for its best literary effect, while at the same time remaining as true as possible to the facts of the world and history. Let's take a look at some of the essayists in our anthology section, and try to see how they establish a pact with the reader early on in their work, combining craft with content:

Joan Didion:

It did not occur to me to call a doctor, because I knew none, and although it did occur to me to call the desk and ask that the air conditioner be turned off, I never called, because I did not know how much to tip whoever might come—was anyone ever so young? I am here to tell you that someone was.

E. B. White:

Seeing him, I would call 'Hello, Parnell!' and he would smile and say 'Hello, Elwyn!' and walk on. Once I remember dashing out of our yard on roller skates and executing a rink turn in front of Parnell, to show off, and he said, 'Well! Quite an artist, aren't you?' I remember the words. I was delighted at praise from an older man and sped away along the flagstone sidewalk, dodging the cracks I knew so well.

Margaret Atwood:

1. Why do you write?"

I've begun this piece nine times. I've junked every beginning.

I hate writing about my writing. I almost never do it. Why am I doing it now? Because I said I would. I got a letter. I wrote back no. Then I was at a party and the same person was there. It's harder to refuse in person. Saying yes had something to do with being nice, as women are taught to be, and something to do with being helpful, which we are also taught.

Bernard Cooper:

You feel a gradual welling up of pleasure, or boredom, or melancholy. Whatever the emotion, it's more abundant than you ever dreamed.

You can no more contain it than your hands can cup a lake. And so you surrender and suck the air. Your esophagus opens, diaphragm expands. Poised at the crest of an exhalation, your body is about to be unburdened, second by second, cell by cell. A kettle hisses. A balloon deflates. Your shoulders fall like two ripe pears, muscles slack at last.

What do you find in common with these four very different essayists? Though they write about quite divergent subjects and from widely varying points of view, they've all constructed an "I" voice that speaks directly to the reader, and they all give the reader some evidence that it will be worthwhile to stay with this conversation. Joan Didion reveals her embarrassment and timidity at being in a city where she knows no one and is unsure of the social conventions. Not only does she reel us in because we might be able to relate to her story, she also laughs at herself and invites the reader to laugh with her: "[W]as anyone ever so young? I am here to tell you that someone was." This one line establishes the fact that Didion has perspective on her experience. She has garnered some wisdom in the time between then and now, and so we won't be subjected to a rendition of raw emotion. Rather, the material will be shaped and presented by someone who can distance herself from the "I" who is a character in her story and the "I" who narrates that story many years later.

E. B. White gains our trust because he's able to describe vividly a scene of childish delight and does it in such a way that we experience the scene along with him. Though we may never have had White's exact experience, he keys us into an experience that might be termed "universal." Surely we've all experienced some moment of delight such as his, some moment when we were recognized by someone we admired. And if we haven't, White makes us wish we had, with his strong verbs ("dashing," "executing," "dodging"), and his powerful sentence structure that leaps and feints and ends in a sigh of nostalgic satisfaction. White, like Didion, also shows us that he understands the difference between creating an "I" character in the story and a narrating "I" with the skills to render this story effectively. The line "I remember the words," while deceptively simple and commonplace, alerts the reader to the fact of the older writer's presence in the scene, looking on and rediscovering it along with the reader.

Margaret Atwood uses the form itself to establish that we're in good hands. She uses the interview question as a reason for writing in the first place, then confesses that she'd rather do anything but write the essay we have in our hands. The tension between the question (which recurs nine times throughout the essay, an insistent voice that spurs the writer and reader on) and her tentative answers to that question provide dramatic suspense for an essay that could, in other hands, easily become clichéd or predictable. Also, by confessing her difficulty, she allows us, again, to relate to her experience. It's as if she's giving voice to the doubts we all carry in our heads—a daring move that we silently applaud. She creates a persona, forthright and strong, who is able to say the things we ourselves might find difficult. With this voice, she's even able to discuss theoretical or political issues in a way that's particular to her, without becoming pedantic.

Bernard Cooper reaches out a hand and tugs us into his essay by starting off with the second-person point of view: "You feel a gradual welling up of pleasure. . . ." He makes us participate in his essay about sighing by re-creating a sigh on the page. Read the passage aloud and see whether you can keep from letting out a long, hearty sigh. And the "you" makes an assertion that's difficult to deny: The experience he creates on the page does indeed become a universal sigh, exhaled in common with thousands of others.

All these writers, along with the multitude of creative nonfiction writers we admire, must immediately make a case for taking up a reader's time and attention. In doing so, they also take care of the "so what?" question that plagues writers of creative nonfiction in general, and of memoir in particular. Why should anyone care about your personal story or your perspective on the world? What use will the essay have for anyone except yourself? By engaging you in their essays through vivid details and an authentic voice, through imaginative uses of form and structure, these essayists show that the personal can indeed become universal. We care about their stories because they have become *our* stories. They've verbalized for us what has previously remained silent or have at least rephrased these issues for us in such a way as to make them new. That's what we're after as readers of literature—a fresh articulation of the world so that we might understand it more thoroughly—and these essayists do so through both personal revelation and careful crafting of their prose.

The Permutations of "Truth": Fact versus Fiction

If you set out to establish a pact with the reader—to gain his or her trust—then you must make some critical decisions about how, or if, you'll use fictional elements in your nonfiction writing. As we've noted earlier, the simple act of writing and the construction of the narrative voice are essentially creative acts that impose a form where none before existed. Beyond that, which kinds of fictions are allowable in creative nonfiction and which aren't? Just how much emphasis do we put on "creative" and how much on "nonfiction?"

On the other hand, some writers believe that nothing at all should ever knowingly be made up in creative nonfiction: If you can't remember what color dress you wore to your sixth-grade graduation, then you'd better leave that detail out or do some research to find the answer. If you had five best friends who helped you through a jam in high school, then you'd better not compress those five into one or two composite characters for the sake of an efficient narrative. On the other hand, there are writers who believe that small details can be fabricated in order to create the scenes of memory, and they knowingly create composite characters because their narrative structures demand it. Some writers willingly admit imagination into factual narratives; others abhor it and see it as a trespass into fiction. It's interesting to note that when a writer publishes a piece of fiction that contains highly autobiographical elements, no one flinches; in fact, such blurring of the boundaries is often presumed. But to admit fictional techniques into autobiographical work creates controversy and furious discussion. The nature of that essential pact with the reader—that sense of trust—demands this kind of scrutiny into the choices we make as nonfiction writers.

We believe that writers must negotiate the boundary between fact and fiction for themselves. What constitutes fabrication for one writer will seem like natural technique to another. But what we can do here is show how some writers employ fictional techniques and what effects these choices might have on your credibility as an essayist.

Memory and Imagination

If your work is rooted in memory, you'll find yourself immediately confronted with imagination. Memory, in a sense, *is* imagination: an "imaging" of the past, re-creating the sights, sounds, smells, tastes, and touches of the past (see chapter 3). In her essay "Memory and Imagination," Patricia Hampl writes: "I am forced to admit that memoir is not a matter of transcription, that memory itself is not a warehouse of finished stories, not a static gallery of framed pictures. I must admit that I invented. But why?"

We invent because our lives, and the world, contain more than simple facts; imagination and the way we imagine are as much a part of ourselves as any factual résumé. In creative nonfiction, the creative aspect involves not only writerly techniques, but also a creative interpretation of the facts of our lives, plumping the skeletal facts with the flesh of imagination. Personal history sometimes demands this kind of elaboration in order for its full significance to emerge on the page. As Hampl continues: "We find, in our details and broken and obscured images, the language of symbol. Here memory impulsively reaches out its arms and embraces imagination. That is the resort to invention. It isn't a lie, but an act of necessity, as the innate urge to locate personal truth always is."

Look ahead to the tonsil story that precedes chapter 3. There's no real way to verify either the fact or fiction of the tonsils floating in a jar on the bedside table. What I (Brenda) can do with this image is admit the bizarre, and unlikely, nature of this mental picture that imagination has called forth in conjunction with memory. I can say, "Why do I remember this jar of tonsils at my hospital bedside?" In so doing, I readily admit the imagination into memory and can then proceed to construct an essay that both interprets the image for metaphorical significance and allows it to become a jumping-off point for a longer meditation on the topics this metaphor suggests. I don't discount or omit this image because its factual veracity is in question; rather, I relish the opportunity to explore that rich boundary zone between memory and imagination. And I do so in full view of my audience, disclosing my intent and so maintaining my pact with the reader.

Or look at Hampl's essay, "The Need to Say It," on the website. To conclude her discussion of why she writes memoirs, Hampl ends with a vivid scene of herself in an elementary school classroom: "Off to the side the whole time, in my lateral sight, has been a single snapshot which I'm convinced possesses the complete explanation. How like a memoirist to believe a solo image, fluttering in the dark, is the rare butterfly that will, at last, complete the collection." She examines this snapshot in precise detail, placing herself in "the blessed outer region far from the blackboard," her schoolmate Mike Maloney whispering behind her. She admits that she does not remember certain details, such as the teacher's question ("It's gone forever . . ."), but she allows herself to elaborate on the details that will bring the scene to life for us. Does she *really* remember the tears welling up in her eyes, the exact sensation in her throat? Does she *really* remember exactly the positions of Tommy Schwartz and Sheila Phalen (or their exact names?) as she sees them blurrily out the classroom window? Does it matter? For the purposes of this essay, do these details really need to correspond to the scene *exactly* as it played out those many years ago? And do these inaccurate details—if they are inaccurate—harm anyone, or aggrandize the writer, or lead the reader astray? Do these kinds of details make you distrust the writer (how could she remember that?) or do you suspend such judgment and accept the scene as a literary device? Decide for yourself. Does Hampl's essay have a truthful *resonance*, what might be called "emotional," or literary, truth? If so, why, and if not, why not? Where do you draw the line?

Emotional Truth versus Factual Truth

Mimi Schwartz, in "Memoir? Fiction? Where's the Line?" writes: "Go for the emotional truth, that's what matters. Yes, gather the facts by all means. Look at old photos, return to old places, ask family members what they remember, look up time-line books for the correct songs and fashion styles, read old newspapers, encyclopedias, whatever—and then use the imagination to fill in the remembered experience." If we allow imagination into memory, then we're naturally aligning ourselves with a stance toward an emotional, or literary, truth; this doesn't mean that we discount factual truth altogether, but that it may be important, for *literary* purposes, to interpret what you can of the facts to get at a truth that resonates with a different kind of veracity on the page. Facts take us only so far.

Schwartz continues: "It may be 'murky terrain,' you may cross the line into fiction and have to step back reluctantly into what really happened—the struggle creates the tensions that make memoir either powerfully true or hopelessly phony. The challenge of this genre is that it hands you characters, plot and setting, and says, 'Go figure them out!'—using fact, memory and imagination to recreate the complexity of real moments, big and small, with no invented rapes or houses burning down." Here, Schwartz herself draws the line. We can reconstruct certain details, imagine ourselves into the stories *behind* the facts, but certain facts, such as a rape or a house burning down, cannot be invented. Or as novelist and memoirist Bret Lott puts it in his essay "Against Technique": "In fiction you get to make up what happens; in creative nonfiction you don't get to mess with what happen*ed*."

Take a look at the case of a highly publicized memoir, *Fragments: Memories of a Wartime Childhood*. In this lyrical narrative told from a child's point of view, Binjamin Wilkomirski re-creates scenes from his experience as a child survivor of the Holocaust. He recounts his father's execution in graphic detail, scenes of rats scurrying over piles of corpses. The prose is beautifully rendered, and some scenes move the reader to tears. But shortly after this memoir was published, critics began to question Wilkomirski's veracity. One journalist investigated and found evidence showing that the writer had never been in a concentration camp at all. Birth certificates and adoption records showed him born in Switzerland in 1941 and adopted into a family shortly thereafter. However, Wilkomirski stood by his memories, which were recovered, he said, in therapy. To him, these memories were just as real—they carried just as much emotional truth—as the factual history.

Few people would argue that Wilkomirski hadn't crossed that ethical line for creative nonfiction. Though we've presented arguments claiming that emotional truths can be just as veracious as facts, it isn't acceptable to appropriate or wholly invent a history with little or no relation to your own. You still need to use your own history as a scaffolding for the emotional truths you'll uncover. While *Fragments* exemplifies this dictum in fairly obvious terms (to appropriate something as horrific and emotionally charged as the Holocaust leaves little room for debate), you need to see how it might operate in smaller ways in your own nonfiction writing. There are facts and then there are *facts*. Which ones are hard and fast?

Annie Dillard, for example, has been brought to task simply for claiming to own a cat she never had. Her book *Pilgrim at Tinker Creek* begins with the line: "I used to have a cat, an old fighting tom, who would jump through the open window by my bed in the middle of the night and land on my chest." Later in the paragraph she writes: "And some mornings I'd wake in daylight to find my body covered with paw prints in blood; I looked as though I'd been painted with roses." This image becomes important to her spiritual explorations throughout the book, and nowhere does she really acknowledge that the cat is a literary device, or a fiction, constructed for this purpose. For many readers, this constitutes a breach of contract; though Dillard uses the fictional cat to good effect, the fact that she deceived the audience in some way undermines her credibility for the rest of the book. "How can we be sure of anything she says from here on out?" these readers would cry. Other readers are willing to forgive Dillard for this fiction, claiming that it isn't an important detail and that the cat is meant as a metaphorical device. After all, the book's subtitle is *A Mystical Excursion into the Natural World*. In the realm of mysticism, even nonexistent fighting toms might materialize to be our spirit guides.

In another case, Dillard makes up a scientific fact in order to fill in the gaps in her narrative. In her essay "Total Eclipse" (see the anthology section), she tells us that the next total eclipse in Yakima will happen in 2019. Years later, in an interview, Dillard admitted to having made up that fact when she couldn't find the date anywhere in her research. For her, it was important to have a date in the paragraph to get across the point she wanted to make and also to establish the rhythm of the prose, so she made one up. It's a short line in a long, complex essay: Does it matter? Does Dillard undermine her pact with the reader? Would you be comfortable inserting such "facts" in your own nonfiction writing?

The Whole Truth?

Sometimes you'll be troubled not by facts that are made up, but by facts that are omitted. In essay writing, it's nearly impossible to tell "the whole truth." Of necessity, you'll find yourself needing to pare away certain details, events, and characters to create an essay that makes narrative sense. For example, if you're writing about something that happened in school when you were ten years old, you'll have to decide just how many members of your fifth-grade class will make it onto the stage. Who's important and who's not for this particular essay?

This is an easy one—you'll naturally choose to flesh out the one or two characters closest to you at the time. More difficult will be knowing when and how to omit the characters that felt important in real life, but just get in the way once you put them on the page. For example, Bernard Cooper included his brothers in his early book *Maps to Anywhere,* but when he wrote the essays collected in *Truth Serum* (which includes "The Fine Art of Sighing"), he made a conscious decision to leave them out. This left him open to criticism from at least one reviewer who accused him of deceiving his audience by implying that he was an only child. Here's his reply:

> I had three brothers, all of whom died of various ailments, a sibling history that strains even my credulity. . . . Very early in the writing of *Truth Serum* I knew that a book concerned with homosexual awakening would sooner or later deal with AIDS and the population of friends I've lost to the disease. . . . To be blunt, I decided to limit the body count in this book in order to prevent it from collapsing under the threat of death. . . . There is only so much loss I can stand to place at the center of the daily rumination that writing requires. . . . Only when the infinite has edges am I capable of making art.

"Only when the infinite has edges am I capable of making art." Perhaps that should be a credo we creative nonfiction writers etch on the walls above our desks. For that is what we're up to all the time: creating those edges, constructing artful containers that will hold some facts and not others.

These edges might also be formed by choosing to create composite characters, or to compress events in time. A composite character is a fictional construction; the author blends the traits of several characters into one or two, thereby streamlining both the cast and the narratives needed to take care of them. Compression of time means that you might conflate anecdotes from several trips home into one composite visit (an alternative is to compose a representative scene; see chapter 1). As a writer and a member of a writing community, you'll want to think about these devices—and talk about them—to see how they conform to your own writing ethics.

Jo Ann Beard, on the flyleaf of the book *The Boys of My Youth* (which includes "The Fourth State of Matter," see the anthology section), states that "several characters are composites" of assorted people she knew. Many people appeared and disappeared during her chaotic adolescence, and she found it difficult to introduce them all in such a way that the reader could keep track of them. Do you have a story that's been difficult to tell because of the number of people involved or the sheer volume of events through which you need to sift? If so, ask yourself whether there's a way of creating composite characters or compressing time that doesn't sacrifice the truth.

Cueing the Reader

As you continue to develop your own guidelines for the permutations of "truth" in creative nonfiction, you'll find that you'll create your own tools for negotiating some of these tricky areas. Some simple ones to keep in mind, however, are tag lines that let the reader in on what exactly you're up to. Phrases such as "I imagine," "I would like to believe," "I don't remember exactly, but," "I would like to remember," or even a simple "Perhaps," alert the reader to your artistic agenda. Once you set the terms of the discussion—once you situate the reader in that boundary zone between fact and fiction—then you'll most likely be free to go wherever you wish.

For example, what would have happened if Annie Dillard had said: "I imagine the next total eclipse, in 2019 perhaps. . . ." Or if she had said, "I never owned a fighting tom, but if I had, I imagine. . . ." For Dillard, these kinds of tag lines might have ruined the effect she was after, lessening their literary effect. But they would certainly have diffused any attacks against her credibility as well.

Cueing the reader can be accomplished more subtly. If you have trouble writing a scene for a family event because it happened ten years ago, try beginning it with a line like, "This is how my father sounded," or "This is what Sundays were like at my house." Then watch the pieces fall into place. These statements are unobtrusive, but they make it clear that you're not claiming to provide a verbatim transcript of an event.

Writers can also tell the reader directly what they're up to: Full disclosure lets readers know what they're in for. Robin Hemley, for instance, begins a memoir about the life of his sister, and to a larger extent his family, by declaring, "I have a larcenous heart." He tells us, essentially, that he will knowingly "steal" his material from his family, shaping it for his own purposes. In a daring move, Lauren Slater titles a book, *Lying: A Metaphorical Memoir.* Though this book is full of details that prove to be untrue, notably her descriptions of having epileptic seizures, Slater stands by her work with an obvious defense: The title tells us bluntly that she's fabricating metaphorical experiences. Even though you may or may not buy this as a reader, you can't claim that she didn't warn you.

Some Pitfalls to Avoid: "Revenge Prose" and "The Therapist's Couch"

Ironically, while creative nonfiction can be a tool of self-discovery, you must also have some distance from the self to write effectively. You must know when you're ready to write about certain subjects and when you are not. If you're crying while crafting a piece of nonfiction, the tears will smudge the ink, making your work ultimately unreadable. If your hand shakes with anger as you write, the words will veer wildly across the page, with no sense of control or design.

This isn't to say that creative nonfiction is devoid of emotion; on the contrary, the most powerful nonfiction is propelled by a sense of urgency, the need to speak about events that touch us deeply, both those in our personal history and those that occur in the world around us. The key to successfully writing about these events is *perspective.* Earlier in the chapter, we aligned creative nonfiction with photography; perspective is the way a photographer chooses to frame and compose a photograph, and perspective is just as vital when you approach tough subjects for personal essays. Perspective defines the difference between a journal entry meant only for private venting and an essay designed for public consumption.

As readers, we rarely want to read an essay that smacks either of "The Therapist's Couch" or "Revenge Prose." In both cases, the writer has not yet gained enough perspective for wisdom, or literature, to emerge from experience. In Therapist's Couch prose, the writer is still weighed down by confusing emotions or feelings of self-pity and wants only to share those emotions with the reader. The depth of these emotions does not allow for a literary design to emerge. In Revenge Prose, the writer's intent seems to be to get back at someone who has wronged him or her. The offender doesn't emerge as a fully developed character, but rather as a flat, one-dimensional incarnation of awful deeds. In both cases, it's the writer who comes out looking bad, because he or she hasn't stepped back enough from the person or the events to gain perspective.

As a writer, it's important for you to start recognizing when you can write about certain material and when you can't. Perhaps it will take another twenty years before you're fully ready to deal with traumatic events in your childhood. It might take years before you're really able to deal with the breakup of your marriage. Or perhaps you'll be able to write about a *small* aspect of the experience, focusing your attention on a particular detail that leads to a larger metaphorical significance outside of the event itself. For instance, David James Duncan, in "The Mickey Mantle Koan" (see the anthology section), deals with the death of his brother years after the fact by focusing his attention on a signed baseball sent to his brother by Mickey Mantle. This baseball leads him to a philosophical rumination on the nature of life itself. This *peripheral vision*—this ability to sidle up to the big issues by way of a side route—is the mark of an accomplished writer, one who has gained enough perspective to use personal experience in the service of a larger literary purpose.

The best writers also show a marked generosity toward the characters in their nonfiction, even those who appear unsympathetic or irredeemable. For example, Terry Tempest Williams, in "The Clan of One-Breasted Women" (see the anthology section), writes an essay that's clearly fueled by anger but that doesn't come across as personally vengeful or mean-spirited. By channeling her energy into research, she shows herself as someone with important information to impart, aside from her own personal history. She creates a metaphor—the clan of one-breasted women—that elevates her own story into a tribal one. By directing her attention to the literary design of her material, she's able to transcend the emotional mine field of that material. "Anger," she has said, "must be channeled so that it becomes nourishing rather than toxic." Her work is passionate, yes, but not shrill in a way that would lose her readers.

In your own work, always be on the lookout for sections that seem too weighed down by the emotions from which they spring. Here are some warning signs: Read the piece aloud and see whether the prose has momentum. Where does it lag and become plodding? Those are the sections that probably haven't been refined enough to avoid melodrama. And seek out any sections that too directly explore your feelings about an event rather than the event itself. Where do you say words such as "I hated," "I felt so depressed," or "I couldn't stand"? The "I" will become intrusive here, repeating itself into infinity—a monologue of old grievances.

If you find yourself telling the reader how to feel, and in a tone that's more like aggrieved chatter at a bar than convincing narrative, then you're probably headed right into Revenge Prose. You don't want to end up sounding like this: "And then you know what else that no-good jerk did? You won't believe this. After *I* was the one to put him through medical school and *I* was the one to have his children, he says *he* needs some space, can you believe that? Space? What the hell does he need *space* for?" Channel your creative energy instead into constructing the scenes, images, and metaphors that will allow the reader to have his or her own reactions, *apart from the ones you had at the time.* On the page, your life isn't just your life anymore; you must put your allegiance now into creating an artifact that will have meaning outside the self.

Try It

1.   Have an individual or group session in which you plumb your own sense of nonfiction ethics. What would you do and what wouldn't you do? Would you re-create a scene or invent dialogue for someone, without a clear cue to the reader? Would you invent a fact, as Annie Dillard did, if it seemed less than critical (or even if it seemed critical)? It's useful for your writing to proceed with a defined sense of your own boundaries.

2.   Practice writing cueing lines. This can be fun to do in a group, while passing one another's essays around, or just writing inventive cueing lines to pass. ("If I dreamed this scene, this is how I would dream it.") Sharing ideas will get you in the habit of using cueing lines creatively.

3.   Try writing out a memory, in scene, from the perspective of at least two people who were present (members of your family, perhaps). Get their memory down as accurately as you can by questioning them about it, and write it as carefully and lovingly as you write your own. Think of this as an exercise in the quirks of individual perspective. If you like the results, try juxtaposing pieces of each narrative, alternating the voices, to create a braided essay (see Chapter 10, "The Lyric Essay").

4.   Try compressing time by creating one scene out of several similar events. For instance, take moments from several Christmas dinners and create one specific scene that encapsulates all of them. What do you gain or lose by doing this to your material?

Suggestions for Further Reading

In Our Anthology

Atwood, Margaret, "Nine Beginnings"

Beard, Jo Ann, "The Fourth State of Matter"

Cooper, Bernard, "The Fine Art of Sighing"

Didion, Joan, "Goodbye to All That"

Dillard, Annie, "Total Eclipse"

Duncan, David James, "The Mickey Mantle Koan"

White, E. B., "Afternoon of an American Boy"

On Our Website

Hampl, Patricia, "The Need to Say It"

Elsewhere

Cooper, Bernard, "Marketing Memory" in *The Business of Memory*

Hampl, Patricia, "Memory and Imagination" in *I Could Tell You Stories*

LeJeune, Philippe, *On Autobiography*

Lott, Bret, "Against Technique" in *Creative Nonfiction*

Schwartz, Mimi, "Memoir? Fiction? Where's the Line?" in *Fourth Genre*

Zinsser, William, *Inventing the Truth: The Art and Craft of Memoir*

PART II

Unearthing Your Material

Chapter Three

The Body of Memory

Memory begins to qualify the imagination, to give it another formation, one that is peculiar to the self. . . . If I were to remember other things, I should be someone else. —**N. Scott Momaday**

- ▊ **The Earliest Memory**
- ▊ **Metaphorical Memory**
- ▊ **"Muscle Memory"**
- ▊ **The Five Senses of Memory**
- ▊ **Try It**

In my earliest memory, I'm a four-year-old girl waking slowly from anesthesia. I lift my head off the damp pillow and gaze blearily through the bars of my hospital crib. I can see a dim hallway with a golden light burning; somehow I know my mother will appear in that hallway any minute now, bearing ice cream and 7 Up. She told me as much before the operation: "All good girls get ice cream and 7 Up when their tonsils come out," she said, stroking my hair. "It's your reward for being brave." I'm vaguely aware of another little girl screaming for her mother in the crib next to mine, but otherwise the room remains dark and hushed, buffered by the footfalls of nurses who stop a moment at the doorway and move on.

I do not turn to face my neighbor, afraid her terror will infect me; I can feel the tickling urge to cry burbling up in my wounded throat, and that might be the end of me, of all my purported bravery and the promised ice cream. I keep my gaze fixed on that hallway, but something glints in my peripheral vision and I turn to face the bedside table. There, in a mason jar, my tonsils float. They rotate in the liquid: misshapen ovals, pink and nubbled, grotesque.

And now my mother has simply appeared, with no warning or announcement. Her head leans close to the crib, and she gently plies the spoon between the bars, places it between my lips, and holds it there while I swallow. I keep my gaze fixed on her face, and she keeps her gaze on mine, though I know we're both aware of those tonsils floating out of reach. The nurses pad about, and one of them enters the room bearing my "Badge of Courage." It's a certificate with a lion in the middle surrounded by laurels, my name scripted in black ink below. My mother holds it out to me, through the bars, and I run a finger across my name, across the lion's mane, across the dry yellowed parchment.—***Brenda***

The Earliest Memory

What's your earliest memory? What's the memory that always emerges from the dim reaches of your consciousness as the *first one,* the beginning to this life you call your own? Most of us can pinpoint them, these images that assume a privileged station in our life's story. Some of these early memories have the vague aspect of a dream, some the vivid clarity of a photograph; whatever form they take, they tend to exert on us a mysterious fascination.

Memory, itself, could be called its own bit of creative nonfiction: We continually, often unconsciously, renovate our memories, shaping them into stories that bring coherence to chaos. Memory's been called the ultimate "mythmaker," continually seeking meaning in the random and often unfathomable events in our lives. "A myth," writes John Kotre, author of *White Gloves: How We Create Ourselves through Memory,* "is not a falsehood but a comprehensive view of reality. It's a story that speaks to the heart as well as the mind, seeking to generate conviction about what it thinks is true."

The first memory, then, becomes the starting point in our own narratives of the self. "Our first memories are like the creation stories that humans have always told about the origins of the earth," Kotre writes. "In a similar way, the individual self—knowing how the story is coming out—selects its earliest memories to say, 'This is who I am because this is how I began.'" As writers, we naturally return again and again to these beginnings and scrutinize them. By paying attention to the illogical, unexpected details of these memories, we just might light upon the odd yet precise images that help our lives make sense—or make sense at least long enough for our purposes as writers.

David James Duncan calls such autobiographical images "river teeth." "There are hard, cross-grained whorls of memory," he writes,

> that remain inexplicably lodged in us long after the straight-grained narrative material that housed them has washed away. Most of these whorls are not stories, exactly: more often they're self-contained moments of shock or of inordinate empathy. . . . These are our "river teeth"—the time-defying knots of experience that remain in us after most of our autobiographies are gone.

Virginia Woolf had her own term for such "shocks" of memory: She calls them "moments of being," and they become essential to our sense of self. They're the times when we get jolted out of our everyday complacency to really *see* the world and all that it contains. This "shock-receiving capacity" is essential for the writer's disposition: "I hazard the explanation," she writes, "that a shock is at once in my case followed by the desire to explain it. . . . I make it real by putting it into words." Woolf's early "moments of being," the vivid first memories from childhood, are of the smallest, most ordinary things: the pattern of her mother's dress, for example, or the pull-cord of the window blind skittering across the floor of their beach house.

The memories that can have the most emotional impact for the writer are those we don't really understand, the images that rise up before us quite without our volition: the flash of our mother's face as she sips from a cooled cup of coffee, for example, her eyes betraying some private grief we've never seen before, or the smell of grapefruit ripening on a tree outside the bedroom window. Perhaps the touch of a stranger's hand reminds you of the way your grandmother casually grasped your hand in her own, the palm so soft but the knuckles so rough, as you sat together watching television, not speaking a word.

These are the "river teeth," the "moments of being," the ones that take your breath away. What repository of memory do you hold in your heart rather than in your head? What are the pictures that rise up to the surface without your bidding? Take these as your cue. Pick up your pen, your net, your magnet, whatever it takes. Be on alert. This is where you begin.

Metaphorical Memory

A metaphor is a way at getting at a truth that exists beyond the literal. By pinpointing certain images as *symbolic,* writers can go deeper than surface truths and create essays that work on many levels at once. This is what writers are up to all the time, not only with memory, but with the material of experience and the world: We resurrect the details not only to describe the surface appearance, but also to make intuitive connections, to articulate some truth that can't be spoken of directly.

If you look at "So Long Ago" in the anthology section, you'll see that Richard Bausch has taken two early images from memory—a short conversation with his father on his seventh birthday and the sight of his great-grandmother in her coffin years later—and expanded them so that these brief flashes now provide jumping-off points to longer meditations on the nature of memory and the passing of time. M. F. K. Fisher, in "A Thing Shared," takes the recollection of a bite of peach pie and transforms it into a vivid illustration of the rare connection between father, daughter, and sisters. These writers, and many others, allow these early memories to impress themselves on the mind. They don't dismiss them as passing details, but rather probe them for any insights they might contain. They ask not only "what," but *"why."* Why do I remember the things I do? Why these memories and not others?

Let's go back to that first memory of the tonsils, that early "river tooth" in the personal essay preceding this chapter. What's important for me, Brenda, as a writer, is not *what* I remember, or even the factual accuracy of the scene, but *why* I remember it the way I do. And I keep coming back to that incongruous jar of tonsils. I doubt the doctors did such a thing (my mother has no recollection of it), but it remains the most stubborn and intractable part of the scene. What I like about this part of my memory is its very illegibility. The best material can't be deciphered in an instant, with a fixed meaning that once pinned down remains immutable. No: What we want, as essayists, is the rich stuff of the inscrutable, those images whose meaning is never clear at first glance, or second, or third.

I could interpret that jar of tonsils in any number of ways, but this is the one I light on most frequently: When I woke from having my tonsils removed, I knew for the first time that my body was not

necessarily a whole unit, always intact. It was the moment I understood the courage it would take to bear this body into a world that
would most certainly do it harm. Of course, as a child I realized no
such thing, but as an adult, *as a writer preserving this memory in lan-*
guage, I begin to create a metaphor that will infiltrate both my writing
and my sense of self from here on out.

Think back on that early memory of yours, the one that came to
mind instantly. Illuminate the details, shine a spotlight on them until
they begin to yield a sense of truth revealed. Where is your body in
this memory? What kind of language does it speak? What metaphor
does it offer for you to puzzle out in writing?

Muscle Memory

The body, the memory, and the mind exist in sublime interdepend-
ence, each part wholly intertwined with the others. There's a term
used in dancing, athletics, parachuting, and other fields that require
sharp training of the body: muscle memory. Once the body learns the
repetitive gestures of a certain movement or skill, the memory of how
to execute these movements is encoded in the muscles. That's why,
for instance, we never forget how to ride a bike. Or why, years after
tap dance lessons, one can still execute a convincing "shuffle-hop-
step" across the kitchen floor.

One cannot speak of memory, and of bodily memory in particular, without trotting out Marcel Proust and his famous madeleine.
Proust dips his madeleine in lime-blossom tea, and *Remembrance of*
Things Past springs forth, all six volumes of it. The moment is worth
recalling here because the connection he makes goes to the very heart
of memory and its residence inside the body:

> [W]hen from a long-distant past nothing subsists, after the people are
> dead, after the things are broken and scattered, taste and smell alone,
> more fragile but more enduring, more unsubstantial, more persistent,
> more faithful, remain poised a long time, like souls, remembering, wait-
> ing, hoping, amid the ruins of all the rest; and bear unflinchingly, in the
> tiny and almost impalpable drop of their essence, the vast structure of
> recollection.

Because memory is so firmly fixed in the body, it takes an object that
appeals to the senses to dislodge memory and allow it to float freely
into the mind or onto the page. *These* are the memories that resonate,
precisely because they haven't been forced into being by a mind insistent on fixed meanings. It's the body's story, and it resonates with
the sense of an inadvertent truth revealed. As writer Terry Tempest

Williams has said, the most potent images and stories are those that "bypass rhetoric and pierce the heart."

So, as far as memory devices go, you could do worse than turn to the body for guidance. It can offer an inexhaustible store of triggers to begin any number of essays, each of which will have greater significance than what appears on the surface. What matters to us most, sometimes, is what has mattered to the body; memory may pretend to live in the cerebral cortex, but memory requires muscle, real muscle, to animate it again for the page.

As a writer, try yielding to the body and all the secrets it harbors. What kind of stories can your body tell? How does your body bear witness to the events of your life? How has it been wounded? Or healed? How does your body connect you to the past and to the future?

The Five Senses of Memory

By paying attention to the sensory gateways of the body, you also begin to write in a way that naturally *embodies* experience, makes it tactile for the reader. Readers tend to care deeply only about those things they *feel*, viscerally, in their body. And so, as a writer, consider your vocation that of a translator: one who renders the abstract into the concrete. We experience the world through our senses; we must translate that experience into the language of the senses as well.

Smell

"Smell is a potent wizard that transports us across thousands of miles and all the years we have lived," wrote Helen Keller in her autobiography. "The odors of fruits waft me to my southern home, to my childhood frolics in the peach orchard. Other odors, instantaneous and fleeting, cause my heart to dilate joyously or contract with remembered grief. Even as I think of smells, my nose is full of scents that start awake sweet memories of summers gone and ripening fields far away."

Though Helen Keller's words are made more poignant by the fact that she was blind and deaf, we all have this innate connection to smell. It seems to travel to our brains directly, without logical or intellectual interference. Physiologically, we *do* apprehend smells more quickly than the other sensations, and the images aroused by smell act as beacons leading to our richest memories, our most private selves. Because smell is so intimately tied up with *breath,* after all, a function of our bodies that works continually, day and night, keeping us alive, it keys us into the memories that evoke the continual ebb and flow of experience. The richest smells can be the most innocent: the smell of a Barbie Doll, the smell of Play-Doh, the smell of the house right after your mother cleaned (the hot dust inside the vacuum, the tart scent of Lemon Pledge), the shoes in your father's closet, redolent of old polish. Or smells can be more complex: the aftershave your father wore the day he lost his job, for instance, or the scent of your baby's head when you first held her in your arms.

What are the smells you remember, the ones that, even in memory, make you stop a moment and breathe deeply, that make your heart beat faster, your palms ache for what's been lost? Write these down. Write as quickly as you can, seeing how one smell leads to another. What kinds of images, memories, or stories might arise from this sensory trigger?

Taste

Food is one of the most social gifts we have. The bond between mother and child forms over the feeding of that child, either at the breast or by bottle, the infant held close, eyes intent on the mother's face. When you choose to unburden yourself to a friend, you often do so over a meal prepared together in the kitchen, the two of you chopping vegetables, sipping wine, as you articulate whatever troubles have come to haunt you. When these troubles grow overwhelming, we turn to "comfort food," those meals that spark in us a memory of an idealized, secure childhood. When we're falling in love, we offer food as our first timid gesture toward intimacy.

In his essay "Afternoon of an American Boy" (see the anthology section), E. B. White vividly remembers the taste of cinnamon toast in conjunction with the first stumbling overtures of a boyhood crush. In "A Thing Shared" (also in that section), M. F. K. Fisher uses something as simple and commonplace as the taste of a peach pie to focus her memories of her father. The food acts as more than mere sustenance; it becomes a moment of communion between her sister, her father, and herself. And this moment transcends personal revelation; through her use of sensory detail, Fisher invokes those kinds of moments that may lie dormant in our own memories. This personal scene becomes an illustration of how we awaken to one another; it's less about her own father than about the fleeting moments of connection that transpire in all families, one way or another.

What are the tastes that carry the most emotion for you—the tastes that, even in memory, make you stop for a moment and run your tongue over your lips and swallow hard? Write these down, as quickly as you can. What scenes, memories, or associations come to the surface?

Hearing

> *The play is memory.*
>
> *Being a memory play, it is dimly lighted, it is sentimental, it is not realistic.*
>
> *In memory everything seems to happen to music. That explains the fiddle in the wings.*
>
> —Tennessee Williams, *The Glass Menagerie*

Sounds often go unnoticed. Since we can't consciously cut off our hearing unless we plug our ears, we've learned to filter sounds, picking and choosing the ones that are important, becoming inured to the rest. But these sounds often make up a subliminal backdrop to our lives, and even the faintest echo of them can tug back moments from the past in their entirety. In his essay "The Fine Art of Sighing" (see the anthology section), Bernard Cooper uses a sound as subtle as a sigh to elucidate his relationship to his family, himself, and the world.

Music isn't subtle, but instead acts as a blaring soundtrack to our emotional lives. Think about the bonds you formed with friends over common musical passions, the days spent listening to the same song over and over as you learned the mundane yet painful lessons of love. Sometimes you turned up that song as loud as you could, so that it might communicate to the world—and to your deepest, deafest self— *exactly* the measure of your emotion.

We often orchestrate our memories around the music that accompanied those pivotal eras of our lives. In "Goodbye to All That" (see the anthology section), Joan Didion uses many of the senses to describe her first experience of New York, but music comes into play as a way of pinpointing both a private experience and a public one. She hears a line from a song that was playing all over the city and to her it exemplifies her own experience: "'Where is the schoolgirl who used to be me?' and if it was late enough I used to wonder that," she writes. In his essay "A Voice for the Lonely" from *In Short*, Stephen Corey (see "Suggestions for Further Reading") writes movingly about how a certain Roy Orbison song can always call him back to his sophomore year of high school, to his friendship with a boy as outcast as himself. He characterizes those moments as "[t]he right singer, the right sadness, the right silence." When you have the soundtrack down, the rest of life seems to fall into place.

Touch

Hospitals rely on volunteers to hold babies in the infant wards. Their only job is to hold and rock any baby who is crying or in distress. They pick these babies up and hold them close, rock with them, stroke their fingertips across faces and hands and bellies. The nurses, of course, don't have time, but they know that this type of touch is as essential as medicine for their patients' healing. As we grow, this need for touch doesn't diminish, but instead gives rise to our raging desire for contact, the subtle and not-so-subtle maneuvers that lead us into skin-to-skin encounters with other living beings.

We're constantly aware of our bodies, of how they feel as they move through the world; without this sense, we become lost, disoriented in space and time. And the people who have affected us the most are the ones who have *touched* us in some way, who have reached beyond this barrier of skin and made contact with our small, isolated selves.

Sometimes an essayist can focus on the tactile feel of objects as a way to explore deeper emotions or memories. For instance, in "Buckeye" (see the anthology section), Scott Russell Sanders focuses his piece on the feel of the buckeye seeds that his father carried with him to ward off arthritis. They are "hollow," he says, "hard as pebbles, yet they still gleam from the polish of his hands." Sanders then allows the sensation of touch to be the way we get to know his father:

> My father never paid much heed to pain. Near the end, when his worn knee often slipped out of joint, he would pound it back in place with a rubber mallet. If a splinter worked into his flesh beyond the reach of tweezers, he would heat the blade of his knife over a cigarette lighter and slice through the skin.

Such sensory details bring the reader almost into the father's body, feeling the pound of that mallet, the slice of the skin. He never needs to tell us his father was a "tough" man; the images do all the work for him. These details allow us to see the narrator, Sanders, watching his father closely, and so this scene also conveys at least a part of their relationship and its emotional tenor.

Think about the people in your life who have *touched* you deeply. What was the quality of their physical touch on your body? How did they touch the objects around them? Why do you think this touch lingers in memory?

Sight

How do you see the world? How do you see yourself? Even linguistically, our sense of sight seems so tied up in our perceptions, our stance, our opinions, our personalities, and our knowledge of the world. To "see" something often means to finally understand, to be enlightened, to have our vision cleared. Many times, what we choose to see—and *not* to see—says more about us than anything else.

When we look back in memory, we *see* those memories. Our minds have catalogued an inexhaustible storehouse of visual images. Now the trick, for you as a writer, is to render those images in writing. Pay attention to the smallest details, the way a tree limb cuts its jagged edge against a winter sky, say, or the dull yellow of the bulldozer that leveled your favorite house down the street. Close your eyes to see these images more clearly. Trace the shape of your favorite toy, the outline of a beloved's face. Turn up the lights in the living room. Go out walking under a full moon. Keep looking.

For Annie Dillard, in her jubilant essay "Seeing" (from *Pilgrim at Tinker Creek*), being able to truly see is akin to spiritual awakening:

> One day I was walking along Tinker Creek thinking of nothing at all and I saw the tree with the lights in it. I saw the backyard cedar where the mourning doves roost charged and transfigured, each cell buzzing with flame. . . . It was less like seeing than like being for the first time seen, knocked breathless by a powerful glance. . . . I had been my whole life a bell, and never knew it until at that moment I was lifted and struck.

What are the moments in your life that have "struck" you? How have they been engraved in memory?

Fortunately, we live in an age where visual memories are routinely preserved in photographs and on videotape. Sometimes these photos and films can act not only as triggers for your memory, reminding you of the visual details of the experience; but also as prompts to help you delve more deeply below the surface. Robin Hemley, for example, in "Reading History to My Mother" (see the anthology section), uses a photograph of his mother at an artists' colony to prompt a deeper exploration of her past and how it connects to the present-day relationship she has with her son. He studies this photograph carefully, noting the facial expressions and the body language, but he doesn't stop there; he uses these surface details not to answer all questions but to raise new ones that propel the essay forward.

In a different way, Lawrence Sutin, in *A Postcard Memoir* (see the anthology section), uses old postcard photographs as a jumping-off point for private meditations. These aren't his own photographs—they don't document his personal history—but he studies them for all the unexpected details, the surprising juxtapositions, the fleeting expression of subtle emotion that will lead him to surprising memories of his own.

Try It

The Earliest Memory

1.   Write a scene of a very early, vivid memory. What calls out for further examination? Are you realistic? What are the odd details, the ones that don't seem to fit with other people's versions of the story? What in this scene seems to matter to you? Should it? What are you leaving out? If you get stuck, keep repeating the phrase "I remember" to start off your sentences; allow this rhythm to take you further than you thought you could go.

   a.   *Variation I:* Do you have an ideal "earliest memory"? Write this out, and see how your imagination and your memory intersect or diverge. Is there an essay in the process of memory itself?

   b.   *Variation II:* Talk with family members about *their* memories of the time you pinpoint as your first memory. How do they corroborate or deny your own memory? How can you create a "collaborative" memory that includes their versions of the events? How does this memory enact a family "myth"? Is there an essay about the way these divergent accounts work together?

What Have You Forgotten?

2.   In the preface to his anthology *The Business of Memory,* Charles Baxter writes: "What we talk about when we talk about memory is—often— what we have forgotten and what has been lost. The passion and torment and significance seem to lie in that direction." What have you forgotten in your life? What are the moments that keep sliding out of reach? Write for 20 minutes, using the phrase "I can't remember" to start off each sentence. Where does such an examination lead you?

You may find that, by using this exercise, you can "back into" the scenes and images you *do* remember but never knew how to approach. Our students have written some very powerful essays based on this prompt, exploring material that seemed too dangerous to examine head-on.

   Variation: After you've settled on some events or times you can't fully articulate, do a little research. Ask others about their memories of that time. Find documents or photographs that may shed some light on the issue. Be a detective, looking for clues. After you've gathered enough evidence, write an essay that focuses on the way your memory and the "reality" either differ or coincide. Why have you forgotten the things you did?

The Beginnings of Things

3.   In her essay "Goodbye to All That," (see the anthology section), Joan Didion writes: "It is easy to see the beginnings of things, and harder to see the ends." For Didion, the beginning, in memory, can be probed, sorted out; endings can prove more slippery. Write about the "beginning" of some period in your life. Try to pinpoint the exact moment you knew you were crossing a threshold.

The First Time

4.   How many different "firsts" can you remember in your life? The first meal you remember enjoying, the first smell you remember wanting to smell again, the first day of school, the first book you remember reading by yourself, the first album you ever bought, the first time you drove a car, the first time you were kissed, the first time you were touched in a sexual way? How does your memory of these "firsts" color your perception of yourself? What kinds of metaphors do they generate for your life story?

The Five Senses of Memory

Smell

5.   Gather articles that you know carry some smell that is evocative for you. One by one, smell them deeply; then write the images that arise in your mind. Write quickly, allowing the smell to trigger other sensory associations.

6.   What smells in your life are gone for you now? Which ones would you give anything to smell again?

7.   Have you ever been "ambushed" by a smell you didn't expect? Opening a box of clothing from a deceased relative, for example, and having the smell of that person's house flood over you. Or walking into a friend's house and smelling a meal exactly like one you remember from childhood. Write a scene about such an incident. If you can't remember anything like that, imagine it. How do these sensory memories differ from memories of the past you'd normally conjure up? Write an essay exploring the idea that your body carries its own dormant memories.

Variation for a group: Have each person bring in an object with some kind of strong smell and take a turn at being the leader. Keep the object hidden until it's your turn. The rest of the group members close their eyes, and the leader brings this object to each person and asks him or her to smell deeply. After everyone has had a chance, the leader hides the object again. Each person immediately writes down the images and associations that the smell evoked in them. Share these writings with each other and see how similarly or differently you reacted to the same object.

Taste

8.   After reading M. F. K. Fisher's "The Measure of My Powers" (see the anthology section), try to remember the first meal you consciously tasted and enjoyed. Describe this meal in detail; make yourself hungry. Who ate this meal with you? If you can't remember any such meal, imagine one.

9.   If you were to write a life history through food, what would be the "touchstone" moments, the meals that represented turning points for you? What meals have you loved? What meals have you hated? What meals marked important transitions in your life?

> *Variation for a group:* Have "food exploration" days set aside for your group meetings. On these days, one person should be responsible for bringing in an item of food for everyone to taste. Try to choose foods that leave strong sensory impressions: a mango, perhaps, or a persimmon. After exploring the sight, texture, and smell of this food, taste it. Describe it in detail, then go on to whatever images and metaphorical associations arise. What in your own life is most like a mango? Begin an essay by outlining what people, feelings, events, and memories this food conjures up for you, and why.

Touch

10.   Take an inventory of the scars or marks on your body. How were they received? How do these external scars relate to any internal "markings"?

11.   After reading Carol Guess's essay "Red" (see the website), write down several moments from your life where the feel of your body played a prominent role in your sense of identity. Choose one of these and write it out in a scene, amplifying the sensation of touch.

12.   In his short essay "Buckeye"(see the anthology section), Scott Russell Sanders uses a buckeye seed to represent his feelings about his father. Find an object that you consider a "talisman," something you either carry with you or keep in a special place in your home. Hold this object in your hand, with your eyes closed, and feel all its textures. Begin to write, using this tactile description to trigger memories, scenes, and metaphors.

Variation for a group: Have each person bring in such an object and do a "show and tell," explaining the story behind the item. Pass these things around the room for everyone to examine, then write based on *someone else's* talisman. What did it feel like in your hand? How does it trigger your own memories?

Sound

13. Try re-creating a scene from your childhood using *only* the sense of hearing. What music is playing in the background? Whose voice is on the radio? How loud is the sound of traffic? What do the trees sound like in the wind? Are there insects, birds, or animals? A hum from a factory? Rain, rivers, the lapping of a lake? What's the quality of the silence? Try to pick out as many ambient sounds as you can, then begin to amplify the ones you think have the most metaphorical significance. What kind of emotional tone do these sounds give to the piece?

14. Put on a piece of music that you strongly associate with a certain era of your life. Using this music as a soundtrack, zero in on a particular scene that arises in your mind. Try writing the scene *without mentioning the music at all,* but convey through your word choices, imagery, and sentence structure the essence of this music's rhythm, its beat.

> *Variation:* Do the same thing, but this time use fragments of the lyrics as "scaffolding" for the essay. Give us a few lines, then write part of the memory those lines evoke in you. Give us a few more, and continue with the memory, so that the song plays throughout the entire piece.

> *Variation for a group:* Have each person bring in a tape or CD of instrumental music that evokes some kind of strong emotion. Put these pieces on in turn, and have everybody write for at least five minutes about each track, trying not to describe the music directly but focusing instead on the images and memories it evokes. Choose a few to read aloud when you're done, but don't mention which piece of music acted as the trigger; have the rest of the group try to guess which music corresponds to which piece of writing.

Sight

15. What do you see when you look in the mirror? Where does your gaze land first? How does this gaze determine your attitude toward yourself and your life? Do you see your younger self beneath your present-day face? Can you determine your future self through this gaze?

16. Using a photograph of yourself, a relative, or a friend, describe every detail of the scene. Then focus on one object or detail that seems unexpected to you in some way. How does this detail trigger specific memories?

Also, imagine what occurred just before and just after this photograph was taken; what's left outside the frame? For instance, write an essay with a title like "After (Before) My Father Is Photographed on the *U.S.S. Constitution*" (insert whatever subject is appropriate for the photographs you've chosen).

> *Variation for a group:* Repeat the above exercise, but then trade photographs with your neighbor. What are the details that strike you? How does any part of the scene remind you of scenes from your own life? Perform a number of these trades around the room to see what kinds of details leap up from other people's photographs.

Suggestions for Further Reading

In Our Anthology

Bausch, Richard, "So Long Ago"

Cooper, Bernard, "The Fine Art of Sighing"

Didion, Joan, "Goodbye to All That"

Fisher, M. F. K., "The Measure of My Powers," and "A Thing Shared"

Hemley, Robin, "Reading History to My Mother"

Sanders, Scott Russell, "Buckeye"

White, E. B., "Afternoon of an American Boy"

On Our Website

Guess, Carol, "Red"

Hampl, Patricia, "The Need to Say It"

Kitchen, Judith, "Things of This Life"

Elsewhere

Ackerman, Diane, *A Natural History of the Senses*

Baxter, Charles, ed., *The Business of Memory* (includes Corey, Stephen, "A Voice for the Lonely" in *In Short*)

Dillard, Annie, *Pilgrim at Tinker Creek*

Duncan, David James, *River Teeth*

Fiffer, Sharon Sloan, ed., *Body: Writers Reflect on Parts of the Body*

Foster, Patricia, ed., *Minding the Body: Women Writers on Body and Soul*

Kitchen, Judith, and Mary Paumier Jones, eds., *In Brief: Short Takes on the Personal*

Kitchen, Judith, and Mary Paumier Jones, eds., *In Short: A Collection of Brief Creative Nonfiction*

Nabokov, Vladimir, *Speak, Memory*

Proust, Marcel, *Remembrance of Things Past*

Woolf, Virginia, *Moments of Being*

Chapter Four

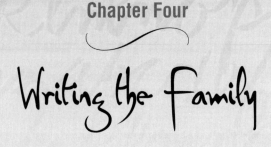

Writing the Family

One thing that we always assume, wrongly, is that if we write about people honestly they will resent it and become angry. If you come at it for the right reasons and you treat people as you would your fictional characters . . . If you treat them with complexity and compassion, sometimes they will feel as though they've been honored, not because they're presented in some ideal way but because they're presented with understanding. —**Kim Barnes**

My brother is swinging the bat and I'm bored in the stands, seven years old. My mother has given me a piece of paper and a pen that doesn't have much ink in it. I've written: "I HAVE TWO BROTHERS. ONE IS A LITTLE ONE. ONE IS A BIG ONE. WE ONLY HAVE TWO GIRLS IN OUR FAMILY. ONE IS ME. ONE IS MY MOTHER." The mothers sit all around me, their straight skirts pulled tight across their knees. My brother is swinging the bat and wiggling his hips on the other side of the mesh. "THE BIG BROTHER IS MEAN. THE LITTLE BROTHER IS SOMETIMES MEAN." Where is my father? I squint to see him near the dugout, his hands cupped around his mouth. My brother swings the bat, and the ball sails, sails, sails out of sight. Everyone stands up, cheering, but I stay seated long enough to write: "THE BIG BROTHER JUST MADE A HOME RUN AND I THINK THATS ALL I'LL WRITE. GOODBYE." My brother prances around the bases, casual and grown-up and intelligent, slapping the hands held out in high-fives as he trots past third. The catcher already sulks unmasked against the backstop. My brother casually taps his foot against home.

On that scrap of paper, I naturally turn toward the people in my life as a way to begin a description of that life. As a child, it's nearly impossible to think of myself as an individual separate from my family. And already, as a novice autobiographer, I see myself spurred by the impulses to document (here is the world, defined by mother, father, brothers), to explore emotion (oh, the harsh treatment I receive at my brothers' hands!), and to transcribe events as they occur (a home run!). In a sense, I'll repeat these impulses over and over throughout the years as I grow into a writer, hopefully refining them a little bit along the way.—**Brenda**

Situating Yourself in Relationship to Family

From the minute we arrive in the world, we're at the mercy of the people who care for us. And we might find the rest of our lives taken up with dual, contradictory impulses: to be an integral part of this clan and to be a separate individual, set apart. Our families, however they're configured, provide our first mirrors, our first definitions of who we are. And they become our first objects of love, anger, and loyalty. No wonder so much creative nonfiction is written about family: How can we really get away from these people? How have they shaped who we are in the world? And how do our particular families reflect issues common to us all?

Several of the writers in the anthology section tackle family issues and do so from widely varying perspectives. In "The Fine Art of Sighing," for example, Bernard Cooper pays attention to his family through the small act of sighing: how his father sighs, how his mother sighs, how Cooper himself sighs. And, paradoxically, by focusing on this small, simple act, Cooper is able to reveal much larger things: his mother's dissatisfaction with domestic life, his father's gruff sensual nature, Cooper's ambivalence about his own body and sexuality. From these particular details, Cooper then expands his essay, much as a sigh expands, to take on the imaginary sighs of strangers. Finally, the essay turns toward metaphor: the Bridge of Sighs, an image that spurs the essay into the realm of poetry. The simple physical act of sighing becomes a way for Cooper not only to make forays into some complex issues in his own family, but to link his personal experience with the greater world. It takes very little time—the essay is only a few paragraphs long—but because Cooper found such a direct line into a way to describe his family, each paragraph works on many levels at once.

In your own writing, you might consider how you can approach the big issues by focusing on the smallest details. It's often tempting, especially if you're dealing with emotionally-charged material, to try to encompass *everything* into one essay. Such a strategy will leave you, and your readers, numb and exhausted. Ask the small questions: Sometimes these are the ones that lead to the biggest answers.

In "Notes of a Native Son" (in the anthology section), James Baldwin approaches writing about his father by focusing on one day: his father's funeral. By situating the essay in this finite time frame, Baldwin is able to contain the many difficult issues that arise in this context: the race riots in Harlem, the conflicts between father and son, the church and his ambivalence toward it. Some of the most telling memories of his father arise during the funeral sermon, fragments that show his father in ways real life never could: the grin on his face as he watched his son sing, the way he teased Baldwin's mother, the comfort the father gave his son when he scraped his knee on a barber chair. These fragments complicate the man, make him more than the forbidding and distant figure he might have been. And Baldwin's emotions become mirrored in the world outside, as violence and hatred rage through the city. In the end, the essay becomes more than a portrait of the father; by placing his personal memories in a historical context, Baldwin gives a greater purpose to his autobiographical impulse.

The Biographer

When we're writing about family, sometimes it's helpful to think of ourselves as biographers, rather than as "autobiographers." This slight shift in perspective just might be enough to create the emotional distance necessary to begin shaping experience into literature on the page. It will also allow you to take a broader view of your subject that encompasses community, culture, and history. It will still be a *subjec-*

tive account—all biographies filter through the mind and emotional perspective of a writer—but it will be an account that has managed to take a wider view.

Look at Brent Staples's essay "The Coroner's Photographs" in the anthology section. In this piece, Staples assumes almost a reporter's role, using the coroner's statistics and graphic photos as a way to begin dealing with his brother's violent death. Because the subject carries so many emotional land mines, Staples makes a conscious decision to step back from the scene. We don't really see a direct emotional reaction from the narrator; rather, he allows the facts to speak for themselves.

Sometimes it's helpful to imagine our relatives as they must have been before we knew them as mother, father, grandmother, and so on. In Paisley Rekdal's essay "The Night My Mother Met Bruce Lee" (see the anthology section), for example, she allows herself to imagine, in vivid detail, her mother as a 16-year-old girl. We move from that imaginative scene into a real one closer to the present day; the contrast between the two allows for a kind of understanding and character development that would otherwise be impossible.

If you were to take on the mantle of the biographer, how could you begin to see the members of your family differently? How can you combine the objectivity of a researcher with the subjectivity of a biographer? We think you'll find that even if you don't end up writing what might be called full-fledged "biography," you'll have been able to find fresh ways to conceptualize the people who are closest to you.

The Obstacle Course

When we write about family, we set ourselves up for a plethora of ethical, emotional, and technical issues that may hinder us from writing altogether. It's one thing to write about your sister in your diary; it's quite another to write about her in an essay published in a national magazine. And when we set out to write about family, we're naturally going to feel compelled to break long silences that may have kept the family together in the first place. In recent years, many creative nonfiction works have taken on child abuse, incest, alcoholic parents, and other emotionally charged issues. When you sit down to write, you may feel obligated to write about the traumas in your family history because you feel that these are the only issues "worth" tackling in literature.

But as you'll see in the essays in the anthology section, and in a plethora of others that deal with family, the writers have instinctively found that they needed to focus their essays on the very small things that might encapsulate the larger issues. Family is an enormous subject, and we must, as writers, find a way to handle it with aplomb and discretion. If your family history is particularly charged, it will be even more essential for you to find the smaller details, the miniscule anecdotes, that will lead the way into a successful essay. This is not to say that you can't, or won't, take on the big issues. But they must arrive on the page less as issues and more as scenes, images, or metaphors that will evoke a strong response from the reader.

As with any good piece of creative nonfiction, the *frame* is essential to getting the story right. Like a photographer, how will you focus your piece? How will you get across to the reader the "occasion," or necessity, for writing this particular essay? Why write about this topic *now*? In the examples we gave earlier, all the writers framed their essays around very small memories and details that carry some urgency, some reason for being on the page at all. The best writers give us the sense that we're entering into a conversation with them that has been going on for a while; the writers take on the authority to tell these stories, and they do so by finding the compelling images and metaphors and narratives that will jump-start experience into literature.

Permission to Speak

While drafting your essay, you must instinctively stifle the voices telling you *not* to write. Your mother, your father, your sisters and brothers—all of them must be banished from the room where you sit at your desk, calling up memories that may be painful or embarrassing. But once you know you have an essay that's more for public consumption than for private venting, you have some difficult decisions to make: How much of this is really your story to tell?

Writers deal with this dilemma in a variety of ways: Some remain in denial, convincing themselves that no one, least of all their families, will ever read their work. Some go to the opposite extreme, confessing to their families about their writing projects and asking permission to divulge certain stories and details, thus giving them complete veto power. Some, like Frank McCourt with *Angela's Ashes*, wait until the major players are dead so they can no longer be hurt by the exposure or pass judgment on the writer. Some decide that writing about this material in a nonfictional form is just too risky and decide to present their work as fiction instead. Others change the names of their characters—or even go so far as to write under a pseudonym—to protect themselves and their families.

Whatever way you choose to negotiate these tricky issues, it's vital to remember that your story *is* your story to tell. Yours is not the *only* story or perspective on your family or on your community, but it's a perfectly valid voice among the chorus. Mimi Schwartz, in her essay "Writing about Family: Is It Worth It?" reminds us that "a memoirist, in particular, must think of truth as having a small 't,' not a big one—as in *my* truth rather than *the* truth." And if you examine this truth with a healthy sense of perspective—and with literary skill—you may be surprised at the reactions you evoke among your subjects. They may feel honored to see themselves in a work of literature and grateful to discover aspects of you that they never recognized before.

Here's how Robin Hemley dealt with these issues when he wrote and published "Reading History to My Mother":

> I think this is one of the few essays I haven't shown my mother. . . . My mother's mental health had started a serious and rapid decline that I was not prepared for emotionally; I took refuge in my writing, specifically in this essay. I felt compelled to write it as a way of sorting through the difficult emotional terrain I faced. I didn't want to show it to my mother because I didn't want to hurt her, and at the time, she was declining so rapidly, I really thought she would be gone, mentally if not physically, in a matter of months.
>
> I don't think that one needs to show everything one writes to those involved—sometimes one can actually do more harm than good with the full-disclosure impulse. Sometimes, one acts more out of one's own need for absolution rather than actually considering the feelings of the person to whom the disclosure is made. To some, this might seem like a dodge or rationalization. I suppose, to some degree it is. But we write for many different reasons, and often our best work is dangerous, edgy, and guilt-inducing. Sometimes we feel it's worth sharing with others, whether the reasons are literary or therapeutic, and I don't think we should necessarily engage in self-censorship simply because we might be unwilling to share our work with the person(s) the work deals with.
>
> Of course, it's tricky territory, and we should be mindful of the feelings of others, I think, without becoming slaves to an inflated sense of propriety. I still would not want my mother to see this essay, though I believe that she would ultimately approve. Knowing her, she might even love it, as she professed to love my memoir, which also dealt with difficult and private subject matter. I'd say that my decision was made of equal measures of love and cowardice.

"Love" and "cowardice": These two words might aptly describe all of us when we find ourselves writing about family or about those close to us in our communities. Complex emotions beset us in this endeavor, and we must remain aware of them before they ambush us altogether.

The Use of Form

Sometimes, the *form* you choose can give you some distance from material that is puzzling or difficult. For example, in "My Children Explain the Big Issues" (see the anthology section), Will Baker gives us sections subtitled with abstract concepts, such as "fate" and "feminism," and uses anecdotes about his children as a way of illustrating those concepts. His children, and his relationship to them as individuals, come into sharp focus through these concrete vignettes, and the title becomes his only commentary on the disparate sections. He turns his family over to us, as readers; the form of the essay reflects the author's guiding impulse, but allows the family to exist independently of him on the page.

In "No Name Woman" (see the anthology section), Maxine Hong Kingston chooses a *peripheral* form by having her mother tell a story about Kingston's aunt, a woman who transgressed the cultural norms of her time. In this way, Kingston creates a portrait of this woman that is richly detailed and that captures the way family histories are traditionally handed down: through stories told to us by past generations. She creates a story within a story, a form that in itself provides some protection for the writer. The form allows her to go places that might be forbidden in a face-to-face encounter.

Finally, in the same vein, in "Reading History to My Mother" (see the anthology section), Robin Hemley chooses a lyrical, fragmented form to focus on his mother as an elderly woman in the present, but through this account he's able to incorporate the past as well. He uses her journal, old photographs, other people's stories, and his own daughters to construct an essay that becomes not just about his mother, but about the issues involved in "reading history." In this way, the essay deals with more than a private family issue; it becomes a case of how we "keep going back over histories, our own and the histories of others, constantly revising."

If we're going to write successfully about family, our motives must be more than simple exposure of family history and secrets. We must have some *perspective* on our experience that spurs the essay beyond our own personal dirty laundry and into the realm of literature (see chapter 2 for a discussion of the dangers of "Revenge Prose" and "The Therapist's Couch"). Like Hemley and the others we've mentioned, we must be able to see our own story in a wider context and to use the *precise* images—such as the reading glasses and the book his daughter reads to him—as propelling forces that raise the essay beyond the commonplace.

Bearing Witness

As we write this chapter, the world has just borne witness to the tragedies that took place at the World Trade Center in New York and the Pentagon in Washington, D.C. Along with millions of others, we watched as the planes hit and the towers collapsed. We watched not only as individuals, but as a part of many different families and communities, trying to figure out how to continue in the face of such an overwhelming disaster.

At times like these, our natural impulse is to hear the personal stories that bear witness not only to the tragedies, but also to the individual people involved in this suffering. We want to understand what happened, yes, but we can't really understand it through the mass media. We seek to understand it by hearing the personal stories of those involved. By hearing such witness accounts, we hope we can understand in a way that will make sense of a world reduced to chaos.

Though our own everyday lives are rarely touched by such traumatic events, our role as writers can be that of witnesses. We continually bear witness to those around us, and sometimes our job is to speak for those who have never spoken for themselves. When we write about our families or take on the mantle of the biographer, we're really writing (and forging) community. As Terry Tempest Williams writes in her essay "A Downwinder in Hiroshima": "I think about . . . how much we need to hear the truth of one another's lives. . . . The Japanese have a word, *aware,* which speaks to both the beauty and pain of our lives, that sorrow is not a grief one forgets or recovers from but is a burning, searing illumination of love for the delicacy and strength of our relations."

Think of yourself as a witness, and your writing will take on greater weight and urgency. As you write about the other people who populate your memories and your life, you'll do so with a clearer sense of purpose that will elevate your writing beyond the purely personal.

Try It

Situating Yourself in Relation to Family

1. Try to reconstruct the names of your matriarchal or patriarchal lineage. For instance, what's the name of your mother, your mother's mother, your mother's mother's mother, and so on? How far back can you go? For instance, I (Brenda) once started an essay with the line: "*I am the daughter of Sandra, the daughter of Beatrice, the daughter of Pearl.*" Naming them brings them to life, and gives you a way to begin writing about them. Where do the names come from? Does your own name have any "inheritance" attached to it? What are the stories behind the names?

Variation: Circle one of the names that intrigues you for whatever reason; then do some research on this person. Find photographs or letters or birth certificates—whatever might be stored in a family archive. Begin an essay that builds a portrait of this person from the name outward.

2.   Describe every member of your family in terms of a part of the body. For instance, describe the hands of your mother, your father, your siblings, your grandparents, and yourself. What kinds of thematic or metaphorical images emerge? How are they alike? How are they different? Push this exercise further by going for the smallest images. Look at belly buttons, fingerprints, moles, toenails, or tongues. If necessary, imagine the details. For instance, imagine your grandmother's hands as they were before she was a grandmother. What traits emerge in your own physical makeup? Which ones do you hate? Which ones do you love? How do you imagine you'll look twenty, forty, or fifty years from now?

The Biographer

3.   Begin an essay by imagining the life of someone close to you—a family member, a friend, a mentor—before you knew that person. Use your imagination coupled with your experience. Use any clues that may exist—objects from the past, documents, photographs, and so on—to form a portrait of this person before you were in the picture. Then complete the essay by contrasting this portrait with the person you know today. How are they similar or different?

4.   Almost all families have some mythic story about someone meeting a famous person. Using Rekdal's "The Night My Mother Met Bruce Lee" (see the anthology section) as a model, try to re-create a relative's encounter with a famous person.

5.   Using Bernard Cooper's "The Fine Art of Sighing" (see the anthology section) as a model, create a picture of your family based on some simple gesture such as the way they sigh, laugh, cry, or kiss. Try to follow Cooper's structure as closely as you can: Begin with a vivid, original description of this gesture, then describe your father, your mother, and yourself (or any other family members you want to write about—sisters, brothers, children, etc.). Try to see how examining these small things reveals larger details about the family.

The Use of Form

6.   Write an imitation of Will Baker's "My Children Explain the Big Issues" (see the anthology section). Including sections labeled with abstract concepts such as "fate," "love," and "evil," use different family members' voices and anecdotes as ways to concretely describe these big issues. For example, you might write an essay entitled "My Mother Explains the Big Issues," then use scenes that involve your mother to illustrate the section titles.

> *Variation:* If you write an essay that shows promise, revise it so that it no longer seems so imitative. Find a structure for the essay that makes it yours.

7.   Like Maxine Hong Kingston, write a family story in a voice other than your own. Create a story within a story as a way of approaching difficult material in a peripheral way.

8.   Write a list of the things you would never write about. What are the silences that can't be broken? Begin each sentence with "I would never write about" or "I am slow to write about." See whether this backward maneuver might actually lead you into scenes, details, and memories you *might* be able to handle in a short essay.

Bearing Witness

9.   Think about a news story that has affected you in the past month or so. Then think about the individual stories that have emerged from that event. Can you imagine yourself in the life of that person? What kinds of details can you imagine that are not in the news reports?

Suggestions for Further Reading

In Our Anthology

Baker, Will, "My Children Explain the Big Issues"

Baldwin, James, "Notes of a Native Son"

Cooper, Bernard, "The Fine Art of Sighing"

Duncan, David James, "The Mickey Mantle Koan"

Fisher, M. F. K., "The Measure of My Powers"

Hemley, Robin, "Reading History to My Mother"

Kingston, Maxine Hong, "No Name Woman"

Rekdal, Paisley, "The Night My Mother Met Bruce Lee"

Staples, Brent, "The Coroner's Photographs"

Williams, Terry Tempest, "The Clan of One-Breasted Women"

Elsewhere

Barnes, Kim, *In the Wilderness*

McCourt, Frank, *Angela's Ashes*

Moore, Honor, "Twelve Years and Counting: Writing Biography," in *Writing Creative Nonfiction*

Schwartz, Mimi, "Writing about Family: Is It Worth It?," *The Writer's Chronicle,* Oct./Nov. 2001

Chapter Five

"Taking Place": Writing the Physical World

*If you live in a place—any place, city or country—long
enough and deeply enough you can learn anything, the
dynamics and inter-connections that exist in every
community, be it plant, human, or animal—you can learn
what a writer needs to know.* —**Gretel Ehrlich**

- ▌ **Start Looking**
- ▌ **Setting Scenes: Place as Character**
- ▌ **Writing about Home**
- ▌ **Writing about Nature**
- ▌ **Writing about the Environment**
- ▌ **Witnesses to Our World**
- ▌ **Travel Writing**
- ▌ **Try It**

I am writing about the first place I remember living, casting
around for a way to write about it that fits in with what I've
learned is acceptable in the literature of place. Elizabeth, New
Jersey: People who know the city shudder and mention the rows
of smokestacks craning along the side of the New Jersey
Turnpike. I spent my early years there, and along with a rickety
shore bungalow, it's the place I have the most visceral childhood
attachment to. But when I think of the writing of childhood
place, I think of Vladimir Nabokov's *Speak, Memory*, with the
majestic beauty of prerevolutionary St. Petersburg, of Annie
Dillard's wooded rambles in *An American Childhood*. How do you
write about a vacant lot glinting with glass, where I spent many

ecstatic hours as a child, a cemetery where my brother and I played? It was as scary and luminous a childhood as any other. Does place matter only when it carries its own transcendent beauty? How do you memorialize the seemingly unbeautiful?

After many false starts, I begin writing about my early home by reflecting on the city's name. "Elizabeth . . . ," I write, "had a queen's name. Every land's an extension of the monarch's body, a great green I Am of the royal person, and Elizabeth's city showed she'd been gone a long time. It was as gassy and bad-smelling as any dead woman."

The Elizabeth of the city, I learned much later, was not Queen Elizabeth, as I'd thought, but some other woman. No matter: it was what I believed at the time of writing and what I believed, for some reason, as a child. The interest of the place was not in its beauty, its own transcendent qualities, but the way it bounced off my life and the lives of those around me: the character it became.—**Suzanne**

Start Looking

Where are you reading this book? Put it down for a second and look around you, taking into account what's both inside and outside the space you're in. Run over in your mind the significance of this place for you—are you somewhere that has meaning for you because it's the place you grew up—or because it's not? Are you somewhere on or near a college campus? Is it the first place you've lived independently, or are you here as a returning student, nourishing yourself after years of working, perhaps raising a family? Does this place represent freedom—or responsibility?

When you force yourself to look around carefully and openly, do you thrill to the natural beauty of the place you're in or respond to its urban excitement? Or are you somewhere you feel you could never call home?

Our responses to place are some of the most complex we'll ever experience. Our sense of visual beauty, our psychological drive for comfort and familiarity in our environment, our complex responses to

loaded concepts such as "nature" and "home" embed place with layers of significance. Although fiction writers typically have driven into
them the importance of location and setting, it's easy for nonfiction
writers to forget that they, too, must be situated physically. We find
that an essayist with a wonderful story to tell—a family story, say, of
a troubled Vietnam-vet father or of raising an autistic child—will typically leave out the vital backdrop of the story: a supportive small
town, a resource-rich city, or a town in which the family's story unfolds against a background of petty bigotry and misunderstanding.

The authors of this book landed—through various academic
tracks—in the smallish city of Bellingham, Washington, on the Puget
Sound, under a volcano called Mt. Baker, which is presently giving off
steam from underground vents called *fumaroles.* On the one hand,
our lives are peaceful: We teach classes, meet with students, attend a
film or concert now and then, and write this book. On the other hand,
every few years the mountain issues this fleecy reminder that it has
more control than we ever give it credit for: Under its crust is enough
molten rock to turn our lives into something else entirely.

Environments tend to function this way: as informing elements we
take for granted and edit out of our stories until they act up. We who
teach here may notice that our classes become quieter and more
lethargic during our gray, rainy winter months and burst back into exuberant life when the sun returns; nevertheless, it takes a certain
amount of awareness to relate the way our lives unfold to the fact that
we live here, in the maritime Northwest, rather than somewhere else.
(And in fact, since the first draft of this chapter was written, we experienced the powerful Nisqually earthquake, which was centered south
of Seattle and sent our computers dancing, and our certainties about
the ground beneath our feet shaking along with them.)

Before proceeding any further in this chapter, pull out an essay
you've already written and check to see how well the "Where?" part
of your story's "Who-What-When-Where-How" has been answered.
Are locations and physical settings established? Can we hear how a
key conversation was heightened by the silence of a forest clearing?
Do we see and smell the eucalyptus trees of California rather than the
cedars of the Northwest? If you write about a town or a city, are its
physical location and socioeconomic character clear?

A student once wrote an essay about sailing in a town where he
kept getting odd, hostile looks. But he failed to mention that the area
he referred to is ultraconservative—a hotbed of militia activity, in fact.
Nonfiction is deceptive: Fiction writers and poets know they have to
provide a depth of information. We often proceed on the assumption
that our readers know all we know. Since essay nonfiction has been,
however wrongly, often associated with ideas, we also may tend to

leave out the sensory side of experience. Even when reading idea-driven nonfiction, we humans must see and feel before we can think. Before going further, check to see what your own tendency is in detailing the places of your nonfiction.

Setting Scenes: Place As Character

In Chapter 1, "The Basics of Good Writing in Any Form," we discuss in depth the techniques of setting a scene and its importance in nonfiction. It seems useful to touch on that topic here as well. Nonfiction writers frequently use place as a primary subject. Even if you never do, however, the place where a story unfolds plays a vital role. In all the elements of setting a scene—character, dialogue, place, action—place can be the easiest to overlook.

Would *Jane Eyre* have been the same book if it didn't unfold against the backdrop of Thornfield, that gabled mansion with its nests of crows? Would Huckleberry Finn's adventures have had the same resonance without the silvery roil of the Mississippi River? Your own story needs the same depth of field. One useful way to judge your own scene-setting is to think of place as a character unto itself. In the excerpt from the essay at the beginning of this chapter, the city takes on the character of a woman: an aging, decayed figure against which the children's exploits take on an incongruous irony.

In Joan Didion's "Goodbye to All That" (see the anthology section), the city of New York becomes a character, one that represents the author at her youngest, most optimistic, and vulnerable age: "[W]as anyone ever so young?" she proclaims. "I am here to tell you that someone was." It's a personal innocence that's embodied by the city that forms her first great geographical love affair, and the turning point in the relationship comes when Didion learns the names of all of New York's many bridges—as if geographical knowledge and knowledge of life's darker side go hand in hand.

Writing about Home

For nonfiction writers, particularly memoirists, the place of childhood has a critical importance. It's the primal map on which we plot life's movements; it's the setting of the rich mythology that constitutes earliest memory (see chapter 3), the enchanted forest in which our benighted characters wander, looking for bread crumbs and clues and facing down their demons. If you draw your earliest place of memory—a bedroom, say, or a favorite hiding place in an apartment or a yard—you will, by the highly selective and emotional process of memory, be drawing an emotional landscape of your childhood.

Maybe you remember the deep, sagging chair that attracted and frightened you because it was sacred to your father and he sank into it in the evening, angry from the day's work; or perhaps you remember the table where your family sat around and ate kimchee, which none of your friends ate and you learned to be vaguely ashamed of. Maybe you recall the soft woolly smell of your covers at night, the dim blue glow of a night-light. This is home, the place where the complex person you are came into being. And understanding the concept of home, and its physical character, is key to understanding the many different individuals you'll write about in your nonfiction.

Bharati Mukherjee, an Indian-American writer, sums up her complex experience of place when she says home to her is a place she has never been and that, in a national sense, no longer exists: her father's natal village, which at the time of his birth was in India and is now part of Bangladesh. Culturally, as a woman of Indian descent, she defines her home patrilineally, making her a citizen of an unknown place, bearing ethnic claims that no longer make any sense.

> I was born into a class that did not live in its native language. I was born into a city that feared its future, and trained me for emigration. I attended a school run by Irish nuns, who regarded our walled-off school compound in Calcutta as a corner (forever green and tropical) of England. My "country"—called in Bengali *desh*, and suggesting more a homeland than a nation of which one is a citizen—I have never seen. It is the ancestral home of my father and is now in Bangladesh. Nevertheless, I speak his dialect of Bengali, and think of myself as "belonging" to Faridpur.

Later in this essay, "A Four-Hundred-Year-Old Woman" (see the anthology section), Mukherjee writes that for her "the all too real Manhattan [her present home] and Faridpur have merged as 'desh.'"

For most Americans, probably, the terms *home* and *native* are loaded with connotations we rarely pause to tease out. We—Brenda and Suzanne—for example, celebrate different holidays. We bake our traditional breads—*challah* and *panettone*—and mark rites of passage with chopped liver or the dried fish called *baccala,* without much awareness of how those foods reflect what was available and affordable in our families' countries of origin, or the poverty and threat reflected in the fact that our not-too-distant forebears came here. There are stories in these deeply personal, everyday connections and disconnections in American lives.

Writing about Nature

If we think of place as character, we should add that no "character" comes with as many preconceptions as nature. Drawing energy from early writers like Thoreau, American essayists have always had a particular affinity for nature writing. This country in its present national incarnation is new—the "new country" that creates by opposition the "old country" of the preceding discussion—and has for much of its life defined itself by its wilderness, by the sense of "frontier" to be explored and frequently controlled. And even as the American wilderness vanishes, literature faces the question of what we've lost with it, along with the buffalo, sequoia, and old-growth forests breathing so recently out of our past.

In his classic memoir *Walden,* Henry David Thoreau's declarations become a charge to nature writers and nature seekers for generations to come:

> I went to the woods because I wished to live deliberately, to front only the essential facts of life, and see if I could not learn what it had to teach, and not, when I came to die, discover that I had not lived.

American literature's historic distrust of civilization (think of Huckleberry Finn) has created a particular reverence for nature writing in our country. Writers like Thoreau teach us that recording the experiences of the individual removed from society, one-on-one with the physical world that created him or her, provides an avenue to "live deep and suck out all the marrow of life."

Thoreau's approach to nature—as a way of paring life down to its essentials, finding oneself—continues in the work of writers like Wendell Berry. In essays like "An Entrance to the Woods" (see the anthology section), Berry describes his feelings on a hiking trip: "Today, as always when I am afoot in the woods, I feel the possibility, the reasonableness, the practicability of living in the world in a way that would enlarge rather than diminish the hope of life."

Nature, to Berry and Thoreau, represents life at its most basic, life at the bone. But there are few subjects in the literary world as complex in their symbolic structure as nature: To Wordsworth, it was the ultimate muse, the "anchor of his purest thoughts"; to others, it's simply the ultimate power, "red in tooth and claw."

What does nature mean to you? For those with a nature-writing bent, it's deceptively simple to wax rhapsodic about the cathedral beauty of old-growth forests or the piercing melodies of the thrush. In other words, we tend to approach nature writing first and foremost as description. While fine description is dandy, however, mere description tends to wear thin after a while. Even if your prose about the soft rosy beauty of the alpenglow is first-rate, if you don't move beyond that, readers are likely to want to put your writing down and go see for themselves. What holds readers in the works of writers like Berry and Thoreau is the sense of a *human consciousness* moving through nature, observing it, reacting to it, and ultimately being transformed by it. Thoreau's description of his cottage at Walden Pond is instructive:

> I was seated by the shore of a small pond. . . . I was so low in the woods that the opposite shore, half a mile off, like the rest, covered with wood, was my most distant horizon. For the first week, whenever I looked out on the pond it impressed me like a tarn high up on the side of a mountain, its bottom far above the surface of other lakes, and, as the sun arose, I saw it throwing off its nightly clothing of mist, and here and there, by degrees, its soft ripples or its smooth reflecting surface was revealed, while the mists, like ghosts, were stealthily withdrawing in every direction into the woods.

Notice how Thoreau embeds his basic concept of living in nature as stripping human life bare in this very description. Not only is it beautifully poetic, but we see Walden Pond looming huge in front of him, throwing off its obscuring mists, as a kind of mirror for Thoreau's consciousness, coming clear in nature and throwing off the obscuring mists of human convention.

In Scott Russell Sanders's essay "Buckeye," (see the anthology section), the author describes how his father, a born naturalist, once stripped the husk from a buckeye to show it to his son: "He picked up one, as fat as a lemon, and peeled away the husk to reveal the shiny seed. He laid it in my palm and closed my fist around it so the seed peeped out from the circle formed by my index finger and thumb." In the essay, Sanders holds on to the memory of his father by saving the buckeyes associated with him; note how the buckeye seems to come alive, almost hatching from the author's hand. It's an image of the life both men find in nature, as well as an image of the father coming alive in the author's memory and, ultimately, in his words.

When you think of your feelings about nature, think about Thoreau and Sanders, and the question of how what you see before you embodies larger forces: an aspect of the human condition, the tenderness and toughness of a person you know. Use that larger element as a way into your essay.

Writing about the Environment

Wendell Berry, in "An Entrance to the Woods," goes beyond merely describing the woods or the way in which his hiking and camping experience lends perspective to his own human existence. As a nonfiction writer who's constantly pushing himself to examine with the broadest possible lens what exists at the tips of his fingers (as all good nonfiction writers do), he asks himself how he as a human being embodies the larger interaction of human and nature. It's an interrelationship that's become problematic at the beginning of the twenty-first century, as we face global warming and the last century's outpouring of industrial pollution.

As Berry, in the woods, hears the roar of a car in the distance he writes: "That roar of the highway is the voice of the American economy; it is sounding also wherever strip mines are being cut in the steep slopes of Appalachia, and wherever cropland is being destroyed to make roads and suburbs, and wherever rivers and marshes and bays and forests are being destroyed for the sake of industry and commerce." It's a wonderful moment in the essay, of opening out and refocusing from a simple, enlightening natural experience to a critique of human intervention in the natural order, the order we've come to label the *ecosystem*.

Typically, a writer sitting down to compose a nature essay like Berry's would erase that car motor from his or her record of this occasion; it's tempting in nonfiction to pare down our experiences to those sights and sounds that make a unified whole. A passing mention of the noise as an anomaly, out of tone with the peaceful surroundings, would also be a natural move to make. It would be a far less important and less honest tack, though, than Berry's turn: discussing how these woods in the essay exist in an uneasy, threatened relationship with the human-dominated world around them.

Witnesses to Our World

In the last chapter, we discussed the emerging sense of much nonfiction as a literature of *witness*—the sense that, in a world flooded with activity and change, and information sources the public (rightly or wrongly) growingly distrusts, the individual voice may provide the ultimate record. In the past decades, nothing has changed faster than the environment. The world's population has burgeoned, and technology has developed the ability to clear lands, pollute the air, and drive species to extinction in record time. Your life has witnessed the eclipse of myriad species, even if they passed out of this world without your awareness. (The current rate of species extinction is matched only by that of the age of the dinosaur's demise, 65 million years ago.) Your life has also seen the destruction of much natural land and its replacement with human habitats, even if this fact, too, only barely crossed your consciousness.

If you *pay attention*, if you notice the small changes that accumulate in the various places you inhabit, you become a witness. For instance, if you can remember a time when Rhode Island spent winters buried under several feet of snow—instead of current light snows and rains—you may be a witness to the phenomenon many would call global warming. Or if you remember capturing Monarch butterflies or frogs as a child—creatures you now see rarely if at all—you've witnessed the severe recent decline of several indigenous creatures.

Travel Writing

Often, a sense of place comes into sharp focus when we leave our own turf and travel to lands foreign to us. Our survival instincts take over, and we grow as alert as cats, turning our heads at the call of the *muezzin* in the mosque, sniffing out the smell of roasted lamb in the market stall, spying an old man bearing a homemade wooden coffin up the alleys of a walled city. In the context of travel, "place" begins to seem not so much the land itself, but anything and everything associated with it: its people, its animals, its food, its music, its religion—all the things that make up life itself.

Pico Iyer, a consummate travel writer, sums it up this way:

> We travel, initially, to lose ourselves; and we travel, next, to find ourselves. We travel to open our hearts and eyes and learn more about the world than our newspapers will accommodate. . . . And we travel, in essence, to become young fools again—to slow time down and get taken in, and fall in love once more.

When traveling, we may find ourselves in precarious situations that require all our attention: the dangerous street we must cross to get to the museum, the twelve-hour bus ride along treacherous mountain roads to the coast, the odd man following you as you wander around lost in the Syrian bazaar. But even while traveling in safe situations, sometimes even in our own town, we can regain that heightened sense of awareness that makes traveling so addictive. Suddenly, our minds slow down enough to take in the slant of light through the trunks of the redwoods, or the smell of sap rising in the maple trees, or the texture of a leaf of aloe dripping its gel. All these perceptions begin to have the force of metaphor, the sting of hard-won revelation.

Your task, as a good travel writer, is both to pay attention to the details of place—in all their glorious particularities, with all their good points and their bad ones—and to render these details in a voice that is wholly your own. You must situate yourself as both participant and observer, always ready for the unexpected, but armed with the many lenses that enable you to interpret this world for your readers in a way they've never heard before.

This mandate requires you to find a purpose for your writing *above and beyond* the travel experience itself. Otherwise, you'll produce a piece of writing akin to those slide shows we all dread: the summons to a friend's living room to view her pictures of last summer's vacation. "And here we are at the Louvre," the hostess quips brightly, while her guests on the couch nod off behind her in the flickering light. If you expect the travels themselves to carry the weight of narrative interest, you'll end up with an essay that looks disconcertingly like, "First I went here, then I went here, and look what an amazing/horrible/fascinating/soul-searing time I had!" No one, eventually, will care. They'll sneak out of your living room the back way, leaving you alone with your out-of-focus slides. The places themselves may be intrinsically fascinating, but if you render them into flat landscapes you'll be left with the lame protest, "Well, you just had to be there."

In a way, the demands of travel writing can epitomize the challenges of any kind of creative nonfiction writing: How do you shape the work—how do you craft it—so that the experience becomes *more* than itself? How do you relinquish the role of the transcriber and take on the mantle of the artist? Critic Paul Fussell answers that question this way: "Successful travel writing mediates between two poles: the individual physical things it describes, on the one hand, and the larger theme that it is 'about' on the other. That is, the particular and the universal."

For instance, to come back to Pico Iyer once more, his books not only describe his travels into places as diverse as the Los Angeles airport, Burmese temples, and suburban Japan, they also become inquiries into the effects of globalization on the world's cultures (see "Where Worlds Collide," in our anthology section). Born to Indian parents in England, then living for a long time in California, Iyer brings with him his deep-seated, almost innate, awareness of how modern cultural boundaries have begun to blur. He begins his book *Video Night in Kathmandu* with a description of how Sylvester Stallone's movie character Rambo had infiltrated every cinema in Asia during his visit there in 1985. By using this one specific example as a focus, he sets the tone and purpose for the book. "I went to Asia," he writes a few pages into the first chapter, "not only to see Asia, but also to see America, from a different vantage point and with new eyes. I left one kind of home to find another: to discover what resided in me and where I resided most fully, and so to better appreciate—in both senses of the word—the home I had left."

With this kind of sensibility, Iyer gains the trust of the reader. We know we're in the hands of a traveler who has experienced a place not only as a tourist, but as an intellectual, an artist, and a pilgrim. We can read his books, yes, to get tips on how to survive those twelve-hour bus trips, or we can read them to enjoy the characters and scenes he reenacts (his description of the bicycle tri-shaw driver in Mandalay will stay with you long after you've finished the book), but these details are held within a much greater context. In this way, he travels with a purpose that allows a sense of place to penetrate him, and his readers, on many levels at once.

What you'll find in all good travel writers is that they avoid the pitfalls that will lead to self-serving or clichéd writing. You'll find not only a heightened perception, a precise attention to language, and a facility with scene-making, but also a marked *generosity* innate in the writer's stance, a perception that sees the foibles of the world and forgives them. In much of the student writing we see about travel, the writer inevitably falls into stereotypes about other tourists and the natives; he or she begins to either make fun of them or put them down. Such a stance not only becomes distasteful to the reader, it betrays a lack of maturity on the part of the writer in not understanding what's important and what's not. Attention to place becomes annoyingly myopic, and the writer becomes a whiner, complaining about "all those tourists" while munching on potato chips in line at the Sistine Chapel. This writer is guilty of just what he or she is complaining about: the tourist mentality that sees only the surfaces and complains when the place fails to live up to expectations.

The other pitfall in travel writing is for the voice to become too much like a guidebook: commenting heavily on the cleanliness of the bathrooms in a hotel in downtown Istanbul, but missing the dawn light on the Blue Mosque. As Fussell puts it: "Guidebooks are not autobiographical but travel books are, and if the personality they reveal is too commonplace and un-eccentric, they will not be very readable." As with any good creative nonfiction, the *self* must be wholly present in the work: A voice must engage us to take this trip along with you, to stand at the windows and gaze out at what you, *and only you*, choose to show us.

Try It

Writing about Home

1. What can you remember? Isolate a single room or outdoor place that, to you, forms the most essential place of childhood. Write down every element of the place you can remember, quickly, with as much detail as possible. What are the patterns of the things you see? Are they old or new? What odd details do you remember (e.g., a gargoyle-shaped knot in the wood, a gray rug with a dark stain the shape of Brazil)? Now fill in an emotional tone for each detail: Did the wallpaper make you feel safe or frightened? What were your favorite things to look at in this place? Your least favorite? Why? What felt like "yours" and what felt like someone else's? Assemble these specifics into an essay about the emotional landscape of your childhood, moving about the room, letting your essay function as an emotional camera.

2.   Many of us, like Mukherjee, find that our sense of *desh* blends real and distant—maybe unseen—places. Is your family one of the many in this country that embodies a divided sense of home? What does home mean to you, your siblings, or your parents? Many contemporary American families are very transient now. As one of our students put it, "Home is where there's a room for me to unpack my things." Her father had been transferred many times while she was growing up. Think about whether there's a single place—a physical location—your family defines as "home," or what you do as you move around to bring the sense of home with you. If you're adopted, your birth family, whether you know them or not, may represent another concept of home. Consider writing an essay in which you unpack the complex layers of meaning in the word "home," with specific references to all the possibilities.

3.   Is there an "old country" in your family profile? How does it affect your family's culture, traditions, and modes of interacting? Write about the ways your family's country or countries of origin cause you to see yourself as different, perhaps straddling very different cultures.

4.   In "Goodbye to All That," in our anthology section, Joan Didion writes about a period of her life in which Manhattan became "home" to her, and what it signified: "It is often said that New York is a city for only the very rich and the very poor. It is less often said that New York is also, at least for those of us who came there from somewhere else, a city for only the very young." Didion writes of the optimism, the sentimental love, the city came to embody for her—the optimism, she writes, of a person's early twenties.

Read "Goodbye to All That" and try to remember a time when a specific *place* embodied a particular period in your life and how the two fed off each other: You could choose the site of first love, first independence, adolescent angst, and so on. Didion ties her emotions clearly to the place in sentences such as, "In retrospect it seems to me that those days before I knew the names of all the bridges were happier than the ones that came later." Write down all the place details you can remember, and draw emotional corollaries for each one.

Setting Scenes: Place as Character

5.   Continuing your look at your own essays for use of place, examine a piece of your writing and scrutinize place as character. Is your setting a developed character? What kind of character is it: positive, nurturing, menacing, indifferent? Imagine setting a scene as a silent character, shaping and nuancing the action surrounding it.

> *Variation:* Write a biography of a place. Choose a street, a forest, an airport (look at Pico Iyer's essay on the Los Angeles airport, "Where Worlds Collide," in the anthology section), a shopping center, anyplace

that has character to you, whether positive or negative. Write a profile (a character study) of that environment. This may lead to a developed essay, like Iyer's; in any event, it's a very useful exercise for characterizing a place.

Writing about Nature

6. Can you articulate what your own vision of nature is? If the outdoors draws you and brings you a special kind of knowledge or contentment, can you put into words what that connection consists of? What metaphor would you use to describe the human/nature interaction that is, in many ways, the ground of our lives here on earth? Can you think of a time when you went into a natural setting to make a difficult decision, work something out in your mind, or somehow come to feel more like yourself? What led you to that place? Did it help you in the way you wanted?

Remember, as you articulate your sense of nature in language, that there's nothing else (besides love, perhaps!) that so easily lends itself to cliché. Tranquil brooks, awesome mountains, trilling birds—these are the stuff of hackneyed authors. Make your description fresh, original, and interesting.

> *Variation: Nature in unexpected places.* Jennifer Price, who wrote the excerpt from "A Brief Natural History of the Plastic Pink Flamingo," in the anthology section, writes about *urban nature*, the aspects of nature that thrive in cities—nature stores at malls, even stuffed birds on women's hats. Write about nature without pursuing nature in the traditional sense: Stay in your apartment building, on your campus, or at a shopping mall, and observe the trees, the crow colonies, even the microclimates created by human development.

Witnesses to Our World

7. In this era of accelerating change, we ask you to think of your life as a piece of living history. Looking at your life as an intersection of personal history and the environment that surrounds you, to what can you bear witness? Write for about ten minutes, associating freely and spontaneously, about a place from your childhood, a place that for you defines your childhood—whether that place is the porch of your house, a creek, the fire escape of an apartment, or a special place in the woods. What did the place smell, taste, or feel like? Include, but don't limit yourself to, the natural elements: air quality and odor, trees, and wildlife (including insects).

8. Now write for ten minutes on what this place is like now, whether from your own experience of it or from what you've been told. How has it changed? What was there before but is gone now? What's there now that wasn't there before? Think of yourself as a living history of this place—what changes did you find between the place of your childhood and the place of your adulthood? Do these changes reflect any changes in your own life?

Remember that even urban areas have a mixture of human and natural components. Suzanne grew up in an urban neighborhood and has fond memories of a vacant lot and a cemetery where she played as a child. Now the lot has been built on and the cemetery is permanently locked. The fireflies that lit up the twilights are much fewer in number, though the neighborhood is still similar to what it was before small changes in it reflected larger changes in American society.

9. As you compare these two quick writings, see what larger elements emerge: Have you and the place of your childhood changed in tandem, or have you gone in different directions? Are you witness to changes that reflect larger, perhaps dangerous, currents of change in our contemporary world? Think about it: Even seemingly small things, like the loss of much of our amphibian life, such as frogs, over time will alter the nature of the planet we live on. Think about your writings in the largest possible sense. Often this short exercise unlocks a valuable essay.

Travel Writing

10. If you have a travel diary or journal, go back to it and pull out sections that give highly sensory descriptions of place: the feel of the air, the taste of the food, the sounds, the smells. Type these out in separate sections, then arrange them on a table and see whether you can find a common theme that could bind an essay together. What can you construe as the greater purpose for your travels? How can you incorporate that purpose into your travel writing? What's the one image that will emerge for metaphorical significance?

11. Take a day to travel your hometown as a tourist. Pretend you've never seen this place before and wander with all your senses heightened. Take a notebook with you and write down your impressions. How can you make the familiar new again?

> *Variation for a group*: As a group, take this trip together. Then compare notes and see how different eyes perceive different things. Take some time at the end of the day, or a few days later, to write together and see where these sensory impressions might lead.

Suggestions for Further Reading

In Our Anthology

Berry, Wendell, "An Entrance to the Woods"

Didion, Joan, "Goodbye to All That"

Iyer, Pico, "Where Worlds Collide"

Mukherjee, Bharati, "A Four-Hundred-Year-Old Woman"

Sanders, Scott Russell, "Buckeye"

Sutin, Lawrence, "Fairchild Tropical Garden" from *A Postcard Memoir*

On Our Website

Miller, Brenda, "Basha Leah"

Paola, Suzanne, "The Human Road"

Elsewhere

Berry, Wendell, "Recollected Essays"

Morris, Jan, *Hong Kong: Epilogue to an Empire* and *Manhattan '45*

Thoreau, Henry David, *Walden*

Chapter Six

Gathering the Threads of History

Everyone has his own story, and everyone could arouse interest in the romance of his life if he but comprehended it. —**George Sand**

History is nothing more than a thin thread of what is remembered stretched out over an ocean of what has been forgotten. —**Milan Kundera**

- ▮ Our Historical, Universal Selves
- ▮ The Ontological Layer
- ▮ You Are a Privileged Observer
- ▮ The Moose at the Window
- ▮ The "When" in Addition to the "What"
- ▮ Try It

I'm working on a short essay about a strange summer I had, when my brother worked for the New Jersey Department of Environmental Protection, running tests on water samples that had been held up for years. He drove a tiny, two-seater Fiat Spyder, the car of choice that year. My start: "It's my brother's Spyder summer. Not dog days but spider days. My brother has a blue Fiat Spyder. It has no back seat but I ride in the back anyway, rolled up in the ten inches or so under the rear window. Spyders aren't much more than human-sized tins so this is risky but it doesn't matter. Let me be a bottle rocket."

What follows is the revised beginning, after a quick search on major events of the year (1974) and surrounding years. I did this search primarily on the Internet, using www.historycentral.com's "This Year in History" service: "It's my brother's Spyder summer. Not dog days but spider days. It's 1974 and things have been crashing. Nixon has resigned or is going to and a few years ago *Apollo 13* crash-landed when an oxygen tank blew (astronauts in there like Spam in a can, Chuck Yeager said.) Karen Silkwood's about to crash. My brother has a blue Fiat Spyder. It has no back seat but I ride in the back anyway, rolled up in the ten inches or so under the rear window. Spyders aren't much more than human-sized tins so this is risky but it doesn't matter. I am a lost person. Let me be a bottle rocket."

What happens when I add these historical details—the space program, the death of Karen Silkwood—is that my story becomes enriched and begins to expand outward: Connections move back and forth, between the closeness of the car and of space capsules, the sense of questing and uncovering and yet danger that marked that time. The reference to Karen Silkwood adds a reference to those who ask difficult questions, particularly environmental questions, as this book goes on to do. The imminent resignation of President Nixon captures the sense of chaos and rebellion, embodied in these teenagers and so prevalent in our country at that time. —**Suzanne**

Our Historical, Universal Selves

Each of us, as this experience shows, exists in both a private and a public way. We're all at once son or daughter, lover, sister, brother, neighbor—the person who must have chocolate cereal in the morning and who absently puts the milky bowl down for the cat to lick. We're also a piece of history. We're the people who witnessed the turn of the millennium; we're the first wave of the world's citizens to see their lives transferred more and more onto computer chips. We're also the people who saw the Berlin Wall dismantled; experienced the Monica Lewinsky scandal; and lived through the tragedy of September 11. If we're citizens of the United States, our country is, for better or worse, the most powerful political entity human civilization has ever made. Our votes, our race, our gender, our sexual orientation, our spending habits—all of these things make us political and historical creatures, as well as the quirky individuals we are.

Often the last thing we do successfully in writing is pinpoint the parts of our own lives that are interesting and worth writing about. In fact, the need for good writing to be somehow "universal" is a rallying cry not just for the creative writing classroom, but also for critics at large. What does universal mean? After all, we must begin with ourselves somehow or other (the other creative writing rallying cry is, of course, "write what you know"). All experience is somehow limited. If you choose to write about childbirth, do you exclude men? Childless women? Couples who adopt?

Naturally, the answer is no. We all have experience with being a child, if not having one. The best nonfiction work gives us a fresh way to view that experience, to see how another human being has processed it, and to witness it unfold on both the personal and the universal levels.

The Ontological Layer

It's essential to the success of an essay that the reader be able to see, in some way, through the surface layer of its immediate subject—like water samples—to a larger, fundamental importance. We could call this deeper significance the *ontological* layer. Ontology is the study of being itself—the questions arising from the fact of our existence. What does it mean to be human, to live and to feel in these ways? How do we exist together and help and hurt one another? The two facets of immediate and deeper significance hold each other in a kind of mutual dignified dance, neither taking the lead. One way to reach this depth is to recognize that your own experience always takes place against a backdrop of larger events.

To look at what it means to exist and be human, at who we are as a species, we must look at history. That historical frame is one that may simply enrich your story. Or—as the Kundera quote at the beginning of the chapter shows—there may be a deep ethical implication to writing creative nonfiction focused on history. Sometimes using our own experience of history is a way of preventing that destructive forgetfulness Kundera describes. As Leslie Brody said simply when discussing her reasons for writing her book *Red Star Sister*, a memoir of her anti–Vietnam War activism, "You have a responsibility to tell history because people forget history."

You Are a Privileged Observer

In the wake of the sales strength of the memoir, there are inevitably critics who complain about the form, the "mob of survivors' stories, both fictional and autobiographical, that publishers have inflicted on us lately," as one critic wrote in response to Kathryn Harrison's memoir *The Kiss*. While in any particular case this criticism may be either true or grossly unfair, critical cries of narcissism and self-indulgence can stem from writers who don't see any significance in what they're doing beyond their own, immediate lives and feelings.

All stories—even extreme stories of personal tragedy—lie embedded in the culture that surrounds them, and culture is always made up of historical events. Historical facts inform the story of these restless teenagers driving recklessly down a highway as the ultimate symbol of authority—the president—is brought down.

First Actors

As creative nonfiction writers, we occupy the ticklish position of being both the authors and, much of the time, the subjects of our own work. We're the shaper and the protagonist—from the Greek *protos* (first) and *agonistes* (actor), that is, the person who generates the action of a drama—and we must learn to assess ourselves as protagonists with all the objectivity we can muster. It's our view that everyone who sits down to write is, in some sense, a *privileged observer*—a writer who has had experiences and witnessed events any reader would be fascinated by, if the writer can learn to uncover and record them.

George Sand tells us to value the unique narrative structure of our own lives. Any of you could write a book that would be treasured in two hundred years, as we treasure the best pioneer diaries, if you could learn, as those authors did, to really *see*.

The Moose at the Window

As writers, we all share the challenge of working to expand our subject matter outward, to embrace the full range of social, cultural, and *historical* significance of our material. Classrooms and private workshops can be one of the best sources of ideas for this expansion.

Bruce Beasley, a Pacific Northwest writer who teaches nonfiction, is having a conference with a student who says she has nothing to write about. The subject for this essay assignment is encountering the natural world. She claims to be utterly without experiences to use.

He tells her they live surrounded by water and mountains.

In reply, she insists that she likes to stay indoors, doesn't hike or camp, and has no feeling for the outdoors.

They go back and forth like this for a while, with Bruce asking question after question about her hobbies, her reaction to her alpine landscape. All are returned with a slightly desperate wail that the subject of nature contains nothing at all she can write about.

"There must be something," he says finally.

"Well," she says hesitantly, "there *was* that moose at the window."

A lost moose had wandered into town and moseyed about for several weeks, making it almost as far as the highway before being rounded up by Animal Control. One morning this student woke up and found him—confused, curious, and hungry—staring in the window of her new apartment. The fascinating aspect of nature in her life turned out to be that it had found her—driven by the historical facts of rapid development and loss of habitat. Thinking about this moment as her subject led to a vivid and colorful essay.

Each of us needs to learn to recognize our moose at the window. We've all experienced meeting someone who claimed to be ordinary while finally slipping into the conversation that he or she had grown up on a commune, sung opera as a child, or—like one student we remember—come of age living inside the Statue of Liberty with his Park Service father. The world he grew into, literally seen through the eyes of the Statue of Liberty, is not the same world the rest of us know.

It's important for you as a writer, particularly a nonfiction writer, to think through what's different and important in your world and what historical events formed the canvas for the fine brush strokes of your own life. You can easily check the highlights of particular dates and years by using resources like www.historycentral.com on the Internet or reference books like *The New York Times Book of Chronologies*.

The "When" in Addition to the "What"

Here is the opening of James Baldwin's essay about racism and family, "Notes of a Native Son" (see the anthology section):

> On the twenty-ninth of July, in 1943, my father died. On the same day, a few hours later, his last child was born. Over a month before this, while

all our energies were concentrated in waiting for these events, there had been, in Detroit, one of the bloodiest race riots of the century. A few hours after my father's funeral, while he lay in state in the undertaker's chapel, a race riot broke out in Harlem. On the morning of the third of August, we drove my father to the graveyard through a wilderness of smashed plate glass.

Notice the author's attention, like a moving camera, panning between familial and national tragedy. Family events come first; then, as if his gaze is forced away, Baldwin takes in the larger chaos of the rioting across the country. At the start of the essay, Baldwin carefully states the season and the year; it's a hot summer month during World War II, black GIs fighting overseas while the same old racism continued back home. By the end of the paragraph, the smashed glass becomes a "wilderness," as if that landscape equals the natural landscape about to close over the body of Baldwin's father. The essay accomplishes an unforgettable weaving of personal tragedy with the period that spawned it.

In a different way, E. B. White's "Afternoon of an American Boy" (see the anthology section) uses what, for him, was a contemporary reference (McCarthyism) as a way to situate himself as the writer in the act of writing. He's not writing in a historical vacuum; rather, he's writing in the midst of what would become a seminal period in our country's history. Being aware of the importance of events as they occur—honing your intuition for what will become solidly entrenched in history and what will pass through with nary a trace—is a skill as important as syntax and punctuation. With this historical backdrop, White creates a context that enables personal memory to take on more weight and significance. He initiates a relationship to the reader as he establishes this connection to our common public history.

It's always important to keep in mind the extent to which history is the individual writ large and the individual life is history writ small. Understanding what shapes how you perceive the world—and how you are perceived—is critical to using your own experiences to create strong nonfiction.

Try It

You'll likely be the last person to recognize what's fascinating—and deeply significant—about you. Your friends will see it, and if you're lucky, your family will too. You, if you're normal, will brush off their interest and tell them that it really wasn't so different—that you don't see what all the fuss is about just because you were on board the *Titanic*.

Here's a tool to help you along: some questions to start yourself off with, whether you choose to answer on paper, in a journal, or in the privacy of your own head. These questions are designed to elicit a greater awareness of the historical events that have shaped your life and also a greater awareness of your *social self*—you as conservative or liberal, member of a disadvantaged group, Buddhist, activist, Rosicrucian. While considering these questions, it's important to remember that this social self *always* functions in a cultural and historical context.

Our Historical, Universal Selves

1.   Many Americans born in the 1950s have powerful early memories of the day President John F. Kennedy was shot—teachers crying in the classroom, the crackling of televisions left on throughout the day. More recently, most of us vividly remember the events of September 11. What event of national or world importance do you remember most clearly? How did you hear of it, and what exactly did you hear? What were other people around you doing? What was going on in your own life that this event bounced off of, resonated with, formed a strange contrast to? Use all of your senses to re-create this memory.

2.   What aspects of your life do people around you consistently find most interesting? What questions do they ask you? What can you tell them that satisfies or dissatisfies them?

3.   At a writer's conference, Leslie Brody talked about living through an unpleasant divorce at a time when the marriage of Diana Spencer to the Prince of Wales dominated the news. She talked about the irony of seeing the two events juxtaposed and how the memories came to fuse together: the painful sundering of a marriage and the artificial romance of the royal wedding. What news events formed a backdrop to the most emotional moments of your life? How do the two stories intersect?

The Ontological Layer

4.   List all of the words you can think of that describe your social qualities, the roles you fill—all that makes up your heritage and identity: daughter, son, husband, friend, roommate, writer, southerner, Methodist, student, atheist, Hispanic, white, black, Asian, adopted, environmentalist, and so on. Write quickly and don't be selective. Try to think of yourself as *everyone* who knows you—classmates, friends, members of your yoga class—would think of you.

5. Look at the list you wrote for number 4 and circle the aspects of yourself that appear in your writing; put a question mark beside those that never appear (for instance, while most writers begin as students and many end up as teachers, we rarely write about learning or teaching). Ask yourself why. Are you selecting "environmentalist" as somehow more worthy of reflection than "Midwesterner"? Maybe it is, but then again, maybe it isn't. Or maybe the two qualities inform each other in a provocative, social/historical way.

You Are a Privileged Observer

6. Try to imagine your own life as someone five hundred years from now might view it. What about your life, the place you live in, and the historical unfoldings you've witnessed do you believe that person would find most interesting? (Hint: What do you find most interesting about life in the past?) How are you a privileged observer?

7. Get into the habit of thinking of yourself in the third person—seeing yourself move through the world as a protagonist—at least once a day. Narrate your daily story to yourself in the third person. As an objective listener (and, to some extent, you can be one), what interests you?

The "When" in Addition to the "What"

This is the exercise that helped Suzanne expand her description of the summer of 1974.

8. For the first part, write a description of several paragraphs about a scene or event you consider critical in your life. It should date from at least a few years in the past or can be from childhood. As in most writing exercises, write quickly and don't censor yourself. Use your senses and be as specific and detailed as possible. If you're sitting on a throw rug in the living room of your childhood, describe in as much detail as you can the weave of the rug, the room, the scents in your childhood home, the people, the drone of the television, if you kept it on, and so on.

9. Now use a list of chronologies, possibly a simple one printed from an Internet site like www.historychannel.com, to date your experience in relation to a corresponding national or world event. Don't worry if you feel you weren't thinking about the event at the time; your first impulses on that question aren't generally accurate, as you wouldn't so much have been thinking about something like the Vietnam War, for example, as living in the atmosphere it created. Also, it isn't necessary for a successful essay that the larger news formed part of your consciousness; your obliviousness to it may be part of what makes the essay fascinating.

10. Once you find a historical corollary, write as many connections, real or metaphoric, as you can. Suzanne might have written "Karen Silkwood, Watergate, authority, secrecy, lies." These are some of the connections that ultimately made their way into her essay.

11. As you look through these ideas for further writing and polishing ideas, remember how rich the field of connections in creative nonfiction can be— literal, linguistic, metaphoric, atmospheric. Don't feel the need to justify to yourself immediately why something feels important. If your gut tells you it's important, then it surely is. You write—we all do—to find out what these connections are, to thread yourself into the intricate web of human existence.

When doing "discovery" work like this, have a notebook or computer file just for your jottings. Don't treat what you place there as polished prose but as seeds, or perhaps even fertilizer, for essays you'll eventually write. Polishing can come later. Scan your notes for comments—descriptions from your self-analysis list, or historical intersections—that spark your interest. Circle these in a notebook, or cut and paste them so these comments/ images/events are at the top of your page. Look through your notes, or free associate, to see what flows out of this start in your imagination.

Suggestions for Further Reading

In Our Anthology

Baldwin, James, "Notes of a Native Son"

Didion, Joan, "Goodbye to All That"

Williams, Terry Tempest, "The Clan of One-Breasted Women"

Elsewhere

Brody, Leslie, *Red Star Sister*

Didion, Joan, *The White Album*

Momaday, N. Scott, *The Names*

Rodriguez, Richard, "Late Victorians," from *A Conversation with My Mexican Father*

Wiesel, Elie, *Night*

Chapter Seven

Writing the Arts

Culture is like a magnetic field, a patterned energy shaping history. It is invisible, even unsuspected, until a receiver sensitive enough to pick up its messages can give it a voice.

—**Guy Davenport**

▮ **The Visual Arts**
▮ **The Moving Image Arts**
▮ **Music**
▮ **Literature: The "Reading Narrative"**
▮ **Try It**

I've put up a new picture, a photograph bought for me at an Edward Weston exhibit last April. The composition shows a young woman, all in black, posed against a high, white fence. She half turns toward the camera; her right hand lies tentatively across her heart. The shadow of a leafless tree (I imagine it to be a young oak) curves up and over this slight figure. Actually, it does more than curve. The shadow arches behind her in a gesture of protection. Almost a bow of respect.

Why do I like this picture so much? I glance at it every day, and every day it puzzles me. What draws me to those dark, shaded eyes? What holds me transfixed by the movement of gray shadows over the straight white planks, the drape of the black coat, the white hand raised to the breast in a stunned gesture of surprise?

These questions led me to write the first essay I ever published, titled "Prologue to a Sad Spring," after Weston's own title for the photograph. In this essay, the photograph's

mysterious title becomes a meditation on what it means to
have a "sad spring," on how our lives are full of losses never
memorialized in photographs. It's a short essay, with a circular
design that leads the reader back to the appeal of black-and-
white photography and to the particular photograph that
started the rumination in the first place. Though it's a simple
piece, with simple ambitions, it remains a favorite essay in my
repertoire. It feels almost like a gift, an ephemeral connection
between myself and the woman in this photograph, a distant
communiqué between a writer and a photographer who would
never meet. —**Brenda**

The Visual Arts

With old glass-plate daguerreotypes—the earliest form of photography—if you tilt the plate just slightly, the image disappears and the
photograph becomes a mirror. This fact seems an apt metaphor for
how the creative nonfiction writer can approach art. Through a close
observation of particular paintings, sculptures, or photographs, you
can reveal your own take on the world or find metaphors in line with
your obsessions. At the same time, you'll elucidate that artwork in
such a way that the piece will forever have a greater significance for
your reader.

Poets perform such literary transformations with paintings so often that the form has an official name: *ekphrastic writing*. Fiction writers, too, often explicate artworks as a basis for their novels: Look at
Girl with a Pearl Earring, for example, or *Girl in Hyacinth Blue,* both
recent novels that use Vermeer paintings as a basis for historical narratives. Creative nonfiction writers, too, can write ekphrastic essays.
This minute examination of artwork often leads to bigger things.

For example, Lawrence Weschler, in his essay "Inventing Peace,"
closely analyzes a Vermeer painting to explicate what happens at the
Bosnian war crimes tribunal in The Hague. He compares the serene,
almost dreamlike settings of Vermeer with the atrocities the judges in
The Hague, just minutes from the Vermeer exhibit, hear about every
day. One particular painting, "The Head of a Young Girl," intrigues
him. He explicates this painting for us:

Has the girl just turned toward us or is she just about to turn away? . . . The answer is that she's actually doing both. This is a woman who has just turned toward us and is already about to look away: and the melancholy of the moment, with its impending sense of loss, is transferred from her eyes to the tearlike pearl dangling from her ear. . . . The girl's lips are parted in a sudden intake of breath—much, we suddenly notice, as are our own as we gaze back upon her.

Weschler studies this painting closely, interpreting the details as he unfolds them for us one by one. He creates a *speculative narrative* that brings this painting to life. In a speculative narrative, the writer infuses a painting, or any situation, with a story that arises both from fact and from imagination. In Weschler's description, it's clear, for instance, that the *facts* of the painting exist as he relates them—the parted lips, the pearl earring—but he allows himself to speculate on the *meaning* of those details. He brings his own interpretation to bear on the portrait—an interpretation that sets up the themes for his piece.

Throughout the essay he brings in other voices—art historians, the judges at The Hague, other art patrons, journalists covering the tribunal—until we have a view of Vermeer and this painting in particular shaped by Weschler's sensibility and by the context in which he chooses to place the painter. In the end, the image of the girl turning away mirrors an image of one of the war criminals, Dusko Tadic, looking up at a TV camera, then turning away. Both images come to be about loss and the ravages of history:

Inventing peace: I found myself thinking of Vermeer with his camera obscura—an empty box fronted by a lens through which the chaos of the world might be drawn in and tamed back to a kind of sublime order. And I found myself thinking of these people here with their legal chamber, the improbably calm site for a similar effort at transmutation.

As you see, Weschler does not sacrifice personal voice, though the topic is external to the self; on the contrary, the "I" remains a guiding force throughout the essay: ruminating, reflecting, and questioning his own fascination.

Weschler does not choose to bring his own life into this essay. But another way to approach art is to allow an artwork to give meaning to personal circumstances. Mary Gordon, in "Still Life: Notes on Pierre Bonnard and My Mother's Ninetieth Birthday"(see the anthology section), writes an essay that is distinctly more self-oriented, but by directing some of that focus outward toward the painting of Bonnard, she creates a piece that works multidimensionally. Like Weschler, she gives us detailed explications of the paintings, but she juxtaposes them against the decline of her mother's condition in a nursing home. Without the parallel narrative about Bonnard—something external to the self—her essay might be in danger of becoming *too* personal or too self-conscious. Gordon allows us to learn something in this essay about Bonnard, and the personal story becomes a backdrop, or support, for this inquiry.

It's important to remember that while nonfiction work about painting is flourishing right now—Terry Tempest William's *Leap* is another example, or Mark Doty's *Still Life with Oysters and Lemon*—photography, sculpture, and installations are all rich subjects for your writing as well. As Tolstoy wrote, art is a language that communicates "soul to soul" on a level that bypasses the intellect. As a writer turning your gaze to the rich, metaphorical world of art, you enter into this dialogue and add to our understanding of the world and ourselves.

The Moving Image Arts

The term "arts" also refers to the moving image arts—TV, film, and video. A vital, and probably the most visible, part of our cultural expression, the moving image arts have been somewhat underrepresented in nonfiction and are due for more serious reflection. Remember that although there is plenty of top-quality film and TV, the art itself doesn't have to be great to warrant your attention. Roland Barthes, in a brilliant essay titled "Leaving the Movie Theater," simply writes about the experience of cinema—the darkness of the theater, the unfolding of a narrative in a giant lighted square—as a way of exploring pleasure and our fascination with images.

In Paisley Rekdal's "The Night My Mother Met Bruce Lee" (see the anthology section), the essay invokes pop culture images of the Chinese and the Chinese-American, particularly the narrator's mother, whose school guidance counselor advises her not to go to Smith, "hinting at some limitation my mother would prefer to ignore." At the same time, a cook in the restaurant where the mother works tells her that he comes from Hong Kong and hence is "*real* Chinese." Rekdal embeds that sense of cultural limbo—appearing Chinese to a white guidance counselor, but not to a recent immigrant—in the artifice of kung fu movies. In the essay, mother and daughter bond watching the martial arts film *Enter the Dragon*.

> Bruce Lee narrows his eyes, ripples his chest muscles under his white turtleneck.
>
> "I knew him," my mother tells me. "I worked with him in a restaurant when I was in high school."
>
> "Really?" This is now officially the only cool thing about her. "What was he like?"

"I don't remember. No one liked him, though. All that kung fu stuff; it looked ridiculous. Like a parody."

Rekdal pays close attention to the film itself in this piece; her prose follows the film's use of lighting—the way Lee's chest "seemed outlined in silver," mirroring the way Rekdal's mother's face "twists into something I do not recognize in the television light." It's as if the cultural distortion created by the movie, and movies like it, distorts the mother even in the eyes of her daughter. Note that Rekdal has been careful to look at the techniques of the films in question and use them throughout her essay—not just the kung fu itself, which becomes picked up by the restaurant chef, but kung fu films' visual style of bright color and exaggerated gesture.

If film or TV is what draws you, consider these as possible essay subjects. Much of what we said in the visual arts section of this chapter applies here as well: Film art can comment on our own lives and on the history surrounding them. And film and TV can capture a cultural moment. Think of how, at times, movies like *Thelma and Louise* or shows like *Seinfeld* seem to speak for the feelings of large numbers of people in our society, generating catchphrases and images that become embedded in our collective consciousness. As Rekdal shows, these arts define us personally as well.

As you draft an essay using the moving image arts, think of how you can use those artistic techniques for their own purposes. Can you borrow the visual style of the work in question? Can you write an essay in which you use scenes from the work you've viewed as a model? Think of your cast of characters as both the films themselves, with their protagonists, and the viewers, including yourself—who must interact somehow with the artificial characters or events on the screen.

You can also take a more analytical approach to TV and film, exploring what they mean in terms of culture and society. For example, Bill McKibben, in his book *The Age of Missing Information,* performs an experiment in which he has friends record every channel on a Virginia cable network for 24 hours; he then goes about analyzing what he sees to create a portrait of the American mind-set: what we learn and, more important, what we don't learn, from what surrounds us on TV. McKibben, who doesn't own a TV himself, spent several months watching these videotapes of a single day's programming:

I began spending eight or ten hour days in front of the VCR—I watched it all, more or less. A few programs repeat endlessly, with half-hour "infomercials" for DiDi 7 spot remover and Liquid Luster car wax leading the list at more than a dozen appearances apiece. Having decided that once or twice was enough to mine their meanings, I would fast-forward through them, though I always slowed down to enjoy the part where the car-wax guy sets fire to the hood of his car.

As you can see, even though McKibben has set himself a huge intellectual task, he doesn't sacrifice his personal voice or his sense of humor to do it. He contrasts what one can learn from a day of TV with what one can learn from a day in the woods, providing highly specific examples of each mode, and revealing his own personality at the same time. He turns his attention and powers of observation to something as common as TV and enables us to perceive its greater meaning.

Music

If you've ever crashed into your room at a bad moment and snapped on a piece of music you had to hear—be it Bach or Alanis Morrisette—or begged for a certain song at your wedding or graduation, you know the emotional strength of music. Pretty much all of us have beloved melodies we replay in our heads or crave powerfully at certain times. These cravings arise from a mix of the power of sound and lyrics and the broader cultural significance of music. Our cave-dwelling ancestors danced, which means they had beat. And ages define themselves partly by their music, whether it's nineteenth-century Vienna with the waltz, or 1960s America with the Beatles.

As we mentioned in chapter 3, music can key us into powerful memories that define the self. And music can serve as a medium to channel some of the most vital issues of our time. We still look back at the 1960s antiwar movement by examining the music that sprang out of it (and what 1960s documentary would be complete without footage of Country Joe and the Fish's "War—What Is It Good For"?). Music is a vessel that holds the emotions of its time.

As an example, let's consider David Margolick, Hilton Als, and Ellis Marsalis's book *Strange Fruit: The Biography of a Song*. "Strange Fruit," a song written for blues singer Billie Holiday, tells the horrendous story of Southern lynchings. Through the lens of this song, Margolick, Als, and Marsalis weave together the tales of Holiday's short, heroin-addicted life; the white communist sympathizer who wrote the song; the struggle for civil rights; New York cafe society; and even the history of lynching. This single song contains within it a story that branches out and out to speak of two extraordinary human beings as well as the thorniest problem in American history—race.

A more personal nonfiction look at a piece of music is Lewis Thomas's *Late Night Thoughts on Listening to Mahler's 9th Symphony*. Mahler's symphony, characteristically dark and plangent, inspires in Thomas thoughts that range from science to psychiatry. He talks about the changes in himself as a listener of Mahler, how the music is, in a sense, made by the listener, and how he has changed Mahler even as Mahler has changed him, particularly in an era threatened by nuclear war:

> There is a short passage near the very end of the Mahler in which the almost vanishing violins, all engaged in a sustained backward glance, are edged aside for a few bars by the cellos. Those lower notes pick up fragments from the first movement, as though prepared to begin everything all over again, and then the cellos subside and disappear, like an exhalation. I used to hear this as a wonderful few seconds of encouragement: we'll be back, we're still here, keep going, keep going.
>
> Now, with a pamphlet in front of me on a corner of my desk, published by the Congressional Office of Technology Assessment, entitled MX Basing, an analysis of all the alternative strategies for placement and protection of hundreds of these missiles, each capable of creating artificial suns to vaporize a hundred Hiroshimas, collectively capable of destroying the life of any continent, I cannot hear the same Mahler. Now, those cellos sound in my mind like the opening of all the hatches and the instant before ignition.

This change speaks poignantly of both artists. Thomas shows the drift of much of the best writing about the arts: unpacking your own emotional responses as a way of unpacking some of the truest parts of yourself. Like Weschler, he also allows himself to be the "speculative narrator"—creating meaning from description and facts.

Another approach might be to mine your obsession with a particular musician or type of music. For example, Geoff Dyer, in his book *But Beautiful: A Book about Jazz,* creates improvisational portraits of eight jazz musicians, getting into their heads and using their points of view. His language and prose style take their cue from jazz, running riffs and hitting discordant notes as he tries to capture the essence of these musicians on paper. As he explains in the introduction: "When I began writing this book I was unsure of the form it should take. This was a great advantage since it meant I had to improvise and so, from the start, the writing was animated by the defining characteristic of its subject." He calls his book "imaginative criticism," and he uses fictional elements along with the facts of these musicians' lives. The result is a speculative narrative, one that roots itself in music and sings itself on the page.

Literature: The "Reading Narrative"

A fascinating new subgenre of nonfiction has emerged in the past few years—we've titled these works *reading narratives*. These essays show the author, in different ways, reading another piece of literature and using it as a springboard for his or her own actions and reflections. Like writers who use the visual arts, authors of reading narratives are somehow grappling with another artist's aesthetics as a means of probing deeper into their own. Though reading narratives sound simple, they aren't; in good hands, they present a beautifully counterpointed music of two different lives, aesthetics, and meanings. Phyllis Rose's book *The Year of Reading Proust* is an excellent example, since the author reads all of Proust's *Remembrance of Things Past* while using it as a means of chronicling her own life, comparing her Key West with Proust's Balbec, the characters inhabiting her life with those in his.

None of us writes in a vacuum. To understand the significance of reading narratives, you have to think for a minute about the enormous debt authors owe to other authors; they are, as a literary journal once dubbed them, our mentors and our tormenters. (How many women have been spurred to write by comments like Robert Southey's to Charlotte Brontë: "Literature cannot be the business of a woman's life"?) We all exist in the current of contemporary literature and the literature we've inherited from past generations—its subjects, its techniques, and its assumptions.

Most of us can remember at least one "eureka" reading moment. That moment may give us permission to do things differently in our own work: use a new voice, dig deeper, or consider new subject matter as potentially ours. Whether we realize it or not, these "eureka" writers are our literary mentors. Moreover, what we read may spur us on in many different ways—other authors inspire us, give us permission, and also irritate us in ways that stimulate us to try something new. You can try writing a literary history of yourself, one that tracks your life through the many different books you've read and loved.

Another way to approach a reading narrative might be to reveal your obsessions with a particular author and how this author has influenced you throughout your life. In *U and I: A True Story,* Nicholson Baker talks us through his obsession with John Updike. "I was trying to record how one increasingly famous writer and his books," he tells us, "read and unread, really functioned in the fifteen or so years of my life since I had first become aware of his existence as I sat at the kitchen table on a Sunday afternoon, watching with envious puzzlement my mother laugh harder than I had ever seen her laugh before . . . as she read an Updike essay on golf in a special edition of the *New York Times Book Review.*" In his funny, self-deprecating style, Baker manages to clue us in that his book is not really *about* Updike (at one point, he writes a confessional list where he admits to having read completely only a handful of Updike's books); rather, it's about how the *idea* of

Updike, and the process of writing this very tale, have influenced his own writing. As we see in the quote above, it's not only his own reading of Updike that matters, but the way Updike shows up in his family history (he makes a note to himself to write: "Mom reading *Too Far to Go* in a hotel when we were visiting some family—maybe around the time she and Dad had decided on a divorce"). Such a narrative enables the writer to approach personal history in a roundabout way that catches us off-guard.

Virginia Woolf's short essay "The Angel in the House" is a good example of a negative reading narrative. Her title and the essay refer to a wildly popular Victorian poem by Coventry Patmore that depicted women as shy, reticent keepers of the home. Woolf's essay states that to become a writer, she had to find her own "angel in the house," a figure who whispered over her shoulder that she ought to be doing things other than writing, and "strangle her." We all sometimes need these kinds of friends and foes to keep our hunger for writing alive.

Try It

The Visual Arts

1. Begin an essay by describing an artwork that has always intrigued you. Feel free to interpret the details, creating a speculative narrative about what's happening in the painting or what was going through the painter's mind. Find other interpretations from art scholars, and begin to create an essay that approaches this artwork from several different angles.

2. Write an essay in which you parallel your interpretation of a particular artwork or artist with events going on in the world around you.

3. Write an essay in which you parallel your interpretation of a particular artwork or artist with events unfolding in your own life.

The Moving Image Arts

4. Think about a film that you love, that you could watch any number of times. Look closely at the conventions and physical experience of the film, and question your obsession. In what ways are you comforted by the artifice of film? Where do you suspend your sense of its unreality, and where do you take comfort in it? Where did you first see the film, and what has it represented to the larger culture? If you like, you can substitute something from TV, but for this exercise you should go for a quality piece.

5. Analyze TV commercials. How do they define their eras? How have they shaped you, perhaps in terms of social relationships, signs of status, or body image?

6. Write a review of a film or a TV show, using specific details that reveal your own voice and vision and that place the show in a larger context.

7. Write an essay that uses popular TV or radio shows to establish the time and place of your piece. What were the shows you watched as a child? How did they establish the routine of your day? Why do you think those particular shows hooked you?

Music

8. This prompt expands on uses of music presented in chapter 3. Identify the piece of music that's been most important to you in your life. First, try to write down why it means so much to you, when and where you can remember hearing it. If there are lyrics, write down all you can remember, and list adjectives that describe the melody. Don't limit yourself to musical words but jot down whatever comes to mind and feels most apt: jittery, spacey, dreamy, grim. You may want to stop here and try an essay about this piece of music, using its importance to you and how you, as a unique individual, interpret its sound. Or you can try one of the following, based on the examples above.

> *Variation:* Try tracing all of the cultural connections of the song, as the authors of *Strange Fruit* did. This may or may not take some research. Here's an obvious example: Suppose you chose Nirvana's "Smells Like Teen Spirit." Myriad connections pop up with a little thought: the widespread shock that followed Kurt Cobain's suicide; the sense in which the song became an anthem to a generation of alienated youth; Cobain's conflicted feelings about fame; the deodorant the title mocks and its place in the culture; and even personal details about Cobain, such as his reverence for the lobotomized actress Frances Farmer.

> *Variation:* Look, as Lewis Thomas did, at how the music has evolved and reshaped itself in your consciousness in response to events in your life. Be as specific and as broad as possible: What was it like before and after the millennium? The World Trade Center attack? The vicissitudes of your own love life?

9. Try to imagine your way into the head of a musician you love. Create a speculative narrative that combines fact and fiction to bring that person's music to life on the page.

Literature: The "Reading Narratives"

10. Think about your reading life. What piece of writing has "taken the top of your head off," to use Emily Dickinson's phrase, or what inspired you to do things differently? Write a reading narrative in which you enter into a dialogue with this writing—feel free to quote it. Where does it guide you? What does it give you permission to do? And where does it leave gaps that you, as a writer, can fill? How has this reading experience changed you and helped you redefine your life and your mission as a writer?

11. Write a history of your life through the books you've read. What was your favorite book at age 5? 10? 16? 20? Write these out in sections, rendering in specific, sensory detail the memories these books inspire in you.

Suggestions for Further Reading

In Our Anthology

Gordon, Mary, "Still Life: Notes on Pierre Bonnard and My Mother's Ninetieth Birthday"

Rekdal, Paisley, "The Night My Mother Met Bruce Lee"

Elsewhere

Baker, Nicholson, *U and I: A True Story*

Barthes, Roland, "Leaving the Movie Theater"

Doty, Mark, *Still Life with Oysters and Lemon*

Dyer, Geoff, *But Beautiful: A Book about Jazz*

Margolick, David, Hilton Als, and Ellis Marsalis, *Strange Fruit: The Biography of a Song*

McKibben, Bill, *The Age of Missing Information*

Rose, Phyllis, *The Year of Reading Proust*

Thomas, Lewis, *Late Night Thoughts on Listening to Mahler's 9th Symphony*

Weschler, Lawrence, "Inventing Peace," *New Yorker*, 20 November 1995, 56–64.

Williams, Terry Tempest, *Leap*

Chapter Eight

Writing the Larger World

Like Flemish miniaturists who reveal the essence of humankind within the confines of a tiny frame, McPhee once again demonstrates that the smallest topic is replete with history, significance, and consequence. —**from a review of John McPhee's** *Oranges*

▌ **Turning Outward: Finding Your Material outside the Self**
▌ **Science**
▌ **The Layperson's Approach**
▌ **The Expert's Approach**
▌ **Sports Writing**
▌ **The Myriad Things around Us**
▌ **The Essay of Ideas**
▌ **Try It**

The first nonfiction book I remember reading and going back to read again was Lewis Thomas's *The Lives of a Cell*. I read it while sitting in my little rented room in Arcata, California; I was a senior in college, a nascent Buddhist brimming with questions about the world and my place in it. Thomas had me thinking about mitochondria—mitochondria!—and the topic had called into question every perception I thought was sound. No longer was I a separate organism, contained within my skin, but a mere continuance of a single cell that erupted eons ago in the primordial soup.

What got to me about these "Notes of a Biology Watcher" was not the information itself (had I read the same information in the encyclopedia, I doubt that it would have affected me so), but *how* that information was presented. Thomas was no mere biologist, but a philosopher and a poet;

his sensibility permeated the information and made it real, made it personal. As I became more and more interested in creative nonfiction, I found this same kind of voice in many of the writers I loved: E. B. White, John McPhee, Tom Wolfe, and Joan Didion, to name just a few. These authors brought their "I" to the world without becoming self-centered; their focus often remained determinedly outward without sacrificing the voice that made their work unique.

Recently, National Public Radio aired a story about the recent spate in nonfiction books that focus on topics one might not expect to find interesting: orchids, tulips, mosquitoes, clouds, ether, and something as diminutive and common as dust. People are reading these books on the bus, at the beach, in a chair by the window; they're coming to the breakfast table and saying to their loved ones, "Did you know about . . . ?" —**Brenda**

Turning Outward: Finding Your Material Outside the Self

Your own private world—if you inhabit it long enough—will become claustrophobic, not only for yourself, but also for your readers. In chapters 6 and 7, we showed how placing yourself in the context of history or art can help diffuse some of the inward focus of creative nonfiction; in this chapter, we encourage you to direct your gaze outward, not leaving the self behind, but perhaps sublimating it in order to discover anew the subjects the world has to offer.

Lee Gutkind, founder and editor of the journal *Creative Nonfiction*, believes that one of the genre's essential missions is "to gather and present information, to teach readers about a person, place, idea or situation combining the creativity of the artistic experience with . . . research. . . . Read the books and essays of the most renowned nonfiction writers in this century and you will read about a writer engaged in a quest for information and discovery." Gutkind himself has written several books of creative nonfiction in which he immerses himself in a topic; from organ transplantation to baseball, he unveils certain aspects of the world that might otherwise remain obscure to us as readers.

A good creative nonfiction writer will be attuned to the things of the world that cry out for examination. In this chapter, we've broken the categories down into a few that interest us, but as with all the prompts we provide in this book, these are mere gateways for your own creative instincts.

Science

A friend said recently that every time he opens up a newspaper these days, he reads something that hits his view of the world with a thunderbolt: Stephen Hawking announces that we must use genetic engineering to evolve faster or computers will make us extinct; there may be infinite parallel universes; a religious group is working to clone human beings.

When you write about science in creative nonfiction, it becomes much more than a recitation or analysis of facts and turns into a means of probing the deepest levels of our common existence. Right now we live steeped in startling scientific and technological advances. These changes signal more than quirky facts to recite; they invade our deepest assumptions about who we are. Here's where literary nonfiction writers become almost essential for our very survival.

We need Lewis Thomas to help us take in the infinite complexities science has found in cell behavior. We need Ursula Goodenough (also a cell biologist), who creates in her *Sacred Depths of Nature* a sophisticated theology out of an examination of cellular life. We need Oliver Sacks, writing books like *The Man Who Mistook His Wife for a Hat,* to teach us how humans cope and remain whole while myriad neurological forces buffet them. Michael Pollan, in *The Botany of Desire*, plants genetically modified potatoes in his garden and maps out the exact nature of genetic modification and its implications for agriculture, as well as how it feels to grow these potatoes, classified by the Environmental Protection Agency as "pesticides," not food. (He doesn't eat them.) Writer–scientists like Stephen Hawking take us by the hand and lead us through a changing cosmos that barely makes sense to physicists now.

The Layperson's Approach

Many personal essayists, such as Annie Dillard, draw heavily on scientific knowledge without being classified as science writers per se.

These authors may flesh out a personal experience with facts that enrich the narrative and that may also be alive with metaphoric significance. Dillard's "Total Eclipse" (see the anthology section) begins with the bald declaration, "It had been like dying, that sliding down the mountain pass." Her approach is personal and vulnerable: She writes of an experience—a total eclipse—that continually threatens to overwhelm her and the other onlookers. The intensity of her reactions ("God save our life," "the last sane moment I remember") continues to emphasize that vulnerability. This passion is matched by that of the cosmos she constantly fits herself into, one in which light and darkness exist in a constant dance of existence and extinguishing.

> The Ring Nebula, in the constellation Lyra, looks, through binoculars, like a smoke ring. It is a star in the process of exploding. Light from its explosion first reached the earth in 1054; it was a supernova then, and so bright it shone in the daytime. Now it is not so bright, but it is still exploding. It expands at the rate of seventy million miles a day. . . . It does not budge. Its apparent size does not increase.

Because Dillard insists on switching from the world of human activity to the world of cosmic activity, we see her sense of being "obliterated" by the eclipse as a coherent response to a cosmos where darkness can signal an ultimate end. Hers becomes a thinking reaction to the universe we're tied to so intimately.

The Expert's Approach

Richard Selzer's perspective is different. He's a practicing surgeon, and rather than recording his own vulnerability in "The Knife" (see the anthology section) he records the fearful power his skills give him. Selzer implies again and again that perhaps no human is fully equipped to have the life and death power of the surgeon: "A stillness settles in my heart and is carried to my hand. It is the quietude of resolve layered over fear." As he operates, he records the following:

> Deeper still. The peritoneum, pink and gleaming and membranous, bulges into the wound. It is grasped with forceps, and opened. For the first time we can see into the cavity of the abdomen. Such a primitive place.

Selzer performs matching surgery on his own emotions, delving deeper and deeper into the emotional and philosophical aspects of his role. "Here is man as microcosm, representing in all his parts the earth, perhaps the universe." "And if the surgeon is like a poet, then the scars you have made on countless bodies are like verses."

In Selzer as in Dillard, the scientific facts recounted become maps for the emotional and philosophical landscapes across which these essays will range. The science is essential to our understanding of both the literal events and their larger, more metaphorical implications. The best science writing functions this way: It provides us with facts about our world that fascinate and that also point to a new way of understanding ourselves.

There's science in everything we do. The act of writing requires magnificently choreographed leaps from the twenty-seven bones in our hands and an intricate, ceaseless dialogue between our two brain hemispheres (one side tends to govern language, the other creativity). Yet none of the writing about writing that we've seen has looked at the basic physiology of the writing process. In the arena of Richard Selzer–type writing, you may feel you lack the expertise to use the expert approach. But you don't have to be a veteran of the surgical theatre to have a topic you can approach with an informed voice. If you have mastered computer technology, been part of a field camp, dissected something, or learned to fix a car, you have a subject you can talk about with expertise.

Sports Writing

It's astonishing how much we reveal about ourselves, personally and as a society, through sports. Think of the social implications of being a "tomboy" or a "klutz," then think of the way sports figures embody our cultural idealizations: There's a reason a great basketball player or an Olympic gymnast can use his or her images to sell almost any product on the market. Reflecting about sports has yielded much great writing on the topic of our societal concepts of success and failure, masculinity and femininity, and race, as well as a way of experiencing through words one of life's great visceral excitements.

David Halberstam, one of the editors of *The Best American Sports Writing of the Century*, describes the sports writing he presents as a portrait "of the nation itself during the explosive period" of the twentieth century. His coeditor Glenn Stout calls ours a "golden age" of sports writing. Both editors—seasoned writers themselves—credit the upsurge in this form to authors like Gay Talese and Tom Wolfe, who refused to sacrifice breadth and literary flair in their sports journalism. As Stout puts it, describing the *Best American Sports Writing* series, "at least once or twice in every edition it was proven, unquestionably, that the best 'sports writing' was . . . just good writing that happened to be about sports." You'll want to keep this in mind as you go through the Try Its at the end of this chapter: Think about how your own sports obsessions reflect yourself and your culture, and what larger questions—of race, violence, and gender—come into play in the sport you choose to write about.

Joyce Carol Oates's book *On Boxing* uses the sport to reflect on larger questions. Sportswriting is a field still dominated by men; it's a little surprising to see a woman writing about sports, especially such a traditionally masculine sport as boxing. She begins the essay by complicating this kind of masculinity:

> No sport is more physical, more direct, than boxing. No sport appears more powerfully homoerotic: the confrontation in the ring—the disrobing—the sweaty heated combat that is part dance, courtship, coupling—the frequent urgent pursuit by one boxer of the other in the fight's natural and violent movement toward the "knockout."

Oates punctures most readers' basic beliefs about boxing, using specific observations of movements in the ring—movements mirrored by her jumpy, fragmented writing—to do so. She observes the embrace the fighters exchange after the fight and goes on to ask, "Are men privileged to embrace with love only after having fought?" She goes on to make the bold statement that this proves man's greatest passion "is for war, not peace." You might disagree with her conclusions, but the essay uses a close observation of a sport she loves to ask questions about gender roles, the nature of love and intimacy, and our human instincts.

David James Duncan, in "The Mickey Mantle Koan " (see the anthology section), uses baseball in a more personal way: to discuss the death of his brother. John Duncan, a sports enthusiast, died at seventeen of a defective heart. In the essay, his talents as a ballplayer and sprinter become compromised by his heart problems, in a way that mirrors the boy's perceptions of the life of his sports hero, Mickey Mantle:

> Mantle was his absolute hero, but his tragic hero. The Mick, my brother maintained, was the greatest raw talent of all time. He was one to whom great gifts were given, from whom great gifts had been ripped away, and the more scarred his knees became, the more frequently he fanned, the more flagrant his limp and apologetic his smile, the more John revered him.

"This has gotten a bit iffy for a sports story," Duncan writes at the end of his essay. It isn't, of course, a traditional sports essay, but an essay that explores sports in order to explore his family: He and his brother bond through their love of baseball.

The day of John's death, an autographed baseball of Mickey Mantle arrives for him. Duncan begins to think of the signed baseball as a *koan*—a Zen riddle the solution to which brings enlightenment. When the author solves this koan for himself, it is, significantly, a season when the "Miracle Mets blitz the Orioles in the World Series." The exhilaration of the games seems to provide the impetus Duncan needs to think through this aspect of his brother's death: Sports victory and personal victory blend. Duncan loves baseball and can write beautifully of "a feeble knuckler, a roundhouse curve, a submarine fastball": Sports writing and family writing intersect and inform each other.

The Myriad Things around Us

Can you imagine writing an entire book about a color? Writing about the *Oxford English Dictionary?* Describing the flight path of a single type of butterfly? How about those clingy grains you thoughtlessly shake off your feet at the beach? Lovely, profound, and popular books have been published in the past few years about such seemingly small things.

Poet Theodore Roethke wrote, "All finite things reveal infinitude." William Blake wrote of seeing eternity "in a grain of sand, and the universe in a flower." These thoughts are not poets' conceits, but philosophical truths nonfiction writers have been among the most successful at plumbing. Annie Dillard's *For the Time Being,* is, on the one hand, a book about everything, and on the other, a book about sand. At least, sand—a solid thing that flows and functions like water—forms a starting point for her long theological look at the flux of the world, Hasidism, and God.

OK, you might say, perhaps sand is interesting, but color? As Simon Garfield, author of *Mauve: How One Man Invented a Color That Changed the World*, discovers, mauve had a lasting impact on the culture of its day (and ours). The color was discovered by an eighteen-year-old chemistry student who found it in a test tube in the course of trying out something else. Mauve, the first synthetic color, soon became a status symbol flaunted by royals, including Queen Victoria. (Contemporaries decried the aristocratic passion for mauve by describing streets pocked by wearers as having a case of "mauve measles.") And, naturally, the invention of synthetic color changed the textile industry and the economy of the day.

In a slightly different way, Fabio Morabito (see the anthology section) turns his attention to the common tools we find in our toolboxes. He anthropomorphizes —gives human qualities to—such tools in "Screw" and "File and Sandpaper." In so doing, he forces us to look at these things not just as the practical things they are, but also as objects of poetry. We humans define ourselves as the animals that make and use tools; by paying such close attention to our tools, the nail that is "heroic and exciting," the screw that's "morose and circumspect," Morabito examines what it means to be human, by our own definition.

Hindus speak reverently of "Indra's net"—a web of interconnectedness with a jewel at each intersection that can be used to embody the interconnectedness of the world. Gifted writers like Dillard and Garfield find the "webs" attached to the subjects that draw them—the flowing and flux suggested by sand, the accident of a test-tube residue changing the fashions and industry of a nineteenth-century imperial power.

Once you as a writer begin to look closely at what's around you—recognizing both the closest details and the larger ways each thing fits into the "Indra's web" that holds us all together—nothing will seem less than a fruitful subject for your writing.

The Essay of Ideas

The essay has long been *the* form for exploring the workings of the human intellect. Essays run the gamut from argument to rumination, and authors have always used them as a vehicle for both developing and expressing ideas, holding political debates, and delving into personal philosophy. Many of us have bad memories of writing "themes" in high school, the five-paragraph essay that rigidly prescribed the way an intellectual essay could work: thesis, three supporting paragraphs, and a tepid conclusion. Here, in the realm of creative nonfiction, you can redeem the essay of ideas and return it to its rightful place in the literary arts.

As is the case with all good creative nonfiction, the important thing to keep in mind is how to make the essay specific to you and your particular voice. Writing about abstract concepts does not need to be done in a dry or dull way; on the contrary, here's an opportunity for you to use the techniques of vivid writing to illuminate difficult topics. You'll seek to uncover the scenes, the details, the images, and the metaphors that make for a memorable essay.

For example, Jeanette Winterson, in her essay "The Semiotics of Sex," begins a highly complex discussion of aesthetics, art, and ideology with a scene in a bookstore:

> I was in a bookshop recently when a young woman approached me.
>
> She told me she was writing an essay on my work and that of Radclyffe Hall. Could I help?

"Yes," I said. "Our work has nothing in common."

"I thought you were a lesbian," she said.

With this brief scene, Winterson provides a compelling example that wholeheartedly admits the "I" into the intellectual discussion to follow. Rather than dryly elucidate her thesis in the first paragraph, *then* provide a support for that thesis, she does the opposite; she finds a scene that encapsulates her argument and she renders that scene in a way that reveals her personality, her voice, and her concerns.

Several of the essays in our anthology section act as essays of ideas, though they may disguise themselves as wholly personal narratives. "The Death of the Moth" (see the anthology section) purports to be a simple description of a moth dying on the windowsill, but in reality Virginia Woolf manages to create a highly nuanced philosophical treatise on the power of death over life. "Notes of a Native Son" (see the anthology section) focuses on the death of James Baldwin's father, but issues of race and violence pulse through the essay, creating a political argument much more effective than any pundit's analysis. Alice Walker's essay "Becoming What We're Called" uses her feelings as a springboard to talk about language, race and gender.

Though all these essayists write about diverse topics, they have something in common: They've observed the world around them closely; then they've taken on the *authority* to write about these issues. They do so through the muscle of their language, the specificity of their examples, and the use of authoritative sources to give texture and credence to their own ideas.

Paradoxically, when you write about abstract concepts—ideas—it's even more important to pay attention to the concrete details that make such things comprehensible. A good essay of ideas will be a mix of argument and reflection, knowledge and experience, so that in the end, the reader has gained some insight into both the ideas and the mind behind them.

Here, more than anywhere else in this book, our message is that it's time to begin to really *see*. Don't brush gnats from your eyes; instead, wonder why they're there, what it is they're attracted to. In the book *Drawing on the Right Side of the Brain,* the authors teach a way to draw a house by finding its shape from what surrounds it: You draw the tree that leans against it, the row of boxwoods in the front, the puff of smoke that defines the chimney, and the house's form arises from those defining shapes. You should try to draw yourself that way too: What people and things and ideas lean into you and change the shape of your mind and your body? We urge you to start seeing even the smallest parts of your world and the largest chains of people and ideas that define you.

Try It

Science

1. Scientific facts, like scientific language, are often rich in metaphor. Great science writing draws the material facts of the universe into the process of reflection on the human experience. How would it inform your writing to know that doctors call the two coverings of the brain the hard mother (*dura mater*) and the tender mother (*pia mater*)? How does it change your sense of your own experience to know that physicists believe that there may be an infinite number of parallel universes, containing what ours contains in somewhat different form?

To speed you in the process of exploring the metaphorical value of scientific facts, do a twenty-minute free-write on any of the following bits of information. Write whatever associations or suggestions come into your head. What experiences of your own crop up when you think of these facts?

　　—The human body contains a vestigial tailbone.

　　—Our galaxy contains a black hole into which our solar system, including earth, will ultimately collapse.

　　—Stephen Hawking has said that if humans don't begin to use genetic engineering to modify themselves—including incorporating computer technology—computers will evolve past us and possibly cause our extinction.

　　—Clones are, for little-known reasons, abnormally large.

Before you begin your free-writing session, whether in a class or a writing group or alone, add to this list any facts that have stuck in your mind as suggestive, fascinating, or just bizarre.

After your free-writing session, assuming that the material interests you, try expanding it into an essay this way: Use a human story (it can be your own or someone else's) to intersperse with the scientific material. At some point in the essay, you must expand on the science, but promise yourself it won't dominate. For example, you might use the Stephen Hawking fact to tell the story of how your father lost his dot-com job as technology changed—a connection suggested by your free-write. The Hawking material, which would come back throughout the piece, would serve to anchor your father's story to the overwhelming tide of change and obsolescence in contemporary human life.

2. Identify an area of expertise you have. This prompt may not work for everybody, but as teachers, we're generally surprised by how much fascinating specialized knowledge newer writers have but take for granted.

Computer technology, advanced science classes that include lab and fieldwork, car repair, part-time jobs in medical institutions—the list is endless. Detail that work as Richard Selzer does so carefully in "The Knife." Examine your role and the larger significance of it, as well as the role this specialized activity plays in human culture and your own life. Think of how it makes you feel, what aspect of your humanity it accentuates.

Sports

3.   Examine a sport in terms of the imagery of its body movements, dress, rituals, and rules. Do any of these seem to defy our stereotypes of this sport? What social significance can you draw from what you see? How do you connect to this sport emotionally?

4.   Think of a way in which a sport has had significance in your own life or that of someone close to you. Are there ways in which this personal experience and the sport, or a sports player's career, have run parallel? How? Can you think of a time when a sporting event had an emotional impact on you as you experienced an important event in your own life?

The Myriad Things around Us

5.   Free-write a list of things you deal with on a daily basis and don't think about very much. Don't be choosy; jot down whatever pops into your head: paper, fluorescent lighting, mosquitoes, slugs, flush toilets. Then select one item from your list to use for more free-writing, examining it from two directions suggested by the work of the writers mentioned throughout this chapter.

6.   What are the larger metaphysical (that is, dealing with the properties of the universe at large) connotations of your item? Look at it if you can. Let's say you've chosen a piece of white paper. What does your paper suggest? What are the implications of its smoothness and whiteness? Of writing on pressed trees? Of writing within a square frame? Don't censor yourself but simply go with your impulses. Be weird. Be funny. Find the universe in the particular "grain of sand" in front of you.

7.   Next, uncover a few facts about your item. They may be things you already know or that classmates or group members can tell you (having a group discussion can really launch a great free-write here; we trivia buffs are many!) or that you can look up quickly on the Internet. (See Chapter 11, "The Basics of Personal Reportage," if you're stymied.) Then do a second free-write, focusing on details about your item that feel interesting or suggestive. How is paper made? What might it mean to the existence of paper that we now have so much writing in cyberspace? Again, don't censor yourself. Feel free to be silly and to be broad. Let yourself move out along the web—if mauve defined a period in Queen Victoria's England, what time period would paper define?

The Essay of Ideas

8. Make a list of the abstract concepts on which you have some opinions: racism, politics, gender wars, and so on. Now circle one of them, and come up with a list of some specific examples from your own experience that elucidate these abstract concepts in a concrete way. How can you gain *authority* to talk about these issues? How can you demonstrate to the reader that you have firsthand knowledge of these topics?

9. Collect newspaper stories and magazine articles that strike you over the course of a few weeks. Gather them together and begin to explore *why* these particular stories grab your attention. Begin to do a little research on the details in these stories to see whether they could lead to a larger essay.

Suggestions for Further Reading

In Our Anthology

Baldwin, James, "Notes of a Native Son"

Dillard, Annie, "Total Eclipse"

Duncan, David James, "The Mickey Mantle Koan"

Morabito, Fabio, "File and Sandpaper" and "Screw"

Price, Jennifer, *A Brief Natural History of the Pink Plastic Flamingo*

Selzer, Richard, "The Knife"

Walker, Alice, "Becoming What We're Called"

Woolf, Virginia, "The Death of the Moth"

Elsewhere

Dillard, Annie, *For the Time Being*

Garfield, Simon, *Mauve: How One Man Invented a Color That Changed the World*

Hawking, Stephen, *A Brief History of Time*

Pollan, Michael, *The Botany of Desire*

Thomas, Lewis, *The Lives of a Cell* and *The Medusa and the Snail*

Winchester, Simon, *The Professor and the Madman*

PART III

The Forms of Creative Nonfiction

The best work speaks intimately to you even though it has been consciously made to speak intimately to thousands of others. The bad writer believes that sincerity of feeling will be enough, and pins her faith on the power of experience. The true writer knows that feeling must give way to form. It is through the form, not in spite of, or accidental to it, that the most powerful emotions are let loose over the greatest number of people. —**Jeanette Winterson**

We began this book with a nod to Emily Dickinson and her mandate to "tell all the Truth but tell it slant. . . ." Part II, we hope, has helped you find out just what kinds of truths you may have to offer. Now, using the techniques for vivid writing we offered in Chapter 1, your job is to find a way to "tell it slant," to find the forms that will contain these truths in the most effective and interesting ways. As a writer of creative nonfiction, you must continually make artistic choices that will finesse life's experience into art that will have lasting meaning for others.

In Part II, we gave you certain triggers to help you mine the material of life and memory; perhaps, as you wrote, you already found yourself confronted with artistic dilemmas: Where do I begin this narrative? Which details do I include; Which do I leave out? Which form do I use? How do I shape this material for its best effect? How do I make a personal story have any relevance for the reader? Here, in Part III, we'll address these kinds of questions, shifting our attention away from content and onto form.

It's through careful attention to form that you'll be able to create art out of your own experience. Understanding how we're structuring our experience forces us to be concrete and vivid. Ironically, the more particular you make your own experience—with sensory details, compelling metaphors, and luscious rhythms—the more fully a reader will feel the personal story along with you. By experiencing it, readers begin to *care* about it, because your experience has now become theirs.

We hope that you'll come to find that form is your friend; that by placing your allegiance in artifact over experience, the material becomes just that: raw material that you'll use to fashion art, rather than the intractable stuff of memory and experience. To come back to our friend Emily Dickinson, in a letter to Thomas Higginson she said, rather cryptically, "My business is circumference." By this she meant, perhaps, that she circled her life, encompassing every hummingbird, every fly, every bit of bread into her art. All creative nonfiction writers should take heed: Observe your life from every angle—cocking your head, squinting your eyes—then fashion what you see through a voice that belongs to you and you alone. Tell us the truth, but shape it in a way that wakes us from our doldrums and startles us into a new grasp of our strange and remarkable lives.

Chapter Nine

The Personal Essay

After a time, some of us learn (and some more slowly than others) that life comes down to some simple things. How we love, how alert we are, how curious we are. Love, attention, curiosity. . . . One way we learn this lesson is by listening to others tell us true stories of their own struggles to come to a way of understanding. It is sometimes comforting to know that others seem to fail as often and as oddly as we do. . . . And it is even more comforting to have such stories told to us with style, the way a writer has found to an individual expression of a personal truth. —**Scott Walker**

I'm a young woman in college, beginning to write. I know I want to write poetry and I do, Sylvia Plath–like free verse, Robert Lowell–style metrics, in the manner of many college poets in the 1970s. At the same time, prose attracts me: I love its rhythms, its wider gait, its capacity. But I know I'm not a fiction writer; I have no gift for character or plot unless I happen upon them in my life. I feel a general attraction to the essay form, but I have a deep sense that I'm not the kind of person who writes essays. When I think of the essay form, even the personal essay form, I think of men, older men: the H. L. Menckens and James Thurbers who populate my 1970s college readers. There are no Maxine Hong Kingstons and Patricia Hampls around yet to give me courage.

Everything changes later when I pick up Annie Dillard's book, *Pilgrim at Tinker Creek*. A book-length, meditative personal essay, *Pilgrim* documents the speaker's observations of the natural world around her home in Virginia. It's at once deeply individual, as she looks at the "rosy, complex" light that fills her kitchen in June, and deeply philosophical, as she draws everything into relationship with the galaxy that is "careening" around her. It's a bold book, drawing on the seemingly small in order to embrace the entire world. More important to me at the time, the speaker is a young woman in her twenties, the author herself. She's not speaking with the authoritative male voice I have come to associate with the essay. She speaks as Annie Dillard, with only the authority of our shared human experience.

I was fascinated to learn later that Annie Dillard originally began *Pilgrim at Tinker Creek* in the voice of a middle-aged male academic, a metaphysician. She didn't trust her own young woman's voice to engage and convince her audience. Other writers persuaded her to trust her own voice and abandon the constructed one, and the book won a Pulitzer Prize, proving that the personal essay form is a broad one. It requires only that you be alert, perceptive, and human.—**Suzanne**

The Personal Essay Tradition

The personal essay is "the way a writer has found to an individual expression of a personal truth." When Scott Walker wrote those words in the 1980s, the personal essay was making a comeback. The reading public seemed hungry for a form that engages us the way fiction does, but that also teaches us something about the way real life works. While the phrase "creative nonfiction" hadn't yet come into popular use, the term "personal essay" seemed adequate to convey that sense of combining a personal voice with a factual story.

In the West, scholars often date the essay tradition back to the sixteenth-century French writer Michel de Montaigne. Montaigne's *Essais*, composed in the author's retirement, laid much of the ground-work for what we now think of as the essay style: Informal, frank (often bawdy), and associative, his book moves easily from a consideration of the classical author Virgil to pieces like "Of Thumbs." His title, *Essais*, plays on the French verb meaning "to try," and it gives us the term we now use routinely in nonfiction writing. The essay writer "tries out" various approaches to the subject, offering tentative forays into an arena where "truth" can be open for debate (see chapter 2).

Phillip Lopate, editor of the historically astute anthology *The Art of the Personal Essay*, puts it this way: "The essayist attempts to surround a something—a subject, a mood, a problematic irritation—by coming at it from all angles, wheeling and diving like a hawk, each seemingly digressive spiral actually taking us closer to the heart of the matter."

As Lopate's anthology illustrates, before Montaigne plenty of writers worked in what we would now consider a personal essay mode. Just a few examples include Sei Shonagon, a tenth-century Japanese courtesan who created elaborately detailed lists that revealed much about herself and her place in the Japanese court; the Japanese monk Kenko's meditative ruminations translated as *Essays in Idleness*; or Roman emperor Marcus Aurelius, whose book *The Meditations of Marcus Aurelius* embodies an aphoristic essay style, creating pithy slogans as advice to those who will succeed him. The Stoic philosopher Seneca the Younger and the Greek biographer Plutarch both wrote "essays in disguise" in the form of letters that ruminated on a range of things, from noise in the marketplace to the proper comportment to maintain in the face of grief.

After Montaigne, British essayists such as Charles Lamb and William Hazlitt made the essay form their own. According to Lopate, "[I]t was the English, rather than Montaigne's own countrymen, who took up his challenge and extended, refined, and cultivated the essay." Lamb wrote about intensely personal material (his sister killed their mother and wounded their father; Lamb himself suffered a nervous breakdown), but he used a fictional persona that gave him some distance from his subject. Hazlitt wrote more in the style of Montaigne, creating essays with titles such as "On Going a Journey," and "On the Pleasure of Hating." In America, at the same time, Thoreau was writing his journals and *Walden,* works that would form the foundation of American nature writing taken up by writers such as Edward Abbey and Annie Dillard.

As an essayist, you should take it on yourself to study the tradition, not only for general knowledge but to situate yourself within that literary lineup. How does your own writing work with or against the stylistic tendencies of a Joan Didion, say, who in turn has a voice that emerges in direct dialogue with the voice of essayists such as George Orwell? Lopate's *The Art of the Personal Essay* is a good place to start, but also look at works of your contemporaries to see how the essay is evolving in your own generation. The literary magazine *Fourth Genre: Explorations in Nonfiction* publishes some of the best contemporary writers in the form, as do the journals *Creative Nonfiction* and *River Teeth: A Journal of Nonfiction Narrative.* You should also avail yourself of the *Best American Essays* series; the editor, Robert Atwan, culls a selection of the strongest essays published by American magazines each year, and a guest editor pares those down further to a select few. While we all have our own definitions of "best," it's useful to read these anthologies to see what your contemporaries are up to. By reading widely, you'll learn not only what's possible, but what still has to be discovered.

You may find, as Lopate has, that "at the core of the essay is the supposition that there is a certain unity to human experience." The personal essay carries the implication that the personal, properly rendered, is universally significant, or should be. Montaigne echoes this: "Every man has within himself the entire human condition." At the same time, Lopate writes that "the hallmark of the personal essay is its intimacy. The writer seems to be speaking directly into your ear, confiding everything from gossip to wisdom." These two poles—intimacy of voice and universality of significance—go to the heart of the personal essay tradition. The essay speaks confidingly, as a whispering friend, and these whispers must be made meaningful in a larger context—capturing a piece of larger human experience within the amber of your own.

The Way Essays Work

What makes an essay an essay? How can you recognize one when you see it? When we study fiction writing or poetry, certain elements of form are easy enough to identify: plot, for instance, or character development in short stories; lineation and rhythm in poems. Essays can be analyzed the same way, but the task is complicated by the wide variety of styles and forms encompassed by the term "personal essay." Many of these forms overlap with content, and perhaps you've already experienced several of them in the first section of this book.

You've already been writing memoir, for example, if you focus on selected memories for a particular metaphorical or narrative effect.
You've already started a nature essay if you described some aspect of
the environment around you. Perhaps you've already tried the travel
piece or a biographical sketch of someone close to you. All of these
are "forms," defined more by content than by craft.

If we turn our attention to craft, we can begin to see some stylistic qualities that help define the essay form. Douglas Hesse, in his essay "The Boundary Zone," describes the difference between essays
and short stories in terms of movement. In any narrative prose piece,
there's some sense of forward movement, visualized as a horizontal
line; this line keeps the story moving forward in some way. For instance, in Jo Ann Beard's "The Fourth State of Matter" (see the anthology section), the horizontal line could be the shooting described in
the piece; she begins the piece before the shooting and continues
through the event and its emotional aftermath. Three other strands
also propel the essay forward: the dying collie, the "vanished" husband, and the squirrels in the attic. All these form miniplots, very
much like a short story. She uses dialogue freely and re-creates scene
with vivid, specific details. And the essay itself reads like a short story
because of the present-tense voice (a narrator) and the sense of horizontal story lines unfolding and intersecting at the same time.

By contrast, a more "essay-like" narrative might have a stronger
"vertical" line to it, the reflective voice that comments on the scenes
it re-creates. David James Duncan works in this mode. In his essay
"The Mickey Mantle Koan," the forward, or horizontal, line of the
narrative—the brother's death—is interrupted, or balanced, by his ruminations on the "koan" of the late-arriving baseball. This reflective
voice runs underneath the horizontal line, creating a sense of movement that delves below the surface of narrative.

While Duncan's essay balances the horizontal and vertical lines,
some essays favor the vertical line almost exclusively. Virginia Woolf's
"The Death of the Moth" (see the anthology section), for example,
spends very little time really on its horizontal thread—the actual death
of the moth—and leans more heavily on the vertical line of reflection.
A more contemporary essayist, Fabio Morabito, takes the vertical line
to the extreme as he forgos horizontal lines altogether; instead,
through close observation, he creates a bizarre new perspective on
tools (see "File and Sandpaper" and "Screw" in the anthology section).
The "I" never directly appears in his meditation, yet the presence of a
first-person sensibility is hard to deny.

Once you begin seeing essays in terms of their movement, you
can decide how your own work might fit, or work against, the categories of personal essay. At one extreme, we have the short-story

style, engaging us with plots and subplots and scenes, and at the other extreme, the analytic meditation, engaging us through the power of the writer's interior voice. Where do you fall on this grid? How can you expand your talents and write essays that create their own definitions?

Memoir

It's important to remember that most essays use elements of different literary approaches—one piece by John McPhee may contain within it nature writing, science writing, and memoir, for instance. But for the purpose of scrutinizing our own work and understanding our traditions, we can discuss nonfiction in terms of categories, bearing in mind all the while that we don't want to allow ourselves or the writers we admire to be limited by those categories.

A nonfiction category strongly linked with the personal essay is memoir. The term comes from the French word for memory; no writer of any stripe is prescient enough to put everything he or she wants to record into notes, so drawing on memory is an essential part of what we all do. Some readers confuse anything written with a first-person "I" that draws on personal experience with memoir, though new journalists like Joan Didion and Tom Wolfe indulge freely in both without necessarily being memoirists. And some writers, reacting to criticism that the form has become overly confessional and prevalent, avoid the term when that's exactly what they're writing (much like the poet Bret Harte, who hated the term "poetry" and punched anyone who didn't refer to his poetry as "lines").

To be memoir, writing must derive its energy and its narrative drive from an exploration of the past. Its lens may be a lifetime or it may be a few hours. Annie Dillard, in "Total Eclipse" (see the anthology section), recollects a past event, but her narrative drive, the "punch" of the piece, is metaphysical meditation, not memoir. E. B. White, however, in "Afternoon of an American Boy" (see the anthology section), writes a piece of pure memoir. His lens is small; he recalls a period in his teenage years when he first got up the courage to ask a girl out to dance—"that precious, brief moment in life before love's pages, through constant reference, had become dog-eared."

William Zinsser, who edited *Inventing the Truth: The Art and Craft of Memoir*, says this: "Unlike autobiography, which moves in a dutiful line from birth to fame, memoir narrows the lens, focusing on a time in the writer's life that was unusually vivid, such as childhood or adolescence, or that was framed by war or travel or public service or some other special circumstance." In other words, memoirists need not have had fascinating lives, worth recounting in every detail.

(Those kinds of books, as Zinsser notes, are generally considered autobiography.)

Memoir mines the past, examining it for shape and meaning, in the belief that from that act can emerge a larger, communal meaning. Memoir can heal, it can warn, and it can provide spiritual direction. Into the last category falls spiritual memoir, like Andre Dubus's "Love In the Morning" (see the website). Memoir can open societal lines of communication on subjects previously held taboo. Richard Hoffman's memoir of child sexual abuse, *Half the House,* for example, eventually led to the prosecution of a child molester.

In his essay "Backtalk," Hoffman provides a defense of the surge of memoir as a corrective to a culture that has accepted the verb "to spin" to mean deliberate distortion of our news: "the ascendance of memoir . . . may be a kind of cultural corrective to the sheer amount of fictional distortion that has accumulated in [our] society." For those of you interested in the memoir form, Hoffman's words may provide a useful starting point; think of yourself as an "unspinner," a voice striving to undo some of the cultural distortion you see around you.

A subset of memoir that has become more and more talked about recently is the *crisis memoir,* which deals with a particular traumatic event, narrowing that memory focus still further. Jo Ann Beard's "The Fourth State of Matter" (see the anthology section) would fall into this category. Much memoir, like E. B. White's, is re-creative, elegiac, and celebratory in its way; crisis memoir serves a different function. It builds support and community and may lift the veil of stigma off painful experiences, as in Richard Hoffman's *Half the House,* or Nancy Mairs's exploration of living with multiple sclerosis. Crisis memoir sometimes, but not always, implies a sense of ultimate victory over the experience, as the writer has gained enough distance and mastery to tell the tale—Kathryn Rhett's anthology of crisis memoir is aptly titled *Survival Stories.*

Though memoir is the nonfiction form most closely associated with an "I," it can be written in second or third person; Judith Kitchen uses third person in her brief memoir "Things of This Life" (see the website). These kinds of techniques—experiments with point of view, use of different tenses (past, present, future), finding just the right metaphorical image to anchor the piece (see Cooper's "The Fine Art of Sighing" in the anthology section)—all serve to help the memoir elevate itself out of self-centered rumination and into the arena of art.

Literary or New Journalism

In 1972, for an article in *New York* magazine, writer Tom Wolfe announced "The Birth of the 'New Journalism.'" This new nonfiction form, Wolfe claimed, would supplant the novel. It allows writers the luxury of a first-person voice and the use of literary devices—scene, imagery, and so forth—in the service of reporting. In other words, Wolfe's new journalism marries traditional journalism with the personal essay. Wolfe cited such new journalists as Hunter S. Thompson, then writing a first-person account of his travels with the Hell's Angels. To Wolfe, acknowledging the reporter's subjectivity is not an indulgence but a recognition that we're always both limited and enriched by the vagaries of our own particular stance.

Before new journalism's emergence, journalists typically shunned the use of the "I" in their stories and strove for an impersonal voice representing objectivity—a "just the facts" approach. Even feature-length, essayistic journalism often followed the same formula. Perhaps our self-conscious, post-Freudian era couldn't sustain for long the fiction that anyone can totally obscure the subjectivity of his or her point of view. Better to let the reader really see you in the story, new journalists implied, in all your subjective, idiosyncratic glory.

Wolfe emerged as one of the leaders of this new journalism, along with other writers like Joan Didion, Gay Talese, and Norman Mailer. Wolfe rode buses with LSD guru Ken Kesey and his Merry Pranksters to write *The Electric Kool-Aid Acid Test,* all the while using his first-person voice liberally and appearing as a character in his own right, in his trademark starched high collars and white suits. Wolfe's insistence on the primacy of his own experience in the act of reporting comes through even in his titles, like this one of an essay about Las Vegas (surely one of the loudest cities in the country): "Las Vegas (What?) Las Vegas (Can't Hear You! Too Noisy) Las Vegas!!!!"

New journalism does stress the act of reporting; its practitioners have done some of the most intense reporting in the nonfiction world, but they also avail themselves of literary techniques and a personal voice. Gay Talese's book *The Bridge* takes an exhaustive look at the building of New York's Verrazano-Narrows Bridge. Talese spent years observing the bridge's construction, to the point that he told the *New York Times,* "I was practically considered one of the staff of U.S. Steel." But look at how he sets up a section of the book describing the bridge workers:

> They drive into town in big cars, and live in furnished rooms, and drink whiskey with beer chasers, and chase women they will soon forget. They linger only a little while, only until they have built the bridge; then they are off again to another town, another bridge, linking everything but their lives.

This prose reads like anything but traditional journalism, which would provide all of the main information in the first few sentences as clearly as possible. Talese relies on the indeterminate pronoun "they," allowing the reader to build a portrait of these unnamed people as the paragraph unfolds. He uses wordplay, like the pun on "beer chasers" and the workers' "chasing" of women, and word repetition, such as the repeated use of "only" and "another." Talese's is a poetic portrait, and one that, although it lacks an "I," is saturated with a sense of a personal point of view.

As research becomes more crucial even to very personal nonfiction, such as Terry Tempest Williams' *Refuge* or Andrew Solomon's *The Noonday Demon* (a heavily researched but intimate look at depression), the line between other forms of nonfiction and the new journalism blur. And in the age of instant information on the Internet, traditional journalism becomes more interpretive and less formulaic. Think of it as a healthy blurring of the categories that can sometimes stifle the evolution of forms.

The Meditative Essay

Montaigne, composing his essays, referred to himself as an "accidental philosopher." The term "essay" carries a double meaning of both *trying* and *proving* or *testing*. To "essay" an action means to attempt it; to "essay" a substance, particularly a metal, means to test it, weigh it, try to determine its composition. The essay itself enfolds this dual nature of the term—essays typically approach their subjects tentatively, allow readers the luxury of seeing the author roll ideas around in his or her mind, *test* conclusions rather than presenting them.

The essay form lends itself to tentative, meditative movement, and the meditative essay derives its power from careful deliberation on a subject, often but not always an abstract one. Some meditative essays, like Abraham Cowley's *Of Greatness,* announce their approach in their title. Annie Dillard, in "Total Eclipse" (see the anthology section), recalls the event of the eclipse in great detail before switching to her true subject, a metaphysical meditation on our relationship to the universe:

> The mind wants to live forever, or to learn a very good reason why not. The mind wants the world to return its love, or its awareness; the mind wants to know all the world, and all eternity, and God. The mind's sidekick [the body], however, will settle for two eggs over easy.

Another example of the meditative essay is Richard Bausch's "So Long Ago," found in our anthology section. The meditative intent comes through in the essay's opening, where Bausch addresses the reader in a conversational tone that both engages us and signals that he's about to take us step-by-step through his thoughts:

Indulge me, a moment.

I have often said glibly that the thing which separates the young from the old is the knowledge of what Time really is; not just how fast, but how illusive and arbitrary and mutable it is. When you are twenty, the idea of twenty years is only barely conceivable, and since that amount of time makes up one's whole life, it seems an enormous thing—a vast, roomy expanse, going on into indefiniteness.

Time—and how we perceive it—is an abstract and slippery subject. Bausch's confiding voice, leading us into his meditation as if we're going into a difficult but rewarding conversation, engages us from the outset. He weaves memories, notably a funeral, among his meditations on the larger importance of time and history: "We come from the chaos of ourselves to the world, and we yearn to know what happened to all the others who came before us. So we impose Time on the flow of events, and call it history."

Without specific events, it's hard to imagine such an abstract meditation holding our interest. The best "meditative essayists" instinctively make this technique their own: They probe concrete events until they yield up the deeper meanings that lie buried beneath the surface.

The Sketch or Portrait

One of the most popular essay forms of the nineteenth century, the sketch or portrait held ground partly because of the lack of other forms of communication—the average person traveled little and, even after the invention of photography, saw far fewer photos than we see today. Writers like Dickens stepped into the breach, offering verbal snapshots of cities, foreign countries, and people.

Today we have newspapers, TV, even the Internet, but the power of language to provide not just verbal pictures but emotional ones keeps the portrait an important form. Immediately after the September 11 attacks on the World Trade Center and the Pentagon, the *New Yorker* magazine commissioned a handful of writers to capture that day in short verbal portraits, collectively titled "First Reactions." The editors realized something crucial about that world-changing event: Photos may best hold the searing image of the buildings, but a writer can also capture the reality of "stumbling out of the smoke into a different world" (Jonathan Franzen).

The character sketch is also an integral part of the portrait form. Originally a kind of verbal photograph, portraits still can capture individuals in a way visual forms cannot, using imagery and description to leap from someone's surface to their essence. Maxine Hong Kingston's

"No Name Woman" (see the anthology section) forms at once a largely imaginary portrait of the author's disgraced aunt and a portrait of her very real mother.

> If I want to learn what clothes my aunt wore, whether flashy or ordinary, I would have to begin, "Remember Father's drowned-in-the-well sister?" I cannot ask that. My mother has told me once and for all the useful parts. She will add nothing unless powered by Necessity, a riverbank that guides her life. She plants vegetable gardens rather than lawns; she carries the odd-shaped tomatoes home from the fields and eats food left for the gods.

What a world of information is packed into this formidable portrait! We see Kingston's mother sketched before us in terms of telling actions—choosing the practical over the ornamental and refusing to waste food, even for presumably religious reasons. We're prepared by this sketch for the tension mother and daughter experience over the suppression of the aunt's story and the way that the story reflects their own uncommunicative relationship.

Character sketches can be of family, of the fascinating, or of the famous. Gore Vidal's "Some Memories of the Glorious Bird and an Earlier Self" and James Baldwin's "Alas, Poor Richard," are character sketches of other writers—Tennessee Williams and Richard Wright, respectively—who influenced Vidal and Baldwin early in their careers.

The Persuasive Essay

In 1970, when illegal drugs first became a very visible part of American society, Gore Vidal shocked readers with an essay that began, "It is possible to stop most drug addiction in the United States within a very short time. Simply make all drugs available and sell them at cost." Vidal is a writer who thrives on provocation, and his suggestion created a stir among readers at the time. Yet he makes in many ways a persuasive argument. "Don't say that marijuana is addictive or dangerous when it is neither," Vidal scolds his audience

The persuasive essay aims to convert us, the readers, to its point of view. It doesn't meander or pretend not to know its own mind, as a meditation or memoir might; it's up-front with a voice that assumes authority and holds a stance on the question at hand. The persuasive essay may not be a personal essay, but it can be. Though it must certainly show, it does tell as well.

One example of a persuasive essay is Alice Walker's "Becoming What We're Called" (see the anthology section), an essay that takes the author's irritation with constantly being addressed by the masculine "guy" or "you guys" as an opportunity to write persuasively on the power of social naming to shape us and, perhaps, disempower us.

> We realized the most exhausting thing was not the travel nor the stress we experienced as we anticipated each audience's response to the film; it was having, at every theater, to endure the following questions: How long did it take "you guys" to do this? What was it like for "you guys" to travel and film in Africa? The women asking us these questions seemed blind to us, and in their blindness we felt our uniqueness as female creators disappear.

Walker urges the reader to consider this kind of everyday language use, touching on the revival of the use of racial slurs by black musicians in their own music. She builds toward a conclusion that persuades the reader away from such seemingly unimportant uses of language: "I don't respect 'guys' enough to obliterate the woman that I see by calling her by their name." What's worth noting here is the way Walker takes the strong position that she has—that the act of naming should always be considered powerful and meaningful—and takes the audience through several proofs of that assertion, in her own and other peoples' lives, threading the argument through her proofs. In your own writing, as you prepare to take a position, list what you would consider to be your proofs and then generate from those, as Walker does, your persuasive statements.

Humor

Of all the audience responses writers may want to elicit, none is harder to gauge than laughter. It's hard to argue about the sentimental value of people falling in love, or the tragedy of war, but we all tend to have a comedy vocabulary peculiarly our own. Emily Dickinson, who lends our book its title, had a peculiar habit of roaring with laughter over the obituaries every day. The use of humor in the personal essay dates back to Montaigne and before. In our anthology section, Anne Lamott's "Why I Don't Meditate" and David Sedaris's "The Drama Bug" exemplify the humorous essay. Let's look at some specifics of what we as a species tend to find funny.

Incongruity

Stephen Leacock, in the book *How to Write,* said, "Humor may be defined as the kindly contemplation of the incongruities of life and the artistic expression thereof." The juxtaposition of odd or unexpected things makes up a lot of what we find comic. Shortly after September 11, an e-mail made the rounds. It described a plan to punish Osama bin Laden by performing a sex change operation on him and returning him to Afghanistan. Given the restrictive treatment of women in that country under the Taliban, the incongruity of a female bin Laden proved grimly funny and cathartic—providing a sort of release—in a tragic time.

In "The Drama Bug," David Sedaris falls in love with theater, and his affected Shakespearean speech in the essay becomes hilarious in juxtaposition to the ordinary things occupying his teenage years. Over a chicken dinner with his family, he proclaims, "Methinks, kind sir, most gentle lady, fellow siblings all, that this barnyard fowl be most tasty and succulent." Humor writers like Sedaris are constantly mining their lives for incongruities to use in their work.

The Twist

Like the incongruity, the twist arises from simple surprise—a verbal rug pulled out from under the reader. In *The Deer on a Bicycle: Excursions into the Writing of Humor,* Patrick McManus describes how he fell in love with writing: "I bore down on my next essay with a diligence and concentration previously unknown to me in any academic subject. The effort paid off. A D-minus!"

Given that McManus is detailing the discovery of his vocation, we expect bells to go off with this essay of his—the D-minus comes as a funny (and self-deprecating) surprise. Anne Lamott also offers the reader wonderful twists; hers help ground a spiritual discussion that threatens to become overly solemn: "I believe that every plane I get on is doomed, and this is why I like to travel with Sam—so that if and when the plane goes down, we will at least be together, and almost certainly get adjoining seats in heaven—ideally, near the desserts."

Life's Irritations

Patrick McManus offers a wonderful piece of advice: Write humor out of your bad experiences, not your good ones. Think about it: Which would make a better essay, your best family car trip, with snacks and singing *Kumbaya,* or the worst, with your father cursing over a flat tire while your little sister screams for a bathroom or else? What was awful then is probably hilarious now. Some of life's most irritating things—telemarketers, computerized voice answering systems, HMOs—yield some of its most reliable humor.

Exaggeration and Understatement

Exaggeration or hyperbole is a classic American form of humor, dear to practitioners like Mark Twain, who once swore that during a tour of Europe, he'd seen the equivalent of a "barrelful" of nails from the True Cross. While the exaggeration is evident, Twain's comment makes a point about the number of false religious relics on display in Europe at the time. Sedaris clearly exaggerates in the long-winded pseudo-Elizabethan speeches he delivers in "The Drama Bug"; no one could remember their own monologues that precisely (and surely his family would have swatted him with the barnyard fowl before listening to all of that!). Lamott is another comic exaggerator. It's a device she uses again and again to great effect, as when she describes a reading in which "I had jet lag, the self-esteem of a prawn, and to top it off, I had stopped breathing. I sounded just like the English Patient."

Comic exaggeration is something we all tend to do in ordinary speech. A friend will say of someone else, "She spends money like Ivana Trump," or of a place, "It sounds like Grand Central Station in here," knowing full well that no one believes those claims to be literally true. Understatement is used a bit less in our speech and in our humor, but it's a wonderful device, and just as effective as exaggeration in delivering laughs. The American humorist Will Rogers tended to use understatement: "One of our pigs," he wrote, "swallowed a stick of dynamite. Later he rubbed against a building. This caused an explosion that razed four city blocks. It sure inconvenienced us. For two or three days we had a mighty sick pig on our hands."

The effect of exaggeration could be called explosive; something small becomes something larger, tickling us as it expands from a chicken dinner to a succulent barnyard fowl. Understatement implodes; that little puff of air as the balloon is popped makes us laugh as it thwarts our expectations.

Self-deprecation

One characteristic the Sedaris and Lamott essays have in common is the self-puncturing qualities of the authors. They laugh at themselves so freely that we feel encouraged to laugh with them—and if we're honest with ourselves, we all have a gold mine of material in self-deprecation. No one knows our foibles better than we do. If you look at the Lamott quote—the "self-esteem of a prawn. . . . I sounded just like the English Patient"—you'll note that she's laughing above all at how seriously she took herself at the time of this bookstore reading. Most comics exemplify Rodney Dangerfield's "I don't get no respect" attitude. They mine their own insecurities and attempts to make themselves larger—like Sedaris adopting the fake Shakespearean diction—to laugh at themselves and encourage us to laugh at those qualities in them, and in the process, at the whole human condition.

Capacity of the Personal Essay

Most of us, in conceptualizing the personal essay, start off by imagining the ten- to twenty-page works typically found in college readers. But the personal essay is an elastic form, capable of holding a great deal; we have yet to explore all of its possibilities. It can proceed through a linear narrative, moving through time; it can braid subjects; it can be a collage or a teasing out of a single idea. Thus, the lyric essay (see chapter 10) can and generally is a personal essay as well. A personal essay can take up an entire book, not just in the form of memoir, but in the form of meditation or persuasion, as in the classic *Meditations of Marcus Aurelius* (or it can be as short as a page or two). Many letters and diaries are considered personal essay classics— Henry David Thoreau's journals and Martin Luther King Jr.'s "Letter from Birmingham Jail," for example. And there's even a book in personal essay form—Mark Doty's *Still Life with Oysters and Lemon*—that stands at eighty-some-odd pages and is billed as "the first nonfiction novella."

Within those two frames of intimacy and universality, the personal essay can move in as many directions as there are individual minds. We reach for it—as the *New Yorker* editors did after September 11—to bring us to those moments when we bridge the gulf between the workings of our own minds and the perceptions of another's and at the same time see our own thoughts perfectly inscribed in someone else's words: those moments of "yes, that's it; that's what I was feeling all along."

Try It

1.   Write a short piece of memoir using a particular event, as E. B. White does in "Afternoon of an American Boy." Write quickly and then examine the piece in light of the above distinctions between the intimate and the universal. Where do you speak as though the reader is a friend, listening at your side? Do you need to reveal more of yourself, of your feelings, as White does in disclosing his embarrassment at his inability to dance? And where is the universality of your experience? You may want to trade with a partner to uncover the answers to these questions.

Variation. With Richard Hoffman's comments in mind, write a memoir of an event that seeks to "unspin" some kind of official version of it.

2.   Write a journalistic story, perhaps about a colorful place nearby or an event in your community (a protest? a festival?) that uses reportorial style to capture the story but also includes your own presence as a character. Use literary devices to describe the people you see; use metaphor to paint their lives. Take advantage of literary devices, while respecting the factuality of journalism.

3.   Write a sketch of a person or a place. Focus on keeping your work vivid and simple—a language portrait. Think of it as being intended for someone who cannot meet this person or visit this area. And remember your personal essayist's challenge to be both intimate and universal—help us see the smallest details, like the buttons on a coat or the ashtrays on a table—while using description that shows how this person or place fits with places or people generally.

4.   Write a short persuasive essay about a subject you have firsthand knowledge of, as Gore Vidal did. Use both your own experience and an authoritative voice.

5.   Practice writing deliberate incongruities, twists, exaggerations, and understatements. What's the strangest sight you've seen over the past year? Was it a Hare Krishna at an airport talking on a cell phone? A Santa Claus withdrawing money from an ATM? What experience in your own life led to the most unexpected conclusion, à la McManus's D-minus essay? Try writing these episodes down as "flash" nonfictions, essays of a page or two. Are there larger humorous subjects—say, the clash of old traditions and modern life suggested by the Santa at the ATM—contained in these episodes?

6.   What irritates you? Write a few paragraphs on the most constant irritants in your life, whether it's your university's computerized registration system, the fact that you have almost the same phone number as the local pizzeria, whatever. Write dialogue and scene; strive to be funny. At the same time, think of the larger subjects this irritant suggests.

7.   Actor Billy Bob Thornton constantly pokes fun at himself for his phobias and obsessions, notably a fear of flying and of antique furniture (!). True or not, these self-lampoons are extremely funny. What are your humorous foibles? What do friends and family lampoon you about? What do these foibles say about you and our human aspirations? See whether there's an essay there.

8.   Write an essay titled "On_____." Fill in the blank yourself and use the title as a way to explore an abstract concept in a personal and concrete way.

9.   Using Fabio Morabito's "Screw" and "File and Sandpaper" (see the anthology section) as a model, write a meditative essay on a common object.

See how you can transform this object through both your attention to detail and your daring with language.

10. All of us have abstract questions we would secretly love to write about. Why are we here? What does it mean to love a child? Why does society exist in the form it does? Write down the abstract question you would most like to explore. Then free-write a group of events you somehow associate with that question: a brush with death, giving birth, living in a different culture. Meditate on the question, alternating your meditations with the actual event, as Bausch moves back and forth between his own memories and larger questions of time in "So Long Ago" (see the anthology section).

Suggestions for Further Reading

In Our Anthology

Baldwin, James, "Notes of a Native Son"

Bausch, Richard, "So Long Ago"

Beard, Jo Ann, "The Fourth State of Matter"

Dillard, Annie, "Total Eclipse"

Duncan, David James, "The Mickey Mantle Koan"

Kingston, Maxine Hong, "No Name Woman"

Lamott, Anne, "Why I Don't Meditate"

Morabito, Fabio, "File and Sandpaper" and "Screw"

Sedaris, David, "The Drama Bug"

Walker, Alice, "Becoming What We're Called"

White, E. B., "Afternoon of an American Boy"

Williams, Terry Tempest, "The Clan of One-Breasted Women"

Woolf, Virginia, "The Death of the Moth"

On Our Website

Kitchen, Judith, "Things of This Life"

Elsewhere

Aurelius, Marcus, *The Meditations of Marcus Aurelius*

Baldwin, James, "Alas, Poor Richard"

Butrym, Alexander, *Essays on the Essay: Reinventing a Genre*

Dillard, Annie, *Pilgrim at Tinker Creek*

Doty, Mark, *Still Life with Oysters and Lemon*

Franzen, Jonathan, from "First Reactions"

Hesse, Douglas, "The Boundry Zone"

Hoffman, Richard, *Half the House*

Kenko, *Essays in Idleness*

Lopate, Phillip, *The Art of the Personal Essay*

Montaigne, Michel de, *Essais*

Roorbach, Bill (ed.), *The Art of Truth*

Root, Robert L. Jr., and Michael Steinberg, *The Fourth Genre: Contemporary Writers of/on Creative Nonfiction*

Shonagon, Sei, *The Pillowbook*

Solomon, Andrew, *The Noonday Demon*

Talese, Gay, *The Bridge*

Vidal, Gore, "Drugs" and "Some Memories of the Glorious Bird and an Earlier Self"

Wolfe, Tom, *The Electric Kool-Aid Acid Test*

Zinsser, William, *Inventing the Truth: The Art and Craft of Memoir*

Chapter Ten

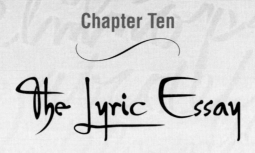
The Lyric Essay

I go out of my way, but rather by license than carelessness.
My ideas follow one another, but sometimes it is from a
distance, and look at each other, but with a sidelong
glance. . . . I love the poetic gait, by leaps and gambols. . . .
—**Michel de Montaigne**

I find myself thumbing through an encyclopedia of Jewish religion I happened to pick up at the library. As I turn the pages of this marvelous book, I'm struck by how little I, a Jewish woman who went to Hebrew school for most of my formative years, know about my own religion. I start writing down the quotes that interest me most, facts about the Kaballah and ritual baths and dybbuks and the Tree of Life. I've also started noodling around with some other stories: a recent trip to Portugal, and the news I received there of my mother's emergency hysterectomy; notes on the volunteer work I perform at the local children's hospital; and musings about my on-again, off-again yoga practice. As I keep all these windows open on my computer, the voice of the encyclopedia emerges as an odd, binding thread, holding together these disparate stories in a way that seems organic. I begin to fragment the stories and to move these fragments around, finding the images that resonate against one another in juxtaposition.

I feel like a poet, creating stanzas and listening for the rhythms of the sentences, using white space, reading aloud to determine when another quote from the encyclopedia is necessary to balance out my personal story. Sometimes I have to throw out whole sections that no longer fit, but this editing leaves room for new segments, new phrases, new images that build and transform over the course of the essay, weaving in and out, but always grounded on the thread of prayer and the body. It takes some time, this shuffling gait, but I finally have an essay, "Basha Leah": a spiritual self-portrait in the form of a complex braid.

This lyric essay allows for the moments of pause, the gaps, the silence. The fragmentation feels correct: It allows for the moments of "not knowing," the unspoken words that seem truer than anything I could ever say aloud. —**Brenda**

What Is the "Lyric Essay?"

"Lyric." "Essay." How do these two terms fit together? At first, they may seem like an oxymoron, diametrically opposed. The lyric implies a poetic sensibility concerned more with language, imagery, sound, and rhythm over the more linear demands of narrative. The word "essay," however, implies a more logical frame of mind, one concerned with a well-wrought story, or a finely tuned argument, over the demands of language. When we put the two together, we come up with a hybrid form that allows for the best of both genres.

One simple way of putting it is this: Lyric essays don't necessarily follow a straight narrative line. The root of the word "lyric" is the lyre, a musical instrument that accompanied ancient song. Lyric poetry and essays are "songlike" in that they hinge on the inherent rhythms of language and sound. Lyric essays favor fragmentation and imagery; they use white space and juxtaposition as structural elements. They're as attuned to silences as they are to utterance. By infusing prose with tools normally relegated to poetic forms, the lyric essayist creates anew, each time, a work that is interactive, alive, and full of new spaces in which meaning can germinate. The *Seneca Review*, in its thirtieth-anniversary issue devoted to lyric essays, characterized them as having "this built-in mechanism for provoking meditation. They require us to complete their meaning."

The lyric essay is quite an ancient form. Classic writers such as Seneca, Bacon, Montaigne, and Emerson all wrote in forms that were inherently lyric. Bacon, in 1597, called his aphoristic essays "dispersed meditations." Sei Shonagon, in the tenth century, wrote lovely works that can be characterized as lyric: She wrote lists of "Depressing Things," "Hateful Things," "Adorable Things": pages and pages of observations that together form a compelling self-portrait. Montaigne ruminates in his castle on everything from the workings of his own digestive system to the state of local politics, the thoughts meandering in an associative style that mirrors the working of the mind and memory. As John D'Agata, lyric essay editor for the *Seneca Review*, puts it:

> The lyric essay takes the subjectivity of the personal essay and objectivity of the public essay, and conflates them both into a literary form that relies on both art and fact—on imagination and observation, rumination and argumentation, human faith and human perception. . . . The result of this ironic parentage is that lyric essays seek answers, yet they seldom seem to find them.

This last statement—"lyric essays seek answers, yet they seldom seem to find them"—could be the credo of the lyric essay. In a lyric essay, the *quest* is the focus, not its fulfillment.

Such a stance leads to a diversity of forms and styles that defy neat categorizations. Many excellent writers and thinkers have tried to pin down the lyric essay, defining it as a collage, a montage, or a mosaic. It's been called disjunctive, segmented, and sectioned. All of these are correct. All of these definitions recognize in the lyric essay a tendency toward fragmentation that invites the reader into those gaps, a structure that emphasizes what is *unknown* rather than the already articulated known.

The writer of the lyric essay brings the reader into an arena where the questions are asked; it's up to the reader to piece together possible answers and interpretations. Fragmentation allows for this type of reader interaction because the writer, by surrendering to the fragmented form, declines a foregone conclusion. Writer and literary theorist Rebecca Faery notes, "In the essays that have in recent years compelled me most, I am summoned, called upon. These essays are choral, polyphonic; there are pauses, rests. . . . The rests in these essays are spaces inviting me in, inviting response."

The Role of Intuition

"The lyric essay chiefly concerns the essayist's perception. . . . And since it's concerned with perception, it is ultimately concerned with the essayist's own mind in action. . . . It must unfold in the very act of writing, and writing should itself be an act (or acts) of unanticipated discovery."
—Sydney Lea

The lyric essay requires an allegiance to intuition. Since we're no longer tied to a logical, linear narrative or argument, we must surrender to the writing process itself to show us the essay's intent. In so doing, we reveal ourselves in a roundabout way. When we write in lyric essay mode, we create not only prose pieces, but a portrait of our subconscious selves, the part of us that speaks in riddles or in brief, imagistic flashes.

As Charles Simic puts it in his book about the work of artist Joseph Cornell: "To submit to chance is to reveal the self and its obsession." Cornell was famous for his "boxes," artworks that bring together disparate objects under glass, three-dimensional collages that make an odd, aesthetic sense. In *Dime Store Alchemy,* Simic elucidates the intuitive stance necessary not only for an artist like Cornell, who brings different objects together to create a sculpture, but for us writers too, the ones who look for the disparate strands of experience to come together and form a lyric essay. As Simic imagines Cornell might put it: "Somewhere in the city of New York there are four or five still-unknown objects that belong together. Once together they'll make a work of art."

We must train ourselves into this state of "meditative expectancy," as poet Carolyn Forché calls the writer's stance; the world, after all, flies by us at millions of miles an hour, spewing out any number of offerings—it's the writer at her desk, the artist out perambulating, who will recognize a gift when she sees one.

Robin Hemley, while writing "Reading History to My Mother" (see the anthology section), immediately knew he had a lyric essay in the making when different incidents and images in his life started resonating against one another: the jumble of eyeglasses on his mother's dresser; his daughter reading books about a mouse going to visit his mother and getting "new feet" for the occasion; the mysterious "L" drawn on the wall of his mother's apartment; the box of macadamia nuts mistaken for a book. A nonwriter would, perhaps, see nothing inherently artistic or coherent in these disparate images, but Hemley saw them as obvious "gifts" that, put together in a segmented essay, create a beautiful and original rendition of what it means to care for an aging parent.

Finding the "Container": Forms of the Lyric Essay

Stephen Dunn, a poet, has written an essay that succinctly describes the way form and content work in concert with one another, especially when we venture into the realm of the lyric essay. Here's his essay in its entirety:

LITTLE ESSAY ON FORM

We build the corral as we reinvent the horse.

In lyric essays, nothing is fixed or predetermined. Lyric essays are fluid forms, bending to fit the content as it arises. Form can also lead to modifications in content, leading you into new areas you never expected. If you glance into the *Seneca Review's* lyric essay issue, you will find a plethora of forms: essays written in fragmented, numbered sections; essays written as interviews; essays written as lists and catalogues; essays that have single lines broken by white space; essays that contain only one single paragraph. As Annie Dillard has written: "The essay is, and has been, all over the map. There's nothing you cannot do with it; no subject matter is forbidden, no structure is proscribed. You get to make up your own structure every time, a structure that arises from the materials and best contains them."

Since the forms of the lyric essay are essentially infinite and still to be known, since you'll create new forms we've never experienced before, we won't be able to delineate them all in this chapter. Part of the fun of the lyric essay will be in making up your own form as you go along. But for the sake of argument, we'll break the lyric essay down into four main categories that seem to encapsulate the lyric essays we see most often: prose poem (or "flash nonfiction"), collage, the braided essay, and a form we've dubbed the "hermit crab."

Prose Poem or "Flash Nonfiction"

For the introduction to their anthology *The Party Train: A Collection of North American Prose Poetry,* the editors begin with this piece by S. C. Hahn:

IF MY FATHER WERE TO ASK

"What's a prose poem?" I would turn my face and look into the distance away from our farm house, into a wild copse of trees which runs from the road's edge and on up the hill to the far fields. Box elder, green ash, and black locust tangle in a net of branches, tied together by thorny greenbrier. I know of a coyote den beneath one old box elder tree, on the edge of a gully cutting through the copse. If I were to stick my hand into the hole, I could feel cool wet air and perhaps the playful teeth of pups.

"Remember when you plowed the fields in the spring," I say to my father, "and the air behind you filled suddenly with sea gulls?" I can see him inhale the aroma of memory: the green and yellow tractor, the motor exhaust and dust, steel blades of the plow sinking into the earth and turning it, the smell all sexual and holy, worms and grubs uncovered into sunlight, then an unexpected slash of white as the gulls materialize behind the plow, a thousand miles and more from any ocean.

This prose poem is a lyric essay in itself and describes the focus and intent of such a form. The piece doesn't provide a logical explanation or a direct answer to a question; rather, "If My Father Were to Ask" prefers to use imagery as a way of getting at possible responses.

What's a prose poem? Well, maybe it's the feeling you get when you're standing in a landscape you know well and love, a landscape where you can imagine what lies hidden behind the trees, beneath the ground. Maybe the prose poem is the "aroma of memory" and all the sensual details such aromas evoke. Or maybe the signature of the prose poem is the unexpected surprise at the end, the improbable appearance of sea birds above the plowed fields of the heartland.

Maybe the prose poem is all these things, but most important, it speaks to the heart rather than the head. The prose poem is about what's possible, not necessarily what has already occurred. Even the title, "If My Father Were to Ask," privileges imagination over experience: The father hasn't asked the question, but what if he did?

In this way, the terms prose poem and flash nonfiction could be nearly interchangeable. Flash nonfiction is a brief essay, usually under a thousand words, that focuses on one particular image. It's tightly focused, with no extraneous words, and it mines its central image in ways that create metaphorical significance. The language is fresh, lyrically surprising, hinged on the workings of the imagination. Lawrence Sutin (see the anthology section) writes discrete pieces of flash nonfiction as he meditates on the old postcards in his collection. Though the pieces themselves are longer than anything one might write on the back of a postcard, they maintain that same kind of *compactness*, that intent to be concise and say only what's important for the moment at hand.

This form is fun both to write and to read. A new on-line magazine, *Brevity,* "publishes concise literary nonfiction of 750 words or less focusing on detail and scene over thought and opinion." W. W. Norton has issued two volumes of short nonfiction, edited by Judith Kitchen and Mary Paumier Jones: *In Short: A Collection of Brief Creative Nonfiction,* and *In Brief: Short Takes on the Personal.* In the introduction to *In Short,* Bernard Cooper elucidates the stance of the lyric essayist working in the flash nonfiction form: "To write short nonfiction requires an alertness to detail, a quickening of the senses, a focusing of the literary lens, so to speak, until one has magnified some small aspect of what it means to be human."

Collage

Do you remember, as a child, making collages out of photographs, images cut from magazines, bits and pieces of text gathered from ticket stubs, documents, and headlines? Often, these mosaics represented the self in a way that no other form could quite accomplish. Our teachers gazed down at us lovingly as we showed them these renderings, our selves displayed in fragments made beautiful by their juxtaposition.

The collage essay works the same way. It brings together many different fragments and assembles them so that they create something wholly new. *Juxtaposition* becomes the key craft element here: One cannot simply throw these pieces down haphazardly—they must be carefully selected for how they'll resonate off one another. In this way, you act as a painter might, scrutinizing how this particular blue will shimmer against this particular yellow. You must listen for the echoes, the repetitions, the way one image organically suggests the next.

The writer must also provide some kind of grounding structure for the reader to hold onto. Going back to those collages you made as a child, they would be useless collections of fragments without the posterboard and glue used to hold the pieces in place. The supporting architecture for a collage essay can take the form of numbered sections, or it can be subtitles that guide the reader along. Or the structure can be as subtle as asterisks delineating the white space between sections. In any case, the structure needs to work in tandem with the content for a certain effect.

For example, in his short essay "My Children Explain the Big Issues" (see the anthology section), Will Baker relies on the title and the subtitles to hold together four stories he has culled from memory about his children. The subtitles—"Feminism," "Fate," "Existentialism," and "East and West"—do all the explaining he needs to do; they act as bridges, or supports, that allow him to write what appears to be four disparate fragments and turn them into one cohesive essay. Without the title or the subtitles, these stories would remain charming vignettes, but they wouldn't carry the impact or hold the focus necessary for an essay. However, if he had decided to *tell* us the meaning of these fragments within the prose itself, the stories would be too earnest, too contrived. The collage structure works well here because each fragment is allowed to stand on its own while still working in concert with the others. The architecture of the piece works on a subtle level: We think we're "reading over" the title and subtitles, barely noticing them, but they work on our subconscious throughout the piece.

In the anthology section, two short essays act as minicollages: "Three Voices," by Bhanu Kapil Rider, and "Three Fragments," by Charles Simic. You'll see that the different sections, though quite separate from one another, remain connected through the reoccurrence of key phrases or images. Collages work through repetition, but not in a monotonous way: You must *transform* your recurring motifs from beginning to end. You must make transitions, but not in the conventional way: In the collage essay, transitions occur through the strategic juxtaposition of images, stories, and phrases. How does one story lead to the next? What image can you pick up from the last section to begin the next? What phrase can act as a repeating, and variable, mantra throughout the piece? You must trust yourself, and your readers, to make sense and meaning out of the gaps between steps, the pauses between words, but you must also act as a guide on this pilgrimage: a pathfinder who directs with a touch we barely notice.

The Braided Essay

On the Jewish Sabbath, we eat a bread called *challah*, a braided egg bread that gleams on its special platter. The braided strands weave in and out, creating a pattern both beautiful and appetizing. We eat a special bread on the Sabbath because this day has been set aside as sacred; the smallest acts must be differentiated from everyday motions.

The braided challah is a fitting symbol for an essay form closely allied with collage: the braided essay. In this form, you fragment your essay into separate strands that repeat and continue. There's more of a sense of weaving about it, of interruption and continuation, like the braiding of bread, or of hair. You must keep your eye on the single strands that come in and out of focus, filaments that glint differently depending on where they've been. At the same time, you must keep your eye focused on the single image or theme that holds them all together. As William Stafford wrote a few weeks before he died, "There's a thread you follow. It goes among/things that change. But it doesn't change." Within the challah itself, once you cut it open, you see nary a sign of the braiding. You have a chunk of bread: whole, fine-grained, delicious.

In his essay "After Yitzl" (see the anthology section), Albert Goldbarth braids several different strands together to create a highly textured essay. Written in numbered sections that at first seem to have little to do with one another, the essay works through a steady accretion of imagery and key repetitions; it speaks in a voice that grows loud, then whispers, that cuts itself off, then rambles. The strands include, among other things, a sleepy conversation in bed with a lover, a fabricated "previous life," facts about the Mormon religion and the Piltdown Man, a story about a cult called the "Unarians," and stories about his own (real) ancestry. The sleepy conversation provides the overall "container" for the essay, an architecture that holds the fragments in place and provides forward momentum. But by fragmenting this narrative, Goldbarth allows for the other strands to have equal weight. He returns to the conversation over and over and repeats phrases from the other strands, so that the essay never seems to veer off topic.

And that topic reveals itself slowly: The essay turns out to be about how we fabricate our own pasts, constantly and continually; how memory itself is a myth; how we create ourselves anew in the stories we tell. The braided form allows this theme to emerge organically, to accrue in the reader's mind until it takes on the aspect of an inevitable truth. He explodes his prose to put it together again in a new pattern that's inordinately pleasurable.

When you write a braided essay, the fragmentation allows you, almost forces you, not to approach this material head-on but to search for a more circuitous way into it. You must expand your peripheral vision, focusing on images that at first seemed oblique to the stories. Sometimes your peripheral vision catches the most important details, those you might not have expected to carry significance. You give yourself over to chance sightings, arresting the image on the verge of skittering away.

The braided form also allows a way for research and outside voices to intertwine with your own voice and experience. Notice how many different sources Goldbarth is able to include in this essay without losing his own voice. When you write a braided essay, find at least one outside voice that will shadow yours; in this way, the essay will gain texture and substance.

For example, Melissa, one of our students, had been trying to write an essay about her mother's death from leukemia when Melissa was just 11. Her attempts to deal with this material head-on tended toward sentimental writing that could not get past the weight of her sorrow. When she turned this experience into a braided essay, however, she found the necessary connections, information, and metaphorical significance to make it work.

Melissa begins with the line: "Only you know what happens at the end of the trail." It's a story about being a camp counselor and telling her charges the myth of the Bat and the Sun. In the essay, she weaves this myth in with memories of her girlhood in Texas and medical facts about leukemia. As she braids these strands together, certain images begin to resonate: the squirrel flying too close to the sun, so that its fur burns off and it becomes a creature of the night; the blood cells forming deep in the bone marrow; the circle of children at the mother's bedside. She carefully stitches these images from one segment to the next, so that the essay never veers off track. In the end, we've experienced a segment of Melissa's life along with her, with all its variant textures, meanings, and emotions. And it becomes an essay not just about Melissa and her mother, but about how we're transformed by things that happen in the night, in the dark, without our really knowing how.

The "Hermit Crab" Essay

Where we—Suzanne and Brenda—live, in the Pacific Northwest, there's a beautiful place called Deception Pass. It's prone to extreme tides, and in the tidepools you can often find hermit crabs skulking about. They look a little like cartoon characters, hiding inside a shell and lifting it up to take it with them when they hurry for cover. They move a few inches, then crouch down and stop, becoming only a shell again. Then they tilt, waver, and scurry away.

A hermit crab is a strange animal, born without the armor to protect its soft, exposed abdomen. And so it spends its life occupying the empty, often beautiful, shells left behind by snails or other mollusks. It reanimates these shells, making of them a strange, new hybrid creature that has its own particular beauty, its own way of moving through the tidepools and among the rocks. Each one is slightly different, depending on the type of shell it decides to inhabit.

In honor of these wonderful creatures and the transformative habitat in which they live, we've dubbed a particular form of lyric essay the "hermit crab essay." This kind of essay appropriates other forms as an outer covering to protect its soft, vulnerable underbelly. It's an essay that deals with material that seems to have been born without its own carapace—material that's soft, exposed, and tender and must look elsewhere to find the form that will best contain it.

The "shells" come from wherever you can find them, anywhere in the world. They may borrow from fiction and poetry, but they also don't hesitate to armor themselves in more mundane structures: the descriptions in a mail order catalog, for example, or the entries in a checkbook register.

For example, in her short story "How to Become a Writer," Lorrie Moore appropriates the form of the "how-to" article to tell a personal narrative. The voice of the narrator catches the cadence of pedagogical manuals, but at the same time winks at the reader: Of course, these are not impersonal instructions, but a way of telling her story. And by using the literary second person, she draws the reader unwittingly along into the place of the narrator. A natural interaction develops:

> First, try to be something, anything, else. A movie star/astronaut. A movie star/missionary. A movie star/kindergarten teacher. President of the World. Fail miserably. It is best if you fail at an early age—say, fourteen. Early, critical disillusionment is necessary so that at fifteen you can write long haiku sequences about thwarted desire. It is a pond, a cherry blossom, a wind brushing against sparrow wing leaving for mountain. Count the syllables. Show it to your mom. She is tough and practical. She has a son in Vietnam and a husband who may be having an affair. She believes in wearing brown because it hides spots. She'll look briefly at your writing, then back up at you with a face blank as donut. She'll say: "How about emptying the dishwasher?" Look away. Shove the forks in the fork drawer. Accidentally break one of the freebie gas station glasses. This is the required pain and suffering. This is only for starters.

Though "How to Become a Writer" is fiction, the story can act as a fine model for innovative lyric essays in the "how-to" mode. What are the aspects of your life that you could render in this form? How will the second person enable you to achieve some distance from the material and thus some perspective? This type of essay can be quite fun to write; the voice takes over and creates its own momentum.

In his essay "Primary Sources," Rick Moody appropriates the form of a footnoted bibliography in order to write an autobiography. In her essay "Nine Beginnings" (see the anthology section), Margaret Atwood takes on two different forms; ostensibly, it's a question/answer piece (with only one persistent, annoying question!), but the title also suggests crumpled first drafts, fished out of the wastebasket. Nancy Willard has written an essay called "The Friendship Tarot," which begins with a sketch of a tarot card layout; she then goes on to insert her autobiographical story into the interpretation of that layout. Several writers have fashioned essays in the form of "to-do" lists. Sei Shonagon has written her lists of "Depressing Things," "Adorable Things," and so on. The possibilities are endless.

Look around you. The world is brimming with forms that await transformation. See how the world constantly orders itself in structures that can be shrewdly turned to your own purposes. A recipe for making soup, handed down by your grandmother, can form the architecture for an essay that fragments a family narrative into the directions for creating something good to eat. An address book that shows the many different places you've lived, or your family has lived, can begin to shape the material of memory and history. A table of contents, an index, an itinerary, a playlist—all these speak with recognizable voices that might work as the right container for your elusive material. The movements of a sonata, the parts of a dance. Your class yearbook from 1976. A wedding album. All these—and endless variations, as infinite as the things of the world themselves—offer to lend you their shells and their voices when your own voice falters and quits.

One of our students, Raven, wrote an essay in the form of complex math problems. He took a difficult subject (his tempestuous relationship with his girlfriend) and "contained" it in the voice and language of the word problems you might find on a test. Form and content work in beautiful harmony here: The relationship often tested the limits of Raven's understanding and also provided complex logical problems almost impossible to solve. The resultant essay is both very funny and very sad, the perfect combination when trying to write about difficult subjects.

By taking on the voice of an exterior form for your internal story, you automatically begin the process of creating an artifact out of experience. The form, while it may seem restrictive, actually allows you a great deal of latitude. Suddenly the second-person or the third-person perspective is available to you. You can take a step back and view your experience through a new lens. Often, the form itself will lead to new material you never even suspected.

Think in terms of *transformation*. The word itself means to move across forms, to be changed. Think of the hermit crab and its soft, exposed abdomen. Think of the experiences you have that are too raw, too dangerous to write about. What if you found the right shell, the right armor? How could you be transformed?

Try It

What Is the "Lyric Essay?"

1. Read "Three Fragments" by Charles Simic and "Three Voices" by Bhanu Kapil in the anthology section. Read them out loud. How are these essays different from a traditional essay such as E. B. White's "Afternoon of an American Boy?" What's the effect of the white space? What images recur in the different fragments? How do you feel as you read these pieces? Is it a satisfying or an unsatisfying experience? Why?

Variation: Using these essays as a model, go back to one of your own pieces and turn it into fragments. Take a pair of scissors to it and cut it up into at least three different sections. Move these around, eliminating what no longer fits, juxtaposing the different sections in various ways. How can you make use of white space? How can you let the images do the talking for you?

The Role of Intuition

2. Pretend, for an afternoon, that you're Joseph Cornell. Wander the streets of your town or the pathways of your campus, looking for objects that "belong together." Gather as many of these as you like, then bring them back to your desk and start arranging them in an artistically pleasing way. Then write for several minutes on each object and see whether you can create a fragmented essay that juxtaposes these elements in the same way.

Variation for a group: Go out and gather objects individually, but come back together as a group to sift through the pile. Use each other's objects to create three-dimensional collages. Then write for an hour to create a collage essay using these objects as a guide.

Prose Poem or "Flash Nonfiction"

3. Write an essay of fewer than five hundred words. Give yourself a time limit—a half-hour, say—and write about one image that comes to mind, or an image that has stayed in your memory from the past couple of days. Use vivid, concrete details. Don't explain the image to us, but instead allow it to evolve into metaphor. If you're stuck, open a book of poetry and write down the first line you see as an epigraph. Write an essay using the epigraph as a starting point for form or content or imagery. If you write over five hundred words (about two pages), trim and cut to stay under the limit. Find out what's essential.

Variation for a group: Each person brings in a line of poetry as an epigraph and offers it to a partner. Write for fifteen minutes, then pass the epigraph to the next person. Write again for fifteen minutes. Continue this process for as long as you like. Try shaping one of these experiments into a complete essay of less than five hundred words.

4. Study a painting or a photograph that you've looked at often. What is it about this image that appeals to you so much? Begin a short essay of under five hundred words that focuses on some unexpected detail that catches your eye in this artwork. Explore this detail for metaphorical significance.

Variation for a group: Each person brings in a postcard of an artwork; these are all set on a table in the front of the room. Each person browses through these postcards and chooses one that intuitively appeals to him or her. Begin writing. You can do this as many times as you like until an image sparks a piece of writing that interests you.

Collage

5. Using Will Baker's "My Children Explain the Big Issues" as a model, take some large concepts (such as "shame," "anger," etc.) and translate them into short, concrete stories. Try this with several different concepts, and see how you might pull them together with a title.

6. Structure an essay around a journey of some sort, using brief, discrete sections to build a collage. This can be a journey to somewhere as commonplace as the mall, or it can be more romantic. What kind of purposeful journey can you imagine taking, such as a visit to the Hall of Fame or a pilgrimage to a sacred place?

7. Choose at least three distinctly separate time periods in your life. Begin each section with "I am _____ years old," and free-write from there. Stay in the present tense. After reading what you've written, see whether you can find any thematic connections or common images that would link the sections together.

8. Experiment with transitions and juxtaposition. Find one image to repeat in the essay from start to finish, but transform this image in some way so that it takes on new characteristics by the end of the essay.

The Braided Essay

9. Read "Basha Leah" (on the website) and "After Yitzl" and "Reading History to My Mother" (in the anthology section). Analyze how these essays weave at least three separate strands throughout the piece. Where do they leave off and pick up again? What's repeated? What's the overall effect?

10. Go back to an essay that's been giving you problems. Look for the one image that seems to encapsulate the abstract ideas or concepts you're trying to develop. Find at least one outside source that will provide new information and details for you. Explode the essay into three or more different strands, each focused on particular aspects of that image, and begin weaving, transforming that image from beginning to end.

11. Cut apart an essay (or two, or three) with scissors and lay the pieces out on the floor or a long table. Start moving them around like pieces of a puzzle and see what kind of patterns you can make through different juxtapositions of the texts.

The "Hermit Crab" Essay

12. Write an essay in the form of a "how-to" guide, using the second person. You can turn anything into a "how-to": Lorrie Moore, in her book *Self-Help,* has stories titled "How to Talk to Your Mother" and "How to Be the Other Woman."

13. Choose a field guide to the natural world as your model ("A Field Guide to Desert Wildflowers," for example, or "A Field Guide to the Atmosphere.") Write an essay in the form of a field guide, inserting your own experience into this format.

14. Write an essay in the form of an interview or a series of letters.

15. Using Bernard Cooper's "The Fine Art of Sighing" (see the anthology section) as a model, write an essay titled "The Fine Art of _____." What mundane act can you transform into art?

16. Brainstorm a list of all the forms in the outer world that you could use as a model for a hermit crab essay. We've done this with classes that have come up with lists of sixty entries and more! The possibilities are endless. Some of the ones they came up with were crossword puzzle clues, horoscopes, fortune cookies, letters to the editor, and missing milk carton kids. Choose one of these forms and begin an essay, using your own material to flesh out the shell. Let the word choices and tone of your shell dictate your own approach to your topic: How would the vague cheeriness of fortunes or horoscopes, for example, inform your family or relationship tale?

17. Write a list of the topics/issues in your life that are forbidden to speak about, things you could never write. Choose one of these and begin to write about it in a hermit crab form.

Suggestions for Further Reading

In Our Anthology

Atwood, Margaret, "Nine Beginnings"

Baker, Will, "My Children Explain the Big Issues"

Cooper, Bernard, "The Fine Art of Sighing"

Goldbarth, Albert, "After Yitzl"

Hemley, Robin, "Reading History to My Mother"

Rider, Bhanu Kapil, "Three Voices"

Sutin, Lawrence, from *A Postcard Memoir*

Simic, Charles, "Three Fragments"

On Our Website

Miller, Brenda, "Basha Leah"

Elsewhere

Alexander, Robert, Mark Vinz, and C. W. Truesdale, eds., *The Party Train: A Collection of North American Prose Poetry*

Brevity: An Online Journal of Concise Creative Nonfiction, *www.creativenonfiction.org/brevity/brevity.html*

Carson, Anne, *Plainwater*

Cooper, Bernard, *Maps to Anywhere*

D'Agata, John, *Halls of Fame*

Dillard, Annie, *For the Time Being*

Kitchen, Judith, and Mary Paumier Jones, *In Brief: Short Takes on the Personal*

Kitchen, Judith, and Mary Paumier Jones, *In Short: A Collection of Brief Creative Nonfiction*

The Lyric Essay. *Seneca Review* 30, no. 1, (2000)

Moore, Lorrie, *Self-Help*

Thomas, Abigail, *Safe Keeping*

Chapter Eleven

The Basics of Personal Reportage

From there to here
From here to there
Funny things
Are everywhere

—Dr. Seuss

- ▮ **Cultivating the Need to Know**
- ▮ **Using Fact as Metaphor**
- ▮ **Researching a Key Fact or Detail**
- ▮ **Research as Credibility: The Detail**
- ▮ **Working with Immersion**
- ▮ **Developing Interview Skills**
- ▮ **Developing Print Research Skills**
- ▮ **Winnowing Down**
- ▮ **Some Last Thoughts**
- ▮ **Try It**

It's a cold but promising April, and a pod of gray whales has swum into Bellingham Bay. Everything about them fascinates me; the sudden emergence of their enormous bodies from the water, the plumes of their breathing, their secrecy and grace. I visit the shoreline each day to watch them live, temporarily, in the small bay I think of as mine. I begin writing about their appearance: "The whales are strips of black rubber separating the water now and then: moving spumes. When they surface and blow, the crowd claps. A young girl in jeans has climbed onto a boulder and dances there, a slow, undulating, arm-waving, feet-on-the-ground dance." I would like to develop this experience into an essay, but as I watch it begin to take shape, I see how much it needs beyond description; my words are accurate, but they don't live—there's no immediacy to this scene, nothing to appeal to anyone who doesn't simply want to read whale description. I need to understand these mammals; I need to see how our lives intersect.

As I learn more about the migration of gray whales, our connections surprise me: "Grays in the Pacific migrate 10,000 miles a year, from the Bering Sea down to Mexico, where they calve and hunger for the cold. The only other gray whale migration route is along the Korean peninsula; grays used to migrate the Atlantic but were hunted to extinction there. Only a few hundred still swim along Korea, but I like thinking that my son, not yet three and born in Seoul, has lived along both their habitats." Later I learn about whale music, and listen to recordings of their sounds, known as *hauntings* and *trumpets*. With these pieces of research—these bits of connective tissue—a real essay starts to form.—**Suzanne**

Cultivating the Need to Know

It should be clear by now that many of the methods we're recommending that you use to expand your subject horizons—placing yourself in history, in the world, braiding, and so on—are probably going to involve research of some sort or another. Our view of research doesn't mean hours in a library poring over dry technical works, unless that's something you want to do. Anything that takes you out of the realm of what you already know is research. All writers need to expand the ideas that feed them: the "flood subjects," as Emily Dickinson called them, which form those subjects dearest to us for meditation and writing. Our flood subjects may never change—if you write about nature, for example, or children, or medicine, you probably always will—but we can and must expand the ground they cover.

Annie Dillard used to teach at our institution, Western Washington University. Science librarians still joke about her weekly forays into the science section and the way she staggered up to the checkout desk with armloads of reference books. Insects, sand, eclipses—nothing escaped her interest. In "Total Eclipse," which we discuss in detail later in this chapter, Dillard demonstrates how a writer's attentiveness to a magazine left carelessly in the lobby of a hotel can create the metaphor needed to complete her meditation on human life and the earthly forces around us.

Perhaps we can equate openness to research with openness to incorporating the world around us, and its events, into our own life meditations: a kind of artistic *porosity* to the world around us. Porous materials, such as fabrics, absorb what comes in contact with them. The best nonfiction writers have a special porosity to what's around them; they're unable to ignore even a motel magazine. We aren't islands, as the poet John Donne famously observed: Our life events are shaped by more externals than we can possibly know. We want to begin the process of knowing them.

Philip Gerard, author of numerous books, including *Secret Soldiers: The Story of World War II's Heroic Army of Deception*, answered a question about the importance of research this way: "Facts in all their glorious complexity make possible creativity. The best nonfiction writers are first-rate reporters, reliable eyewitnesses focused on the world, not themselves, and relentless researchers with the imagination to understand the implications of their discoveries."

Not everyone will want to do full-bore investigative journalism. It's worth remembering that sometimes the best research we can do involves going somewhere we wouldn't normally go and talking to people we wouldn't normally talk to—and, of course, really listening. Are you writing an essay about someone who lifts weights? Get a day pass to a gym and absorb the culture of weight lifting—how lifters push themselves, how muscle curves out of itself when flexed. Imaginatively, see your subject there.

If you want to write about your childhood, don't settle for your memories but look at all the media that shaped your world—check out magazines from the early years of your life from a library, watch Nickelodeon reruns from that period on television, go to *www. historychannel.com* and look up the key songs, plays, films, and news events of those years. Confront primary sources, such as documents, photos, films, newspapers, and even gravestones; you'll often find discrepancies between the stories people tell you and the facts you uncover, discrepancies that reveal a lot about your stories and your subjects.

If you're writing about your parents, think about them as human beings at that earlier time—what messages were they hearing? How did those messages help shape them into the people they were?

Using Fact as Metaphor

Factual research will most often be used for what it is: fact. Water may contain a certain complex of chemicals; weight lifting may have such-and-such an effect on the body. These facts can become the basis of an essay that explores the physical wonders and limitations of our world. At times, however, fact will also function as metaphor, inform-ing the essay both on its own terms—information about the physical world the reader may need or find interesting—and as a basis for comparison for a more intangible part of the piece.

One of our students, Jen Whetham, turned in an essay titled "Swimming Pool Hedonist," chronicling how swimming and swimming pools have defined her and held her milestones: learning to trust, early sports success, even a first sexual encounter. The first draft of the essay began by saying "My earliest memory is at a swimming pool" and in-cluded a passing reference to the odor of chlorine. That odor turned up again and again, and Suzanne made the suggestion that maybe chlorine itself mattered in some larger way. Jen, studying the chemistry of chlorine, came up with this section in her final version:

> My skin has always smelled like chlorine. . . .
>
> Chlorine is missing one electron from its outer shell: this makes it highly attractive to other molecules. Chlorine's extreme reactivity makes it a powerful disinfectant: it bonds with the outer surfaces of bacteria and viruses and destroys them. When it kills the natural flora on human skin, the reaction creates the stuffy, cloudy smell we associate with chlorine.
>
> Chlorine marks us in ways we cannot see.

The essay goes on to use the touchstone of chlorine—odorless, changing forever everything it comes into contact with—as a metaphor for all the invisible ways life touches and changes us, and we touch and change one another. It's a subtle and nuanced use of fact as fact and fact as metaphor.

Researching a Key Fact or Detail

Peter Balakian set out to write a family memoir in his book *Black Dog of Fate*. Yet as he probed memories of life with his immigrant family in New Jersey—communal meals, days spent at his grandmother's helping her as she baked—he began to notice that the real story of his family lay in a subject they did *not* discuss: their now-vanished home-land of Armenia, including the fate of the family members who had remained there. Finally, by asking questions of his family and doing his own historical research, Balakian came to grips with the real story haunting him: the massacre of the Armenians by the Turks early in the twentieth century, a massacre so successful it gave Hitler the confidence to conceive the Holocaust.

In "The Clan of One-Breasted Women" (see the anthology section), Terry Tempest Williams begins to examine the larger forces that may be contributing to her family's high rate of breast cancer. In the following excerpt, you can see her seamless and organic movement from personal history into researched analysis. She has, as this dialogue begins, told her father of a recurring dream she has of a flash of light in the desert.

> "You did see it," he said.
>
> "Saw what?"
>
> "The bomb. The cloud. We were driving home from Riverside, California. You were sitting on Diane's lap. She was pregnant. . . . We pulled over and suddenly, rising from the desert floor, we saw it, clearly, this golden-stemmed cloud, the mushroom. The sky seemed to vibrate with an eerie pink glow. Within a few minutes, a light ash was raining on the car. . . ."
>
> It is a well-known story in the Desert West, "The Day We Bombed Utah," or more accurately, the years we bombed Utah: above ground atomic testing in Nevada took place from January 27, 1951 through July 11, 1962. Not only were the winds blowing north covering "low-use segments of the population" with fallout and leaving sheep dead in their tracks, but the climate was right.

Tempest goes on to provide an analysis of the political climate of the period—the growth of McCarthyism, the Korean War. She summarizes litigation stemming from the tests and returns seamlessly to her own story. Note that here she has clearly researched the dates of the bomb testing, as well as the wind patterns during those years, but she weaves those facts unobtrusively into her own narrative.

Research as Credibility: The Detail

Both Balakian and Williams use research into a large and emotionally complex event to deepen and expand the family stories they've already told in their books. In both cases, the last chapters of their books open the personal narratives up into complex and historically important stories. Research can be just as vital when it's operating on a smaller level—even providing power and credibility to a single detail.

In her essay "Total Eclipse" (see the anthology section), Annie Dillard describes a trip to view a total eclipse of the sun in eastern Washington. She communicates in perfectly pitched language the deep dislocation of seeing the sun "going" and the daytime world appearing "wrong," contrasting this with a meditation on our human need for predictability and order. Readers are set up for this contrast by a casual mention of an article she reads in the lobby of her motel:

> In South Africa, in India, and in South Dakota, the gold mines extend so deeply into the earth's crust that they are hot. The rock walls burn the miners' hands. The companies have to air-condition the mines; if the air conditioners break, the miners die. The elevators in the mineshafts run very slowly, down, and up, so the miners' ears will not pop in their skulls. When the miners return to the surface, their faces are deathly pale.

Dillard's careful reading—and no doubt, note-taking—on this article prepares us for the terror she experiences at the eclipse.

Later in the essay, trying to justify a terror that evoked "screams" from onlookers, Dillard describes the swift descent of the eclipse shadow:

> The second before the sun went out, we saw a wall of dark shadow come speeding at us. We no sooner saw it than it was upon us, like thunder. It roared up the valley. It slammed our hill and knocked us out. It was the monstrous swift shadow cone of the moon. I have since read that this wave of shadow moves 1,800 miles an hour. Language can give no sense of this sort of speed—1,800 miles an hour. It was 195 miles wide. . . . It rolled at you across the land at 1,800 miles an hour, hauling darkness like plague behind it.

Mentally remove the facts from this description, and if you're like most readers, you'll turn off, not quite believing the ferocity of the description. But that repetition of 1,800 miles an hour convinces us with its factual magnitude—the darkness of the eclipse becomes like a terrifying dark comet from space falling on the crowd of onlookers.

Working with Immersion

Immersion refers to the technique of actually living an experience—usually briefly—in order to write about it. George Plimpton, writer and editor of the *Paris Review*, lived for a while as a football player to research the book *Paper Lion*. Lee Gutkind, writer and editor of the journal *Creative Nonfiction*, has done a great deal of immersion writing: He has lived as a circus clown and followed transplant doctors and umpires on their rounds. Several years ago, Robert Sullivan lived for months with the Makah Indian tribe and observed their hunt for gray whales in his book *A Whale Hunt*.

Writers differ in their approach to immersion research. Gutkind writes of the writer's need to become invisible, almost a piece of furniture in the room: "I like to compare myself to a rather undistinguished and utilitarian end table in a living room or office," he writes. Didion, however, is often a presence in her research, one whose shy, questioning self forms another character in the piece.

Several years ago, a student of ours named Katy read about an adult nightclub in Seattle; it was one of the few clubs in the United States owned and run entirely by women, with an atmosphere that was woman-friendly and safe. She visited the place; the dancers were mainly college women and single mothers. The women saved plenty of their salaries and felt good about their work. She asked the owners and employees of the club if they would mind her hanging around for a few days and asking them questions. They were delighted, and her immersion experience resulted in an essay uncovering a fascinating side of a business generally viewed as degrading and exploiting to women.

Developing Interview Skills

There are as many interview styles as there are writers in this world. Writer Gay Talese's polished assurance invites confidence. On the other side of the spectrum are writers like Joan Didion and John McPhee, both of whom describe themselves (or are described by others) as so shy and unsure that interviewees tend to underrate them. It's important to remember artistically as well as ethically that when you conduct research and interview people, their words may ultimately be used in ways they won't like. Didion puts it bluntly: "Writers are always selling somebody out."

Regardless of your style, there are some tips that will help any interview go more productively. Most researchers ask a few throw-off questions—those with simple and unimportant answers—to relax their subjects before moving on to more difficult questions. And as far as that goes, the toughest questions should be saved for last. If someone shuts down because you asked why he or she supported the Gulf War, for example, you don't want that confrontation to ruin the entire interview. Begin with the simplest and least emotional information, and move forward from there.

Always begin an interview with a list of questions you want to ask; a prepared list will prevent you from forgetting to ask something important because of nerves or simple absent-mindedness. It's also helpful to end interviews with an open-ended question that will direct you to your next research source, for example, "What do you think the best place to go for information about the war is?" "Are there other people I should speak to about this subject?"

Philip Gerard advises that you always strive to use interviews to find primary sources. "An interview may be a great start," he says, "but will that person also let you read his or her diary, letters, business correspondence?" Gerard tells the story of a scholar who found that the most valuable document in studying F. Scott Fitzgerald turned out to be his tax returns, chronicling his inflated lifestyle and his debt.

Above all, put your questions out there, pause, and really listen. Have your list of questions ready, but be prepared to change course when you get an answer—or a partial answer—that intrigues you. If your subject says casually, "Well, of course John wasn't around then because he was in jail for a while," follow up on that point right away; don't continue with your checklist. You may forget to come back to it, or the person you're speaking to may regret having let it slip. Listen carefully and follow up on what you hear.

You can learn a great deal about effective interview techniques by listening to some of the better talk shows on the radio or TV. Terry Gross, for example, in her show *Fresh Air* (aired on most National Public Radio stations), provides a model for interview techniques. She's genuinely interested in her interviewees, and this enthusiasm comes through in her voice. In turn, her subjects feel comfortable and open up to her in ways that lead to in-depth interviews. Gross obviously comes prepared with questions, but she doesn't hesitate to pick up on what might be a "throw-away" comment; she often says "wait a minute" and goes back to these comments and probes for more detail. She manages to do this without coming across as confrontational or adversarial; rather she acts as a helpful guide, gently leading her subjects into areas that may have seemed peripheral to the main topic. Often, these are the moments when we, as listeners, perk up our ears, hearing the "real" stuff that might otherwise have remained hidden.

Developing Print Research Skills

The Library

The best thing about libraries, we think, is reference librarians. The smallest library contains a wealth of information. There are newspapers from all over, going back many years; reference books from the obvious World Book–type books to dictionaries of chronologies and disasters; specialized encyclopedias; works on microfilm; and tapes and videos. When you know just what you want, the computer or card catalogue will steer you to it. When you don't—say you have a general question about molecular physics or weather or genealogical research—reference librarians will point you to the right sources and help you find what you need.

We went to several of our favorite librarians for advice on how to use the resources of the library most effectively. According to Western Washington University's Paul Piper, the first tip is to develop a relationship with your research librarian—introduce yourself, and try to keep working with the same person. He or she will get a sense of what you want and keep on the lookout for materials you can use. Piper also recommends spending time articulating to yourself what you're really looking for. He remembers a patron who asked for books on dogs, but then, after wasting quite a bit of time in the dog section, complained she couldn't find anything about the life cycle of the flea! Dogs are dogs, and fleas are fleas. Articulate your interest to yourself as clearly as you can.

Al Cordle, a reference librarian in Portland, gave us this piece of advice: "I have a favorite technique for locating books in my library. I always go to the online catalogue and type in one or two keywords to describe my topic and the word *dictionary* or *encyclopedia*. Almost without fail I find specialized reference books devoted to my research topics." Cordle notes that keyword searches, as opposed to subject searches, can be more successful because the search engines operate more flexibly with keywords. Keyword searching should be an option offered by any library computer's toolbar. "So, for example," says Cordle, "if I type *encyclopedia* and *Native Americans*, I may come up with *Encyclopedia of Minorities in American Politics; Native Americans: An Encyclopedia of History, Culture, and Peoples;* and the *Encyclopedia of North American Indians.*"

Even without the help of a reference librarian, libraries aren't hard to navigate if you keep in mind that most print information can be tracked through master sources found in the library's reference section. Before you start, articulate to yourself as specifically as you can what information you're looking for. If you had to ask one question to move forward on this writing project, what would it be? Once you have that specific question (or questions) in mind, identify the major reference works that might help you.

Here are some basic categories, taken from *Rules of Thumb for Research* by Jay Silverman, Elaine Hughes and Diana Roberts Wienbroer. Say you're Annie Dillard, beginning your essay "Total Eclipse." For general information, you could look for an encyclopedia, where you'd find a compact and readable definition of a phenomenon like an eclipse. If you wanted biographical information (say, on the first astronomer to study eclipses), you might start with *Who's Who* or the *Dictionary of American Biography*. For further reading, you could check out the *Biography and General Master Index*, which lists articles in many other places; you can locate whatever looks interesting through your library's computer system or card catalogue. Finally, most fields have specialized reference books; you could try names like *Astronomy Abstracts* or *Dictionary of Astronomy* and see what comes up.

One more major library resource consists of indexes, which track the thousands of news articles written and archived every day. The most basic is the *Reader's Guide to Periodical Literature,* which covers articles written in magazines aimed at the general public (in other words, something like a specialized medical or scientific journal wouldn't be covered in the *Reader's Guide*). Anything relevant to your search that's been published in a venue like *Time, Newsweek,* or even *Scientific American* would appear in the *Reader's Guide,* so it's a tremendously useful volume to consult. Newspapers also publish annual indexes of their articles, and libraries house many of these. If your search covers a specific area, such as Chicago, check to see whether your library has the *Chicago Tribune* or *Sun-Times* indexes. If you're seeking information on a national news event, check the indexes for the *Washington Post* or the *New York Times.* For a major newspaper like the *Times,* your library should have its back issues archived on microfilm. If not, you can try the newspaper's on-line archives.

If you delve deeply into reference sources covering books and periodical literature, you'll come across print sources that sound tantalizingly perfect for your research but that your library doesn't hold and that aren't available in on-line archives either. Go to the information desk and inquire about your library's interlibrary loan policy. Almost anything, including out-of-print books and old newspapers on microfilm, can be borrowed through interlibrary loan. You may have to wait a while and do a lot of reading rather quickly once it arrives, since these items can generally be kept only for a few weeks. But knowing you've solved a puzzle, or put together information no one else has, by tracking little-known sources is part of the thrill of research.

The Internet

Most researchers agree that the Internet is the most important new research tool we now have, offering access to trillions of pages of material at the touch of a finger. This massive access also forms the Internet's biggest drawback: the large volume of unsorted material it turns up. Still, it's one of the best quick sources of information available, especially for facts that don't hold too much ambiguity. If you want to know the migration habits of the gray whale, a quick search will get this information for you, along with maps and sound (if your computer has speakers) that will enable you to hear the grays making their way along the coast. This is quite a large payoff for very little effort.

Reva Basch, coauthor of *Researching Online for Dummies*, breaks down the areas in which Internet research is most useful: The first is to get background information on a subject, and the second is for fact-checking. AskJeeves and *www.refdesk.com* are both highly recommended sites for fact-checking, and a site like the Library of Congress's American Memory (*www.memory.loc.gov/ammem/amhome.html*) will give you an excellent overview of any subject that could be considered historical, such as Watergate or more recent topics like the last election. Like many other resource sites, American Memory even houses video and audio clips.

A number of search engines, much like the *Reader's Guide to Periodical Literature*, track what's published in thousands of print sources, and many offer abstracts or summaries of the articles (some even offer complete copies). Check your library for its list of on-line resources to see what specialized search engines you can use there, if the right ones aren't available on your home computer (assuming that you have one). A few to look for are Infotrak, which is an exhaustive list of periodical publications; PDQ, which offers abstracts and complete articles in many cases; and Northern Light's Special Collections (*www.northernlight.com*), which gives access to many specialized magazines (Northern Light charges a small fee, but your library may offer it for free).

If you can think of an institution that would house information you need, consider checking its website. Museums, government organizations, and the Library of Congress all offer immense amounts of information on the Internet. You might wonder, for instance, what the Smithsonian Institution in Washington, DC, a premier science source, could tell you about eclipses. Use a search engine to access the Smithsonian's site, then follow its navigation instructions to access its on-line resources. You can often figure out web addresses even without search engines; if you want information on nuclear energy, you might start with the U.S. Department of Energy. Put its abbreviation (DOE), with the *.gov* suffix used by all government agencies, after the basic World Wide Web address of *www.*, and voilà—there it is.

Services, called research services, which find articles for free and then make money by charging you for copies, are also available on the Internet. One that uses a powerful search engine, doesn't require an initial fee, and is recommended by *Rules of Thumb for Research* is CARL (Colorado Alliance of Research Libraries) at *www.carl.org*. If you find a helpful-looking article, you can either pay the small fee charged by CARL for a copy or try to find the article through a local library. A final resource you may want to try is Internet gophers, portal sites that link you to research facilities grouped by subject. The first and main gopher is the one maintained by the University of Minnesota (*gopher.//gopher.tc.umn.edu*). Once you've accessed the gopher, you type in a general subject heading and get a list of related sites, all links you can click on for instant access.

You can begin playing with Internet research—assuming you haven't done so already—by choosing a good browser and search engine and typing in keywords or phrases that capture your interest. Give this process a dry run just to see how it feels—choose a subject that has either interested you for a long time or is something you take absolutely for granted, maybe "the molecular structure of DNA" or "the electoral college." (We don't think much of the vagaries of how we vote; we just do it.)

Learn to scrutinize both the search engine summaries and the sites themselves for clues to how useful or downright flaky they are. The suffixes *.edu* and *.gov,* for instance, indicate sites run by educational institutions and the U.S. government, respectively. A number of sites run by leading-edge universities like the Massachusetts Institute of Technology have pages on the molecular structure of DNA, as does the World Book online (*www.worldbookonline.com*); the identities of these sources are clear from their Uniform Resource Locators or URLs. Several government sites, denoted by their *.gov* suffix, have good explanations of the electoral college. Lots of sites will also come up that you'll probably want to ignore—sites not relevant to your question, personal on-line diaries, even stories about alien DNA! Or maybe these are another essay altogether.

Remember that computers are literal creatures. The woman searching for information on fleas could stumble on an explanation by looking for dog books, however much time she may lose by approaching the subject that way. No search engine, however, can intuit the leap from "dog" to "flea." Phrase your search as precisely as you can without narrowing it down too much. "AIDS in Africa" will result in hundreds of thousands of sites; "AIDS in unwed mothers between the ages of 28 and 30 in the lower Volta Delta" probably won't yield any. And try alternative terms to see whether you uncover more or better results—both "FBI" and "Federal Bureau of Investigation," for example.

Primary Sources

One writer we know wanted to research a point in family history about which he'd heard conflicting stories—his grandparents' marriage and the birth of his mother. Visiting the courthouse in the county where the marriage took place, he requested his grandmother's marriage license and was handed a license for a marriage other than the

one to his grandfather. Intrigued, he recovered copies of both marriage licenses, wedding announcements that ran in the newspapers of
the time, and his mother's birth certificate—and discovered that his
grandmother had been pregnant and just divorcing when she married
his grandfather. Back in the 1930s, both events would have prompted
a great deal of scandal. Tensions in family relationships suddenly fell
into place.

You may not discover anything quite this interesting, or you may
find something far more interesting, but the fact is that courthouses
keep records of births, adoptions, marriages, divorces, deaths, and
more. Anyone can request copies; you visit the town or county courthouse, ask to see the directory of records, and request copies of what
you want. Or you can register with an on-line service like Courtlink
(*www.lexisnexis.com/courtlink*), which can generally obtain legal documents on file anywhere in the country for a fairly low fee. If you're
researching a topic in a particular town, you might want to try the historical society; most towns have them, and they keep all sorts of documents, including deeds, photographs, and, frequently, diaries and
old publications. Old newspapers, too, which are full of information,
are kept in local libraries on microfilm. You may want to back up your
family interviews with research into what really happened.

There are so many other print sources of information that we
can't list them all here. The Government Printing Office, for example,
has reports and statistics available on everything imaginable, from
congressional testimony to government-sponsored research. The Television Archives housed at Vanderbilt University contain tapes of
broadcasts, news broadcasts as well as programs, going back to the
earliest days of TV. You can also request written transcripts of old
broadcasts. Through intelligent research, it's possible to immerse yourself completely in another place and time.

Brent Staples, author of "The Coroner's Photographs," (see the anthology section) describes how he went to a commonwealth attorney's
office to request the documents on his brother Blake's murder. Included in the documents he obtains are the Roanoke coroner's photographs and his report on Blake's death from a gunshot wound. Staples
builds this essay out of juxtaposing his own trips to Roanoke—first to
plead with his brother to leave the drug business and next to obtain
the details of Blake's death—with the coroner's dry, institutional inventory of the body: "HEART: 300 grams. No valve or chamber lesions"
and so on.

Staples's use of the documents reveals a justice system in which the
death of a poor black drug dealer is "an ordinary death," a crime nobody takes too seriously. It also becomes a self-indictment, however,
a reflection of the part of him that "told myself to feel nothing. I had

already mourned Blake and buried him and was determined not to suffer his death a second time." Brent Staples becomes both a mirror image of the man in the coroner's photographs, whose family resemblance to himself he carefully catalogues, and a mirror of the institutional indifference to the crime, which he finally faces. The research he conducts into Blake's death becomes essential in understanding his own, and society's, reactions to it.

Winnowing Down

Here's an example of the genesis of a research-driven essay. Jennifer Price, the author of "A Brief Natural History of the Plastic Pink Flamingo" (see the anthology section), commented that she had "no desire to write about the flamingo until I learned the guy who invented it was named Featherstone, he and his wife wore matching outfits every day that his wife sewed, and they had a poodle named Bourgeois." These stray facts convinced Price that the lawn flamingo, brainchild of an eccentric inventor, might hold a story she wanted to tell.

In the course of her investigation, she learned that people from film directors to *New Yorker* editors held cherished collections of the birds and that a pair of flamingos had been kidnapped; the kidnappers sent back photographs from the birds as they traveled the world, against backdrops like the Eiffel Tower in Paris. "I couldn't believe one lawn ornament could represent so much," said Price, who stumbled into this story through a casual bit of research.

From those beginnings, where we fall in love with a piece of information, essays begin; the shaping that follows, however, can be difficult. Jennifer Price, at this early stage of research, had to ask herself which story she really wanted to tell, Featherstone's or the flamingo's. (As the title indicates, she chose the latter.) The toughest thing about research is learning to sort through what you find, particularly now, in the midst of the Internet explosion and the Information Age. Imagine that you're Jennifer Price, feeling just a tickle of interest in writing an essay about pink plastic lawn flamingos. A search on a powerful search engine—*www.google.com*—takes several seconds and unearths almost three hundred sites on the Internet, each one loaded with information on lawn flamingos.

Without looking any further, you can scan the search engine summaries and learn all these facts: that lawn flamingos were initially designed using photographs from *National Geographic,* that they've stirred up dissent when used to create Nativity scenes at Christmas, and that their creator got an award from the satirical *Journal of Irreproducible Results.* This quick scan creates practically an essay in itself, without bothering to click on the sites and learn even more.

What do you do with it all? First of all, keep close to you the initial impulse that made you want to do this research—the first fact or hint that gave you a sense that you had a subject for an essay you could live with, even grow obsessive about, for a while. It's important to avoid the temptation to drop into your essay everything you learn that's strange or amusing. Jennifer Price began her essay with an interest in flamingo creator Don Featherstone, but she found, sorting through her material, that it was the flamingos' borderline between artifice and nature that captured her.

> The deepest meanings of each of these flamingos, I've become convinced, owe their logic and fervor to deep meanings and big definitions of nature. The story of the pink lawn bird is the tale of how Americans converted a plastic object into the very symbol of what is artificial. It is a story of the meanings of Artifice. And that is a history, at the same time, of the meanings of Nature.

What's closest to your own heart, your own obsessions? What in this research do you feel most qualified and eager to talk about? Sit with your papers, including interview notes, in front of you, and circle or highlight the material that seems most to draw you or belong to you. You can try making piles in order of urgency: what you *must* write about, what you probably should include, what's iffier, and so on.

Once you've done some basic highlighting and sorting, if you're working on a piece that requires a great deal of research—not just a key fact here and there like the eclipse shadow—it helps to create a computer file or notebook page with a list of material you want to use. Put facts in an order that feels like it might correspond to the order you'll use them in, but don't burden yourself by treating this as an outline. Your writing should always stay fluid, flexible, and open to your best intuitive leaps. Consult the list as you draft, to see whether there are any exciting facts—those that help explain or offer metaphorical possibilities, for example—which you've forgotten.

Some Last Thoughts

We've given you tools for collecting and organizing your research and ways of thinking about what interests you. Whatever direction your research takes, here are some final thoughts for creating a strong research essay.

1. *Begin with what you love.* Question your impulses a little bit. Wanting to write about the environment, for instance, is very different from writing about nature. Because you love the water and find it a source of inspiration doesn't mean that your interest level will stay high up as you wade through papers about PCBs

(polychlorinated biphenyls) and mercury levels. Some of us thrive on the challenge of understanding what's really going on at the chemical level, and some of us don't. As we said earlier, be sure that the research is such that you'll find it pleasurable, at least when you start pulling the results together.

2. *Be sure the research is key to the writing impulse.* Annie Dillard's "Total Eclipse" needed facts about the eclipse shadow to justify the power of her description. Jen Whetham's essay needed the chemical information on chlorine to serve as a metaphor for the changing power of touch. We have, however, read essays about sailing where the author suddenly drops in the fact that Bellingham Bay is polluted with chlorine and mercury, then blithely carries on with a sailing story. As readers, we're not sure what to do with that, unless the thread of water pollution is picked up again or bounces off something in the essay as metaphor. Sometimes knowing a fact is irresistible; as writers, we need to find our moments, not simply tell everything we know.

3. *Interact with your research.* What you learn must change you, change your sense of the story. Here are the words of Robin Hemley, who wrote a memoir of his deeply spiritual and schizophrenic sister, called *Nola*:

> When I began the book, I thought I could escape more or less unscathed, that I was writing about other people and their secrets, not my own. But I soon realized that I had to apply the same scrutiny to myself as I applied to everyone else. Otherwise, the book would have been a failure on the literary level, an emotional failure and maybe a moral one, too.

Creative nonfiction is ultimately the story of the journeying mind, the individual in transition. Make sure that you do as Hemley did—apply the same scrutiny to yourself that you apply to your other fields of inquiry, and your research will always be successful.

Try It

Research as Credibility: The Detail

Research is an addictive process. Most writers go from resisting the idea of research to finding that they have to limit the amount of time they spend on it. It's easy to become obsessed with discovering exactly why the corpse flower blooms one day every few years with an odor of decaying meat or how IBM's supercomputer Deep Blue beat the reigning World Chess

Champion Garry Kasparov. We suggest the following process to help you discover how research can enrich your own writing.

1.   Pull out an essay you've been working on, one that has promise but doesn't feel quite finished yet. Make a list of facts that inform this piece— none of these facts needs to be present in the work, but rather can be implied through location, time, action, or characters. Here's a sample opening paragraph and the list it generates:

> It is 1963 and I am watching, for what seems like the hundredth time, Lee Harvey Oswald collapse as he is shot by Jack Ruby. I am wearing my Winnie the Pooh pajamas and listening to the ice clink in my mother's glass as she drinks another gin in the kitchen. I've told her I'm watching Rocky & Bullwinkle but by this time of night she's too far gone to pay attention.

This is a very promising start: emotional without any trace of self-indulgence, nicely detailed. Here's a list of possible research areas:

- Kennedy assassination: political climate of the time? Bay of Pigs?
- Media in the early 1960s
- The Midwest (unstated in the opening, but this is the location)
- Alcoholism, particularly during this period. What was the medical view of alcoholism? The social view? How was alcohol portrayed in the media of the time?

Going down the list, you decide that alcoholism is the most promising avenue for further study. You begin by looking at advertisements and films from the period, seeing how alcohol is portrayed: as an everyday diversion, the province of sophisticates and James Bond types. You explore medical textbooks dating from the 1960s to see how alcohol dependence was viewed then: You find it less a disease model and much more a character-driven view than today. Finally, you browse Alcoholics Anonymous (AA) literature to see how a sense of the disease of alcoholism has evolved.

None of these sources is particularly hard to come by or unpleasant to research: Any video store will have films from different periods, any decent library will stock old magazines and medical texts, and organizations like AA are pleased to send literature through the mail. (It's doubly worth noting that our compassion as well as our writing grows through this kind of research.) The final step is highlighting information worth using and then working it into the author's story without a change of voice: It's important not to sound like a textbook, as if another author has come in to serve as newscaster. Compare two moves you could make next:

> In 1963, more than half of Americans, current experts agree, use alcohol to excess, and 75% of films show characters drinking alcoholic drinks.

Or:

> This year, everybody is in love with James Bond, who drinks martini after martini in his movies without any change in behavior. James Bond has made

"shaken, not stirred" a mantra for this martini-smitten culture. My mother simply eliminates the vermouth.

What began as a delicate, personal essay can't afford to switch into the sociological language of the first example, not to mention the fact that its dry tone is distancing and hard to care about. The second attempt contains a real detail of the period that ties intimately to the author's story, a detail that's engaging and sets the mother within the context of acceptable social behavior at the time. Nevertheless, it's a detail the author wouldn't have found without a little digging.

2.   Look at an essay like Jennifer Price's "A Brief Natural History of the Plastic Pink Flamingo" or Joan Didion's "On the Mall" (from *The White Album*), or any essay organized around a quirky piece of research. In "On the Mall," Didion spins an essay out of the subcategory of urban planning known as shopping-center theory, which she finds in a textbook. She blends odd facts from shopping-center theory—such as the use of overly large parking spaces to make a lot look full—with a personal meditation on the way shopping centers have created her own postwar baby boom landscape:

> They float on the landscape like pyramids to the boom years, all those Plazas and Malls and Esplanades. All those Squares and Fairs. . . . They are toy garden cities in which no one lives but everyone consumes, profound equalizers, the perfect fusion of the profit motive and the egalitarian ideal.

The next time a strange fact grabs your attention, write it down or cut out the source, if it appears in a newspaper or magazine. Ask yourself why this fact seems to demand your attention. Does it resonate with a chord in your own life, as shopping centers do with Didion's? How does this fact speak to you? Does it have a metaphorical value? (Didion's shopping centers become metaphors for postwar idealism.) Write an essay based on this fact, using additional research if necessary. If you're trolling for odd facts, try almanacs or Harper's Index, which holds a plethora of bizarre tidbits, like the fact that the Pentagon spends $100 a minute on Viagra®.

Working with Immersion

3.   Chances are that you've already had at least one terrific immersion experience, even if you didn't call it that: maybe it was the wedding you attended where the bride and groom were Goths who married in black robes with white powder on their faces; maybe it was the time your uncle dragged you along to a meeting of the local Elks Club.

Fascinating immersion experiences exist everywhere. Do you live near a hospital? A casino? A group of Wiccans? A branch of the Society for Creative Anachronism? Ask them if they would mind your observing them a while for an essay. Keep notes, use a tape recorder, or both.

Before you begin your immersion experience, decide how you see your role. Will you take Didion's approach and acknowledge your presence in the events you write about, or, like Gutkind, will you try to keep yourself out of the narrative? Adjust your presence accordingly.

Developing Interview Skills

To hone your interview skills and create a body of information you'll almost certainly want to come back to, try family interviews. These are generally far less intimidating than tracking down your local physicist to ask questions about the implications of the Big Bang. Families also tend to be repositories of fascinating hidden information—uncles who had more money than they should have, cousins who disappeared in disgrace.

4.   Start with a question you've always wanted to get an answer, or a clearer answer, to. It may be the life story of the family scapegrace, an immigration story, or a detailed picture of a parent's early years. Make a list of questions; keep them fairly simple. If you're pursuing the story of a family member in legal trouble, your questions might include the year the trouble first occurred, the full details, the way family members responded, and so forth.

5.   Ask your questions of two or three different family members—preferably from several generations, such as a cousin, a parent, a grandparent—and make note of the discrepancies between their versions of events. Unless your family is very different from most, there will be plenty. Follow up on your initial interviews with further questions, to see whether you can explain differing versions of the story.

Suggestions for Further Reading

In Our Anthology

Dillard, Annie, "Total Eclipse"

Hemley, Robin, "Reading History To My Mother"

Price, Jennifer, "A Brief Natural History of the Plastic Pink Flamingo"

Staples, Brent, "The Coroner's Photographs"

Williams, Terry Tempest, "The Clan Of One-Breasted Women"

Elsewhere

Balakian, Peter, *Black Dog of Fate*

Didion Joan, *The White Album*

Dillard, Annie, *The Annie Dillard Reader*

Gerard, Philip, *Brilliant Passage: A Schooning Memoir* and *Secret Soldiers: The Story of World War II's Heroic Army of Deception*

Gutkind, Lee, *The Best Seat in Baseball But You Have To Stand: The Game as Umpires See It*

Harr, Jonathan, *A Civil Action*

Hemley, Robin, *Nola*

McPhee, John, *The John McPhee Reader*

Plimpton, George, *Paper Lion*

Silverman, Jay, Elaine Hughes and Diana Roberts Wienbroer, *Rules of Thumb for Research*

Chapter Twelve

The Writing Process and Revision

The writing has changed, in your hands, and in a twinkling, from an expression of your notions to an epistemological tool. The new place interests you because it is not clear. You attend. In your humility, you lay down the words carefully, watching all the angles. Now the earlier writing looks soft and careless. Process is nothing; erase your tracks. The path is not the work. I hope your tracks have grown over; I hope birds ate the crumbs; I hope you will toss it all and not look back. —**Annie Dillard**

- ▍ **The Drafting Process**
- ▍ **Global Revision versus Line Editing**
- ▍ **The Role of the Audience**
- ▍ **Three Quick Fixes for Stronger Prose**
- ▍ **An Example of the Writing Process**
- ▍ **Try It**

In graduate school, I once submitted a workshop story that nobody liked—not one person. I remember one woman in particular: She dangled my work in front of her and said, her lip curling in distaste, "I don't understand why this story even exists!" Of course, at the time, I huffed and I puffed, and I spoke derisively of this woman at the bar that night. My friends cooed words of support, patted me on the back, and scanned the bar for more lively company. But even as I walked home that night, I could tell that her comment, though poorly worded, had something in it that I needed to hear. It has stayed with me throughout the years, and now, when I'm at the revision stage, it's her question that I hear in my head: *Why does this essay exist?* I go back to work with grim determination. No longer do I coddle the newborn prose, but hold it up roughly, probing for weakness, drawing blood. I try to identify and slash out all that is mere indulgence or platitude.

At this stage in the writing process, the draft becomes nothing more than a fruitful scavenging ground. Right now, as a I write, I'm in the middle of Wyoming, and down the road a huge junkyard lies at the intersection of two minor highways. Against the rolling fields of wheat grass, this junkyard rises as ten acres of glinting metal, bent chrome, colors of every hue. One of my fellow colonists, a sculptor, began buying scraps to incorporate in her work: gorgeous landscapes with ribbons of rusted metal juxtaposed across blue skies. Now I've come to see the junkyard as a place of infinite possibilities. What useful parts still hum in the innards of these machines? How will they be unearthed? What kind of work would it take to make them shine? —**Brenda**

The Drafting Process

> *Writing is easy; all you do is sit staring at a blank sheet of paper until the drops of blood form on your forehead.*
>
> —*Gene Fowler*

When you first sit down to work, you may have no idea what the writing will bring. Maybe it even scares you a little, the thought of venturing into that unknown territory. Perhaps you circle your desk for a while, wary of the task at hand. You pick up your cup of coffee in both hands and gaze out the window; you remember a letter you meant to write or an e-mail you meant to answer. You get up and check the mailbox, while you're at it, picking a few dead leaves off the coleus plant in the window. You sit down. You get up and change your shirt, appraise yourself in the mirror for a long time, and come back to your desk. Maybe you pick up a book of poetry and read a few lines, then put it down. You pick up your pen and write a word, then another. You go back and revise. You begin again.

Or maybe you're the type who can sit down and start writing without hesitation, training yourself to write at least one full paragraph before you stop. You know you'll go back and trim and revise, so you just keep the words coming. You give yourself an hour, and you don't move from your chair during that time. If the writing goes well, that hour turns into two or three. You work steadily and pile up the pages.

Either way, the important thing to know, for yourself, is your own style. In the first case, to the untrained eye, you may appear to be engaged in mere procrastination; certainly you're not writing. But if you know yourself well, you understand that this puttering is essential to your writing process. Some thought has been brewing in your brain for several days now, perhaps even weeks or months. This idea needs your body to occupy itself while the essay forms itself into something sturdy enough to survive outside the mind and on the bleak terrain of the page. Or in the second case, you act more like an athlete in training, knowing that routine and discipline are essential for your creative process. You write quickly because that's the only way to outrun your inner critic. Neither way is "correct." The only correct way to write is the one that works for you.

The writing process is just that: a *process*. You must have the patience to watch the piece evolve, and you need an awareness of your own stages: You must know when you can go pell-mell with the heat of creation and when you must settle down, take a wider view, and make some choices that will determine the essay's final shape.

First drafts can be seen as "discovery drafts"; much of the writing you did from the prompts in part II will fall into this category. You're writing to discover what you know or to recover memories and images that may have been lost to you. You're going for the details, the unexpected images, the story line that reveals itself only as you go along. The best writing you do will have this sense of exploration about it; you allow yourself to go into the unknown, to excavate what lies beneath the surface. It's important to give yourself permission to write *anything* in a first draft; otherwise, you might censor yourself into silence. The first draft is the place where you just might light on the right *voice* for telling this particular story; once you're onto that voice, you can write for hours.

No matter how good (or bad) this material seems at first glance, most often it will need some shaping and revision before it's ready for public scrutiny. Writer Natalie Goldberg calls revision "envisioning again," and this gets at the heart of true revision: you see your work in a new light and rework it for a specific effect. Revision, perhaps, is an acquired taste, but you may find that revision actually becomes the most "creative" part of creative nonfiction. At this stage, you've already produced the raw material; now you have the opportunity to roll up your sleeves and dig into it, all your tools sharpened and at the ready. It's in revision that the real work begins. Short story writer Raymond Carver often wrote twenty to thirty drafts of a piece before he was satisfied. "It's something I love to do," he said, "putting words in and taking words out." Or listen to Vladimir Nabokov: "I have re-written—often several times—every word I have ever published. My pencils outlast their erasers."

Global Revision versus Line Editing

Revision can often be mistaken for line editing. There's a time, naturally, for going back to your prose to fine-tune the grammar, change a few words, and fix typos. But first you need to look at the essay as a whole and decide what will make it matter. What's the *real* subject of the piece? Where does the voice ring out most strongly? What image takes on more metaphorical significance than you realized? What now seems superfluous, mere dead weight that hinders the essay's momentum?

It's beneficial to take some time between drafts at this stage. After that first, heady flush of creation settles down, you'll better be able to pinpoint the areas that sing and those that fall flat. You'll be able to notice an unexpected theme that emerges organically through the imagery you chose. You'll hear how the ending may actually be the beginning of your piece—or how the beginning may make for a better ending. At this point, you need to see the work as a fluid thing, with infinite possibilities yet to come. What you may have intended to write may not be the most interesting part of the essay now. Be open to what has developed in the writing process itself, and don't be afraid to cut out those areas that no longer work. Natalie Goldberg calls this becoming the "Samurai, a great warrior with courage to cut out anything that is not present."

Ask yourself this question: What's the essence of the topic *for this particular essay?* Many times, it's easy to think that we have to put in everything we know or feel about a topic in one essay. For instance, if you're writing about a big issue, such as sexual abuse in childhood, you may be tempted to write a gigantic essay that incorporates every incident, every feeling you ever had, the entire cast of characters involved. Or if you're writing about a life-changing travel experience, you might feel you need to put in every stop along the way. You have to figure out what's necessary for this essay *and this essay alone.* Don't worry, you'll write other essays about the topic. As Goldberg puts it: "Your main obsessions have power; they are what you will come back to in your writing over and over again. And you'll create new stories around them."

You may end up keeping only a small portion of the original work, perhaps just one line. But by doing this kind of pruning, you enable new growth, sturdier and more beautiful growth, to emerge. Take comfort in knowing that the old work may find its way into new essays yet to come. Keep a file on your desk, or in your computer, called "Fragments." If it's hard for you to let go of a section completely, put it in the file and know that you can call it back in a new incarnation sometime in the future. Time and again, we—Suzanne and Brenda—have found new homes for those bits and pieces of prose that just didn't work in their original homes.

The Role of the Audience

As we mentioned in chapter 2, the connection between reader and writer is particularly important in creative nonfiction. You create a strong personal voice, and through this voice you make a certain pact with the reader. As you revise, it can be helpful to begin thinking of your reader as a way to focus the essay's intent, hone its structure, and amplify its voice.

When you're writing a first draft, it's often necessary to ignore any concept of audience just so you can get the material out. At that stage of the writing process, an attentive audience, hanging on your every word, can be inhibiting. But when you're revising, having some concept of audience can help you gain the necessary distance to do the hard work that needs to be done. This audience can be a single person: For example, what would your writing teacher from high school, the one who drove you into writing in the first place, think of this essay? Where would she say you're being lazy or timid? What would your most trusted friend say about that last paragraph? Sometimes by merely placing yourself in another person's perspective, the problems of the piece become readily apparent and you can fix them with ease.

Or the audience can be much larger. Many times, having some kind of reading venue or publication in mind can focus your attention in a way that nothing else can. Many towns have open mike readings in cafes or bookstores where beginning and experienced writers are invited to read their work to an audience. If you're brave enough to commit yourself to reading like this, you'll find yourself in a fever of revision, reading the piece aloud many times and getting every word just right. Or you might decide that you're ready to start sending your work out for publication (see the website for publication information). Find one journal and read as many copies as you can; then revise your piece with this publication in mind. You'll surprise yourself with the focus you can generate once the piece leaves the personal arena and goes public.

Three Quick Fixes for Stronger Prose

After you've done the big labor on your essay, you'll want to do the finish work, the small things that make the prose really shine. (We don't mean to suggest that these two processes are mutually exclusive; naturally, you'll find yourself adjusting the prose as you go along.) We have three quick fixes that make any piece stronger—we call these "Search and Destroy," the "Adjective/Adverb Purge," and the "Punch."

1. *Search and Destroy*

   The most overused verbs in the English language are the forms of "to be"—"is," "are," "were," "was," and so on. While these verbs are necessary (note how we just used two of them in the two pre-ceding sentences!), you can often sharpen your prose by going over the piece carefully and eliminating as many of them as you can. To do this, you'll need to look closely at the words sur-rounding the "to be" verbs; frequently you can find stronger verbs, or juicier nouns, to take their place. Even if you only elim-inate one or two of these, the resultant prose will seem much cleaner and lighter. It's the kind of work the reader won't notice (except for word nuts like us!), but it will immediately make your prose more professional.

   Take a draft of an essay that's nearly finished. Go through it with a red pen and circle all the forms of "to be." Go back and see whether you can rework any of the sentences to eliminate these verbs and replace them with words that feel more "muscled" or have more impact. Sometimes you'll find you don't need the sen-tence at all, and you'll have eliminated some deadweight. If you're working in a group, exchange essays with one another and do the same thing. Suggest new lines that eliminate the forms of "to be."

2. *The Adjective/Adverb Purge*

   Often adjectives are your enemy rather than your friend. Adjec-tives or adverbs can act like crutches, holding up weak nouns or verbs, and they actually water down your prose rather than inten-sify it. As with the "Search and Destroy" exercise above, the point here is not to eliminate every adjective and adverb, but to scruti-nize each one and see whether it's necessary for the point you want to get across.

Take an essay you think is nearly finished and circle every adjective and adverb. Go back and see whether you can rework the sentences to eliminate these words and replace them with stronger verbs or nouns. Or you can take stronger measures: For at least one writing session, ban adjectives and adverbs from your vocabulary. See how this exercise forces you to find more vivid nouns and verbs for your prose.

3. *The Punch*

Professional writers develop a fine ear for language. Writers are really musicians, "aural" artists attuned to every rhythm and nuance of their prose. And if you study the writers you admire, you'll invariably find that they tend to end most of their sentences, all of their paragraphs, and certainly the closing line of their essays with potent words that pack a punch. They don't allow their sentences to trail off, but instead close them firmly and strongly with words that leave the reader satisfied. When you work toward strong closing words in your sentences, the prose also takes on a new sense of momentum and trajectory, the sentences rearranging themselves in fresh ways to wield that satisfying "crack" at the end.

Read your essay aloud, paying attention to the sounds of the words at the ends of sentences and paragraphs. Do they ring clearly and cleanly, firmly ending your thought? Or do they trail off into abstraction? Circle any words that seem weak to you; then go back and rework these sentences for better closing effects. Pay particular attention to the word you use to end the entire essay. How do you leave your reader? What will he or she remember?

An Example of the Writing Process

We asked writer Bernard Cooper (see "The Fine Art of Sighing" in the anthology section) for his thoughts on the writing process. Here's what he had to say:

A friend of mine once said that she needed two things in order to write: paper, and Liquid Paper. This was before she used a computer, or course, but I think her statement illustrates the importance of revision, the necessity to change and perfect what one has written down. I edit relentlessly—have already revised this very statement. My prose itself tends to come in short bursts, while the bulk of my time is involved in trying different words and sentence structures and punctuation so those word-bursts say exactly what I want them to. Revision seems to me the writer's most crucial task; you are given the chance to make your work as powerful as possible. "Words are all we have," said novelist Evan Connell, "and they'd better be the right ones." Anyone who has written for long knows the pleasure in finding the word that makes a description suddenly more vivid, or finding the structure that makes a sentence more taut, surprising, rhythmic, or funny.

"The Fine Art of Sighing," like much of my work, came to me as a vague idea, and then the substance of it was worked out as I went along. I had no idea where the idea would lead me—I certainly didn't suspect to Venice—and I arrived at my conclusion sentence by sentence. I listened to my sentences, worked with them until they expressed sentiments impossible to put in any other way. I do remember how excited I was by the sentence where my mother scratches my father's back because "found on his back and scratched" puts such finality and emphasis on the word "scratched," which is such a wonderfully onomatopoeic word. The sound of the words seemed important in this piece, since it was about the sound of sighing. The various people I describe sighing were a fairly arbitrary lot, but I wanted to give the reader a sense they represent all of us, so I played with their occupations and their locations and the reasons for their sighs. That play was revision.

When you write well, you'll feel the same sense of "play." Revision becomes not a chore, but the essence of the writing act itself. What came before cleared the way for what's to come; no writing is ever wasted, no time spent at the desk is ever useless. Writing creates its own rhythm and momentum, and you must be willing to go with it, to become absorbed in the task, to let go of the writing you once thought precious. It's exhausting work, requiring stamina and rigor, but the rewards keep you going.

At one time or another, many writers experience what they call "gifts"—essays or poems or stories that seem to come effortlessly, full-blown onto the page with little revision or effort. But as the poet Richard Hugo puts it, "Lucky accidents seldom happen to writers who don't work. . . . The hard work you do on one poem is put in on all poems. The hard work on the first poem is responsible for the sudden ease of the second. If you just sit around waiting for the easy ones, nothing will come. Get to work."

Try It

The Drafting Process

1. Take a writing session to observe everything you do. What's your routine? How does it serve or sabotage you? What keeps you from writing? What helps you? What happens when you change your routine?

2. Do you have an "inner critic" that immediately censors or criticizes your writing? Take a piece of paper and draw a line down the center. On the right side, begin writing, perhaps from one of the writing exercises in part II. On the left side, write down any "critic" thoughts that come to mind as you write. (Don't worry if the session becomes only "critic" thoughts; it happens all the time!) Do this for about five or ten minutes; then go back and read what the critic has to say to you.

On a new sheet of paper, begin a dialogue with your inner critic. How does the critic both enable and sabotage your writing? For example, one of our students realized that the critic was merely trying to protect her from the harsh criticism the world might heap on her; rather than a hostile presence, the critic was actually quite benevolent. Once she realized this, she was better able to circumvent the thoughts that stopped her from writing.

Global Revision versus Line Editing

3. Take out a piece you wrote at least a month ago. Read it aloud, either to yourself or to a kind audience. Make note of the paragraphs that feel rich and full and those that are not as strong. Are there any areas that surprise you? What's the essay really about? What can be cut out and saved for another time? What should be included but was left out at first?

Here are some specific questions to ask yourself as you go about the global revision process:

- Is there one image that can be used as a cohesive thread throughout the piece? How can you amplify this image and transform it from beginning to end?

- Have you chosen the most effective point of view for telling the story? What happens if you experiment with third person or second person? (See chapter 1 for a discussion of point of view in creative nonfiction.)

- Look closely at the beginning paragraph of your essay. Do you begin in a way that draws the reader in? Often the first few paragraphs of a rough draft merely "clear the throat." Is the true beginning really a few pages in?

- Look closely at the ending. Do you end in a way that leaves the reader with a compelling image? Often it's tempting to "sum up" the essay in a way that can be wholly unsatisfying to the reader. Can you end on an image rather than an idea?

- How do the beginning and ending paragraphs mirror or echo one another? The first and last paragraphs act as a "frame" for the piece as a whole. They are, in a way, the most important places in the essay, because they determine everything that happens in between. If you make an effort to connect them in some way—repeating a key image from the beginning, bringing back on stage the major players for a final bow—you'll find a stunning finish to the piece.

Suggestions for Further Reading

In Our Anthology

Atwood, Margaret, "Nine Beginnings"

Cooper, Bernard, "The Fine Art of Sighing"

On Our Website

Dubus, Andre, "Love in the Morning"

Hampl, Patricia, "The Need to Say It"

Elsewhere

Dillard, Annie, *The Writing Life*

Goldberg, Natalie, *Writing Down the Bones*

Hugo, Richard, *The Triggering Town*

Lamott, Anne, *Bird by Bird*

Sternburg, Janet, *The Writer on Her Work*, Vols. I and II

Strunk, William Jr., and White, E. B., *The Elements of Style*

Ueland, Brenda, *If You Want to Write*

Writers at Work, *The Paris Review Interview Series*

Epilogue

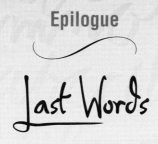

Last Words

Starting here, what do you want to remember?
How sunlight creeps along a shining floor?
What scent of old wood hovers, what softened
sound from outside fills the air?

Will you ever bring a better gift for the world
than the breathing respect that you carry
wherever you go right now? Are you waiting
for time to show you some better thoughts?

—William Stafford, from "You Reading This, Be Ready"

Lately I've been reading the selected poems of William Stafford, including some of the poetry he wrote the year before he died. Stafford was in the habit of getting up every day at 4 A.M.; he wrote, by hand, during the dark, quiet hours in his study. He wrote about the simple things, the small things, in a voice that carries with it that sense of early morning meditation.

I don't know whether Stafford felt his approaching death (he was 80, after all, and perhaps at some point we can no longer deny that particular specter at our door), but the poems written during those final days have the quality of "last words": stripped of artifice, speaking from a self that wants only to understand and be understood. These are poems that want us to pay attention—not to abstract ideas and philosophies, not to idle worries or regrets, but to the world as it unfolds before us, every minute, every day. And as I read these poems, I'm thinking that all of our writing, perhaps, could be written with this kind of disposition: with the tenor of last words, the essays we would leave behind if no further writing were possible. —**Brenda**

These days, whenever I visit one of my friends, her twelve-year-old daughter begs for my stories. My own son, at four-and-a-half, is already too jaded to listen to me for very long, but suddenly my baby boom New York–area history fascinates Elisabeth. I find it hard to come up with enough anecdotes to satisfy her curiosity. She's mesmerized that I saw the Rolling Stones and the Grateful Dead when they were young bands; she fires questions at me about *Apollo 11,* or how I watched Richard Nixon's motorcade once as his thick makeup sweated down in the heat. She wants to know about the antiwar protests and race riots I grew up with. These are topics she's studying in school, and I reach deep into that trusty and unquestioned valise—my life—to find material to satisfy her.

It's hard to believe, but our lives—secret, banal, and full of Kleenexes and bus schedules as they are—form stepping stones to the future and vital links to the past. What we've lived through and done will define the world as it exists hundreds of years from now. We're the only witnesses to this, our time, which is as wondrous and banal as any moment in history and which carries its full complement of world-changing events: wars fought, great art made, rights hard won. Value your own life, and the experiences you've had: they're priceless. At the same time, learn to love the world you live in: Hike urban streets, mountain trails, or, better yet, both. Go to places you've never thought of going before; talk to everyone you meet with the assumption that his or her life is just as interesting as yours. Fall in love, be passionate, and the stories of your time will be yours to tell. —**Suzanne**

Regaining Passion

Sometimes when you're in a writing class or studying writing intensively, it's easy to lose, temporarily, the passion that brought you to writing in the first place. It's easy to feel as if you've taken all the magic out of it, and you sit at your desk, bored or resistant, unable to find one single thing worth writing about. Especially when you write creative nonfiction, it's easy to feel you've used up all your material, plumbed all your memories, reflected on everything there is to reflect about. Your mirror has lost its luster; your pen has run dry of ink.

When this happens (and it happens to all of us), you must do whatever it takes to "refill the well." This might mean just taking some time out to roam the city or spending a week on the couch with your favorite books and comfort food. It might mean making a date with your writing group or deciding to write poetry or fiction for a while instead. The important thing to remember is that *your passion for writing will come back.* Your passion for writing will always return, doubled in force, after a period of dormancy. The writing life is one of patience and faith.

As you've read through this book, you've received all kinds of writing prompts to trigger new work; you've read about techniques, and you've learned a bit about the philosophical and ethical challenges of creative nonfiction. You've read some writers you admire and some that you don't. You've perhaps learned new ways to approach your own memories, your research interests, and your ideas. Now, with all this knowledge still settling inside your head, we want to tell you one last thing:

Forget it all.

Don't forget it forever. But just forget it for now. Take a moment to be quiet in the space where you do your best work, at the time when the muses are most present. Try to remember what it's like to be a beginner; regain what the Zen masters call "beginner's mind," open to all possibilities. When you're ready, we offer you this one last

Try It

What are your "last words?" What would you write if you knew your time was up? What would you notice in the world around you? What's important for us to hear?

PART IV

Anthology

Preface to the Anthology

Read, read, read. Read everything—trash, classics, good and bad, and see how they do it. Just like a carpenter who works as an apprentice and studies the master. Read! You'll absorb it. Then write. If it is good, you'll find out. If it's not, throw it out the window. —**William Faulkner**

There's no getting around it: Reading and writing go hand in hand. You can't be a good writer without also being a good reader. You *must* read widely, with the eye of a writer, engrossed not only in the plot or the characters or the descriptions, but attuned to the craft that makes these things come alive on the page. You read to hear other writers' voices, but you also read to tune your *own* voice, to remember what gets you excited about writing in the first place.

Sometimes reading can act as your muse for writing. The two of us often warm up to the writing task by reading a little first, to remind ourselves of the sounds and rhythms of literature. Sometimes we read *while* we're writing—getting up from the desk to roam the house, reading in short bursts like marathon runners downing their Dixie cups of Gatorade. We pick up poetry, short stories, essays, novels, or magazines. Then we hurry back to our desks and write the line or, if we're lucky, the whole paragraph we've been waiting for.

Sometimes, when you're writing, you can feel as if you suffer from momentary bouts of amnesia in between the few sentences you manage to get down at a time. You forget how to put one word in front of the other, so you go to the voices you love to remind yourself. You continually learn the craft all over again.

The anthology section that follows contains work that models the particular aspects of creative nonfiction we've discussed throughout *Tell It Slant*. This mini-collection is by no means meant to be a comprehensive survey of the genre (there are many terrific anthologies out there for that; see the suggested reading in Chapter 9, "The Personal Essay"), but only a way to get you started. If you find authors you admire in this section, we encourage you to go out and find their books. Read literary journals from the library to see what your contemporaries are up to.

Take it upon yourself to become a scholar of creative nonfiction; take on the mantle of the "apprentice." Writer Nicholas DelBanco puts it this way: "I have carried with me for some time . . . the notion of writers as artisans, or artists engaged in a guild . . . with its compelling triad of apprentice, then journeyman laborer, then master craftsman—this last attained after a lifetime's study and practice of the craft." The writers you read become your larger community and provide the standards by which you can begin to measure your own work.

Questions for Reading Like a Writer

Here's a list of questions to ask yourself as you read the works in this anthology. These lines of inquiry will lead you past your surface reaction as a reader ("gee, I really liked that ending," or "god, I *hated* that line!") and into a more rigorous engagement with the craft issues at work in the prose. Read an essay once for the content; then read it again with a pen or pencil in hand to make note of *how* these writers make literature out of experience.

Questions to Ask Yourself

- What are the major themes of the piece? Are there any minor themes as well? Is there any kind of "subtext" to the essay? What kind of murmur runs below the surface?

- What specific details stay in your mind? Why? How do these small details lead to larger ideas?

- Does any particular image repeat throughout the essay? If so, why did the author choose it? Does it have "metaphorical significance"? Is it transformed in any way from beginning to end?

- Find specific examples of abstract (ideas and concepts) and concrete (specific details, sensory impressions) language. What are the effects?

- How does the writer create characters?

- Identify where the writer chooses to expand into a full-fledged scene. Is it a "representative" scene or a "specific" one?

- What kind of rhythm does the writer create? Is there a variety in the sentence structure? Read the piece aloud to get a sense of the writer's voice.

- How does the writer structure the essay and to what effect? (Why does it begin where it does? Why does it end with the image or scene the writer chose? Is it a linear narrative? Or one that is fragmented or circular?)

- Break the piece down paragraph by paragraph (or section by section). How does each piece act as a "building block"? How does the writer create dramatic tension or interest through these building blocks?

- Look at the transitions the writer makes, either between paragraphs or between sections. How does he or she make these transitions? What effect do they have on the forward momentum of the piece?

- Look at the first and last paragraphs. Are they linked in any way? Do they echo each other?

- How does the writer create significance? How does the piece move from the personal to the universal?

- Are there any moments that seem weak or clichéd to you? If so, why? If this were your essay, how would you change those moments?

- Is there anything about this essay that provides a model for your own writing?

Nine Beginnings

Margaret Atwood

1. *Why do you write?*

I've begun this piece nine times. I've junked each beginning.

I hate writing about my writing. I almost never do it. Why am I doing it now? Because I said I would. I got a letter. I wrote back *no*. Then I was at a party and the same person was there. It's harder to refuse in person. Saying *yes* had something to do with being nice, as women are taught to be, and something to do with being helpful, which we are also taught. Being helpful to women, giving a pint of blood. With not claiming the sacred prerogatives, the touch-me-not self-protectiveness of the artist, with not being selfish. With conciliation, with doing your bit, with appeasement. I was well brought up. I have trouble ignoring social obligations. Saying you'll write about your writing is a social obligation. It's not an obligation to the writing.

2. *Why do you write?*

I've junked each of nine beginnings. They seemed beside the point. Too assertive, too pedagogical, too frivolous or belligerent, too falsely wise. As if I had some special self-revelation that would encourage others, or some special knowledge to impart, some pithy saying that

199

would act like a talisman for the driven, the obsessed. But I have no such talismans. If I did, I would not continue, myself, to be so driven and obsessed.

3. *Why do you write?*

I hate writing about my writing because I have nothing to say about it. I have nothing to say about it because I can't remember what goes on when I'm doing it. That time is like small pieces cut out of my brain. It's not time I myself have lived. I can remember the details of the rooms and places where I've written, the circumstances, the other things I did before and after, but not the process itself. Writing about writing requires self-consciousness; writing itself requires the abdication of it.

4. *Why do you write?*

There are a lot of things that can be said about what goes on around the edges of writing. Certain ideas you may have, certain motivations, grand designs that don't get carried out. I can talk about bad reviews, about sexist reactions to my writing, about making an idiot of myself on television shows. I can talk about books that failed, that never got finished, and about why they failed. The one that had too many characters, the one that had too many layers of time, red herrings that diverted me when what I really wanted to get at was something else, a certain corner of the visual world, a certain voice, an inarticulate landscape.

I can talk about the difficulties that women encounter as writers. For instance, if you're a woman writer, sometime, somewhere, you will be asked: *Do you think of yourself as a writer first, or as a woman first?* Look out. Whoever asks this hates and fears both writing and women.

Many of us, in my generation at least, ran into teachers or male writers or other defensive jerks who told us women could not really write because they couldn't be truck drivers or Marines and therefore didn't understand the seamier side of life, which included sex with women. We were told we wrote like housewives, or else we were treated like honorary men, as if to be a good writer was to suppress the female.

Such pronouncements used to be made as if they were the simple truth. Now they're questioned. Some things have changed for the better, but not all. There's a lack of self-confidence that gets instilled very early in many young girls, before writing is even seen as a possibility. You need a certain amount of nerve to be a writer, an almost physical nerve, the kind you need to walk a log across a river. The horse throws you and you get back on the horse. I learned to swim by being dropped into the water. You need to know you can sink, and survive it. Girls should be allowed to play in the mud. They should be released from the obligations of perfection. Some of your writing, at least, should be as evanescent as play.

A ratio of failures is built into the process of writing. The wastebasket has evolved for a reason. Think of it as the altar of the Muse Oblivion, to whom you sacrifice your botched first drafts, the tokens of your human imperfection. She is the tenth Muse, the one without whom none of the others can function. The gift she offers you is the freedom of the second chance. Or as many chances as you'll take.

5. *Why do you write?*

In the mid-eighties I began a sporadic journal. Today I went back through it, looking for something I could dig out and fob off as pertinent, instead of writing this piece about writing. But it was useless. There was nothing in it about the actual composition of anything I've written over the past six years. Instead there are exhortations to myself—to get up earlier, to walk more, to resist lures and distractions. *Drink more water,* I find. *Go to bed earlier.* There were lists of how many pages I'd written per day, how many I'd retyped, how many yet to go. Other than that, there was nothing but descriptions of rooms, accounts of what we'd cooked and/or eaten and with whom, letters written and received, notable sayings of children, birds and animals seen, the weather. What came up in the garden. Illnesses, my own and those of others. Deaths, births. Nothing about writing.

> January 1, 1984. Blakeny, England. As of today, I have about 130 pp. of the novel done and it's just beginning to take shape & reach the point at which I feel that it exists and can be finished and may be worth it. I work in the bedroom of the big house, and here, in the sitting room, with the wood fire in the fireplace and the coke fire in the dilapidated Roeburn in the kitchen. As usual I'm too cold, which is better than being too hot—today is grey, warm for the time of year, damp. If I got up earlier maybe I would work more, but I might just spend more time procrastinating—as now.

And so on.

6. *Why do you write?*

You learn to write by reading and writing, writing and reading. As a craft it's acquired through the apprentice system, but you choose your own teachers. Sometimes they're alive, sometimes dead.

As a vocation, it involves the laying on of hands. You receive your vocation and in your turn you must pass it on. Perhaps you will do this only through your work, perhaps in other ways. Either way, you're part of a community, the community of writers, the community of storytellers that stretches back through time to the beginning of human society.

As for the particular human society to which you yourself belong—sometimes you'll feel you're speaking for it, sometimes—when it's taken an unjust form—against it, or for that other community, the community of the oppressed, the exploited, the voiceless. Either way, the pressures on you will be intense; in other countries, perhaps fatal. But even here—speak "for women," or for any other group which is feeling the boot, and there will be many at hand, both for and against, to tell you to shut up, or to say what they want you to say, or to say it a different way. Or to save them. The billboard awaits you, but if you succumb to its temptations you'll end up two-dimensional.

Tell what is yours to tell. Let others tell what is theirs.

7. *Why do you write?*

Why are we so addicted to causality? *Why do* you *write?* (Treatise by child psychologist, mapping your formative traumas. Conversely: palm-reading, astrology and genetic studies, pointing to the stars, fate, heredity.) *Why do you write?* (That is, why not do something useful instead?) If you were a doctor, you could tell some acceptable moral tale about how you put Band-Aids on your cats as a child, how you've always longed to cure suffering. No one can argue with that. But writing? What is it *for?*

Some possible answers: *Why does the sun shine? In the face of the absurdity of modern society, why do anything else? Because I'm a writer. Because I want to discover the patterns in the chaos of time. Because I must. Because someone has to bear witness. Why do you read?* (This last is tricky: maybe they don't.) *Because I wish to forge in the smithy of my soul the uncreated conscience of my race. Because I wish to make an axe to break the frozen sea within.* (These have been used, but they're good.)

If at a loss, perfect the shrug. Or say: *It's better than working in a bank.* Or say: *For fun.* If you say this, you won't be believed, or else you'll be dismissed as trivial. Either way, you'll have avoided the question.

8. *Why do you write?*

Not long ago, in the course of clearing some of the excess paper out of my workroom, I opened a filing cabinet drawer I hadn't looked into for years. In it was a bundle of loose sheets, folded, creased, and grubby, tied up with leftover string. It consisted of things I'd written in the late fifties, in high school and the early years of university. There were scrawled, inky poems, about snow, despair, and the Hungarian Revolution. There were short stories dealing with girls who'd had to get married, and dispirited, mousy-haired high-school English teach-ers—to end up as either was at that time my vision of Hell—typed finger-by-finger on an ancient machine that made all the letters half-red.

There I am, then, back in grade twelve, going through the writers' magazines after I'd finished my French Composition homework, typ-ing out my lugubrious poems and my grit-filled stories. (I was big on grit. I had an eye for lawn-litter and dog turds on sidewalks. In these stories it was usually snowing damply, or raining; at the very least there was slush. If it was summer, the heat and humidity were always wiltingly high and my characters had sweat marks under their arms; if it was spring, wet clay stuck to their feet. Though some would say all this was just normal Toronto weather.)

In the top right-hand corners of some of these, my hopeful seventeen-year-old self had typed, "First North American Rights Only." I was not sure what "First North American Rights" were; I put it in be-cause the writing magazines said you should. I was at that time an afi-cionado of writing magazines, having no one else to turn to for professional advice.

If I were an archeologist, digging through the layers of old paper that mark the eras in my life as a writer, I'd have found, at the lowest or Stone Age level—say around ages five to seven—a few poems and sto-ries, unremarkable precursors of all my frenetic later scribbling. (Many children write at that age, just as many children draw. The strange thing is that so few of them go on to become writers or painters.) After that there's a great blank. For eight years, I simply didn't write. Then, sud-denly, and with no missing links in between, there's a wad of manu-scripts. One week I wasn't a writer, the next I was.

Who did I think I was, to be able to get away with this? What did I think I was doing? How did I get that way? To these questions I still have no answers.

9. *Why do you write?*

There's the blank page, and the thing that obsesses you. There's the story that wants to take you over and there's your resistance to it. There's your longing to get out of this, this servitude, to play hooky, to do anything else: wash the laundry, see a movie. There are words and their inertias, their biases, their insufficiencies, their glories. There are the risks you take and your loss of nerve, and the help that comes when you're least expecting it. There's the laborious revision, the scrawled-over, crumpled-up pages that drift across the floor like spilled litter. There's the one sentence you know you will save.

Next day there's the blank page. You give yourself up to it like a sleepwalker. Something goes on that you can't remember afterwards. You look at what you've done. It's hopeless.

You begin again. It never gets any easier.

Margaret Atwood

Canadian author Margaret Atwood has written over twenty-five books, including The Handmaid's Tale *and bestsellers* The Robber Bride, Alias Grace, *and* The Blind Assassin. *Atwood has also published numerous volumes of poetry, short fiction, children's literature, and essays, as well as critical articles in* The Washington Post, The Nation, *and other periodicals. She lives in Toronto, and was born on November 18, 1939 in Ottawa, Ontario.*

My Children Explain the Big Issues

Will Baker

Feminism

I am walking up a long hill toward our water tank and pond. My daughter Montana, 23 months, has decided to accompany me. It is a very warm day, so she wears only diapers, cowboy boots, and a floral-print bonnet. At the outset I offer to carry her but she says "I walk," and then, "You don't have to hold my hand, daddy."

This is the longest walk she has taken, without assistance. I see droplets of sweat on the bridge of her nose. Just before the water tank there is a steep pitch and loose gravel on the path, so I offer again to help.

She pulls away and says, "You don't have to hold me, daddy." A moment later she slips and falls flat. A pause while she rolls into a sitting position and considers, her mouth bent down. But quickly she scrambles up and slaps at the dirty places on her knees, then looks at me sidelong with a broad grin. "See?"

Fate

I first explained to Cole that there was no advantage in dumping the sand from his sandbox onto the patio. He would have more fun bulldozing and trucking inside the two-by-twelve frame. Heavy-equipment guys stayed within the boundaries, part of their job, and the sand would be no good scattered abroad, would get mixed with dead beetles and cat poop.

Next I warned him firmly not to shovel out his patrimony, warned him twice. The third time I physically removed him from the box and underscored my point very emphatically. At this stage, he was in danger of losing important privileges. Reasonable tolerance had already been shown him and there was no further room for negotiation. There was a line in the sand. Did he understand the gravity of the situation? Between whimpers, he nodded.

The last time I lifted him by his ear, held his contorted face close to mine, and posed a furious question to him: "*Why? Why are you doing this?*"

Shaking all over with sobs of deep grief, he tried to answer.

"*Eyeadhoo.*"

"What?"

"Eyeadhoo, eyeadhoo!"

One more second, grinding my teeth, and the translation came to me. I had to. I had to.

Existentialism

Cole is almost three and has had a sister now for four months. All his old things have been resurrected. Crib, changing table, car seat, backpack, bassinet. There have been visitors visiting, doctors doctoring, a washer and dryer always washing and drying.

He has taken to following me around when I go to work on a tractor or pump, cut firewood, or feed the horses. We are out of the house. It doesn't matter if it is raining. In our slickers and rubber boots we stride through a strip of orchard, on our way to some small chore. I am involved with a problem of my own, fooling with a metaphor or calculating if it's time to spray for leaf curl. The rain drumming on the hood of the slicker, wet grass swooshing against the boots, I completely forget my son is there.

"Hey dad," he says suddenly, and I wake up, look down at him, and see that he is in a state of serious wonder, serious delight. "We're *alone* together, aren't we dad?"

East and West

My other daughter, Willa, is a Tibetan Buddhist nun on retreat. For three years I cannot see her. She writes me to explain subtle points of the doctrine of emptiness, or the merit in abandoning ego, serving others unselfishly.

I will write back to remind her of a party I took her to in 1970. The apartment was painted entirely in black, and candles were burning. There was loud music and a smell of incense and skunky weed. It was very crowded, some dancing and others talking and laughing. People were wearing ornaments of turquoise, bone, feather, and stained glass.

I glimpsed my six-year-old daughter, at midnight, sitting cross-legged on the floor opposite a young man with very long blond hair. He had no shoes and his shirt was only a painted rag. They were in very deep conversation, eyes locked. I did not hear what the young man had just said, but I overheard my daughter very clearly, her voice definite and assured.

"But," she was saying, "you and I are not the same person."

Will Baker
Born in Idaho, Will Baker grew up in the West and taught at the University of California at Davis from 1969 to 1995. He currently operates a small farm in northern California.

Notes of a Native Son

James Baldwin

On the 29th of July, in 1943, my father died. On the same day, a few hours later, his last child was born. Over a month before this, while all our energies were concentrated in waiting for these events, there had been, in Detroit, one of the bloodiest race riots of the century. A few hours after my father's funeral, while he lay in state in the undertaker's chapel, a race riot broke out in Harlem. On the morning of the 3rd of August, we drove my father to the graveyard through a wilderness of smashed plate glass.

The day of my father's funeral had also been my nineteenth birthday. As we drove him to the graveyard, the spoils of injustice, anarchy, discontent, and hatred were all around us. It seemed to me that God himself had devised, to mark my father's end, the most sustained and brutally dissonant of codas. And it seemed to me, too, that the violence which rose all about us as my father left the world had been devised as a corrective for the pride of his eldest son. I had declined to believe in that apocalypse which had been central to my father's vision; very well, life seemed to be saying, here is something that will certainly pass for an apocalypse until the real thing comes along. I had inclined to be contemptuous of my father for the conditions of his life, for the conditions of our lives. When his life had ended I began to wonder about that life and also, in a new way, to be apprehensive about my own.

I had not known my father very well. We had got on badly, partly because we shared, in our different fashions, the vice of stubborn pride. When he was dead I realized that I had hardly ever spoken to him. When he had been dead a long time I began to wish I had. It seems to be typical of life in America, where opportunities, real and fancied, are thicker than anywhere else on the globe, that the second generation has no time to talk to the first. No one, including my father, seems to have known exactly how old he was, but his mother had been born during slavery. He was of the first generation of free men. He, along with thousands of other Negroes, came North after 1919 and I was part of that generation which had never seen the landscape of what Negroes sometimes call the Old Country.

He had been born in New Orleans and had been a quite young man there during the time that Louis Armstrong, a boy, was running errands for the dives and honky-tonks of what was always presented to me as one of the most wicked of cities—to this day, whenever I think of New Orleans, I also helplessly think of Sodom and Gomorrah. My father never mentioned Louis Armstrong, except to forbid us to play his records; but there was a picture of him on our wall for a long time. One of my father's strong-willed female relatives had placed it there and forbade my father to take it down. He never did, but he eventually maneuvered her out of the house and when, some years later, she was in trouble and near death, he refused to do anything to help her.

He was, I think, very handsome. I gather this from photographs and from my own memories of him, dressed in his Sunday best and on his way to preach a sermon somewhere, when I was little. Handsome, proud, and ingrown, "like a toe-nail," somebody said. But he looked to me, as I grew older, like pictures I had seen of African tribal chieftains: he really should have been naked, with war-paint on and barbaric mementos, standing among spears. He could be chilling in the pulpit and indescribably cruel in his personal life and he was certainly the most bitter man I have ever met; yet it must be said that there was something else in him, buried in him, which lent him his tremendous power and, even, a rather crushing charm. It had something to do with his blackness, I think—he was very black—with his blackness and his beauty, and with the fact that he knew that he was black but did not know that he was beautiful. He claimed to be proud of his blackness but it had also been the cause of much humiliation and it had fixed bleak boundaries to his life. He was not a young man when we were growing up and he had already suffered many kinds of ruin; in his outrageously demanding and protective way he loved his children, who were black like him and menaced, like him; and all these things sometimes showed in his face when he tried, never to my knowledge with any success, to establish contact with any of us. When he took one of his children on his knee to play, the child always became fretful and began to cry; when he tried to help one of us with our homework the absolutely unabating tension which emanated from him caused our minds and our tongues to become paralyzed, so that he, scarcely knowing why, flew into a rage and the child, not knowing why, was punished. If it ever entered his head to bring a surprise home for his children, it was, almost unfailingly, the wrong surprise and even the big watermelons he often brought home on his back in the summertime led to the most appalling scenes. I do not remember, in all those years, that one of his children was ever glad to see him come home. From what I was able to gather of his early life, it seemed that this inability to establish contact with other people had always marked him and had been one of the things which had driven him out of New Orleans. There was something in him, therefore, groping and tentative, which was never expressed and which was buried with him. One saw it most clearly when he was facing new people and hoping to impress them. But he never did, not for long. We went from church to smaller and more improbable church, he found himself in less and less demand as a minister, and by the time he died none of his friends had come to see him for a long time. He had lived and died in an intolerable bitterness of spirit and it frightened me, as we drove him to the graveyard through those unquiet, ruined streets, to see how powerful and overflowing this bitterness could be and to realize that this bitterness now was mine.

When he died I had been away from home for a little over a year. In that year I had had time to become aware of the meaning of all my father's bitter warnings, had discovered the secret of his proudly pursed lips and rigid carriage: I had discovered the weight of white people in the world. I saw that this had been for my ancestors and now would be for me an awful thing to live with and that the bitterness which had helped to kill my father could also kill me.

He had been ill a long time—in the mind, as we now realized, reliving instances of his fantastic intransigence in the new light of his affliction and endeavoring to feel a sorrow for him which never, quite, came true. We had not known that he was being eaten up by paranoia, and the discovery that his cruelty, to our bodies and our minds, had been one of the symptoms of his illness was not, then, enough to enable us to forgive him. The younger children felt, quite simply, relief that he would not be coming home anymore. My mother's observation that it was he, after all, who had kept them alive all these years meant nothing because the problems of keeping children alive are not real for children. The older children felt, with my father gone, that they could invite their friends to the house without fear that their friends would be insulted or, as had sometimes happened with me, being told that their friends were in league with the devil and intended to rob our family of everything we owned. (I didn't fail to wonder, and it made me hate him, what on earth we owned that anybody else would want.)

His illness was beyond all hope of healing before anyone realized that he was ill. He had always been so strange and had lived, like a prophet, in such unimaginably close communion with the Lord that his long silences which were punctuated by moans and hallelujahs and snatches of old songs while he sat at the living-room window never seemed odd to us. It was not until he refused to eat because, he said, his family was trying to poison him that my mother was forced to accept as a fact what had, until then, been only an unwilling suspicion. When he was committed, it was discovered that he had tuberculosis and, as it turned out, the disease of his mind allowed the disease of his body to destroy him. For the doctors could not force him to eat, either, and, though he was fed intravenously, it was clear from the beginning that there was no hope for him.

In my mind's eye I could see him, sitting at the window, locked up in his terrors; hating and fearing every living soul including his children who had betrayed him, too, by reaching towards the world which had despised him. There were nine of us. I began to wonder what it could have felt like for such a man to have had nine children whom he could barely feed. He used to make little jokes about our poverty, which never, of course, seemed very funny to us; they could not have seemed very funny to him, either, or else our all too feeble response to them would never have caused such rages. He spent great energy and achieved, to our chagrin, no small amount of success in keeping us away from the people who surrounded us, people who had all-night rent parties to which we listened when we should have been sleeping, people who cursed and drank and flashed razor blades on Lenox Avenue. He could not understand why, if they had so much energy to spare, they could not use it to make their lives better. He treated almost everybody on our block with a most uncharitable asperity and neither they, nor, of course, their children were slow to reciprocate.

The only white people who came to our house were welfare workers and bill collectors. It was almost always my mother who dealt with them, for my father's temper, which was at the mercy of his pride, was never to be trusted. It was clear that he felt their very presence in his home to be a violation: this was conveyed by his carriage, almost ludicrously stiff, and by his voice, harsh and vindictively polite. When I was around nine or ten I wrote a play which was directed by a young, white schoolteacher, a woman, who then took an interest in me, and gave me books to read and, in order to corroborate my theatrical bent, decided to take me to see what she somewhat tactlessly referred to as "real" plays. Theater-going was forbidden in our house, but, with the really cruel intuitiveness of a child, I suspected that the color of this woman's skin would carry the day for me. When, at school, she suggested taking me to the theater, I did not, as I might have done if she had been a Negro, find a way of discouraging her, but agreed that she should pick me up at my house one evening. I then, very cleverly, left all the rest to my mother, who suggested to my father, as I knew she would, that it would not be very nice to let such a kind woman make the trip for nothing. Also, since it was a schoolteacher, I imagine that my mother countered the idea of sin with the idea of "education," which word, even with my father, carried a kind of bitter weight.

Before the teacher came my father took me aside to ask *why* she was coming, what *interest* she could possibly have in our house, in a boy like me. I said I didn't know but I, too, suggested that it had something to do with education. And I understood that my father was waiting for me to say something—I didn't quite know what; perhaps that I wanted his protection against this teacher and her "education." I said none of these things and the teacher came and we went out. It was clear, during the brief interview in our living room, that my father was agreeing very much against his will and that he would have refused permission if he had dared. The fact that he did not dare caused me to despise him: I had no way of knowing that he was facing in that living room a wholly unprecedented and frightening situation.

Later, when my father had been laid off from his job, this woman became very important to us. She was really a very sweet and generous woman and went to a great deal of trouble to be of help to us, particularly during one awful winter. My mother called her by the highest name she knew: she said she was a "christian." My father could scarcely disagree but during the four or five years of our relatively close association he never trusted her and was always trying to surprise in her open, Midwestern face the genuine, cunningly hidden, and hideous motivation. In later years, particularly when it began to be clear that this "education" of mine was going to lead me to perdition, he became more explicit and warned me that my white friends in high school were not really my friends and that I would see, when I was older, how white people would do anything to keep a Negro down. Some of them could be nice, he admitted, but none of them were to be trusted and most of them were not even nice. The best thing was to have as little to do with them as possible. I did not feel this way and I was certain, in my innocence, that I never would.

But the year which preceded my father's death had made a great change in my life. I had been living in New Jersey, working in defense plants, working and living among southerners, white and black. I knew about the south, of course, and about how southerners treated Negroes and how they expected them to behave, but it had never entered my mind that anyone would look at me and expect *me* to behave that way. I learned in New Jersey that to be a Negro meant, precisely, that one was never looked at but was simply at the mercy of the reflexes the color of one's skin caused in other people. I acted in New Jersey as I had always acted, that is as though I thought a great deal of myself—I had to *act* that way—with results that were, simply, unbelievable. I had scarcely arrived before I had earned the enmity, which was extraordinarily ingenious, of all my superiors and nearly all my co-workers. In the beginning, to make matters worse, I simply did not know what was happening. I did not know what I had done, and I shortly began to wonder what *anyone* could possibly do, to bring about such unanimous, active, and unbearably vocal hostility. I knew about jim-crow but I had never experienced it. I went to the same self-service restaurant three times and stood with all the Princeton boys before the counter, waiting for a hamburger and coffee; it was always an extraordinarily long time before anything was set before me; but it was not until the fourth visit that I learned that, in fact, nothing had ever been set before me: I had simply picked something up. Negroes were not served there, I was told, and they had been waiting for me to realize that I was always the only Negro present. Once I was told this, I determined to go there all the time. But now they were ready for me and, though some dreadful scenes were subsequently enacted in that restaurant, I never ate there again.

It was the same story all over New Jersey, in bars, bowling alleys, diners, places to live. I was always being forced to leave, silently, or with mutual imprecations. I very shortly became notorious and children giggled behind me when I passed and their elders whispered or shouted—they really believed that I was mad. And it did begin to work on my mind, of course; I began to be afraid to go anywhere and to compensate for this I went places to which I really should not have gone and where, God knows, I had no desire to be. My reputation in town naturally enhanced my reputation at work and my working day became one long series of acrobatics designed to keep me out of trouble. I cannot say that these acrobatics succeeded. It began to seem that the machinery of the organization I worked for was turning over, day and night, with but one aim: to eject me. I was fired once, and contrived, with the aid of a friend from New York, to get back on the payroll; was fired again, and bounced back again. It took a while to fire me for the third time, but the third time took. There were no loopholes anywhere. There was not even any way of getting back inside the gates.

That year in New Jersey lives in my mind as though it were the year during which, having an unsuspected predilection for it, I first contracted some dread, chronic disease, the unfailing symptom of which is a kind of blind fever, a pounding in the skull and fire in the bowels. Once this disease is contracted, one can never be really care-free again, for the fever, without an instant's warning, can recur at any moment. It can wreck more important things than race relations. There is not a Negro alive who does not have this rage in his blood—one has the choice, merely, of living with it consciously or surrendering to it. As for me, this fever has recurred in me, and does, and will until the day I die.

My last night in New Jersey, a white friend from New York took me to the nearest big town, Trenton, to go to the movies and have a few drinks. As it turned out, he also saved me from, at the very least, a violent whipping. Almost every detail of that night stands out very clearly in my memory. I even remember the name of the movie we saw because its title impressed me as being so patly ironical. It was a movie about the German occupation of France, starring Maureen O'Hara and Charles Laughton and called *This Land Is Mine*. I remember the name of the diner we walked into when the movie ended: It was the "American Diner." When we walked in the counterman asked what we wanted and I remember answering with the casual sharpness which had become my habit: "We want a hamburger and a cup of coffee, what do you think we want?" I do not know why, after a year of such rebuffs, I so completely failed to anticipate his answer, which was, of course, "We don't serve Negroes here." This reply failed to discompose me, at least for the moment. I made some sardonic comment about the name of the diner and we walked out into the streets.

This was the time of what was called the "brown-out," when the lights in all American cities were very dim. When we re-entered the streets something happened to me which had the force of an optical illusion, or a nightmare. The streets were very crowded and I was facing north. People were moving in every direction but it seemed to me, in that instant, that all of the people I could see, and many more than that, were moving toward me, against me, and that everyone was white. I remember how their faces gleamed. And I felt, like a physical sensation, a *click* at the nape of my neck as though some interior string connecting my head to my body had been cut. I began to walk. I heard my friend call after me, but I ignored him. Heaven only knows what was going on in his mind, but he had the good sense not to touch me—I don't know what would have happened if he had—and to keep me in sight. I don't know what was going on in my mind, either; I certainly had no conscious plan. I wanted to do something to crush these white faces, which were crushing me. I walked for perhaps a block or two until I came to an enormous, glittering, and fashionable restaurant in which I knew not even the intercession of the Virgin would cause me to be served. I pushed through the doors and took the first vacant seat I saw, at a table for two, and waited.

I do not know how long I waited and I rather wonder, until today, what I could possibly have looked like. Whatever I looked like, I frightened the waitress who shortly appeared, and the moment she appeared all of my fury flowed towards her. I hated her for her white face, and for her great, astounded, frightened eyes. I felt that if she found a black man so frightening I would make her fright worthwhile.

She did not ask me what I wanted, but repeated, as though she had learned it somewhere, "We don't serve Negroes here." She did not say it with the blunt, derisive hostility to which I had grown so accustomed, but, rather, with a note of apology in her voice, and fear. This made me colder and more murderous than ever. I felt I had to do something with my hands. I wanted her to come close enough for me to get her neck between my hands.

So I pretended not to have understood her, hoping to draw her closer. And she did step a very short step closer, with her pencil poised incongruously over her pad, and repeated the formula: ". . . don't serve Negroes here."

Somehow, with the repetition of that phrase, which was already ringing in my head like a thousand bells of a nightmare, I realized that she would never come any closer and that I would have to strike from a distance. There was nothing on the table but an ordinary water-mug half full of water, and I picked this up and hurled it with all my strength at her. She ducked and it missed her and shattered against the mirror behind the bar. And, with that sound, my frozen blood abruptly thawed, I returned from wherever I had been, I *saw,* for the first time, the restaurant, the people with their mouths open, already, as it seemed to me, rising as one man, and I realized what I had done, and where I was, and I was frightened. I rose and began running for the door. A round, potbellied man grabbed me by the nape of the neck just as I reached the doors and began to beat me about the face. I kicked him and got loose and ran into the streets. My friend whispered, "*Run!*" and I ran.

My friend stayed outside the restaurant long enough to misdirect my pursuers and the police, who arrived, he told me, at once. I do not know what I said to him when he came to my room that night. I could not have said much. I felt, in the oddest, most awful way, that I had somehow betrayed him. I lived it over and over and over again, the way one relives an automobile accident after it has happened and one finds oneself alone and safe. I could not get over two facts, both equally difficult for the imagination to grasp, and one was that I could have been murdered. But the other was that I had been ready to commit murder. I saw nothing very clearly but I did see this: that my life, my *real* life, was in danger, and not from anything other people might do but from the hatred I carried in my own heart.

II

I had returned home around the second week in June—in great haste because it seemed that my father's death and my mother's confinement were both but a matter of hours. In the case of my mother, it soon became clear that she had simply made a miscalculation. This had always been her tendency and I don't believe that a single one of us arrived in the world, or has since arrived anywhere else, on time. But none of us dawdled so intolerably about the business of being born as did my baby sister. We sometimes amused ourselves, during those endless, stifling weeks, by picturing the baby sitting within in the safe, warm dark, bitterly regretting the necessity of becoming a part of our chaos and stubbornly putting it off as long as possible. I understood her perfectly and congratulated her on showing such good sense so soon. Death, however, sat as purposefully at my father's bedside as life stirred within my mother's womb and it was harder to understand why he so lingered in that long shadow. It seemed that he had bent, and for a long time, too, all of his energies towards dying. Now death was ready for him but my father held back.

All of Harlem, indeed, seemed to be infected by waiting. I had never before known it to be so violently still. Racial tensions throughout this country were exacerbated during the early years of the war, partly because the labor market brought together hundreds of thousands of ill-prepared people and partly because Negro soldiers, regardless of where they were born, received their military training in the south. What happened in defense plants and army camps had repercussions, naturally, in every Negro ghetto. The situation in Harlem had grown bad enough for clergymen, policemen, educators, politicians, and social workers to assert in one breath that there was no "crime wave" and to offer, in the very next breath, suggestions as to how to combat it. These suggestions always seemed to involve playgrounds, despite the fact that racial skirmishes were occurring in the playgrounds, too. Playground or not, crime wave or not, the Harlem police force had been augmented in March, and the unrest grew—perhaps, in fact, partly as a result of the ghetto's instinctive hatred of policemen. Perhaps the most revealing news item, out of the steady parade of reports of muggings, stabbings, shootings, assaults, gang wars, and accusations of police brutality, is the item concerning six Negro girls who set upon a white girl in the subway because, as they all too accurately put it, she was stepping on their toes. Indeed she was, all over the nation.

I had never before been so aware of policemen, on foot, on horseback, on corners, everywhere, always two by two. Nor had I ever been so aware of small knots of people. They were on stoops and on corners and in doorways, and what was striking about them, I think, was that they did not seem to be talking. Never, when I passed these groups, did the usual sound of a curse or a laugh ring out and neither did there seem to be any hum of gossip. There was certainly, on the other hand, occurring between them communication extraordinarily intense. Another thing that was striking was the unexpected diversity of the people who made up these groups. Usually, for example, one would see a group of sharpies standing on the street corner, jiving the passing chicks; or a group of older men, usually, for some reason, in the vicinity of a barber shop, discussing baseball scores, or the numbers, or making rather chilling observations about women they had known. Women, in a general way, tended to be seen less often together—unless they were church women, or very young girls, or prostitutes met together for an unprofessional instant. But that summer I saw the strangest combinations: large, respectable, churchly matrons standing on the stoops or the corners with their hair tied up, together with a girl in sleazy satin whose face bore the marks of gin and the razor, or heavy-set, abrupt, no-nonsense older men, in company with the most disreputable and fanatical "race" men, or these same "race" men with the sharpies, or these sharpies with the churchly women. Seventh Day Adventists and Methodists and Spiritualists seemed to be hobnobbing with Holyrollers and they were all, alike, entangled with the most flagrant disbelievers; something heavy in their stance seemed to indicate that they had all, incredibly, seen a common vision, and on each face there seemed to be the same strange, bitter shadow.

The churchly women and the matter-of-fact, no-nonsense men had children in the Army. The sleazy girls they talked to had lovers there, the sharpies and the "race" men had friends and brothers there. It would have demanded an unquestioning patriotism, happily as uncommon in this country as it is undesirable, for these people not to have been disturbed by the bitter letters they received, by the newspaper stories they read, not to have been enraged by the posters, then to be found all over New York, which described the Japanese as "yellowbellied Japs." It was only the "race" men, to be sure, who spoke ceaselessly of being revenged—how this vengeance was to be exacted was not clear—for the indignities and dangers suffered by

Negro boys in uniform; but everybody felt a directionless, hopeless bitterness, as well as that panic which can scarcely be suppressed when one knows that a human being one loves is beyond one's reach, and in danger. This helplessness and this gnawing uneasiness does something, at length, to even the toughest mind. Perhaps the best way to sum all this up is to say that the people I knew felt, mainly, a peculiar kind of relief when they knew that their boys were being shipped out of the south, to do battle overseas. It was, perhaps, like feeling that the most dangerous part of a dangerous journey had been passed and that now, even if death should come, it would come with honor and without the complicity of their countrymen. Such a death would be, in short, a fact with which one could hope to live.

It was on the 28th of July, which I believe was a Wednesday, that I visited my father for the first time during his illness and for the last time in his life. The moment I saw him I knew why I had put off this visit so long. I had told my mother that I did not want to see him because I hated him. But this was not true. It was only that I *had* hated him and I wanted to hold on to this hatred. I did not want to look on him as a ruin: it was not a ruin I had hated. I imagine that one of the reasons people cling to their hates so stubbornly is because they sense, once hate is gone, that they will be forced to deal with pain.

We traveled out to him, his older sister and myself, to what seemed to be the very end of a very Long Island. It was hot and dusty and we wrangled, my aunt and I, all the way out, over the fact that I had recently begun to smoke and, as she said, to give myself airs. But I knew that she wrangled with me because she could not bear to face the fact of her brother's dying. Neither could I endure the reality of her despair, her unstated bafflement as to what had happened to her brother's life, and her own. So we wrangled and I smoked and from time to time she fell into a heavy reverie. Covertly, I watched her face, which was the face of an old woman; it had fallen in, the eyes were sunken and lightless; soon she would be dying, too.

In my childhood—it had not been so long ago—I had thought her beautiful. She had been quick-witted and quick-moving and very generous with all the children and each of her visits had been an event. At one time one of my brothers and myself had thought of running away to live with her. Now she could no longer produce out of her handbag some unexpected and yet familiar delight. She made me feel pity and revulsion and fear. It was awful to realize that she no longer caused me to feel affection. The closer we came to the hospital the more querulous she became and at the same time, naturally, grew more dependent on me. Between pity and guilt and fear I began to feel that there was another me trapped in my skull like a jack-in-the-box who might escape my control at any moment and fill the air with screaming.

She began to cry the moment we entered the room and she saw him lying there, all shriveled and still, like a little black monkey. The great, gleaming apparatus which fed him and would have compelled him to be still even if he had been able to move brought to mind, not beneficence, but torture; the tubes entering his arm made me think of pictures I had seen when a child, of Gulliver, tied down by the pygmies on that island. My aunt wept and wept, there was a whistling sound in my father's throat; nothing was said; he could not speak. I wanted to take his hand, to say something. But I do not know what I could have said, even if he could have heard me. He was not really in that room with us, he had at last really embarked on his journey; and though my aunt told me that he said he was going to meet Jesus, I did not hear anything except that whistling in his throat. The doctor came back and we left, into that unbearable train again, and home. In the morning came the telegram saying that he was dead. Then the house was suddenly full of relatives, friends, hysteria, and confusion and I quickly left my mother and the children to the care of those impressive women, who, in Negro communities at least, automatically appear at times of bereavement armed with lotions, proverbs, and patience, and an ability to cook. I went downtown. By the time I returned, later the same day, my mother had been carried to the hospital and the baby had been born.

III

For my father's funeral I had nothing black to wear and this posed a nagging problem all day long. It was one of those problems, simple, or impossible of solution, to which the mind insanely clings in order to avoid the mind's real trouble. I spent most of that day at the downtown apartment of a girl I knew, celebrating my birthday with whiskey and wondering what to wear that night. When planning a birthday celebration one naturally does not expect that it will be up against competition from a funeral and this girl had anticipated taking me out that night, for a big dinner and a night club afterwards. Sometime during the course of that long day we decided that we would go out anyway, when my father's funeral service was over. I imagine *I* decided it, since, as the funeral hour approached, it became clearer and clearer to me that I would not know what to do with myself when it was over. The girl, stifling her very lively concern as to the possible effects of the whiskey on one of my father's chief mourners, concentrated on being conciliatory and practically helpful. She found a black shirt for me somewhere and ironed it and, dressed in the darkest pants and jacket I owned, and slightly drunk, I made my way to my father's funeral.

The chapel was full, but not packed, and very quiet. There were, mainly, my father's relatives, and his children, and here and there I saw faces I had not seen since childhood, the faces of my father's one-time friends. They were very dark and solemn now, seeming somehow to suggest that they had known all along that something like this would happen. Chief among the mourners was my aunt, who had quarreled with my father all his life; by which I do not mean to suggest that her mourning was insincere or that she had not loved him. I suppose that she was one of the few people in the world who had, and their incessant quarreling proved precisely the strength of the tie that bound them. The only other person in the world, as far as I knew, whose relationship to my father rivaled my aunt's in depth was my mother, who was not there.

It seemed to me, of course, that it was a very long funeral. But it was, if anything, a rather shorter funeral than most, nor, since there were no overwhelming, uncontrollable expressions of grief, could it be called—if I dare to use the word—successful. The minister who preached my father's funeral sermon was one of the few my father had still been seeing as he neared his end. He presented to us in his sermon a man whom none of us had ever seen—a man thoughtful, patient, and forbearing, a Christian inspiration to all who knew him, and a model for his children. And no doubt the children, in their disturbed and guilty state, were almost ready to believe this; he had been remote enough to be anything and, anyway, the shock of the incontrovertible, that it was really our father lying up there in that casket, prepared the mind for anything. His sister moaned and this grief-stricken moaning was taken as corroboration. The other faces held a dark, non-committal thoughtfulness. This was not the man they had known, but they had scarcely expected to be confronted with *him;* this was, in a sense deeper than questions of fact, the man they had not known, and the man they had not known may have been the real one. The real man, whoever he had been, had suffered and now he was dead: this was all that was sure and all that mattered now. Every man in the chapel hoped that when his hour came he, too, would be eulogized, which is to say forgiven, and that all of his lapses, greeds, errors, and strayings from the truth would be invested with coherence and looked upon with charity. This was perhaps the last thing human beings could give each other and it was what they demanded, after all, of the Lord. Only the Lord saw the midnight tears, only He was present when one of His children, moaning and wringing hands, paced up and down the room. When one slapped one's child in anger the recoil in the heart reverberated through heaven and became part of the pain of the universe. And when the children were hungry and sullen and distrustful and one watched them, daily, growing wilder, and further away, and running headlong into danger, it was the Lord who knew what the charged heart endured as the strap was laid to the backside; the Lord alone who knew what one *would* have said if one had had, like the Lord, the gift of the living word. It was the Lord who knew of the impossibility every parent in that room faced: how to prepare the child for the day when the child would be despised and how to *create* in the child—by what means?—a stronger antidote to this poison than one had found for oneself. The avenues, side streets, bars, billiard halls, hospitals, police stations, and even the playgrounds of Harlem—not to mention the houses of correction, the jails, and the morgue—testified to the potency of the poison while remaining silent as to the efficacy of whatever antidote, irresistibly raising the question of whether or not such an antidote existed; raising, which was worse, the question of whether or not an antidote was desirable; perhaps poison should be fought with poison. With these several schisms in the mind and with more terrors in the heart than could be named, it was better not to judge the man who had gone down under an impossible burden. It was better to remember: *Thou knowest this man's fall; but thou knowest not his wrassling.*

While the preacher talked and I watched the children—years of changing their diapers, scrubbing them, slapping them, taking them to school, and scolding them had had the perhaps inevitable result of making me love them, though I am not sure I knew this then—my mind was busily breaking out with a rash of disconnected impressions. Snatches of popular songs, indecent jokes, bits of books I had read, movie sequences, faces, voices, political issues—I thought I was going mad; all these impressions suspended, as it were, in the solution of the faint nausea produced in me by the heat and liquor. For a moment I had the impression that my alcoholic breath, inefficiently disguised with chewing gum, filled the entire chapel. Then someone began singing one of my father's favorite songs and, abruptly, I was with him, sitting on his knee, in the hot, enormous, crowded church which was the first church we attended. It was the Abyssinia Baptist Church on 138th Street. We had not gone there long. With this image, a host of others came. I had forgotten, in the rage of my growing up, how proud my father had been of me when I was little. Apparently, I had had a voice and my father had liked to show me off before the members of the church. I had forgotten what he had looked like when he was pleased but now I remembered that he had always been grinning with pleasure when my solos ended. I even remembered certain expressions on his face when he teased my mother—had he loved her? I would never know. And when had it all begun to change? For now it seemed that he had not always been cruel. I remembered being taken for a haircut and scraping my knee on the footrest of the barber's chair and I remembered my father's face as he soothed my crying and applied the stinging iodine. Then I remembered our fights, fights which had been of the worst possible kind because my technique had been silence.

I remembered the one time in all our life together when we had really spoken to each other.

It was on a Sunday and it must have been shortly before I left home. We were walking, just the two of us, in our usual silence, to or from church. I was in high school and had been doing a lot of writing and I was, at about this time, the editor of the high school magazine. But I had also been a Young Minister and had been preaching from the pulpit. Lately, I had been taking fewer engagements and preached as rarely as possible. It was said in the church, quite truthfully, that I was "cooling off."

My father asked me abruptly, "You'd rather write than preach, wouldn't you?"

I was astonished at his question—because it was a real question. I answered, "Yes."

That was all we said. It was awful to remember that that was all we had *ever* said.

The casket now was opened and the mourners were being led up the aisle to look for the last time on the deceased. The assumption was that the family was too overcome with grief to be allowed to make this journey alone and I watched while my aunt was led to the casket and, muffled in black, and shaking, led back to her seat. I disapproved of forcing the children to look on their dead father, considering that the shock of his death, or, more truthfully, the shock of death as a reality, was already a little more than a child could bear, but my judgment in this matter had been overruled and there they were, bewildered and frightened and very small, being led, one by one, to the casket. But there is also something very gallant about children at such moments. It has something to do with their silence and gravity and with the fact that one cannot help them. Their legs, somehow, seem *exposed,* so that it is at once incredible and terribly clear that their legs are all they have to hold them up.

I had not wanted to go to the casket myself and I certainly had not wished to be led there, but there was no way of avoiding either of these forms. One of the deacons led me up and I looked on my father's face. I cannot say that it looked like him at all. His blackness had been equivocated by powder and there was no suggestion in that casket of what his power had or could have been. He was simply an old man dead, and it was hard to believe that he had ever given anyone either joy or pain. Yet, his life filled that room. Further up the avenue his wife was holding his newborn child. Life and death so close together, and love and hatred, and right and wrong, said something to me which I did not want to hear concerning man, concerning the life of man.

After the funeral, while I was downtown desperately celebrating my birthday, a Negro soldier, in the lobby of the Hotel Braddock, got into a fight with a white policeman over a Negro girl. Negro girls, white policemen, in or out of uniform, and Negro males—in or out of uniform—were part of the furniture of the lobby of the Hotel Braddock and this was certainly not the first time such an incident had occurred. It was destined, however, to receive an unprecedented publicity, for the fight between the policeman and the soldier ended with the shooting of the soldier. Rumor, flowing immediately to the streets outside, stated that the soldier had been shot in the back, an instantaneous and revealing invention, and that the soldier had died protecting a Negro woman. The facts were somewhat different—for example, the soldier had not been shot in the back, and was not dead, and the girl seems to have been as dubious a symbol of womanhood as her white counterpart in Georgia usually is, but no one was interested in the facts. They preferred the invention because this invention expressed and corroborated their hates and fears so perfectly. It is just as well to remember that people are always doing this. Perhaps many of those legends, including Christianity, to which the world clings began their conquest of the world with just some such concerted surrender to distortion. The effect, in Harlem, of this particular legend was like the effect of a lit match in a tin of gasoline. The mob gathered before the doors of the Hotel Braddock simply began to swell and to spread in every direction, and Harlem exploded.

The mob did not cross the ghetto lines. It would have been easy, for example, to have gone over Morningside Park on the west side or to have crossed the Grand Central railroad tracks at 125th Street on the east side, to wreak havoc in white neighborhoods. The mob seems to have been mainly interested in something more potent and real than the white face, that is, in white power, and the principal damage done during the riot of the summer of 1943 was to white business establishments in Harlem. It might have been a far bloodier story, of course, if, at the hour the riot began, these establishments had still been open. From the Hotel Braddock the mob fanned out, east and west along 125th Street, and for the entire length of Lenox, Seventh, and Eighth avenues. Along each of these avenues, and along each major side street—116th, 125th, 135th, and so on—bars, stores, pawnshops, restaurants, even little luncheonettes had been smashed open and entered and looted—looted, it might be added, with more haste than efficiency. The shelves really looked as though a bomb had struck them. Cans of beans and soup and dog food, along with toilet paper, corn flakes, sardines, and milk tumbled every which way, and abandoned cash registers and cases of beer leaned crazily out of the splintered windows and were strewn along the avenues. Sheets, blankets, and clothing of every description formed a kind of path, as though people had dropped them while running. I truly had not realized that Harlem *had* so many stores until I saw them all smashed open; the first time the word *wealth* ever entered my mind in relation to Harlem was when I saw it scattered in the streets. But one's first, incongruous impression of plenty was countered immediately by an impression of waste. None of this was doing anybody any good. It would have been better to have left the plate glass as it had been and the goods lying in the stores.

It would have been better, but it would also have been intolerable, for Harlem had needed something to smash. To smash something is the ghetto's chronic need. Most of the time it is the members of the ghetto who smash each other, and themselves. But as long as the ghetto walls are standing there will always come a moment when these outlets do not work. That summer, for example, it was not enough to get into a fight on Lenox Avenue, or curse out one's cronies in the barber shops. If ever, indeed, the violence which fills Harlem's churches, pool halls, and bars erupts outward in a more direct fashion, Harlem and its citizens are likely to vanish in an apocalyptic flood. That this is not likely to happen is due to a great many reasons, most hidden and powerful among them the Negro's real relation to the white American. This relation prohibits, simply, anything as uncomplicated and satisfactory as pure hatred. In order really to hate white people, one has to blot so much out of the mind—and the heart—that this hatred itself becomes an exhausting and self-destructive pose. But this does not mean, on the other hand, that love comes easily: the white world is too powerful, too complacent, too ready with gratuitous humiliation, and, above all, too ignorant and too innocent for that. One is absolutely forced to make perpetual qualifications and one's own reactions are always canceling each other out. It is this, really, which has driven so many people mad, both white and black. One is always in the position of having to decide between amputation and gangrene. Amputation is swift but time may prove that the amputation was not necessary—or one may delay the amputation too long. Gangrene is slow, but it is impossible to be sure that one is reading one's symptoms right. The idea of going through life as a cripple is more than one can bear, and equally unbearable is the risk of swelling up slowly, in agony, with poison. And the trouble, finally, is that the risks are real even if the choices do not exist.

"But as for me and my house," my father had said, "we will serve the Lord." I wondered, as we drove him to his resting place, what this line had meant for him. I had heard him preach it many times. I had preached it once myself, proudly giving it an interpretation different from my father's. Now the whole thing came back to me, as though my father and I were on our way to Sunday school and I were memorizing the golden text: *And if it seem evil unto you to serve the Lord, choose you this day whom you will serve; whether the gods which your fathers served that were on the other side of the flood, or the gods of the Amorites, in whose land ye dwell: but as for me and my house, we will serve the Lord.* I suspected in these familiar lines a meaning which had never been there for me before. All of my father's texts and songs, which I had decided were meaningless, were arranged before me at his death like empty bottles, waiting to hold the meaning which life would give them for me. This was his legacy: nothing is ever escaped. That bleakly memorable morning I hated the unbelievable streets and the Negroes and whites who had, equally, made them that way. But I knew that it was folly, as my father would have said, this bitterness was folly. It was necessary to hold on to the things that mattered. The dead man mattered, the new life mattered; blackness and whiteness did not matter; to believe that they did was to acquiesce in one's own destruction. Hatred, which could destroy so much, never failed to destroy the man who hated and this was an immutable law.

It began to seem that one would have to hold in the mind forever two ideas which seemed to be in opposition. The first idea was acceptance, the acceptance, totally without rancor, of life as it is, and men as they are: in the light of this idea, it goes without saying that injustice is a commonplace. But this did not mean that one could be complacent, for the second idea was of equal power: that one must never, in one's own life, accept these injustices as commonplace but must fight them with all one's strength. This fight begins, however, in the heart and it now had been laid to my charge to keep my own heart free of hatred and despair. This intimation made my heart heavy and, now that my father was irrecoverable, I wished that he had been beside me so that I could have searched his face for the answers which only the future would give me now.

James Baldwin

Novelist, essayist, and playwright, James Baldwin produced a body of writing that is often a blend of autobiography and social commentary, focusing on sexual and racial identity. In the 1960s, Baldwin's writings on the civil rights movement caught the attention of the FBI, and they kept a 1,750-page file on him. He published numerous essays in The New Leader, The Nation, Commentary, *and* Partisan Review *before getting his first novel,* Go Tell It On the Mountain, *published in 1953.* Notes of a Native Son *was published in 1955. His numerous other works include* Another Country, If Beale Street Could Talk, The Devil Finds Work, *and* Perspectives: Angles on African Art. *His collected essays, edited by Toni Morrison, were published posthumously in 1998. Born in Harlem in 1924, Baldwin spent almost a decade in France as a young man. He returned to that country in old age and died in 1987 on the French Riviera.*

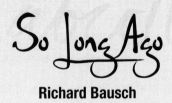

So Long Ago

Richard Bausch

Indulge me, a moment.

I have often said glibly that the thing which separates the young from the old is the knowledge of what Time really is; not just how fast, but how illusive and arbitrary and mutable it is. When you are twenty, the idea of twenty years is only barely conceivable, and since that amount of time makes up one's whole life, it seems an enormous thing—a vast, roomy expanse, going on into indefiniteness. One arrives at forty with a sense of the error in this way of seeing, and maturity, um, can be said to have set in.

And the truest element of this aspect of the way we experience time, of course, is the sense of the nearness of time past.

I have a memory of being bathed by my father on my seventh birthday. Morning, rainy light at a window. The swish and wash of lukewarm water. My own body, soft-feeling and small under the solid strong hands, lathered with soap. I said, "Well, I guess I'm a big boy now."

He said, "No, not quite."

I remember feeling a bit surprised, perhaps even downcast, that he didn't simply agree with me, as most of the adults in our large family usually did. He ran the towel over me, ruffled my hair with it, drying me off. I went across the hall into my room, and dressed for the April day. Baseball season was starting.

Let me go back there for a little while, to that bath, my seventh birthday. At the time, I wasn't old enough to understand the difference between the humoring of children, which is a large part of any talk with them, and truth telling, which is what my father did. I loved his rough hands on me, and the smell of him—aftershave, and cigarettes, and sometimes the redolence of my mother's Chanel.

He hated lies, and lying. He was a storyteller, and he must have learned early how to exaggerate and heighten things, to make the telling go better, to entertain and enthrall. He was so good at it. He could spin it out and do all the voices and set the scene and take you to the laughs, and there simply *had* to have been elements that he fabricated. And yet he hated lies. Any trouble you ever got into in our house always had to do with that: you learned very early that even if you *had* done something wrong, something for which you wanted some kind of an excuse, or explanation, it had better not involve telling a lie.

I was often in some kind of mischief at school—my twin, Robert, and I had a talent for making other kids laugh, and for imitating our teachers' gestures and voice mannerisms. Well, we were the sons of a storyteller. Neither of us liked school very much; and the teachers, the nuns of Saint Bernadette's, knew it. They kept tabs on us. They were at some pains to discipline us. And whenever we got into a scrape at school, we lived in dread that our father would ask us, that evening, how things had gone at school. I remember sitting at the dinner table as he and my mother told stories, or commented happily on the various people—friends and family—who inhabited our lives then. Bobby and I would sit there in awful anticipation of the question: "How was school today?" You couldn't gloss over anything—you couldn't use a cover-all word like *fine*. You had to be specific, and you had to tell it all, the truth. You were *compelled* to do so by what you knew of the value he set upon the truth. And never mind philosophical truth, or the truth of experience, really; he wanted to know what happened in the day, what was said and done, and how it went—*that* kind of truth.

I have no memory—not even a glimmer—of how and when we learned that this was what he expected from us, and that the surest way to earn his displeasure was by lying to him. I don't have much of a memory of him telling us this; I recall him talking about how it was a thing *his* father expected, but by then I was in my teens, and I understood it then as an echo of a kind, a source.

All right.

I remember being surprised that in my father's truthful opinion I was not a big boy yet. I remember that we had two boys our age living next door to us, and that this took place on Kenross Avenue in Montgomery County, Maryland. I know intellectually that the year was 1952, and that Truman was still president. I could not have said who Truman was then, and I recall that a few months later, in the summer, when the Republican Convention was on our little General Electric black-and-white television, I saw all those people in the arena, with Eisenhower standing there on the podium, and I guessed the number to be everyone in the world. "No," my father said, "It's not even a small fraction of the number." I didn't know the word *fraction* and yet I understood what he meant.

Sometime around then I saw film of the war that had just ended, and I was told by my mother that another war was going on, in Korea. A summer evening—we were driving past an army post, and I had seen the antiaircraft guns, the olive drab barrels aimed at the sky. I wondered aloud why we couldn't hear the guns.

"It's on the other side of the world, honey. Thousands of miles away."

In 1952, my mother was thirty-four years old. Now, I'm almost twenty years older than that, and this is the math I'm always doing—have been doing, like a kind of mental nerve-tic, since I was twenty-seven years old, and a father for the first time myself.

When my son Wes was fourteen months old, we moved to Iowa, where I attended the Writers' Workshop. I spent a lot of time with him that year, and as he grew slightly older I decided to conduct a sort of experiment: I'd see if I could manage to keep in his memory the times we had at Iowa—the swing set and sandbox outside the Hawkeye Court Apartments, the little amusement park by the river in Iowa City, with its Ferris wheel and its kiddie train. I'd ask him about it, almost daily: "Do you remember the swing set? The sandbox? Do you remember how I used to push you on the swings, and you didn't want to go in the house? Remember the summer nights when it would be getting dark, and we'd go to that park and ride in the kiddie train?" Yes, he remembered. He was three, and then four, and then five, and he remembered. He offered elements of that time, so he wasn't merely remembering *my* memory: yes, the swing set and the sandbox—but did I remember the red wagon that got stuck there, and then buried there by the other children? I did. Yes, the kiddie train, but remember the buffalo? Yes, there had been a small enclosure with Bison standing in it; the big Ferris wheel, yes, but did I remember riding it and being stopped at the very top?

Oh, yes.

I had begun to think I might be able to help my son carry that part of his life with him into his own adulthood—earliest memories that have chronological shape. It became important that he have it all to keep. And then one winter evening, as we were riding in the car on the way to a movie, I asked him about Iowa again, and he recalled nothing—it was all simply gone. I asked him about the swing set, the sandbox, the park, the train, the Ferris wheel, even the buffalo. To each one he said, "No." Innocently, simply, without the slightest trace of perplexity or anything of what I was feeling, which was sorrow. You could see him striving to get something of it back, but it was like a game, and there was nothing. No, he had no recollection of any of it. I don't think it had been more than a week or two since we had gone through this little litany of memory, and even so it had all disappeared from his mind, and my description of it was only a story, now.

When I was fifteen, my great-grandmother, Minnie Roddy, died. Minnie had for the most part raised my mother, because Minnie's daughter had had to go to work for the government when my mother was still a baby. They all lived with my aunt Daisy, Minnie's sister, in a big sprawling Victorian house with a wide porch that had blue-gray painted boards and white trim. When Minnie began to fail, my mother went over there, and we later learned, through the talk of the adults in the rooms of the two houses, that she was holding the old woman in her arms in the last moments. Minnie used to tell me stories, sitting in the breakfast nook, by the windows where younger children ran. Summer evenings, the cousins and aunts and uncles out on the lawn, throwing horseshoes. The bell-like clang of the metal on metal when someone hit one of the posts, or scored a ringer or a leaner. Fireflies rising in the shallow pools of shade in the spaces between the houses, in the cloud-shaped willow tree—you couldn't see its trunk for the drooping filamental mass of its branches—at the edge of the property. Minnie talking, telling me about coming from Ireland on a ship; about her husband—who had come to America after killing a man in a fight one afternoon in a pub in Dublin. Her voice would trail off, and the louder voices out the window would distract me. I'd nod and pretend to listen. I was always reading books, as Bobbie was, but it showed more on me, and I was the one, after all, who believed that I had a vocation. I was planning for the priesthood. Minnie Roddy would say, "You'll grow up and tell these stories. You'll grow up and be a writer."

And she would go on talking, unscrolling her memory of earlier days, of my mother as a young girl; of Ireland, and a childhood spent, for the most part, in the latter part of the nineteenth century. I didn't hear most of it. I nodded and pretended to listen, while this woman—this tiny slip of a lady with her wire-framed glasses and her clear large blue eyes—tried to give me treasure, something to store up, for the arrival of a season I was not and am not ready for.

When she died, it was decided that Bobby and I were old enough to attend the funeral. I felt a strange detached curiosity about the whole thing: I was actually going to see a dead person. I told one of the other boys in my class, speaking it out with a sort of quiet, fake-brave shrug. "I'm going to see a dead person today."

"Who?"

"My great-grandmother."

"Jesus, no kidding?"

I was, I suppose, even a little proud of the fact. Minnie had lived to great age, and her going seemed natural enough, and so far away from my own life and world that I could only think of it in a sort of abstract haze. I was still young enough and egocentric enough to be unable quite to imagine my own demise.

The day of the funeral was bright and chilly. I don't recall whether it was spring or fall. It wasn't summer, because I was in school. I think it was fall. We rode with our parents to the funeral home, and I was like a secret traveler in the backseat, planning my exploration of this curiosity, death, this unreal element of the life I was in so permanently. I was wildly curious; I understood, according to the tenets of the faith I had been raised in that Minnie Roddy would not be there, but only her body, the empty vessel she had vacated. She was in that blue elsewhere that I associated with the sky, and we could now pray to her.

Blue is the important color, here.

Standing over the box where she lay, looking like a bad likeness of herself, I saw the forking, colorless veins in her bony hands, the fingers of which were wound with a black rosary; and I saw the blue place at her earlobe, where blue did not belong. I marked it, and knew that I would never forget it.

This sounds as though I were marking things with the flaccid, nervous sensitivity of one of those pretentious people who like to think of themselves as a romantic central figure in their own drama: the incipient artist, observing everything with the intention of later recording it. I do not mean it this way at all, and it was not like that at all. I was a child, still. I knew next to nothing about anything, especially about myself. And I don't know that I have learned much since then, either.

I suppose I have to admit that it might just be impossible to have it both ways: To claim that I was not that hypersensitive romantic figure, the artist-as-a-young-man, and still report the impressions of a moment like that one, standing over the body of a woman who had lived a life so separate from mine, and nothing like mine, and whose reality could not have anticipated that she would be a figure in my speech, a character in a story I would tell, even as she told me about all the living she had seen and done, and I pretended to listen. In any case, I do not mean this the way it will sound. I mean to express the quality of a memory, in order to say something about this life we live, so much of which is fugitive, so much of which is lost in the living of it.

The room we were in was banked with flowers, and there were chairs in rows, as though someone might give a lecture, or a homily. Minnie's coffin looked to have been where it was long enough for this prodigious wall of flowers to grow up on three sides of it. There was a dim light, a candle burning at one end. The light was brightest where she lay, with her eyes shut in a way that made you understand they would not open again. The skin looked oddly transparent, like the synthetic skin of a doll. And there was the blue place at the ear, the place, I knew, where the cosmetics of the mortician hadn't quite taken. I stood there and looked with a kind of detached, though respectful silence at this, aware of it not as death, quite, but death's signature. I was conscious of the difference. I spent my minute there, head bowed, and then walked back to my seat at the rear of the room, with the other young people, all in their early teens, like me. I saw my mother and my aunt Florence come from where I had just been, and my mother had a handkerchief that she held to her nose. She sobbed, once. Earlier, when we had arrived, Florence had come up to my mother and said, "You scared the bejesus out of me." I don't know— or I don't remember—what this was about; I think it had something to do with what had gone on last night, at the viewing. Perhaps my mother had gotten woozy, or swooned. It was the first time I had ever heard the word *bejesus.*

Florence and my mother sat down, and a priest led us in the rosary. If he said anything about the woman who lay behind him in the long box, I don't recall it. We were in the room for a time, and then people began to file out. I remained in my seat, and I have no idea why. Others crossed in front of me, and maybe I was saying my own prayers—it seems to me now that I must have felt some pang of guilt for my oddly remote observation of everything, and was trying to say the words of a prayer, repeating them inwardly in an attempt to say them not out of automatic memory but actually to enter into the meaning of them:

Hail Mary, full of grace, the Lord is with thee. Blessed art thou among women and blessed is the fruit of thy womb, Jesus. Holy Mary, Mother of God, pray for us sinners, now and at the hour of our death, Amen.

The others were all filing quietly out of the long room, and I saw the mortician step to the side of the casket, where we had each stood only moments before. With a practical sureness, the nearly offhand familiarity of experience, he reached into the white satin that ringed Minnie Roddy's head, and pushed downward on it, a tucking motion, and Minnie slipped from her sleeping pose. Her head dropped down into that box like a stone.

Something must have shown in my face; and the mortician's wife—let us call them the Hallorans, because I no longer recall the name—saw the change in my features. Later, as I was getting into the back of my father's car, Aunt Florence leaned in and said, "Honey, Mrs. Halloran wanted me to tell you that Mr. Halloran was only making it so Minnie could rest better."

I nodded. I don't believe I said anything. It was almost as if I had stumbled upon someone in a privy act; I felt the same kind of embarrassment. But there was something else in it, too, a kind of species-thrill: this was the human end, a reality I was not expecting. I am trying to express this as exactly as I can, and it is finally inexpressible. I know that all my fascination was gone, and I sat there in the back of the car, looking out at the sunny streets of Washington, D.C., and felt numb, far down.

That memory is as present to me as the moment, almost a decade earlier, when I said to my father that I was a big boy, and he told me the truth, that I was not a big boy. Not yet. And those memories are as near as the memory of asking, in the first line of this story, for your indulgence.

Of course, this is not an original perception; yet one arrives at it in life—doesn't one?—with the sense of having had a revelation: one's personal past is a *place,* and everything that resides there does so in contemporaneous time. What then, of the collective past? The collective memory? That is where chronology really is. We come from the chaos of ourselves to the world, and we yearn to know what happened to all the others who came before us. So we impose Time on the flow of events, and call it history. For me, Memory is always *story.* True memory is nothing like the organized surface of a story, yet that is all we have to tell it, and know it, and experience it again: but if we are doomed to put our remembered life into stories, we are blessed by it, too.

I never spoke to my mother and father, or even to my brothers and sisters, about what I had seen at the funeral home. I don't know why, now. I can't recall why. Perhaps it was too private, finally; and perhaps I did not want to have it in memory, didn't want to fix it there in the telling. But it has never left me. It is with all the others, large and small, important and meaningless, all waiting in the same timeless dark, to drift toward the surface when I write, or daydream, or sleep.

Richard Bausch

Richard Bausch plays the steel guitar and once dreamed of being a singer/songwriter. He has used his voice in other ways, publishing nine novels, including Hello to the Cannibals, *and five volumes of short stories, including* Someone to Watch Over Me. *Bausch, who is widely regarded as a contemporary master of short fiction, has had stories and essays appear in many journals and magazines, including* The New Yorker, The Atlantic, Ploughshares, *and* Esquire, *as well as in anthologies such as* Best American Short Stories. *Today, Bausch holds the Heritage Chair in Writing at George Mason University.*

The Fourth State of Matter

Jo Ann Beard

The collie wakes me up about three times a night, summoning me from a great distance as I row my boat through a dim, complicated dream. She's on the shoreline, barking. Wake up. She's staring at me with her head slightly tipped to the side, long nose, gazing eyes, toenails clenched to get a purchase on the wood floor. We used to call her the face of love.

She totters on her broomstick legs into the hallway and over the doorsill into the kitchen, makes a sharp left at the refrigerator—careful, almost went down—then a straightaway to the door. I sleep on my feet, in the cold of the doorway, waiting. Here she comes. Lift her down the two steps. She pees and then stands, Lassie in a ratty coat, gazing out at the yard.

In the porchlight the trees shiver, the squirrels turn over in their sleep. The Milky Way is a long smear on the sky, like something erased on a chalkboard. Over the neighbor's house Mars flashes white, then red, then white again. Jupiter is hidden among the anonymous blinks and glitterings. It has a moon with sulfur-spewing volcanoes and a beautiful name: Io. I learned it at work, from the group of men who surround me there. Space physicists, guys who spend days on end with their heads poked through the fabric of the sky, listening to the sounds of the universe. Guys whose own lives are ticking like alarm clocks getting ready to go off, although none of us is aware of it yet.

The collie turns and looks, waits to be carried up the two steps. Inside the house, she drops like a shoe onto her blanket, a thud, an adjustment. I've climbed back under my covers already but her leg's stuck underneath her, we can't get comfortable. I fix the leg, she rolls over and sleeps. Two hours later I wake up again and she's gazing at me in the darkness. The face of love. She wants to go out again. I give her a boost, balance her on her legs. Right on time: 3:40 A.M.

There are squirrels living in the spare bedroom upstairs. Three dogs also live in this house, but they were invited. I keep the door of the spare bedroom shut at all times, because of the squirrels and because that's where the vanished husband's belongings are stored. Two of the dogs—the smart little brown mutt and the Labrador—spend hours sitting patiently outside the door, waiting for it to be opened so they can dismantle the squirrels. The collie can no longer make it up the stairs, so she lies at the bottom and snores or stares in an interested manner at the furniture around her.

I can take almost anything at this point. For instance, that my vanished husband is neither here nor there; he's reduced himself to a troubled voice on the telephone three or four times a day.

Or that the dog at the bottom of the stairs keeps having mild strokes which cause her to tilt her head inquisitively and also to fall over. She drinks prodigious amounts of water and pees great volumes onto the folded blankets where she sleeps. Each time this happens I stand her up, dry her off, put fresh blankets underneath her, carry the peed-on blankets down to the basement, stuff them into the washer and then into the dryer. By the time I bring them back upstairs they are needed again. The first few times this happened I found the dog trying to stand up, gazing with frantic concern at her own rear. I praised her and patted her head and gave her treats until she settled down. Now I know whenever it happens because I hear her tail thumping against the floor in anticipation of reward. In retraining her I've somehow retrained myself, bustling cheerfully down to the basement, arms drenched in urine, the task of doing load after load of laundry strangely satisfying. She is Pavlov and I am her dog.

I'm fine about the vanished husband's boxes stored in the spare bedroom. For now the boxes and the phone calls persuade me that things could turn around at any moment. The boxes are filled with thirteen years of his pack-rattedness: statistics textbooks that still harbor an air of desperation, smarmy suitcoats from the Goodwill, various old Halloween masks and one giant black papier-mâché thing that was supposed to be Elvis's hair but didn't turn out. A collection of ancient Rolling Stones T-shirts. You know he's turning over a new leaf when he leaves the Rolling Stones behind.

What I can't take are the squirrels. They come alive at night throwing terrible parties in the spare bedroom, making thumps and crashes. Occasionally a high-pitched squeal is heard amid bumps and the sound of scrabbling toenails. I've taken to sleeping downstairs, on the blue vinyl dog couch, the sheets slipping off, my skin stuck to the cushions. This is an affront to two of the dogs, who know the couch belongs to them; as soon as I settle in they creep up and find their places between my knees and elbows.

I'm on the couch because the dog on the blanket gets worried at night. During the day she sleeps the catnappy sleep of the elderly, but when it gets dark her eyes open and she is agitated, trying to stand whenever I leave the room, settling down only when I'm next to her. We are in this together, the dying game, and I read for hours in the evening, one foot on her back, getting up only to open a new can of beer or take peed-on blankets to the basement. At some point I stretch out on the vinyl couch and close my eyes, one hand hanging down, touching her side. By morning the dog-arm has become a nerveless club that doesn't come around until noon. My friends think I'm nuts.

One night, for hours, the dog won't lie down, stands braced on her rickety legs in the middle of the living room, looking at me and slowly wagging her tail. Each time I get her situated on her blankets and try to stretch out on the couch she stands up, looks at me, wags her tail. I call my office pal, Mary, and wake her up. "*I'm weary,*" I say, in italics.

Mary listens, sympathetic, on the other end. "Oh my God," she finally says, "*what* are you going to do?"

I calm down immediately. "Exactly what I'm doing," I tell her. The dog finally parks herself with a thump on the stack of damp blankets. She sets her nose down and tips her eyes up to watch me. We all sleep then, for a bit, while the squirrels sort through the boxes overhead and the dog on the blanket keeps nervous watch.

I've called in tired to work. It's midmorning and I'm shuffling around in my long underwear, smoking cigarettes and drinking coffee. The whole house is bathed in sunlight and the faint odor of used diapers. The collie is on her blanket, taking one of her vampirish daytime naps. The other two dogs are being mild-mannered and charming. I nudge the collie with my foot.

"Wake up and smell zee bacons," I say. She startles awake, lifts her nose groggily, and falls back asleep. I get ready for the office.

"I'm leaving and I'm never coming back," I say while putting on my coat. I use my mother's aggrieved, underappreciated tone. The little brown dog wags her tail, transferring her gaze from me to the table, which is the last place she remembers seeing toast. The collie continues her ghoulish sleep, eyes partially open, teeth exposed, while the Labrador, who understands English, begins howling miserably. She wins the toast sweepstakes and is chewing loudly when I leave, the little dog barking ferociously at her.

Work is its usual comforting green-corridored self. There are three blinks on the answering machine, the first from an author who speaks very slowly, like a kindergarten teacher, asking about reprints. "What am I, the village idiot?" I ask the room taking down his number in large backward characters. The second and third blinks are from my husband, the across-town apartment dweller.

The first makes my heart lurch in a hopeful way. "I have to talk to you right *now*," he says grimly. "Where *are* you? I can never find you."

"Try calling your own house," I say to the machine. In the second message he has composed himself.

"I'm *fine* now," he says firmly. "Disregard previous message and don't call me back, please; I have meetings." Click, dial tone, rewind.

I feel crestfallen, the leaping heart settles back into its hole in my chest. I say damn it out loud, just as Chris strides into the office.

"What?" he asks defensively. He tries to think if he's done anything wrong recently. He checks the table for work; none there. He's on top of it. We have a genial relationship these days, reading the paper together in the mornings, congratulating ourselves on each issue of the journal. It's a space physics quarterly and he's the editor and I'm the managing editor. I know nothing about the science part; my job is to shepherd the manuscripts through the review process and create a journal out of the acceptable ones.

Christoph Goertz. He's hip in a professorial kind of way, tall and lanky and white-haired, forty-seven years old, with an elegant trace of accent from his native Germany. He has a great dog, a giant black outlaw named Mica who runs through the streets of Iowa City at night, inspecting garbage. She's big and friendly but a bad judge of character and frequently runs right into the arms of the dog catcher. Chris is always bailing her out.

"They don't understand dogs," he says.

I spend more time with Chris than I ever did with my husband. The morning I told him I was being dumped he was genuinely perplexed.

"He's leaving *you?*" he asked.

Chris was drinking coffee, sitting at his table in front of the chalk-board. Behind his head was a chalk drawing of a hip, professorial man holding a coffee cup. It was a collaborative effort; I drew the man and Chris framed him, using brown chalk and a straightedge. The two-dimensional man and the three-dimensional man stared at me intently.

"He's leaving *you?*" And for an instant I saw myself from their vantage point across the room—Jo Ann—and a small bubble of self-esteem percolated up from the depths. Chris shrugged. "You'll do fine," he said.

During my current turmoils, I've come to think of work as my own kind of zen practice, the constant barrage of paper hypnotic and sooth-ing. Chris lets me work an erratic, eccentric schedule, which gives me time to pursue my nonexistent writing career. In return I update his publications list for him and listen to stories about outer space.

Besides being an editor and a teacher, he's the head of a theoret-ical plasma physics team made up of graduate students and research scientists. During the summers he travels all over the world telling people about the magnetospheres of various planets, and when he comes back he brings me presents—a small bronze box from Africa with an alligator embossed on the top, a big piece of amber from Poland with the wings of flies preserved inside it, and, once, a set of delicate, horrifying bracelets made from the hide of an elephant.

Currently he is obsessed with the dust in the plasma of Saturn's rings. Plasma is the fourth state of matter. You've got your solid, your liquid, your gas, and then your plasma. In outer space there's the plas-masphere and the plasmapause. I like to avoid the math when I can and put a layperson's spin on these things.

"Plasma is blood," I told him.

"Exactly," he agreed, removing the comics page and handing it to me.

Mostly we have those kinds of conversations around the office, but today he's caught me at a weak moment, tucking my heart back inside my chest. I decide to be cavalier.

"I wish my *dog* was out tearing up the town and my *husband* was home peeing on a blanket," I say.

Chris thinks the dog thing has gone far enough. "Why are you let-ting this go on?" he asks solemnly.

"I'm not *letting* it, that's why," I tell him. There are stacks of man-uscripts everywhere and he has all the pens over on his side of the room. "It just *is*, is all. Throw me a pen." He does, I miss it, stoop to pick it up, and when I straighten up again I might be crying.

You have control over this, he explains in his professor voice. You can decide how long she suffers.

This makes my heart pound. Absolutely not, I cannot do it. And then I weaken and say what I really want. For her to go to sleep and not wake up, just slip out of her skin and into the other world.

"Exactly," he says.

I have an ex-beauty queen coming over to get rid of the squirrels for me. She has long red hair and a smile that can stop trucks. I've seen her wrestle goats, scare off a giant snake, and express a dog's anal glands, all in one afternoon. I told her on the phone that a family of squirrels is living in the upstairs of my house and there's nothing I can do about it.

"They're making a monkey out of me," I said.

So Caroline climbs in her car and drives across half the state, pulls up in front of my house, and gets out carrying zucchinis, cigarettes, and a pair of big leather gloves. I'm sitting outside with my sweet old dog, who lurches to her feet, staggers three steps, sits down, and falls over. Caroline starts crying.

"Don't try to give me zucchini," I tell her.

We sit companionably on the front stoop for a while, staring at the dog and smoking cigarettes. One time I went to Caroline's house and she was nursing a dead cat that was still breathing. At some point that afternoon I saw her spoon baby food into its mouth and as soon as she turned away the whole pureed mess plopped back out. A day later she took it to the vet and had it euthanized. I remind her of this.

"You'll do it when you do it," she says firmly.

I pick the collie up like a fifty-pound bag of sticks and feathers, stagger inside, place her on the damp blankets, and put the other two nutcases in the backyard. From upstairs comes a crash and a shriek. Caroline stares up at the ceiling.

"It's like having the Wallendas stay at your house," I say cheerfully. All of a sudden I feel fond of the squirrels and fond of Caroline and fond of myself for heroically calling her to help me. The phone rings four times. It's the husband, and his voice over the answering machine sounds frantic. He pleads with whoever Jo Ann is to pick up the phone.

"Please? I think I might be freaking out," he says. "Am I ruining my life here, or what? Am I making a *mistake?* Jo?" He breathes raggedly and sniffs into the receiver for a moment then hangs up with a muffled clatter.

Caroline stares at the machine like it's a copperhead.

"Holy fuckoly," she says, shaking her head. "You're *living* with this crap?"

"He wants me to reassure him that he's strong enough to leave me," I tell her. "Else he won't have fun on his bike ride. And guess what; I'm too tired to." Except that now I can see him in his dank little apartment, wringing his hands and staring out the windows. He's wearing his Sunday hairdo with baseball cap trying to scrunch it down. In his rickety dresser is the new package of condoms he accidentally showed me last week.

Caroline lights another cigarette. The dog pees and thumps her tail.

I need to call him back because he's suffering.

"You call him back and I'm forced to kill you," Caroline says. She exhales smoke and points to the phone. "That is evil shit," she says.

I tend to agree. It's blanket time. I roll the collie off onto the floor and put the fresh ones down, roll her back. She stares at me with the face of love. I get her a treat, which she chews with gusto and then goes back to sleep. I carry the blankets down to the basement and stuff them into the machine, trudge back up the stairs. Caroline has finished smoking her medicine and is wearing the leather gloves which go all the way to her elbows. She's staring at the ceiling with determination.

The plan is that I'm supposed to separate one from the herd and get it in a corner. Caroline will take it from there. Unfortunately, my nerves are shot, and when I'm in the room with her and the squirrels are running around all I can do is scream. I'm not even afraid of them, but my screaming button is stuck on and the only way to turn it off is to leave the room.

"How are you doing?" I ask from the other side of the door. All I can hear is Caroline crashing around and swearing. Suddenly there is a high-pitched screech that doesn't end. The door opens and Caroline falls out into the hall, with a gray squirrel stuck to her glove. Brief pandemonium and then she clatters down the stairs and out the front door and returns looking triumphant.

The collie appears at the foot of the stairs with her head cocked and her ears up. She looks like a puppy for an instant, and then her feet start to slide. I run down and catch her and carry her upstairs so she can watch the show. They careen around the room, tearing the ancient wallpaper off the walls. The last one is a baby, so we keep it for a few minutes, looking at its little feet and its little tail. We show it to the collie, who stands up immediately and tries to get it.

Caroline patches the hole where they got in, cutting wood with a power saw down in the basement. She comes up wearing a toolbelt and lugging a ladder. I've seen a scrapbook of photos of her wearing evening gowns with a banner across her chest and a crown on her head. Curled hair, lipstick. She climbs down and puts the tools away. We eat nachos.

"I only make food that's boiled or melted these days," I tell her.

"I know," she replies.

We smoke cigarettes and think. The phone rings again but who-ever it is hangs up.

"Is it him?" she asks.

"Nope."

The collie sleeps on her blankets while the other two dogs sit next to Caroline on the couch. She's looking through their ears for mites. At some point she gestures to the sleeping dog on the blanket and remarks that it seems like just two days ago she was a puppy.

"She was never a puppy," I say. "She's always been older than me."

When they say good-bye, she holds the collie's long nose in one hand and kisses her on the forehead; the collie stares back at her gravely. Caroline is crying when she leaves, a combination of squirrel adrenaline, and sadness. I cry, too, although I don't feel particularly bad about anything. I hand her the zucchini through the window and she pulls away from the curb.

The house is starting to get dark in that terrible early evening twilit way. I turn on lights, get a cigarette, and go upstairs to the for-mer squirrel room. The black dog comes with me and circles the room, snorting loudly, nose to floor. There is a spot of turmoil in an open box—they made a nest in some old disco shirts from the seven-ties. I suspect that's where the baby one slept. The mean landlady has evicted them.

Downstairs, I turn the lights back off and let evening have its way with me. Waves of pre-nighttime nervousness are coming from the collie's blanket. I sit next to her in the dimness touching her ears, and listen for feet at the top of the stairs.

They're speaking in physics so I'm left out of the conversation. Chris apologetically erases one of the pictures I've drawn on the blackboard and replaces it with a curving blue arrow surrounded by radiating chalk waves of green.

"If it's plasma, make it in red," I suggest helpfully. We're all smok-ing illegally in the journal office with the door closed and the window open. We're having a plasma party.

"We aren't discussing *plas*ma." Bob says condescendingly. He's smoking a horrendously smelly pipe. The longer he stays in here the more it feels like I'm breathing small daggers in through my nose. He and I don't get along; each of us thinks the other needs to be taken down a peg. Once we had a hissing match in the hallway which ended with him suggesting that I could be fired, which drove me to tell him he was *already* fired, and both of us stomped into our offices and slammed our doors.

"I had to fire Bob," I tell Chris later.

"I heard," he says noncommittally. Bob is his best friend. They spend at least half of each day standing in front of chalkboards, writing equations and arguing about outer space. Then they write theoretical papers about what they come up with. They're actually quite a big deal in the space physics community, but around here they're just two guys who keep erasing my pictures.

Someone knocks on the door and we put our cigarettes out. Bob hides his pipe in the palm of his hand and opens the door.

It's Gang Lu, one of their students. Everyone lights up again. Gang Lu stands stiffly talking to Chris while Bob holds a match to his pipe and puffs fiercely; nose daggers waft up and out, right in my direction. I give him a sugary smile and he gives me one back. Unimaginable, really, that less than two months from now one of his colleagues from abroad, a woman with delicate, birdlike features, will appear at the door to my office and identify herself as a friend of Bob's. When she asks, I take her down the hall to the room with the long table and then to his empty office. I do this without saying anything because there's nothing to say, and she takes it all in with small, serious nods until the moment she sees his blackboard covered with scribbles and arrows and equations. At that point her face loosens and she starts to cry in long ragged sobs. An hour later I go back and the office is empty. When I erase the blackboard finally, I can see where she laid her hands carefully, where the numbers are ghostly and blurred.

Bob blows his smoke discreetly in my direction and waits for Chris to finish talking to Gang Lu, who is answering questions in a monotone—yes or no, or I don't know. Another Chinese student named Shan lets himself in after knocking lightly. He nods and smiles at me and then stands at a respectful distance waiting to ask Chris a question.

It's like a physics conference in here. I wish they'd all leave so I could make my usual midafternoon spate of personal calls. I begin thumbing through papers in a businesslike way.

Bob pokes at his pipe with a bent paper clip. Shan yawns hugely and then looks embarrassed. Chris erases what he put on the blackboard and tries unsuccessfully to redraw my pecking parakeet. "I don't know how it goes," he says to me.

Gang Lu looks around the room idly with expressionless eyes. He's sick of physics and sick of the buffoons who practice it. The tall glacial German, Chris, who tells him what to do; the crass idiot Bob who talks to him like he is a dog; the student Shan whose ideas about plasma physics are treated with reverence and praised at every meeting. The woman who puts her feet on the desk and dismisses him with her eyes. Gang Lu no longer spends his evenings in the computer lab, running simulations and thinking about magnetic forces and invisible particles; he now spends them at the firing range, learning to hit a moving target with the gun he purchased last spring. He pictures himself holding the gun with both hands, arms straight out and steady; Clint Eastwood, only smarter. Clint Eastwood as a rocket scientist.

He stares at each person in turn, trying to gauge how much respect each of them has for him. One by one. Behind black-rimmed glasses, he counts with his eyes. In each case the verdict is clear: not enough.

The collie fell down the basement stairs. I don't know if she was disoriented and looking for me or what. But when I was at work she used her long nose like a lever and got the door to the basement open and tried to go down there except her legs wouldn't do it and she fell. I found her sleeping on the concrete floor in an unnatural position, one leg still awkwardly resting on the last step. I repositioned the leg and sat down next to her and petted her. We used to play a game called Maserati, where I'd grab her nose like a gearshift and put her through all the gears, first second third fourth, until we were going a hundred miles an hour through town. She thought it was funny.

Now I'm at work but this morning there's nothing to do, and every time I turn around I see her sprawled, eyes mute, leg bent upward. We're breaking each other's hearts. I draw a picture of her on the blackboard using brown chalk. I make Xs where her eyes should be. Chris walks in with the morning paper and a cup of coffee. He looks around the clean office.

"Why are you here when there's no work to do?" he asks.

"I'm hiding from my life, what else," I tell him. This sounds perfectly reasonable to him. He gives me part of the paper.

His mother is visiting from Germany, a robust woman of eighty who is depressed and hoping to be cheered up. In the last year she has lost her one-hundred-year-old mother and her husband of sixty years. She mostly can't be cheered up, but she likes going to art galleries so Chris has been driving her around the Midwest, to our best cities, showing her what kind of art Americans like to look at.

"How's your mom?" I ask him.

He shrugs and makes a flat-handed so-so motion.

We read, smoke, drink coffee, and yawn. I decide to go home.

"Good idea," he says encouragingly.

It's November 1, 1991, the last day of the first part of my life. Before I leave I pick up the eraser and stand in front of the collie's picture on the blackboard, thinking. I can feel him watching me, drinking his coffee. He's wearing a gold shirt and blue jeans and a gray cardigan sweater. He is tall and lanky and white-haired, forty-seven years old. He has a wife named Ulrike, a daughter named Karein, and a son named Goran. A dog named Mica. A mother named Ursula. A friend named me.

I erase the *X*s.

Down the hall, Linhua Shan feeds numbers into a computer and watches as a graph is formed. The computer screen is brilliant blue, and the lines appear in red and yellow and green. Four keystrokes and the green becomes purple. More keystrokes and the blue background fades to the azure of a summer sky. The wave lines arc over it, crossing against one another. He asks the computer to print, and while it chugs along he pulls up a golf game on the screen and tees off.

One room over, at a desk, Gang Lu works on a letter to his sister in China. *The study of physics is more and more disappointing,* he tells her. *Modern physics is self-delusion and all my life I have been honest and straightforward, and I have most of all detested cunning, fawning sycophants and dishonest bureaucrats who think they are always right in everything.* Delicate Chinese characters all over a page. She was a kind and gentle sister, and he thanks her for that. He's going to kill himself. *You yourself should not be too sad about it, for at least I have found a few traveling companions to accompany me to the grave.* Inside the coat on the back of his chair are a .38-caliber handgun and a .22-caliber revolver. They're heavier than they look and weigh the pockets down. *My beloved elder sister, I take my eternal leave of you.*

The collie's eyes are almond-shaped; I draw them in with brown chalk and put a white bone next to her feet.

"That's better," Chris says kindly.

Before I leave the building I pass Gang Lu in the hallway and say hello. He has a letter in his hand and he's wearing his coat. He doesn't answer and I don't expect him to. At the end of the hallway are the double doors leading to the rest of my life. I push them open and walk through.

Friday afternoon seminar, everyone is glazed over, listening as someone explains something unexplainable at the head of the long table. Gang Lu stands up and leaves the room abruptly; goes down one floor to see if the chairman, Dwight, is sitting in his office. He is. The door is open. Gang Lu turns and walks back up the stairs and enters the meeting room again. Chris Goertz is sitting near the door and takes the first bullet in the back of the head. There is a loud popping sound and then blue smoke. Shan gets the second bullet in the forehead, the lenses of his glasses shatter. More smoke and the room rings with the popping. Bob Smith tries to crawl beneath the table. Gang Lu takes two steps, holds his arms straight out, and levels the gun with both hands. Bob looks up. The third bullet in the right hand, the fourth in the chest. Smoke. Elbows and legs, people trying to get out of the way and then out of the room.

Gang Lu walks quickly down the stairs, dispelling spent cartridges and loading new ones. From the doorway of Dwight's office: the fifth bullet in the head, the sixth strays, the seventh also in the head. A slumping. More smoke and ringing. Through the cloud an image comes forward—Bob Smith, hit in the chest, hit in the hand, still alive. Back up the stairs. Two scientists, young men, crouched over Bob, loosening his clothes, talking to him. From where he lies, Bob can see his best friend still sitting upright in a chair, head thrown back at an unnatural angle. Everything is broken and red. The two young scientists leave the room at gunpoint. Bob closes his eyes. The eighth and ninth bullets in his head. As Bob dies, Chris Goertz's body settles in his chair, a long sigh escapes his throat. Reload. Two more for Chris, one for Shan. Exit the building, cross two streets, run across the green, into building number two and upstairs.

The administrator, Anne Cleary, is summoned from her office by the receptionist. She speaks to him for a few seconds, he produces the gun and shoots her in the face. The receptionist, a young student working as a temp, is just beginning to stand when he shoots her in the mouth. He dispels the spent cartridges in the stairwell, loads new ones. Reaches the top of the steps, looks around. Is disoriented suddenly. The ringing and the smoke and the dissatisfaction of not checking all the names off the list. A slamming and a running sound, the shout of police. He walks into an empty classroom, takes off his coat, folds it carefully and puts it over the back of the chair. Checks his watch; twelve minutes since it began. Places the barrel against his right temple. Fires.

The first call comes at four o'clock. I'm reading on the bench in the kitchen, one foot on a sleeping dog's back. It's Mary, calling from work. There's been some kind of disturbance in the building, a rumor that Dwight was shot; cops are running through the halls carrying rifles. They're evacuating the building and she's coming over.

Dwight, a tall likable oddball who cut off his ponytail when they made him chair of the department. Greets everyone with a famous booming hello in the morning, studies plasma, just like Chris and Bob. Chris lives two and half blocks from the physics building; he'll be home by now if they've evacuated. I dial his house and his mother answers. She tells me that Chris won't be home until five o'clock, and then they're going to a play. Ulrike, her daughter-in-law, is coming back from a trip to Chicago and will join them. She wants to know why I'm looking for Chris; isn't he where I am?

No, I'm at home and I just had to ask him something. Could he please call me when he comes in.

She tells me that Chris showed her a drawing I made of him sitting at his desk behind a stack of manuscripts. She's so pleased to meet Chris's friends, and the Midwest is lovely, really, except it's very brown, isn't it?

It *is* very brown. We hang up.

The Midwest is very brown. The phone rings. It's a physicist. His wife, a friend of mine, is on the extension. Well, he's not sure, but it's possible that I should brace myself for bad news. I've already heard, I tell him, something happened to Dwight. There's a long pause and then his wife says, Jo Ann. It's possible that Chris was involved.

I think she means Chris shot Dwight. No, she says gently, killed too.

Mary is here. I tell them not to worry and hang up. I have two cigarettes going. Mary takes one and smokes it. She's not looking at me. I tell her about the phone call.

"They're out of it," I say. "They thought Chris was involved."

She repeats what they said: I think you should brace yourself for bad news. Pours whiskey in a coffee cup.

For a few minutes I can't sit down, I can't stand up. I can only smoke. The phone rings. Another physicist tells me there's some bad news. He mentions Chris and Bob and I tell him I don't want to talk right now. He says okay but to be prepared because it's going to be on the news any minute. It's 4:45.

"Now they're trying to stir Bob into the stew," I tell Mary. She nods; she's heard this, too. I have the distinct feeling there is something going on that I can either understand or not understand. There's a choice to be made.

"I don't understand," I tell Mary.

We sit in the darkening living room, smoking and sipping our cups of whiskey. Inside my head I keep thinking *Uh-oh,* over and over. I'm in a rattled condition; I can't calm down and figure this out.

"I think we should brace ourselves in case something bad has happened," I say to Mary. She nods. "Just in case. It won't hurt to be braced." She nods again. I realize that I don't know what *braced* means. You hear it all the time but that doesn't mean it makes sense. Whiskey is supposed to be bracing but what it is is awful. I want either tea or beer, no whiskey. Mary nods and heads into the kitchen.

Within an hour there are seven women in the dim living room, sitting. Switching back and forth between CNN and the special reports by the local news. There is something terrifying about the quality of the light and the way voices are echoing in the room. The phone never stops ringing, ever since the story hit the national news. Physics,

University of Iowa, dead people. Names not yet released. Everyone I've ever known is checking in to see if I'm still alive. California calls, New York calls, Florida calls, Ohio calls twice. All the guests at a party my husband is having call, one after the other, to ask how I'm doing. Each time, fifty times, I think it might be Chris and then it isn't.

It occurs to me once that I could call his house and talk to him directly, find out exactly what happened. Fear that his mother would answer prevents me from doing it. By this time I am getting reconciled to the fact that Shan, Gang Lu, and Dwight were killed. Also an administrator and her office assistant. The Channel 9 newslady keeps saying there are six dead and two in critical condition. They're not saying who did the shooting. The names will be released at nine o'clock. Eventually I sacrifice all of them except Chris and Bob; they are the ones in critical condition, which is certainly not hopeless. At some point I go into the study to get away from the terrible dimness in the living room, all those eyes, all that calmness in the face of chaos. The collie tries to stand up but someone stops her with a handful of Fritos.

The study is small and cold after I shut the door, but more brightly lit than the living room. I can't remember what anything means. The phone rings and I pick up the extension and listen. My friend Michael is calling from Illinois for the second time. He asks Shirley if I'm holding up okay. Shirley says it's hard to tell. I go back into the living room.

The newslady breaks in at nine o'clock, and of course they drag it out as long as they can. I've already figured out that if they go in alphabetical order Chris will come first. Goertz, Lu, Nicholson, Shan, Smith. His name will come on first. She drones on, dead University of Iowa professors, lone gunman named Gang Lu.

Gang Lu. Lone gunman. Before I have a chance to absorb that she says, The dead are.

Chris's picture.

Oh no, oh God. I lean against Mary's chair and then leave the room abruptly. I have to stand in the bathroom for a while and look at myself in the mirror. I'm still Jo Ann, white face and dark hair. I have earrings on, tiny wrenches that hang from wires. In the living room she's pronouncing all the other names. The two critically wounded are the administrator and her assistant, Miya Sioson. The administrator is already dead for all practical purposes, although they won't disconnect the machines until the following afternoon. The student receptionist will survive but will never again be able to move more than her head. She was in Gang Lu's path and he shot her in the mouth and the bullet lodged in the top of her spine and not only will she never dance again, she'll never walk or write or spend a day alone. She got to keep her head but lost her body. The final victim is

Chris's mother, who will weather it all with a dignified face and an erect spine, then return to Germany and kill herself without further words or fanfare.

I tell the white face in the mirror that Gang Lu did this, wrecked everything and killed all those people. It seems as ludicrous as everything else. I can't get my mind to work right, I'm still operating on yesterday's facts; today hasn't jelled yet. "It's a good thing none of this happened," I say to my face. A knock on the door and I open it.

The collie is swaying on her feet, toenails clenched to keep from sliding on the wood floor. Julene's hesitant face. "She wanted to come visit you," she tells me. I bring her in and close the door. We sit by the tub. She lifts her long nose to my face and I take her muzzle and we move through the gears slowly, first second third fourth, all the way through town, until what happened has happened and we know it has happened. We return to the living room. The second wave of calls is starting to come in, from those who just saw the faces on the news. Shirley screens. A knock comes on the door. Julene settles the dog down again on her blanket. It's the husband at the door, looking frantic. He hugs me hard but I'm made of cement, arms stuck in a down position.

The women immediately clear out, taking their leave, looking at the floor. Suddenly it's only me and him, sitting in our living room on a Friday night, just like always. I realize it took quite a bit of courage for him to come to the house when he did, facing all those women who think he's the Antichrist. The dogs are crowded against him on the couch and he's wearing a shirt I've never seen before. He's here to help me get through this. Me. He knows how awful this must be. Awful. He knows how I felt about Chris. Past tense. I have to put my hands over my face for a minute.

We sit silently in our living room. He watches the mute television screen and I watch him. The planes and ridges of his face are more familiar to me than my own. I understand that he wishes even more than I do that he still loved me. When he looks over at me, it's with an expression I've seen before. It's the way he looks at the dog on the blanket.

I get his coat and follow him out into the cold November night. There are stars and stars and stars. The sky is full of dead men, drifting in the blackness like helium balloons. My mother floats past in a hospital gown, trailing tubes. I go back inside where the heat is.

The house is empty and dim, full of dogs and cigarette butts. The collie has peed again. The television is flickering *Special Report* across the screen and I turn it off before the pictures appear. I bring blankets up, fresh and warm from the dryer.

After all the commotion the living room feels cavernous and dead. A branch scrapes against the house and for a brief instant I feel a surge of hope. They might have come back. And I stand at the foot of the stairs staring up into the darkness, listening for the sounds of their little squirrel feet. Silence. No matter how much you miss them. They never come back once they're gone.

I wake her up three times between midnight and dawn. She doesn't usually sleep this soundly but all the chaos and company in the house tonight have made her more tired than usual. The Lab wakes and drowsily begins licking her lower region. She stops and stares at me, trying to make out my face in the dark, then gives up and sleeps. The brown dog is flat on her back with her paws limp, wedged between me and the back of the couch.

I've propped myself so I'll be able to see when dawn starts to arrive. For now there are still planets and stars. Above the black branches of a maple is the dog star, Sirius, my personal favorite. The dusty rings of Saturn. Io, Jupiter's moon.

When I think I can't bear it for one more minute I reach down and nudge her gently with my dog-arm. She rises slowly, faltering, and stands over me in the darkness. My peer, my colleague. In a few hours the world will resume itself, but for now we're in a pocket of silence. We're in the plasmapause, a place of equilibrium, where the forces of the Earth meet the forces of the sun. I imagine it as a place of silence, where the particles of dust stop spinning and hang motionless in deep space.

Around my neck is the stone he brought me from Poland. I hold it out. *Like this?* I ask. Shards of fly wings, suspended in amber.

Exactly, he says.

Jo Ann Beard
Jo Ann Beard was born in Illinois in 1955 and attended the Nonfiction Writing Program at the University of Iowa. She received a Whiting Award in 1997 and has published work in The New Yorker, Story, *and other magazines. She currently resides in upstate New York.*

An Entrance to the Woods

Wendell Berry

On a fine sunny afternoon at the end of September I leave my work in Lexington and drive east on I-64 and the Mountain Parkway. When I leave the Parkway at the little town of Pine Ridge I am in the watershed of the Red River in the Daniel Boone National Forest. From Pine Ridge I take Highway 715 out along the narrow ridgetops, a winding tunnel through the trees. And then I turn off on a Forest Service Road and follow it to the head of a foot trail that goes down the steep valley wall of one of the tributary creeks. I pull my car off the road and lock it, and lift on my pack.

It is nearly five o'clock when I start walking. The afternoon is brilliant and warm, absolutely still, not enough air stirring to move a leaf. There is only the steady somnolent trilling of insects, and now and again in the woods below me the cry of a pileated woodpecker. Those, and my footsteps on the path, are the only sounds.

From the dry oak woods of the ridge I pass down into the rock. The foot trails of the Red River Gorge all seek these stony notches that little streams have cut back through the cliffs. I pass a ledge overhanging a sheer drop of the rock, where in a wetter time there would be a waterfall. The ledge is dry and mute now, but on the face of the rock below are the characteristic mosses, ferns, liverwort, meadow

250

rue. And here where the ravine suddenly steepens and narrows, where the shadows are long-lived and the dampness stays, the trees are different. Here are beech and hemlock and poplar, straight and tall, reaching way up into the light. Under them are evergreen thickets of rhododendron. And wherever the dampness is there are mosses and ferns. The faces of the rock are intricately scalloped with veins of ironstone, scooped and carved by the wind.

Finally from the crease of the ravine I am following there begins to come the trickling and splashing of water. There is a great restfulness in the sounds these small streams make; they are going down as fast as they can, but their sounds seem leisurely and idle, as if produced like gemstones with the greatest patience and care.

A little later, stopping, I hear not far away the more voluble flowing of the creek. I go on down to where the trail crosses and begin to look for a camping place. The little bottoms along the creek here are thickety and weedy, probably having been kept clear and cropped or pastured not so long ago. In the more open places are little lavender asters, and the even smaller-flowered white ones that some people call beeweed or farewell-summer. And in low wet places are the richly flowered spikes of great lobelia, the blooms an intense startling blue, exquisitely shaped. I choose a place in an open thicket near the stream, and make camp.

It is a simple matter to make camp. I string up a shelter and put my air mattress and sleeping bag in it, and I am ready for the night. And supper is even simpler, for I have brought sandwiches for this first meal. In less than an hour all my chores are done. It will still be light for a good while, and I go over and sit down on a rock at the edge of the stream.

And then a heavy feeling of melancholy and lonesomeness comes over me. This does not surprise me, for I have felt it before when I have been alone at evening in wilderness places that I am not familiar with. But here it has a quality that I recognize as peculiar to the narrow hollows of the Red River Gorge. These are deeply shaded by the trees and by the valley walls, the sun rising on them late and setting early; they are more dark than light. And there will often be little rapids in the stream that will sound, at a certain distance, exactly like people talking. As I sit on my rock by the stream now, I could swear that there is a party of campers coming up the trail toward me, and for several minutes I stay alert, listening for them, their voices seeming to rise and fall, fade out and lift again, in happy conversation. When I finally realize that it is only a sound the creek is making, though I have not come here for company and do not want any, I am inexplicably sad.

These are haunted places, or at least it is easy to feel haunted in them, alone at nightfall. As the air darkens and the cool of the night rises, one feels the immanence of the wraiths of the ancient tribesmen who used to inhabit the rock houses of the cliffs; of the white hunters from east of the mountains; of the farmers who accepted the isolation of these nearly inaccessible valleys to crop the narrow bottoms and ridges and pasture their cattle and hogs in the woods; of the seekers of quick wealth in timber and ore. For though this is a wilderness place, it bears its part of the burden of human history. If one spends much time here and feels much liking for the place, it is hard to escape the sense of one's predecessors. If one has read of the prehistoric Indians whose flint arrowpoints and pottery and hominy holes and petroglyphs have been found here, then every rock shelter and clifty spring will suggest the presence of those dim people who have disappeared into the earth. Walking along the ridges and the stream bottoms, one will come upon the heaped stones of a chimney, or the slowly filling depression of an old cellar, or will find in the spring a japonica bush or periwinkles or a few jonquils blooming in a thicket that used to be a dooryard. Wherever the land is level enough there are abandoned fields and pastures. And nearly always there is the evidence that one follows in the steps of the loggers.

That sense of the past is probably one reason for the melancholy that I feel. But I know that there are other reasons.

One is that, though I am here in body, my mind and my nerves too are not yet altogether here. We seem to grant to our high-speed roads and our airlines the rather thoughtless assumption that people can change places as rapidly as their bodies can be transported. That, as my own experience keeps proving to me, is not true. In the middle of the afternoon I left off being busy at work, and drove through traffic to the freeway, and then for a solid hour or more I drove sixty or seventy miles an hour, hardly aware of the country I was passing through, because on the freeway one does not have to be. The landscape has been subdued so that one may drive over it at seventy miles per hour without any concession whatsoever to one's whereabouts. One might as well be flying. Though one is in Kentucky one is not experiencing Kentucky; one is experiencing the highway, which might be in nearly any hill country east of the Mississippi.

Once off the freeway, my pace gradually slowed, as the roads became progressively more primitive, from seventy miles an hour to a walk. And now, here at my camping place, I have stopped altogether. But my mind is still keyed to seventy miles an hour. And having come here so fast, it is still busy with the work I am usually doing. Having come here by the freeway, my mind is not so fully here as it would have been if I had come by the crookeder, slower state roads; it is incalculably farther away than it would have been if I had come all the way on foot, as my earliest predecessors came. When the Indians and the first white hunters entered this country they were altogether here as soon as they arrived, for they had seen and experienced fully everything between here and their starting place, and so the transition was gradual and articulate in their consciousness. Our senses, after all, were developed to function at foot speeds; and the transition from foot travel to motor travel, in terms of evolutionary time, has been abrupt. The faster one goes, the more strain there is on the senses, the more they fail to take in, the more confusion they must tolerate or gloss over—and the longer it takes to bring the mind to a stop in the presence of anything. Though the freeway passes through the very heart of this forest, the motorist remains several hours' journey by foot from what is living at the edge of the right-of-way.

But I have not only come to this strangely haunted place in a short time and too fast. I have in that move made an enormous change: I have departed from my life as I am used to living it, and have come into the wilderness. It is not fear that I feel; I have learned to fear the everyday events of human history much more than I fear the everyday occurrences of the woods; in general, I would rather trust myself to the woods than to any government that I know of. I feel, instead, an uneasy awareness of severed connections, of being cut off from all familiar places and of being a stranger where I am. What is happening at home? I wonder, and I know I can't find out very easily or very soon.

Even more discomforting is a pervasive sense of unfamiliarity. In the places I am most familiar with—my house, or my garden, or even the woods near home that I have walked in for years—I am surrounded by associations; everywhere I look I am reminded of my history and my hopes; even unconsciously I am comforted by any number of proofs that my life on the earth is an established and a going thing. But I am in this hollow for the first time in my life. I see nothing that I recognize. Everything looks as it did before I came, as it will when I am gone. When I look over at my little camp I see how tentative and insignificant it is. Lying there in my bed in the dark tonight, I will be absorbed in the being of this place, invisible as a squirrel in his nest.

Uneasy as this feeling is, I know it will pass. Its passing will produce a deep pleasure in being here. And I have felt it often enough before that I have begun to understand something of what it means:

Nobody knows where I am. I don't know what is happening to anybody else in the world. While I am here I will not speak, and will have no reason or need for speech. It is only beyond this lonesomeness for the places I have come from that I can reach the vital reality of a place such as this. Turning toward this place, I confront a presence that none of my schooling and none of my usual assumptions have prepared me for: the wilderness, mostly unknowable and mostly alien, that is the universe. Perhaps the most difficult labor for my species is to accept its limits, its weakness and ignorance. But here I am. This wild place where I have camped lies within an enormous cone widening from the center of the earth out across the universe, nearly all of it a mysterious wilderness in which the power and the knowledge of men count for nothing. As long as its instruments are correct and its engines run, the airplane now flying through this great cone is safely within the human freehold; its behavior is as familiar and predictable to those concerned as the inside of a man's living room. But let its instruments or its engines fail, and at once it enters the wilderness where nothing is foreseeable. And these steep narrow hollows, these cliffs and forested ridges that lie below, are the antithesis of flight.

Wilderness is the element in which we live encased in civilization, as a mollusk lives in his shell in the sea. It is a wilderness that is beautiful, dangerous, abundant, oblivious of us, mysterious, never to be conquered or controlled or second-guessed, or known more than a little. It is a wilderness that for most of us most of the time is kept out of sight, camouflaged, by the edifices and the busyness and the bothers of human society.

And so, coming here, what I have done is strip away the human facade that usually stands between me and the universe, and I see more clearly where I am. What I am able to ignore much of the time, but find undeniable here, is that all wildernesses are one: there is a profound joining between this wild stream deep in one of the folds of my native country and the tropical jungles, the tundras of the north, the oceans and the deserts. Alone here, among the rocks and the trees, I see that I am alone also among the stars. A stranger here, unfamiliar with my surroundings, I am aware also that I know only in the most relative terms my whereabouts within the black reaches of the universe. And because the natural processes are here so little qualified by anything human, this fragment of the wilderness is also joined to other times; there flows over it a nonhuman time to be told by the growth and death of the forest and the wearing of the stream. I feel drawing out beyond my comprehension perspectives from which the growth and the death of a large poplar would seem as continuous and sudden as the raising and the lowering of a man's hand, from which men's history in the world, their brief clearing of the ground, will seem no more than the opening and shutting of an eye.

And so I have come here to enact—not because I want to but because, once here, I cannot help it—the loneliness and the humbleness of my kind. I must see in my flimsy shelter, pitched here for two nights, the transience of capitols and cathedrals. In growing used to being in this place, I will have to accept a humbler and a truer view of myself than I usually have.

A man enters and leaves the world naked. And it is only naked—or nearly so—that he can enter and leave the wilderness. If he walks, that is; and if he doesn't walk it can hardly be said that he has entered. He can bring only what he can carry—the little that it takes to replace for a few hours or a few days an animal's fur and teeth and claws and functioning instincts. In comparison to the usual traveler with his dependence on machines and highways and restaurants and motels—on the economy and the government, in short—the man who walks into the wilderness is naked indeed. He leaves behind his work, his household, his duties, his comforts—even, if he comes alone, his words. He immerses himself in what he is not. It is a kind of death.

The dawn comes slow and cold. Only occasionally, somewhere along the creek or on the slopes above, a bird sings. I have not slept well, and I waken without much interest in the day. I set the camp to rights, and fix breakfast, and eat. The day is clear, and high up on the points and ridges to the west of my camp I can see the sun shining on the woods. And suddenly I am full of an ambition: I want to get up where the sun is; I want to sit still in the sun up there among the high rocks until I can feel its warmth in my bones.

I put some lunch into a little canvas bag, and start out, leaving my jacket so as not to have to carry it after the day gets warm. Without my jacket, even climbing, it is cold in the shadow of the hollow, and I have a long way to go to get to the sun. I climb the steep path up the valley wall, walking rapidly, thinking only of the sunlight above me. It is as though I have entered into a deep sympathy with those tulip poplars that grow so straight and tall out of the shady ravines, not growing a branch worth the name until their heads are in the sun. I am so concentrated on the sun that when some grouse flush from the undergrowth ahead of me, I am thunderstruck; they are already planing down into the underbrush again before I can get my wits together and realize what they are.

The path zigzags up the last steepness of the bluff and then slowly levels out. For some distance it follows the backbone of a ridge, and then where the ridge is narrowest there is a great slab of bare rock lying full in the sun. This is what I have been looking for. I walk out into the center of the rock and sit, the clear warm light falling unobstructed all around. As the sun warms me I begin to grow comfortable not only in my clothes, but in the place and the day. And like those light-seeking poplars of the ravines, my mind begins to branch out.

Southward, I can hear the traffic on the Mountain Parkway, a steady continuous roar—the corporate voice of twentieth-century humanity, sustained above the transient voices of its members. Last night, except for an occasional airplane passing over, I camped out of reach of the sounds of engines. For long stretches of time I heard no sounds but the sounds of the woods.

Near where I am sitting there is an inscription cut into the rock:

A · J · SARGENT
fEB · 2ƀ · 1903

Those letters were carved there more than sixty-six years ago. As I look around me I realize that I can see no evidence of the lapse of so much time. In every direction I can see only narrow ridges and narrow deep hollows, all covered with trees. For all that can be told from this height by looking, it might still be 1903—or, for that matter, 1803 or 1703, or 1003. Indians no doubt sat here and looked over the country as I am doing now; the visual impression is so pure and strong that I can almost imagine myself one of them. But the insistent, the overwhelming, evidence of the time of my own arrival is in what I can hear—that roar of the highway off there in the distance. In 1903 the continent was still covered by a great ocean of silence, in which the sounds of machinery were scattered at wide intervals of time and space. Here, in 1903, there were only the natural sounds of the place. On a day like this, at the end of September, there would have been only the sounds of a few faint crickets, a woodpecker now and then, now and then the wind. But today, two-thirds of a century later, the continent is covered by an ocean of engine noise, in which silences occur only sporadically and at wide intervals.

From where I am sitting in the midst of this island of wilderness, it is as though I am listening to the machine of human history—a huge flywheel building speed until finally the force of its whirling will break it in pieces, and the world with it. That is not an attractive thought, and yet I find it impossible to escape, for it has seemed to me for years now that the doings of men no longer occur within nature, but that the natural places which the human economy has so far spared now survive almost accidentally within the doings of men. This wilderness of the Red River now carries on its ancient processes *within* the human climate of war and waste and confusion. And I know that the distant roar of engines, though it may *seem* only to be passing through this wilderness, is really bearing down upon it. The machine is running now with a speed that produces blindness—as to the driver of a speeding automobile the only thing stable, the only thing not a mere blur on the edge of the retina, is the automobile itself—and the blindness of a thing with power promises the destruction of what cannot be seen. That roar of the highway is the voice of the American economy; it is sounding also wherever strip mines are being cut in the steep slopes of Appalachia, and wherever cropland is being destroyed to make roads and suburbs, and wherever rivers and marshes and bays and forests are being destroyed for the sake of industry or commerce.

No. Even here where the economy of life is really an economy—where the creation is yet fully alive and continuous and self-enriching, where whatever dies enters directly into the life of the living—even here one cannot fully escape the sense of an impending human catastrophe. One cannot come here without the awareness that this is an island surrounded by the machinery and the workings of an insane greed, hungering for the world's end—that ours is a "civilization" of which the work of no builder or artist is symbol, nor the life of any good man, but rather the bulldozer, the poison spray, the hugging fire of napalm, the cloud of Hiroshima.

Though from the high vantage point of this stony ridge I see little hope that I will ever live a day as an optimist, still I am not desperate. In fact, with the sun warming me now, and with the whole day before me to wander in this beautiful country, I am happy. A man cannot despair if he can imagine a better life, and if he can enact something of its possibility. It is only when I am ensnarled in the meaningless ordeals and the ordeals of meaninglessness, of which our public and political life is now so productive, that I lose the awareness of something better, and feel the despair of having come to the dead end of possibility.

Today, as always when I am afoot in the woods, I feel the possibility, the reasonableness, the practicability of living in the world in a way that would enlarge rather than diminish the hope of life. I feel the possibility of a frugal and protective love for the creation that would be unimaginably more meaningful and joyful than our present destructive and wasteful economy. The absence of human society, that made me so uneasy last night, now begins to be a comfort to me. I am afoot in the woods. I am alive in the world, this moment, without the help or the interference of any machine. I can move without reference to anything except the lay of the land and the capabilities of my own body. The necessities of foot travel in this steep country have stripped away all superfluities. I simply could not enter into this place and assume its quiet with all the belongings of a family man, property holder, etc. For the time, I am reduced to my irreducible self. I feel the lightness of body that a man must feel who has just lost fifty pounds of fat. As I leave the bare expanse of the rock and go in under the trees again, I am aware that I move in the landscape as one of its details.

Walking through the woods, you can never see far, either ahead or behind, so you move without much of a sense of getting anywhere or of moving at any certain speed. You burrow through the foliage in the air much as a mole burrows through the roots in the ground. The views that open out occasionally from the ridges afford a relief, a recovery of orientation, that they could never give as mere "scenery," looked at from a turnout at the edge of a highway.

The trail leaves the ridge and goes down a ravine into the valley of a creek where the night chill has stayed. I pause only long enough to drink the cold clean water. The trail climbs up onto the next ridge.

It is the ebb of the year. Though the slopes have not yet taken on the bright colors of the autumn maples and oaks, some of the duller trees are already shedding. The foliage has begun to flow down the cliff faces and the slopes like a tide pulling back. The woods is mostly quiet, subdued, as if the pressure of survival has grown heavy upon it, as if above the growing warmth of the day the cold of winter can be felt waiting to descend.

At my approach a big hawk flies off the low branch of an oak and out over the treetops. Now and again a nuthatch hoots, off somewhere in the woods. Twice I stop and watch an ovenbird. A few feet ahead of me there is a sudden movement in the leaves, and then quiet. When I slip up and examine the spot there is nothing to be found. Whatever passed there has disappeared, quicker than the hand that is quicker than the eye, a shadow fallen into a shadow.

In the afternoon I leave the trail. My walk so far has come perhaps three-quarters of the way around a long zigzagging loop that will eventually bring me back to my starting place. I turn down a small unnamed branch of the creek where I am camped, and I begin the loveliest part of the day. There is nothing here resembling a trail. The best way is nearly always to follow the edge of the stream, stepping from one stone to another. Crossing back and forth over the water, stepping on or over rocks and logs, the way ahead is never clear for more than a few feet. The stream accompanies me down, threading its way under boulders and logs and over little falls and rapids. The rhododendron overhangs it so closely in places that I can go only by stooping. Over the rhododendron are the great dark heads of the hemlocks. The streambanks are ferny and mossy. And through this green tunnel the voice of the stream changes from rock to rock; subdued like all the other autumn voices of the woods, it seems sunk in a deep contented meditation on the sounds of *l*.

The water in the pools is absolutely clear. If it weren't for the shadows and ripples you would hardly notice that it is water; the fish would seem to swim in the air. As it is, where there is no leaf floating, it is impossible to tell exactly where the plane of the surface lies. As I walk up on a pool the little fish dart every which way out of sight. And then after I sit still a while, watching, they come out again. Their shadows flow over the rocks and leaves on the bottom. Now I have come into the heart of the woods. I am far from the highway and can hear no sound of it. All around there is a grand deep autumn quiet, in which a few insects dream their summer songs. Suddenly a wren sings way off in the underbrush. A redbreasted nuthatch walks, hooting, headfirst down the trunk of a walnut. An ovenbird walks out along the limb of a hemlock and looks at me, curious. The little fish soar in the pool, turning their clean quick angles, their shadows seeming barely to keep up. As I lean and dip my cup in the water, they scatter. I drink, and go on.

When I get back to camp it is only the middle of the afternoon or a little after. Since I left in the morning I have walked something like eight miles. I haven't hurried—have mostly poked along, stopping often and looking around. But I am tired, and coming down the creek I have got both feet wet. I find a sunny place, and take off my shoes and socks and set them to dry. For a long time then, lying propped against the trunk of a tree, I read and rest and watch the evening come.

All day I have moved through the woods, making as little noise as possible. Slowly my mind and my nerves have slowed to a walk. The quiet of the woods has ceased to be something that I observe; now it is something that I am a part of. I have joined it with my own quiet. As the twilight draws on I no longer feel the strangeness and uneasiness of the evening before. The sounds of the creek move through my mind as they move through the valley, unimpeded and clear.

When the time comes I prepare supper and eat, and then wash kettle and cup and spoon and put them away. As far as possible I get things ready for an early start in the morning. Soon after dark I go to bed, and I sleep well.

I wake long before dawn. The air is warm and I feel rested and wide awake. By the light of a small candle lantern I break camp and pack. And then I begin the steep climb back to the car.

The moon is bright and high. The woods stands in deep shadow, the light falling soft through the openings of the foliage. The trees appear immensely tall, and black, gravely looming over the path. It is windless and still; the moonlight pouring over the country seems more potent than the air. All around me there is still that constant low singing of the insects. For days now it has continued without letup or inflection, like ripples on water under a steady breeze. While I slept it went on through the night, a shimmer on my mind. My shoulder brushes a low tree overhanging the path and a bird that was asleep on one of the branches startles awake and flies off into the shadows, and I go on with the sense that I am passing near to the sleep of things.

In a way this is the best part of the trip. Stopping now and again to rest, I linger over it, sorry to be going. It seems to me that if I were to stay on, today would be better than yesterday, and I realize it was to renew the life of that possibility that I came here. What I am leaving is something to look forward to.

Wendell Berry
Wendell Berry, a farmer, was born on August 5, 1934 in Newcastle, Kentucky. A poet, novelist, and essayist, he is the author of over thirty books, including Home Economics *and* Another Turn of the Crank. *Berry taught English at New York University and the University of Kentucky. He is a recipient of numerous awards, including the T. S. Eliot Award. The* New York Review of Books *called him "the great moral essayist of our day."*

The Fine Art of Sighing

Bernard Cooper

You feel a gradual welling up of pleasure, or boredom, or melancholy. Whatever the emotion, it's more abundant than you ever dreamed. You can no more contain it than your hands can cup a lake. And so you surrender and suck the air. Your esophagus opens, diaphragm expands. Poised at the crest of an exhalation, your body is about to be unburdened, second by second, cell by cell. A kettle hisses. A balloon deflates. Your shoulders fall like two ripe pears, muscles slack at last.

My mother stared out the kitchen window, ashes from her cigarette dribbling into the sink. She'd turned her back on the rest of the house, guarding her own solitude. I'd tiptoe across the linoleum and fix my lunch without making a sound. Sometimes I saw her back expand, then heard her let loose one plummeting note, a sigh so long and weary it might have been her last. Beyond our backyard, above telephone poles and apartment buildings, rose the brown horizon of the city; across it glided an occasional bird, or the blimp that advertised Goodyear tires. She might have been drifting into the distance, or lamenting her separation from it. She might have been wishing she were somewhere else, or wishing she could be happy where she was, a middle-aged housewife dreaming at her sink.

My father's sighs were more melodic. What began as a somber sigh could abruptly change pitch, turn gusty and loose, and suggest by its very transformation that what begins in sorrow might end in relief. He could prolong the rounded vowel of *oy,* or let it ricochet like an echo, as if he were shouting in a tunnel or a cave. Where my mother sighed from ineffable sadness, my father sighed at simple things: the coldness of a drink, the softness of a pillow, or an itch that my mother, following the frantic map of his words, finally found on his back and scratched.

A friend of mine once mentioned that I was given to long and ponderous sighs. Once I became aware of this habit, I heard my father's sighs in my own and knew for a moment his small satisfactions. At other times, I felt my mother's restlessness and wished I could leave my body with my breath, or be happy in the body my breath left behind.

It's a reflex and a legacy, this soulful species of breathing. Listen closely: My ancestors' lungs are pumping like bellows, men towing boats along the banks of the Volga, women lugging baskets of rye bread and pike. At the end of each day, they lift their weary arms in a toast; as thanks for the heat and sting of vodka, their aahs condense in the cold Russian air.

At any given moment, there must be thousands of people sighing. A man in Milwaukee heaves and shivers and blesses the head of his second wife, who's not too shy to lick his toes. A judge in Munich groans with pleasure after tasting again the silky bratwurst she ate as a child. Every day, meaningful sighs are expelled from schoolchildren, driving instructors, forensic experts, certified public accountants, and dental hygienists, just to name a few. The sighs of widows and widowers alone must account for a significant portion of the carbon dioxide released into the atmosphere. Every time a girdle is removed, a foot is submerged in a tub of warm water, or a restroom is reached on a desolate road . . . you'd think the sheer velocity of it would create mistrals, siroccos, hurricanes; arrows should be swarming over satellite maps, weathermen talking a mile a minute, ties flapping from their necks like flags.

Before I learned that Venetian prisoners were led across it to their execution, I imagined that the Bridge of Sighs was a feat of invisible engineering, a structure vaulting above the earth, the girders and trusses, the stay ropes and cables, the counterweights and safety rails, connecting one human breath to the next.

Bernard Cooper

Bernard Cooper, art critic for Los Angeles Magazine, *explores in his writing the delicate relationship between identity and memory. Born in California in 1951, Cooper is the author of two collections of memoirs (*Truth Serum *and* Maps to Anywhere*), a novel (*A Year of Rhymes*), a book of short stories (*Guess Again*), as well as many works in anthologies and journals, including* The Paris Review *and* The Best American Essays. *Cooper has taught creative writing at Antioch University and at the UCLA Writer's Program, and he has received the PEN/Hemingway Award and the O. Henry Prize.*

Goodbye to All That

Joan Didion

How many miles to Babylon?
Three score miles and ten—
Can I get there by candlelight?
Yes, and back again—
If your feet are nimble and light
You can get there by candlelight.

It is easy to see the beginnings of things, and harder to see the ends. I can remember now, with a clarity that makes the nerves in the back of my neck constrict, when New York began for me, but I cannot lay my finger upon the moment it ended, can never cut through the ambiguities and second starts and broken resolves to the exact place on the page where the heroine is no longer as optimistic as she once was. When I first saw New York I was twenty, and it was summertime, and I got off a DC-7 at the old Idlewild temporary terminal in a new dress which had seemed very smart in Sacramento but seemed less smart already, even in the old Idlewild temporary terminal, and the warm air smelled of mildew and some instinct, programmed by all the movies I had ever seen and all the songs I had ever heard sung and all the stories I had ever read about New York, informed me that it would never be quite the same again. In fact it never was. Some time later there was a song on all the jukeboxes on the upper East Side that went "but where is the schoolgirl who used to be me," and if it was late enough at night I used to wonder that. I know now that almost everyone wonders something like that, sooner or later and no matter what he or she is doing, but one of the mixed blessings of being twenty and twenty-one and even twenty-three is the conviction that nothing like this, all evidence to the contrary notwithstanding, has ever happened to anyone before.

Of course it might have been some other city, had circumstances been different and the time been different and had I been different, might have been Paris or Chicago or even San Francisco, but because I am talking about myself I am talking here about New York. That first night I opened my window on the bus into town and watched for the skyline, but all I could see were the wastes of Queens and the big signs that said MIDTOWN TUNNEL THIS LANE and then a flood of summer rain (even that seemed remarkable and exotic, for I had come out of the West where there was no summer rain), and for the next three days I sat wrapped in blankets in a hotel room air-conditioned to 35° and tried to get over a bad cold and a high fever. It did not occur to me to call a doctor, because I knew none, and although it did occur to me to call the desk and ask that the air conditioner be turned off, I never called, because I did not know how much to tip whoever might come—was anyone ever so young? I am here to tell you that someone was. All I could do during those three days was talk long-distance to the boy I already knew I would never marry in the spring. I would stay in New York, I told him, just six months, and I could see the Brooklyn Bridge from my window. As it turned out the bridge was the Triborough, and I stayed eight years.

In retrospect it seems to me that those days before I knew the names of all the bridges were happier than the ones that came later, but perhaps you will see that as we go along. Part of what I want to tell you is what it is like to be young in New York, how six months can become eight years with the deceptive ease of a film dissolve, for that is how those years appear to me now, in a long sequence of sentimental dissolves and old-fashioned trick shots—the Seagram Building fountains dissolve into snowflakes, I enter a revolving door at twenty and come out a good deal older, and on a different street. But most particularly I want to explain to you, and in the process perhaps to myself, why I no longer live in New York. It is often said that New York is a city for only the very rich and the very poor. It is less often said that New York is also, at least for those of us who came there from somewhere else, a city for only the very young.

I remember once, one cold bright December evening in New York, suggesting to a friend who complained of having been around too long that he come with me to a party where there would be, I assured him with the bright resourcefulness of twenty-three, "new faces." He laughed literally until he choked, and I had to roll down the taxi window and hit him on the back. "New faces," he said finally, "don't tell me about *new faces*." It seemed that the last time he had gone to a party where he had been promised "new faces," there had been fifteen people in the room, and he had already slept with five of the women and owed money to all but two of the men. I laughed with him, but the first snow had just begun to fall and the big Christmas trees glittered yellow and white as far as I could see up Park Avenue and I had a new dress and it would be a long while before I would come to understand the particular moral of the story.

It would be a long while because, quite simply, I was in love with New York. I do not mean "love" in any colloquial way, I mean that I was in love with the city, the way you love the first person who ever touches you and never love anyone quite that way again. I remember walking across Sixty-second Street one twilight that first spring, or the second spring, they were all alike for a while. I was late to meet someone but I stopped at Lexington Avenue and bought a peach and stood on the corner eating it and knew that I had come out of the West and reached the mirage. I could taste the peach and feel the soft air blowing from a subway grating on my legs and I could smell lilac and garbage and expensive perfume and I knew that it would cost something sooner or later—because I did not belong there, did not come from there—but when you are twenty-two or twenty-three, you figure that later you will have a high emotional balance, and be able to pay whatever it costs. I still believed in possibilities then, still had the sense, so peculiar to New York, that something extraordinary would happen any minute, any day, any month. I was making only $65 or $70 a week then ("Put yourself in Hattie Carnegie's hands," I was advised without the slightest trace of irony by an editor of the magazine for which I worked), so little money that some weeks I had to charge food at Bloomingdale's gourmet shop in order to eat, a fact which went unmentioned in the letters I wrote to California. I never told my father that I needed money because then he would have sent it, and I would never know if I could do it by myself. At that time making a living seemed a game to me, with arbitrary but quite inflexible rules. And except on a certain kind of winter evening—six-thirty in the Seventies, say, already dark and bitter with a wind off the river, when I would be walking very fast toward a bus and would look in the bright windows of brownstones and see cooks working in clean kitchens and imagine women lighting candles on the floor above and beautiful children being bathed on the floor above that—except on nights like those, I never felt poor; I had the feeling that if I needed money I could always get it. I could write a syndicated column for teenagers under the name "Debbi Lynn" or I could smuggle gold into India or I could become a $100 call girl, and none of it would matter.

Nothing was irrevocable; everything was within reach. Just around every corner lay something curious and interesting, something I had never before seen or done or known about. I could go to a party and meet someone who called himself Mr. Emotional Appeal and ran The Emotional Appeal Institute or Tina Onassis Blandford or a Florida cracker who was then a regular on what he called "the Big C," the Southampton–El Morocco circuit ("I'm well-connected on the Big C, honey," he would tell me over collard greens on his vast borrowed terrace), or the widow of the celery king of the Harlem market or a piano salesman from Bonne Terre, Missouri, or someone who had already made and lost two fortunes in Midland, Texas. I could make promises to myself and to other people and there would be all the time in the world to keep them. I could stay up all night and make mistakes, and none of it would count.

You see I was in a curious position in New York: it never occurred to me that I was living a real life there. In my imagination I was always there for just another few months, just until Christmas or Easter or the first warm day in May. For that reason I was most comfortable in the company of Southerners. They seemed to be in New York as I was, on some indefinitely extended leave from wherever they belonged, disinclined to consider the future, temporary exiles who always knew when the flights left for New Orleans or Memphis or Richmond or, in my case, California. Someone who lives always with a plane schedule in the drawer lives on a slightly different calendar. Christmas, for example, was a difficult season. Other people could take it in stride, going to Stowe or going abroad or going for the day to their mothers' places in Connecticut; those of us who believed that we lived somewhere else would spend it making and canceling airline reservations, waiting for weatherbound flights as if for the last plane out of Lisbon in 1940, and finally comforting one another, those of us who were left, with the oranges and mementos and smoked-oyster stuffings of childhood, gathering close, colonials in a far country.

Which is precisely what we were. I am not sure that it is possible for anyone brought up in the East to appreciate entirely what New York, the idea of New York, means to those of us who came out of the West and the South. To an Eastern child, particularly a child who has always had an uncle on Wall Street and who has spent several hundred Saturdays first at F. A. O. Schwarz and being fitted for shoes at Best's and then waiting under the Biltmore clock and dancing to Lester Lanin, New York is just a city, albeit *the* city, a plausible place for people to live. But to those of us who came from places where no one had heard of Lester Lanin and Grand Central Station was a Saturday radio program, where Wall Street and Fifth Avenue and Madison Avenue were not places at all but abstractions ("Money," and "High Fashion," and "The Hucksters"), New York was no mere city. It was instead an infinitely romantic notion, the mysterious nexus of all love and money and power, the shining and perishable dream itself. To think of "living" there was to reduce the miraculous to the mundane; one does not "live" at Xanadu.

In fact it was difficult in the extreme for me to understand those young women for whom New York was not simply an ephemeral Estoril but a real place, girls who bought toasters and installed new cabinets in their apartments and committed themselves to some reasonable future. I never bought any furniture in New York. For a year or so I lived in other people's apartments; after that I lived in the Nineties in an apartment furnished entirely with things taken from storage by a friend whose wife had moved away. And when I left the apartment in the Nineties (that was when I was leaving everything, when it was all breaking up) I left everything in it, even my winter clothes and the map of Sacramento County I had hung on the bedroom wall to remind me who I was, and I moved into a monastic four-room floor-through on Seventy-fifth Street. "Monastic" is perhaps misleading here, implying some chic severity; until after I was married and my husband moved some furniture in, there was nothing at all in those four rooms except a cheap double mattress and box springs, ordered by telephone the day I decided to move, and two French garden chairs lent me by a friend who imported them. (It strikes me now that the people I knew in New York all had curious and self-defeating sidelines. They imported garden chairs which did not sell very well at Hammacher Schlemmer or they tried to market hair straighteners in Harlem or they ghosted exposés of Murder Incorporated for Sunday supplements. I think that perhaps none of us was very serious, *engagé* only about our most private lives.)

All I ever did to that apartment was hang fifty yards of yellow theatrical silk across the bedroom windows, because I had some idea that the gold light would make me feel better, but I did not bother to weight the curtains correctly and all that summer the long panels of transparent golden silk would blow out the windows and get tangled and drenched in the afternoon thunderstorms. That was the year, my twenty-eighth, when I was discovering that not all of the promises would be kept, that some things are in fact irrevocable and that it had counted after all, every evasion and every procrastination, every mistake, every word, all of it.

That is what it was all about, wasn't it? Promises? Now when New York comes back to me it comes in hallucinatory flashes, so clinically detailed that I sometimes wish that memory would effect the distortion with which it is commonly credited. For a lot of the time I was in New York I used a perfume called *Fleurs de Rocaille,* and then *L'Air du Temps,* and now the slightest trace of either can short-circuit my connections for the rest of the day. Nor can I smell Henri Bendel jasmine soap without falling back into the past, or the particular mixture of spices used for boiling crabs. There were barrels of crab boil in a Czech place in the Eighties where I once shopped. Smells, of course, are notorious memory stimuli, but there are other things which affect me the same way. Blue-and-white striped sheets. Vermouth cassis. Some faded nightgowns which were new in 1959 or 1960, and some chiffon scarves I bought about the same time.

I suppose that a lot of us who have been young in New York have the same scenes on our home screens. I remember sitting in a lot of apartments with a slight headache about five o'clock in the morning. I had a friend who could not sleep, and he knew a few other people who had the same trouble, and we would watch the sky lighten and have a last drink with no ice and then go home in the early morning light, when the streets were clean and wet (had it rained in the night? we never knew) and the few cruising taxis still had their headlights on and the only color was the red and green of traffic signals. The White Rose bars opened very early in the morning; I recall waiting in one of them to watch an astronaut go into space, waiting so long that at the moment it actually happened I had my eyes not on the television screen but on a cockroach on the tile floor. I liked the bleak branches above Washington Square at dawn, and the monochromatic flatness of Second Avenue, the fire escapes and the grilled storefronts peculiar and empty in their perspective.

It is relatively hard to fight at six-thirty or seven in the morning without any sleep, which was perhaps one reason we stayed up all night, and it seemed to me a pleasant time of day. The windows were shuttered in that apartment in the Nineties and I could sleep a few hours and then go to work. I could work then on two or three hours' sleep and a container of coffee from Chock Full O' Nuts. I liked going to work, liked the soothing and satisfactory rhythm of getting out a magazine, liked the orderly progression of four-color closings and two-color closings and black-and-white closings and then The Product, no abstraction but something which looked effortlessly glossy and could be picked up on a newsstand and weighed in the hand. I liked all the minutiae of proofs and layouts, liked working late on the nights the magazine went to press, sitting and reading *Variety* and waiting for the copy desk to call. From my office I could look across town to the weather signal on the Mutual of New York Building and the lights that alternately spelled out TIME and LIFE above Rockefeller Plaza; that pleased me obscurely, and so did walking uptown in the mauve eight o'clocks of early summer evenings and looking at things, Lowestoft tureens in Fifty-seventh Street windows, people in evening clothes trying to get taxis, the trees just coming into full leaf, the lambent air, all the sweet promises of money and summer.

Some years passed, but I still did not lose that sense of wonder about New York. I began to cherish the loneliness of it, the sense that at any given time no one need know where I was or what I was doing. I liked walking, from the East River over to the Hudson and back on brisk days, down around the Village on warm days. A friend would leave me the key to her apartment in the West Village when she was out of town, and sometimes I would just move down there, because by that time the telephone was beginning to bother me (the canker, you see, was already in the rose) and not many people had that number. I remember one day when someone who did have the West Village number came to pick me up for lunch there, and we both had hangovers, and I cut my finger opening him a beer and burst into tears, and we walked to a Spanish restaurant and drank Bloody Marys and *gazpacho* until we felt better. I was not then guilt-ridden about spending afternoons that way, because I still had all the afternoons in the world.

And even that late in the game I still liked going to parties, all parties, bad parties, Saturday-afternoon parties given by recently married couples who lived in Stuyvesant Town, West Side parties given by unpublished or failed writers who served cheap red wine and talked about going to Guadalajara, Village parties where all the guests worked for advertising agencies and voted for Reform Democrats, press parties at Sardi's, the worst kinds of parties. You will have perceived by now that I was not one to profit by the experience of others, that it was a very long time indeed before I stopped believing in new faces and began to understand the lesson in that story, which was that it is distinctly possible to stay too long at the Fair.

I could not tell you when I began to understand that. All I know is that it was very bad when I was twenty-eight. Everything that was said to me I seemed to have heard before, and I could no longer listen. I could no longer sit in little bars near Grand Central and listen to someone complaining of his wife's inability to cope with the help while he missed another train to Connecticut. I no longer had any interest in hearing about the advances other people had received from their publishers, about plays which were having second-act trouble in Philadelphia, or about people I would like very much if only I would come out and meet them. I had already met them, always. There were certain parts of the city which I had to avoid. I could not bear upper Madison Avenue on weekday mornings (this was a particularly inconvenient aversion, since I then lived just fifty or sixty feet east of Madison), because I would see women walking Yorkshire terriers and shopping at Gristede's, and some Veblenesque gorge would rise in my throat. I could not go to Times Square in the afternoon, or to the New York Public Library for any reason whatsoever. One day I could not go into a Schrafft's; the next day it would be Bonwit Teller.

I hurt the people I cared about, and insulted those I did not. I cut myself off from the one person who was closer to me than any other. I cried until I was not even aware when I was crying and when I was not, cried in elevators and in taxis and in Chinese laundries, and when I went to the doctor he said only that I seemed to be depressed, and should see a "specialist." He wrote down a psychiatrist's name and address for me, but I did not go.

Instead I got married, which as it turned out was a very good thing to do but badly timed, since I still could not walk on upper Madison Avenue in the mornings and still could not talk to people and still cried in Chinese laundries. I had never before understood what "despair" meant, and I am not sure that I understand now, but I understood that year. Of course I could not work. I could not even get dinner with any degree of certainty, and I would sit in the apartment on Seventy-fifth Street paralyzed until my husband would call from his office and say gently that I did not have to get dinner, that I could meet him at Michael's Pub or at Toots Shor's or at Sardi's East. And then one morning in April (we had been married in January) he called and told me that he wanted to get out of New York for a while, that he would take a six-month leave of absence, that we would go somewhere.

It was three years ago that he told me that, and we have lived in Los Angeles since. Many of the people we knew in New York think this a curious aberration, and in fact tell us so. There is no possible, no adequate answer to that, and so we give certain stock answers, the answers everyone gives. I talk about how difficult it would be for us to "afford" to live in New York right now, about how much "space" we need. All I mean is that I was very young in New York, and that at some point the golden rhythm was broken, and I am not that young any more. The last time I was in New York was in a cold January, and everyone was ill and tired. Many of the people I used to know there had moved to Dallas or had gone on Antabuse or had bought a farm in New Hampshire. We stayed ten days, and then we took an afternoon flight back to Los Angeles, and on the way home from the airport that night I could see the moon on the Pacific and smell jasmine all around and we both knew that there was no longer any point in keeping the apartment we still kept in New York. There were years when I called Los Angeles "the Coast," but they seem a long time ago.

Joan Didion

Born in Sacramento, California in 1934, Joan Didion worked at Vogue *in the 1950s and then became a freelance writer. Her essays are a highly charged blend of personal narrative, and cultural-political commentary. Didion's essay collections include* Slouching Towards Bethlehem *and* The White Album, *and she is the author of a number of novels, including* Play It As It Lays *and* The Last Thing He Wanted. *She also co-authored several screenplays, including* A Star is Born *and* Up Close *and* Personal. *Didion has been awarded the Columbia Journalism Award and the Edward MacDowell Medal. She lives in New York and contributes to* The New Yorker *and* The New York Review of Books.

Total Eclipse

Annie Dillard

I

It had been like dying, that sliding down the mountain pass. It had been like the death of someone, irrational, that sliding down the mountain pass and into the region of dread. It was like slipping into fever, or falling down that hole in sleep from which you wake yourself whimpering. We had crossed the mountains that day, and now we were in a strange place—a hotel in central Washington, in a town near Yakima. The eclipse we had traveled here to see would occur early the next morning.

I lay in bed. My husband, Gary, was reading beside me. I lay in bed and looked at the painting on the hotel-room wall. It was a print of a detailed and lifelike painting of a smiling clown's head, made out of vegetables. It was a painting of the sort that you do not intend to look at and that, alas, you never forget. Some tasteless fate presses it upon you; it becomes part of the complex interior junk you carry with you wherever you go. Two years have passed since the total eclipse of which I write. During those years I have forgotten, I assume, a great many things I wanted to remember—but I have not forgotten that clown painting or its lunatic setting in the old hotel.

The clown was bald. Actually, he wore a clown's tight rubber wig, painted white; this stretched over the top of his skull, which was a cabbage. His hair was bunches of baby carrots. Inset in his white clown makeup, and in his cabbage skull, were his small and laughing human eyes. The clown's glance was like the glance of Rembrandt in some of the self-portraits: lively, knowing, deep, and loving. The crinkled shadows around his eyes were string beans. His eyebrows were parsley. Each of his ears was a broad bean. His thin, joyful lips were red chili peppers; between his lips were wet rows of human teeth and a suggestion of a real tongue. The clown print was framed in gilt and glassed.

To put ourselves in the path of the total eclipse, that day we had driven five hours inland from the Washington coast, where we lived. When we tried to cross the Cascades range, an avalanche had blocked the pass.

A slope's worth of snow blocked the road; traffic backed up. Had the avalanche buried any cars that morning? We could not learn. This highway was the only winter road over the mountains. We waited as highway crews bulldozed a passage through the avalanche. With two-by-fours and walls of plyboard, they erected a one-way, roofed tunnel through the avalanche. We drove through the avalanche tunnel, crossed the pass, and descended several thousand feet into central Washington and the broad Yakima valley, about which we knew only that it was orchard country. As we lost altitude, the snows disappeared; our ears popped; the trees changed, and in the trees were strange birds. I watched the landscape innocently, like a fool, like a diver in the rapture of the deep who plays on the bottom while his air runs out.

The hotel lobby was a dark, derelict room, narrow as a corridor, and seemingly without air. We waited on a couch while the manager vanished upstairs to do something unknown to our room. Beside us, on an overstuffed chair, absolutely motionless, was a platinum-blond woman in her forties, wearing a black silk dress and a strand of pearls. Her long legs were crossed; she supported her head on her fist. At the dim far end of the room, their backs toward us, sat six bald old men in their shirtsleeves, around a loud television. Two of them seemed asleep. They were drunks. "Number six!" cried the man on television, "Number six!"

On the broad lobby desk was a ten-gallon aquarium, lighted and bubbling, that contained one large fish; the fish tilted up and down in its water. Against the long opposite wall sang a live canary in its cage. Beneath the cage, among spilled millet seeds on the carpet, were a decorated child's sand bucket and matching sand shovel.

Now the alarm was set for six. I lay awake remembering an article I had read downstairs in the lobby, in an engineering magazine. The article was about gold mining.

In South Africa, in India, and in South Dakota, the gold mines extend so deeply into the earth's crust that they are hot. The rock walls burn the miners' hands. The companies have to air-condition the mines; if the air conditioners break, the miners die. The elevators in the mine shafts run very slowly, down, and up, so the miners' ears will not pop in their skulls. When the miners return to the surface, their faces are deathly pale.

Early the next morning we checked out. It was February 26, 1979, a Monday morning. We would drive out of town, find a hilltop, watch the eclipse, and then drive back over the mountains and home to the coast. How familiar things are here; how adept we are; how smoothly and professionally we check out! I had forgotten the clown's smiling head and the hotel lobby as if they had never existed. Gary put the car in gear and off we went, as off we have gone to a hundred other adventures.

It was before dawn when we found a highway out of town and drove into the unfamiliar countryside. By the growing light we could see a band of cirrostratus clouds in the sky. Later the rising sun would clear these clouds before the eclipse began. We drove at random until we came to a range of unfenced hills. We pulled off the highway, bundled up, and climbed one of these hills.

II

The hill was five hundred feet high. Long winter-killed grass covered it, as high as our knees. We climbed and rested, sweating in the cold; we passed clumps of bundled people on the hillside who were setting up telescopes and fiddling with cameras. The top of the hill stuck up in the middle of the sky. We tightened our scarves and looked around.

East of us rose another hill like ours. Between the hills, far below, was the highway that threaded south into the valley. This was the Yakima valley; I had never seen it before. It is justly famous for its beauty, like every planted valley. It extended south into the horizon, a distant dream of a valley, a Shangri-la. All its hundreds of low, golden slopes bore orchards. Among the orchards were towns, and roads, and plowed and fallow fields. Through the valley wandered a thin, shining river; from the river extended fine, frozen irrigation ditches. Distance blurred and blued the sight, so that the whole valley looked like a thickness or sediment at the bottom of the sky. Directly behind us was more sky, and empty lowlands blued by distance, and Mount Adams. Mount Adams was an enormous, snow-covered volcanic cone rising flat, like so much scenery.

Now the sun was up. We could not see it; but the sky behind the band of clouds was yellow, and, far down the valley, some hillside orchards had lighted up. More people were parking near the highway and climbing the hills. It was the West. All of us rugged individualists were wearing knit caps and blue nylon parkas. People were climbing the nearby hills and setting up shop in clumps among the dead grasses. It looked as though we had all gathered on hilltops to pray for the world on its last day. It looked as though we had all crawled out of spaceships and were preparing to assault the valley below. It looked as though we were scattered on hilltops at dawn to sacrifice virgins, make rain, set stone stelae in a ring. There was no place out of the wind. The straw grasses banged our legs.

Up in the sky where we stood, the air was lusterless yellow. To the west the sky was blue. Now the sun cleared the clouds. We cast rough shadows on the blowing grass; freezing, we waved our arms. Near the sun, the sky was bright and colorless. There was nothing to see.

It began with no ado. It was odd that such a well-advertised public event should have no starting gun, no overture, no introductory speaker. I should have known right then that I was out of my depth. Without pause or preamble, silent as orbits, a piece of the sun went away. We looked at it through welders' goggles. A piece of the sun was missing; in its place we saw empty sky.

I had seen a partial eclipse in 1970. A partial eclipse is very interesting. It bears almost no relation to a total eclipse. Seeing a partial eclipse bears the same relation to seeing a total eclipse as kissing a man does to marrying him, or as flying in an airplane does to falling out of an airplane. Although the one experience precedes the other, it in no way prepares you for it. During a partial eclipse the sky does not darken—not even when 94 percent of the sun is hidden. Nor does the sun, seen colorless through protective devices, seem terribly strange. We have all seen a sliver of light in the sky; we have all seen the crescent moon by day. However, during a partial eclipse the air does indeed get cold, precisely as if someone were standing between you and the fire. And blackbirds do fly back to their roosts. I had seen a partial eclipse before, and here was another.

What you see in an eclipse is entirely different from what you know. It is especially different for those of us whose grasp of astronomy is so frail that, given a flashlight, a grapefruit, two oranges, and fifteen years, we still could not figure out which way to set the clocks for daylight saving time. Usually it is a bit of a trick to keep your knowledge from blinding you. But during an eclipse it is easy. What you see is much more convincing than any wild-eyed theory you may know.

You may read that the moon has something to do with eclipses. I have never seen the moon yet. You do not see the moon. So near the sun, it is as completely invisible as the stars are by day. What you see before your eyes is the sun going through phases. It gets narrower and narrower, as the waning moon does, and, like the ordinary moon, it travels alone in the simple sky. The sky is of course background. It does not appear to eat the sun; it is far behind the sun. The sun simply shaves away; gradually, you see less sun and more sky.

The sky's blue was deepening, but there was no darkness. The sun was a wide crescent, like a segment of tangerine. The wind freshened and blew steadily over the hill. The eastern hill across the highway grew dusky and sharp. The towns and orchards in the valley to the south were dissolving into the blue light. Only the thin river held a trickle of sun.

Now the sky to the west deepened to indigo, a color never seen. A dark sky usually loses color. This was a saturated, deep indigo, up in the air. Stuck up into that unworldly sky was the cone of Mount Adams, and the alpenglow was upon it. The alpenglow is that red light of sunset which holds out on snowy mountaintops long after the valleys and tablelands are dimmed. "Look at Mount Adams," I said, and that was the last sane moment I remember.

I turned back to the sun. It was going. The sun was going, and the world was wrong. The grasses were wrong; they were platinum. Their every detail of stem, head, and blade shone lightless and artificially distinct as an art photographer's platinum print. This color has never been seen on earth. The hues were metallic; their finish was matte. The hillside was a nineteenth-century tinted photograph from which the tints had faded. All the people you see in the photograph, distinct and detailed as their faces look, are now dead. The sky was navy blue. My hands were silver. All the distant hills' grasses were finespun metal that the wind laid down. I was watching a faded color print of a movie filmed in the Middle Ages; I was standing in it, by some mistake. I was standing in a movie of hillside grasses filmed in the Middle Ages. I missed my own century, the people I knew, and the real light of day.

I looked at Gary. He was in the film. Everything was lost. He was a platinum print, a dead artist's version of life. I saw on his skull the darkness of night mixed with the colors of day. My mind was going out; my eyes were receding the way galaxies recede to the rim of space. Gary was light-years away, gesturing inside a circle of darkness, down the wrong end of a telescope. He smiled as if he saw me; the stringy crinkles around his eyes moved. The sight of him, familiar and wrong, was something I was remembering from centuries hence, from the other side of death: yes, *that* is the way he used to look, when we were living. When it was our generation's turn to be alive. I could not hear him; the wind was too loud. Behind him the sun was going. We had all started down a chute of time. At first it was pleasant; now there was no stopping it. Gary was chuting away across space, moving and talking and catching my eye, chuting down the long corridor of separation. The skin on his face moved like thin bronze plating that would peel.

The grass at our feet was wild barley. It was the wild einkorn wheat that grew on the hilly flanks of the Zagros Mountains, above the Euphrates valley, above the valley of the river we called *River*. We harvested the grass with stone sickles, I remember. We found the grasses on the hillsides; we built our shelter beside them and cut them down. That is how he used to look then, that one, moving and living and catching my eye, with the sky so dark behind him, and the wind blowing. God save our life.

From all the hills came screams. A piece of sky beside the crescent sun was detaching. It was a loosened circle of evening sky, suddenly lighted from the back. It was an abrupt black body out of nowhere; it was a flat disk; it was almost over the sun. That is when there were screams. At once this disk of sky slid over the sun like a lid. The sky snapped over the sun like a lens cover. The hatch in the brain slammed. Abruptly it was dark night, on the land and in the sky. In the night sky was a tiny ring of light. The hole where the sun belongs is very small. A thin ring of light marked its place. There was no sound. The eyes dried, the arteries drained, the lungs hushed. There was no world. We were the world's dead people rotating and orbiting around and around, embedded in the planet's crust, while the earth rolled down. Our minds were light-years distant, forgetful of almost everything. Only an extraordinary act of will could recall to us our former, living selves and our contexts in matter and time. We had, it seems, loved the planet and loved our lives, but could no longer remember the way of them. We got the light wrong. In the sky was something that should not be there. In the black sky was a ring of light. It was a thin ring, an old, thin silver wedding band, an old, worn ring. It was an old wedding band in the sky, or a morsel of bone. There were stars. It was all over.

III

It is now that the temptation is strongest to leave these regions. We have seen enough; let's go. Why burn our hands any more than we have to? But two years have passed; the price of gold has risen. I return to the same buried alluvial beds and pick through the strata again.

I saw, early in the morning, the sun diminish against a backdrop of sky. I saw a circular piece of that sky appear, suddenly detached, blackened, and backlighted; from nowhere it came and overlapped the sun. It did not look like the moon. It was enormous and black. If I had not read that it was the moon, I could have seen the sight a hundred times and never thought of the moon once. (If, however, I had not read that it was the moon—if, like most of the world's people throughout time, I had simply glanced up and seen this thing—then I doubtless would not have speculated much, but would have, like Emperor Louis of Bavaria in 840, simply died of fright on the spot.) It did not look like a dragon, although it looked more like a dragon than the moon. It looked like a lens cover, or the lid of a pot. It materialized out of thin air—black, and flat, and sliding, outlined in flame.

Seeing this black body was like seeing a mushroom cloud. The heart screeched. The meaning of the sight overwhelmed its fascination. It obliterated meaning itself. If you were to glance out one day and see a row of mushroom clouds rising on the horizon, you would know at once that what you were seeing, remarkable as it was, was intrinsically not worth remarking. No use running to tell anyone. Significant as it was, it did not matter a whit. For what is significance? It is significance for people. No people, no significance. This is all I have to tell you.

In the deeps are the violence and terror of which psychology has warned us. But if you ride these monsters deeper down, if you drop with them farther over the world's rim, you find what our sciences cannot locate or name, the substrate, the ocean or matrix or ether that buoys the rest, that gives goodness its power for good, and evil its power for evil, the unified field: our complex and inexplicable caring for each other, and for our life together here. This is given. It is not learned.

The world that lay under darkness and stillness following the closing of the lid was not the world we know. The event was over. Its devastation lay round about us. The clamoring mind and heart stilled, almost indifferent, certainly disembodied, frail, and exhausted. The hills were hushed, obliterated. Up in the sky, like a crater from some distant cataclysm, was a hollow ring.

You have seen photographs of the sun taken during a total eclipse. The corona fills the print. All of those photographs were taken through telescopes. The lenses of telescopes and cameras can no more cover the breadth and scale of the visual array than language can cover the breadth and simultaneity of internal experience. Lenses enlarge the sight, omit its context, and make of it a pretty and sensible picture, like something on a Christmas card. I assure you, if you send any shepherds a Christmas card on which is printed a three-by-three photograph of the angel of the Lord, the glory of the Lord, and a multitude of the heavenly host, they will not be sore afraid. More fearsome things can come in envelopes. More moving photographs than those of the sun's corona can appear in magazines. But I pray you will never see anything more awful in the sky.

You see the wide world swaddled in darkness; you see a vast breadth of hilly land, and an enormous, distant, blackened valley; you see towns' lights, a river's path, and blurred portions of your hat and scarf; you see your husband's face looking like an early black-and-white film; and you see a sprawl of black sky and blue sky together, with unfamiliar stars in it, some barely visible bands of cloud, and, over there, a small white ring. The ring is as small as one goose in a flock of migrating geese—if you happen to notice a flock of migrating geese. It is one 360th part of the visible sky. The sun we see is less than half the diameter of a dime held at arm's length.

The Ring Nebula, in the constellation Lyra, looks, through binoculars, like a smoke ring. It is a star in the process of exploding. Light from its explosion first reached the earth in 1054; it was a supernova then, and so bright it shone in the daytime. Now it is not so bright, but it is still exploding. It expands at the rate of seventy million miles a day. It is interesting to look through binoculars at something expanding seventy million miles a day. It does not budge. Its apparent size does not increase. Photographs of the Ring Nebula taken fifteen years ago seem identical to photographs of it taken yesterday. Some lichens are similar. Botanists have measured some ordinary lichens twice, at fifty-year intervals, without detecting any growth at all. And yet their cells divide; they live.

The small ring of light was like these things—like a ridiculous lichen up in the sky, like a perfectly still explosion 5,000 light-years away: it was interesting, and lovely, and in witless motion, and it had nothing to do with anything.

It had nothing to do with anything. The sun was too small, and too cold, and too far away, to keep the world alive. The white ring was not enough. It was feeble and worthless. It was as useless as a memory; it was as off kilter and hollow and wretched as a memory.

When you try your hardest to recall someone's face, or the look of a place, you see in your mind's eye some vague and terrible sight such as this. It is dark; it is insubstantial; it is all wrong.

The white ring and the saturated darkness made the earth and the sky look as they must look in the memories of the careless dead. What I saw, what I seemed to be standing in, was all the wrecked light that the memories of the dead could shed upon the living world. We had all died in our boots on the hilltops of Yakima and were alone in eternity. Empty space stoppered our eyes and mouths; we cared for nothing. We remembered our living days wrong. With great effort we had remembered some sort of circular light in the sky—but only the outline. Oh, and then the orchard trees withered, the ground froze, the glaciers slid down the valleys and overlapped the towns. If there had ever been people on earth, nobody knew it. The dead had forgotten those they had loved. The dead were parted one from the other and could no longer remember the faces and lands they had loved in the light. They seemed to stand on darkened hilltops, looking down.

IV

We teach our children one thing only, as we were taught: to wake up. We teach our children to look alive there, to join by words and activities the life of human culture on the planet's crust. As adults we are almost all adept at waking up. We have so mastered the transition, we have forgotten we ever learned it. Yet it is a transition we make a hundred times a day, as, like so many will-less dolphins, we plunge and surface, lapse and emerge. We live half our waking lives and all of our sleeping lives in some private, useless, and insensible waters we never mention or recall. Useless, I say. Valueless, I might add—until someone hauls the wealth up to the surface and into the wide-awake city, in a form that people can use.

I do not know how we got to the restaurant. Like Roethke, "I take my waking slow." Gradually I seemed more or less alive, and already forgetful. It was now almost nine in the morning. It was the day of a solar eclipse in central Washington, and a fine adventure for everyone. The sky was clear; there was a fresh breeze out of the north.

The restaurant was a roadside place with tables and booths. The other eclipse-watchers were there. From our booth we could see their cars' California license plates, their University of Washington parking stickers. Inside the restaurant we were all eating eggs or waffles;

people were fairly shouting and exchanging enthusiasms, like fans after a World Series game. Did you see . . . ? Did you see . . . ? Then somebody said something that knocked me for a loop.

A college student, a boy in a blue parka who carried a Hasselblad, said to us, "Did you see that little white ring? It looked like a Life Saver. It looked like a Life Saver up in the sky."

And so it did. The boy spoke well. He was a walking alarm clock. I myself had at that time no access to such a term. He could write a sentence, and I could not. I grabbed that Life Saver and rode it to the surface. And I had to laugh. I had been dumbstruck on the Euphrates River, I had been dead and gone and grieving, all over the sight of something that, if you could claw your way up to that level, you would grant looked very much like a Life Saver. It was good to be back among people so clever; it was good to have all the world's words at the mind's disposal, so the mind could begin its task. All those things for which we have no words are lost. The mind—the culture—has two little tools, grammar and lexicon: a decorated sand bucket and a matching shovel. With these we bluster about the continents and do all the world's work. With these we try to save our very lives.

There are a few more things to tell from this level, the level of the restaurant. One is the old joke about breakfast. "It can never be satisfied, the mind, never." Wallace Stevens wrote that, and in the long run he was right. The mind wants to live forever, or to learn a very good reason why not. The mind wants the world to return its love, or its awareness; the mind wants to know all the world, and all eternity, and God. The mind's sidekick, however, will settle for two eggs over easy.

The dear, stupid body is as easily satisfied as a spaniel. And, incredibly, the simple spaniel can lure the brawling mind to its dish. It is everlastingly funny that the proud, metaphysically ambitious, clamoring mind will hush if you give it an egg.

Further: while the mind reels in deep space, while the mind grieves or fears or exults, the workaday senses, in ignorance or idiocy, like so many computer terminals printing out market prices while the world blows up, still transcribe their little data and transmit them to the warehouse in the skull. Later, under the tranquilizing influence of fried eggs, the mind can sort through these data. The restaurant was a halfway house, a decompression chamber. There I remembered a few things more.

The deepest, and most terrifying, was this: I have said that I heard screams. (I have since read that screaming, with hysteria, is a common reaction even to expected total eclipses.) People on all the hillsides, including, I think, myself, screamed when the black body of the moon detached from the sky and rolled over the sun. But something else was happening at that same instant, and it was this, I believe, that made us scream.

The second before the sun went out, we saw a wall of dark shadow come speeding at us. We no sooner saw it than it was upon us, like thunder. It roared up the valley. It slammed our hill and knocked us out. It was the monstrous swift shadow cone of the moon. I have since read that this wave of shadow moves 1,800 miles an hour. Language can give no sense of this sort of speed—1,800 miles an hour. It was 195 miles wide. No end was in sight—you saw only the edge. It rolled at you across the land at 1,800 miles an hour, hauling darkness like plague behind it. Seeing it, and knowing it was coming straight for you, was like feeling a slug of anesthetic shoot up your arm. If you think very fast, you may have time to think: Soon it will hit my brain. You can feel the deadness race up your arm; you can feel the appalling, inhuman speed of your own blood. We saw the wall of shadow coming, and screamed before it hit.

This was the universe about which we have read so much and never before felt: the universe as a clockwork of loose spheres flung at stupefying, unauthorized speeds. How could anything moving so fast not crash, not veer from its orbit amok like a car out of control on a turn?

Less than two minutes later, when the sun emerged, the trailing edge of the shadow cone sped away. It coursed down our hill and raced eastward over the plain, faster than the eye could believe; it swept over the plain and dropped over the planet's rim in a twinkling. It had clobbered us, and now it roared away. We blinked in the light. It was as though an enormous, loping god in the sky had reached down and slapped the earth's face.

Something else, something more ordinary, came back to me along about the third cup of coffee. During the moments of totality, it was so dark that drivers on the highway below turned on their cars' headlights. We could see the highway's route as a strand of lights. It was bumper-to-bumper down there. It was eight-fifteen in the morning, Monday morning, and people were driving into Yakima to work. That it was as dark as night, and eerie as hell, an hour after dawn apparently meant that in order to *see* to drive to work, people had to use their headlights. Four or five cars pulled off the road. The rest, in a line at least five miles long, drove to town. The highway ran between hills; the people could not have seen any of the eclipsed sun at all. Yakima will have another total eclipse in 2019. Perhaps, in 2019, businesses will give their employees an hour off.

From the restaurant we drove back to the coast. The highway crossing the Cascades range was open. We drove over the mountain like old pros. We joined our places on the planet's thin crust; it held. For the time being, we were home free.

Early that morning at six, when we had checked out, the six bald men were sitting on folding chairs in the dim hotel lobby. The television was on. Most of them were awake. You might drown in your own spittle, God knows, at any time; you might wake up dead in a small hotel, a cabbage head watching TV while snows pile up in the passes, watching TV while the chili peppers smile and the moon passes over the sun and nothing changes and nothing is learned because you have lost your vomit bucket and shovel and no longer care. What if you regain the surface and open your sack and find, instead of treasure, a beast, which jumps at you? Or you may not come back at all. The winches may jam, the scaffolding buckle, the air-conditioning collapse. You may glance up one day and see by your headlamp the canary keeled over in its cage. You may reach into a cranny for pearls and touch a moray eel. You yank on your rope; it is too late.

Apparently people share a sense of these hazards, for when the total eclipse ended, an odd thing happened.

When the sun appeared as a blinding bead on the ring's side, the eclipse was over. The black lens cover appeared again, backlighted, and slid away. At once the yellow light made the sky blue again; the black lid dissolved and vanished. The real world began there. I remember now: we all hurried away. We were born and bored at a stroke. We rushed down the hill. We found our car; we saw the other people streaming down the hillsides; we joined the highway traffic and drove away.

We never looked back. It was a general vamoose, and an odd one, for when we left the hill, the sun was still partially eclipsed—a sight rare enough, and one that, in itself, we would probably have driven five hours to see. But enough is enough. One turns at last even from glory itself with a sigh of relief. From the depths of mystery, and even from the heights of splendor, we bounce back and hurry for the latitudes of home.

Annie Dillard
Annie Dillard, whose writings are infused with influences from a multitude of religions, refers to herself as "spiritually promiscuous." Dillard has published nine books of both fiction and creative nonfiction, including The Living, An American Childhood, *and* Pilgrim at Tinker Creek, *which won the Pulitzer Prize for nonfiction in 1975. Born in 1945 in Pittsburgh, she now teaches at Wesleyan University.*

The Mickey Mantle Koan

David James Duncan

On April 6, 1965, my brother Nicholas John Duncan died of what his surgeons called "complications" after three unsuccessful open-heart operations. He was seventeen at the time—four years my elder to the very day. He'd been the fastest sprinter in his high school class till the valve in his heart began to close, but he was so bonkers about baseball that he'd preferred playing a mediocre JV shortstop to starring at varsity track. As a ballplayer he was a competent fielder, had a strong and fairly accurate arm and stole bases with ease—when he reached them. But no matter how much he practiced or what stances, grips or self-hypnotic tricks he tried, he lacked the hand-eye magic that consistently lays bat-fat against ball, and remained one of the weakest hitters on his team.

John lived his entire life on the outskirts of Portland, Oregon—650 miles from the nearest Major League team—and in franchiseless cities in the fifties and early sixties there were really just two types of fans: those who thought the Yankees stood for everything right with America, and those who thought they stood for everything wrong with it. My brother was an extreme manifestation of the former type. He conducted a one-man campaign to notify the world that Roger Maris's sixty-one homers in '61 came in three fewer at-bats than Babe

Ruth's sixty in '27. He maintained—all statistical evidence to the contrary—that Clete Boyer was a better third baseman than his brother, Ken, simply because Clete was a Yankee. He combed the high school every October for fools willing to bet against Whitey Ford in the World Series, and if he couldn't find one there he knew he'd find one at home: me. He tried to enhance our games of catch by portraying the first two-thirds of Kubek to Richardson to Skowron double plays, but the intensity of his Kubek for some reason caused his Richardson to imagine my "Moose" to be the genuine six-four article—so off the ball would sail into the neighbor's apple orchard. He may not have been the only kid on the block who considered Casey Stengel the greatest sage since Solomon, but I'm sure he was the only one who considered Yogi Berra the second greatest. And though he would concede that Ted Williams, and later Willie Mays, had slightly more productive careers than Mickey Mantle, even this was for a pro-Yankee reason: Mantle was his absolute hero, but his tragic hero. The Mick, my brother maintained, was the greatest raw talent of all time. He was one to whom great gifts were given, from whom great gifts had been ripped away, and the more scarred his knees became, the more frequently he fanned, the more flagrant his limp and apologetic his smile, the more John revered him. And toward this single Yankee I too was able to feel a touch of reverence, if only because, on the subject of scars, I considered my brother an unimpeachable authority: he'd worn one from the time he was eight, compliments of the Mayo Clinic, that wrapped clear around his chest in a wavy line, like stitching round a clean white baseball.

Yankees aside, John and I had more in common than a birthday. We bickered regularly with our middle brother and little sister but almost never with each other. We were both bored, occasionally to insurrection, by school-going, church-going and any game or sport that didn't involve a ball. We both preferred, as a mere matter of style, Indians to cowboys, knights of the road to Knights of Columbus, Buster Keaton to Charlie Chaplin, Gary Cooper to John Wayne, deadbeats to brown-nosers, and even brown-nosers to Elvis Presley. We shared a single devil's food chocolate cake on our joint birthday, invariably annihilating the candle flames with a tandem blowing effort, only to realize that we'd once again forgotten to make a wish. And whenever the parties were over or the house was stuffy, the parents cranky or the TV insufferably dumb, whenever we were restless, punchy or just feeling the "nuthin' to do" feeling, catch—with a hardball—was the nuthin' John and I chose to do.

We were not exclusive, or not by intention: our father and middle brother and an occasional cousin or friend would join us now and then. But something in most people's brains or bloodstreams sent them bustling off to more industrious endeavors before the real rhythm of the thing ever took hold. Genuine catch-playing occurs in a double-limbo between busyness and idleness, and between the imaginary and the real. As with any contemplative pursuit, it takes time, and the ability to forget time, to slip into this dual limbo, and to discover (i.e. lose) oneself in the music of the game.

It helps to have a special spot to play. Ours was a shaded, ninety-foot corridor between one neighbor's apple orchard and the other's stand of old-growth Douglas firs, on a stretch of lawn so lush and mossy it sucked the heat out of even the hottest grounders. I always stood in the north, John in the south. When I had to chase his wild throws into the orchard I'd sometimes hide the ball in my shirt and fire back a Gravenstein, leaving him to judge, while it was in the air, whether it was fit to catch and eat or an overripe rotter about to splatter in his mitt. When he chased my dud pegs into the firs, he'd give me an innocent, uncomplaining smile as he trotted back into position—then rifle a cone, dirt clod or stone at my head.

But these antics were the exception. The deep shade, the two-hundred-foot firs, the mossy footing and fragrance of apples all made it a setting more conducive to mental-vacationing than to any kind of disciplined effort, so a vigorous serenity was the rule. We might call balls and strikes for an imaginary inning or two, throw each other a few pop-ups or grounders or maybe count the number of errorless catches and throws we could make (three-hundreds were common, and our record was high in the eight-hundreds). But as our movements became fluid and the throws brisk and accurate, the pretense of practice would inevitably fade, and we'd just aim for the chest and fire, *hisssss pop! hisssss pop!* till a meal, a duty or total darkness forced us to recall that this is the world in which even timeless pursuits come to an end.

Our talk must have seemed strange to eavesdroppers. We lived in our bodies during catch, and our minds and mouths, though still operative, were just along for the ride. Most of the noise I made was with the four or five pieces of Bazooka I was invariably working over, though once the gum lost its sugar I'd sometimes narrate our efforts in a stream-of-doggerel play-by-play. My brother's speech was a bit more coherent, but of no greater didactic intent: he poured out idle litanies of Yankee worship or even idler braggadocio à la Dizzy Dean, all of it artfully spiced with spat sunflower-seed husks.

Dan Jenkins defined the catch-player perfectly when he spoke of athletes who "mostly like to stand around, chew things, spit and scratch their nuts." Not too complimentary a definition, perhaps, yet from the catch-playing point of view, what are the alternatives? Why run around wrecking the world for pay when you could be standing in one place transcending time? Why chew Rolaids, swallow your spit and feel too inhibited to scratch where it itches when you could be chewing Day's Work or Double Bubble, shooting end-over-enders, easing the itch and firing off hisses and pops? Whatever he really meant, Yogi Berra defended catch-players best. He said: "If you can't copy 'em, don't imitate 'em."

But one day, when we were sixteen and twelve respectively, my big brother surprised me out there in our corridor. Snagging a low throw, he closed his mitt round the ball, stuck it under his arm, stared off into the trees and got serious for a minute. All his life, he said, he'd struggled to be a shortstop and a hitter, but he was older now, had a clearer notion of what he could and couldn't do, and it was time to get practical. Time to start developing obvious strengths and evading flagrant weaknesses. "So I've decided," he concluded, "to become a junk pitcher."

I didn't believe a word of this. My brother had been a slugger worshiper from birth. He went on embellishing his idea, though, and even made it sound rather poetic: to foil some muscle-bound fence-buster with an off-speed piece of crap that blupped off his bat like a cow custard—this, he maintained, was the pluperfect pith of an attribute he called "Solid Cool." What was neither poetic nor cool was the errant garbage he began winging my way, or the whining I did as I took so many ball-hunting excursions back into the apples that I was finally moved to stage a sit-down strike and tell him to go hunt his own junk.

But to my surprise, he did go hunt it. And to my regret, I didn't recognize till months later just how carefully considered this new junk-pitching jag had been. That John's throwing arm was better than his batting eye had always been obvious, and it made sense to exploit that. But there were other factors he didn't mention: like the sharp pains in his chest every time he took a full swing, or the new ache that half-blinded and sickened him whenever he ran full speed. Finding the high arts of slugging and base-stealing physically impossible, he'd simply lowered his sights enough to keep his baseball dreams alive. No longer able to emulate his heroes, he set out to bamboozle those who thought they could. To that end he'd learned a feeble knuckler, a roundhouse curve, a submarine fastball formidable solely for its lack of accuracy, and was trashing his arm and my patience with his would-be screwball, when his doctors informed our family that a valve in his heart was rapidly closing. He might live as long as five years if we let it go, they said, but immediate surgery was best, since his recuperative powers were greatest now. John said nothing to any of this. He just waited till the day he was due at the hospital, snuck down to the stable where he kept his horse, saddled her up and galloped away. He rode about twenty miles, to the farm of a friend, and stayed there in hiding for nearly two weeks. But when he stole home one morning for clean clothes and money, my father caught him, and first tried to force him, but finally convinced him, to have the operation and be done with it.

Once in the hospital he was cooperative, cheerful and unrelentingly courageous. He survived second, third and fourth operations, several stoppings of the heart and a nineteen-day coma. He recovered enough at one point, even after the coma, to come home for a week or so. But the overriding "complication" to which his principal surgeon kept making oblique references turned out to be a heart so ravaged by scalpel wounds that an artificial valve had nothing but shreds and wounds to be sutured to. Bleeding internally, pissing blood, he was moved into an oxygen tent in an isolated room, where he remained fully conscious, and fully determined to heal, for two months after his surgeons had abandoned him. And, against all odds, his condition stabilized, then began to improve. The doctors reappeared and began to discuss the feasibility of a fifth operation.

Then came a second complication: staph. We were reduced overnight from genuine hope to awkward pleas for divine intervention. We invoked no miracles. Two weeks after contracting the infection, my brother died.

At his funeral, a preacher who didn't know John from Judge Kenesaw Mountain Landis eulogized him so lavishly and inaccurately that I was moved to a state of tearlessness that lasted for years. It's an unenviable task, certainly, trying to make public sense of a private catastrophe you know little about. But had I been in that preacher's shoes I think I might have mentioned one or two of my brother's actual attributes, if only to assure late-arriving mourners that they hadn't wandered into the wrong funeral. The person we were endeavoring to miss had, for instance, been a C student but an excellent horseman, had smothered every kind of meat he ate, including chicken and fish, with ketchup, and had often gone so far as to wear sunglasses indoors in the relentless quest for Solid Cool. He'd had the disconcerting habit of sound-testing his pleasant baritone by bellowing *Beeee-Ooooooooooo!* down any alley or hall that looked like it might contain an echo. He'd had an interesting, slangy obliviousness to proportion: any altercation from a fistfight to a world war was "a rack," any authority from our mother to the head of the UN was "the Brass," any pest from the neighbor kid to Khrushchev was "a butt wipe," and any kind of ball from a BB to the sun was "the orb." He was brave: whenever anyone his age harassed me, John warned them once and punched them out the second time, or got punched trying. He was also unabashedly, majestically vain. He referred to his person, with obvious pride and in spite of his teen acne, as "the Bod." He was an immaculate dresser. And he loved to stare at himself, publicly or privately, in mirrors, windows, puddles, chrome car fenders, upside down in teaspoons, and to solemnly comb his long auburn hair over and over, like his hero, "Kookie" Kookson, on "77 Sunset Strip."

His most astonishing attribute, to me at least, was his never-ending skein of girlfriends. What struck me when I was small was that he wanted them around at all; what impressed me later was that he was able to be so relaxed and natural around them. He had a simple but apparently efficient rating system for all female acquaintances: he called it "percentage of Cool versus percentage of Crud." A steady girl-friend usually weighed in at around 95 percent Cool, 5 percent Crud, and if the Crud level reached 10 percent it was time to start quietly looking elsewhere. Only two girls ever made his 100 percent Cool List, and I was struck by the fact that neither was a girlfriend, and one wasn't even pretty: whatever 100 percent Cool was, it was not skin deep. No girl ever came close to a 100 percent Crud rating, by the way: my brother was chivalrous.

He was not religious. The devout wing of our family believed in resurrection of the body, provided a preacher had at some point im-mersed the whole sinful thing, so my brothers and I were baptized en masse in the winter of '62, in a frigid outdoor swimming pool. The only revelatory moment for John and me, however, occurred in the shower room afterward, when we simultaneously noticed—then no-ticed each other noticing—that the icy immersion had caused the pri-vates of our NFL-tackle-sized pastor to shrivel into an object a hungry rodent could have mistaken for a peanut, shelled no less, and clearly in no kind of shape for sin. John believed in God, but passively, with nothing like the passion he had for the Yankees. He seemed a little more friendly with Jesus. "Christ is cool," he'd say, if forced to show his hand. But I don't recall him speaking of any sort of goings-on be-tween them till he casually mentioned, a day or two before he died, a conversation they'd just had there in the oxygen tent. And even then John was John: what impressed him even more than the fact of Christ's presence or the consoling words He spoke were the natty suit and tie He was wearing.

John had a girlfriend right up to the end—a tall, pretty blonde with the highest rating yet: only 1.5 percent Crud. He was my most in-timate friend, but a hero to me even so. In fact my faith in his heroism was so complete that when my mother woke me one spring morning by saying he'd just died, I was unable to feel grief. What my orthodox, baseball-worshiping brain fixed upon instead was the top-of-the-line

Wilson outfielder's glove I would now be inheriting, and the dreams and courage I believed I'd keep alive by simply sliding it onto my left hand.

But on the morning after his death, April 7, 1965, a small brown-paper package arrived at our house, special delivery from New York City, addressed to John. I brought it to my mother, leaned over her shoulder as she sat down to open it. Catching a whiff of antiseptic, I thought at first that it came from her hair: she'd spent the last four months of her life in a straight-back chair by my brother's bed, and hospital odors had permeated her. But the smell grew stronger as she began unwrapping the brown paper, till I realized it came from the object inside.

It was a small, white, cylindrical cardboard bandage box. "Johnson & Johnson," it said in red letters. "12 inches $\times$ 10 yards," it added in blue. Strange. Then I saw that it had been slit in half by a knife or scalpel and bound back together with adhesive tape: there was another layer, something hiding inside. My mother smiled as she began to rip the tape away. At the same time, tears were landing in her lap. Then the tape was gone, the little cylinder fell in two, and inside, nested in tissue, was a baseball. Immaculate white leather. Perfect red stitching. On one cheek, in faint green ink, the signature of Joseph Cronin and the trademark, REACH, THE SIGN OF QUALITY. And on the opposite cheek, with bright blue ballpoint ink, a tidy but flowing hand had written.

To John—
My Best Wishes
Your Pal
Mickey Mantle
April 6, 1965.

The ball proceeded to perch upon our fireplace mantel—an unintentional pun on my mother's part. We used half the Johnson & Johnson box as a pedestal for it, and for years saved the other half, figuring that the bandage it once contained held Mantle's storied knee together for a game. Even after my mother explained that the ball came not out of the blue but in response to a letter, I considered it a treasure, told all my friends about it, invited the closest to stop by and gawk at it. But gradually I began to see that the public reaction to the ball was disconcertingly predictable. The first response was usually "Wow! Mickey Mantle!" But then they'd get the full story: "Mantle signed it the day he died? Your brother never even *saw* it?" And that made them uncomfortable. This was not at all the way an autographed baseball was supposed to behave. How could an immortal call himself your pal, how could you be the recipient of the Mick's best wishes and still just lie back and die?

I began to share the discomfort. Over the last three of my thirteen years I'd devoured scores of baseball books, fiction and nonfiction, all of which agreed that a bat, program, mitt or ball signed by a Big League hero is a sacred relic, that we *should* expect such relics to have magical properties, and that they *would* prove pivotal in a young protagonist's life. Yet here I was, the young protagonist. Here was my relic. And all the damned thing did before long was depress and confuse me. I stopped showing the ball to people, tried ignoring it, found this impossible, tried instead to pretend that the blue ink was an illegible scribble and that the ball was just a ball. But the ink *wasn't* illegible: it never stopped saying what it said. So finally I tried picking the ball up and studying it, *hard,* hoping to discover exactly why it haunted me so. But it was far too easy to come up with reasons. The hospital reek of the entire package. The date of its arrival. The even crueler date of the inscription. The way the box, like my brother, had been sliced in half, then bound clumsily back together. Severed white skin. Brilliant red stitches.

Best Wishes . . . Pal . . .

A lot of us strive, in a crisis, to fall back on reason. But when our dreams come false and our prayers become unanswerable questions, the reason we fall back on has a tendency to turn caustic, and so becomes a tool which, in trying to explain our crisis, merely explains it away. Applying my reason to the ball, I told myself that a standard sports hero had received a letter from a standard distraught mother, had signed, packaged and mailed off the standard, ingratiatingly heroic response, had failed to realize that the boy he inscribed the ball to might be dead when it arrived, and so had mailed us a blackly comic non sequitur. "That's all there is to it," reason told me. Which left me no option but to pretend that I wasn't hurting, that I hadn't expected or wanted any more from the ball than I got, that I'd harbored no desire for any sort of sign, any imprimatur, any flicker of recognition from an Above or a Beyond.

I then began falling to pieces, for lack of that sign.

The bad thing about falling to pieces is that it hurts. The good thing about it is that once you're lying there in shards you've got nothing left to protect, and so have no reason not to be honest. I finally got honest with Mantle's baseball: I finally picked the thing up, read it once more and admitted for the first time that I was *pissed.* As is always the case with arriving baseballs, timing is the key—and this cheery orb was inscribed on the day its recipient lay dying and arrived

on the day he was being embalmed! This was *not* a "harmless coinci-
dence." It was the shabbiest, most embittering joke that Providence
had ever played on me. My best friend and brother was dead, dead,
dead, Mantle's damned ball and best wishes made that loss far less tol-
erable, and *that,* I told myself, really *was* all there was to it.

I hardened my heart, quit the baseball team, went out for golf. I
practiced like a zealot, cheated like hell, kicked my innocuous, naive
little opponents all over the course. I sold my beautiful inherited mitt
for a pittance.

But, as is usual in baseball stories, that wasn't all there was to it.

I'd never heard of Zen koans at the time, and Mickey Mantle is
certainly no *roshi.* But baseball and Zen are two things that Americans
and Japanese have each imported without embargo; and *roshis* are
men famous for hitting things hard with a big wooden stick; and a
koan is a perfectly nonsensical or nonsequacious statement given by
an old pro (*roshi*) to a rookie (layman or monk); and the stress of living with and meditating upon one of these mind-numbing pieces of
nonsense is said to eventually prove illuminating. So I know of no
better way to describe what the message on the ball became for me
than to call it a koan.

In the first place, the damned thing's batteries just wouldn't run
down. For weeks, months, *years,* every time I saw those ten blithe,
blue-inked words they knocked me off balance like a sudden shove
from behind. They were an emblem of all the false assurances of surgeons, all the futile prayers of preachers, all the hollowness of good-
guys-can't-lose baseball stories I'd ever heard or read. They were
graffiti scrawled across my brother's ruined chest. They were a throw
I'd never catch And yet—REACH, the ball said, THE SIGN OF QUALITY. So
year after year I kept trying, kept struggling to somehow answer the
koan.

I hit adolescence, enrolled in the school of pain-without-dignity
called "puberty," nearly flunked, then graduated almost without noticing. In the process I discovered that there was life after baseball, that
America was not the Good Guy, that Jesus was not a Christian and
that some girls, contrary to boyhood certainty, were nothing like 95
percent Crud; I discovered Europe and metaphysics, high lakes and
wilderness, black tea, rock, Bach, trout streams, the Orient, my life's
work and a hundred other grown-up tools and toys. But amid these
maturations and transformations there was an unwanted constant: in
the presence of that confounded ball, I remained thirteen years old.
One peek at the "Your Pal" koan and whatever maturity or equanim-
ity I possessed was repossessed, leaving me irked as any stumped
monk or slumping slugger.

It took four years to solve the riddle on the ball. It was autumn when it happened—the same autumn during which I'd grown a little older than my big brother would ever be. As often happens with koan solutions, I wasn't even thinking about the ball when it came. As is also the case with koans, I can't possibly paint in words the impact of the response, the instantaneous healing that took place or the ensuing sense of lightness and release. But I'll say what I can.

The solution came during a fit of restlessness brought on by a warm Indian summer evening. I'd just finished watching the Miracle Mets blitz the Orioles in the World Series and was standing alone in the living room, just staring out at the yard and fading sunlight, feeling a little stale and fidgety, when I realized that these were just the sort of fidgets I'd never had to suffer when John was alive—because we'd always work our way through them with a long game of catch. With that thought, and at that moment, I simply saw my brother catch, then throw a baseball. It occurred in neither an indoors nor an outdoors. It lasted a couple of seconds, no more. But I saw him so clearly, and he then vanished so completely, that my eyes blurred, my throat and chest ached, and I didn't need to see Mantle's baseball to realize exactly what I'd wanted from it all along:

From the moment I'd first laid eyes on it, all I'd wanted was to take that immaculate ball out to our corridor on an evening just like this one, to take my place near the apples in the north and to find my brother waiting beneath the immense firs to the south. All I'd wanted was to pluck that too-perfect ball off its pedestal and proceed, without speaking, to play catch so long and hard that the grass stains and nicks and the sweat of our palms would finally obliterate every last trace of Mantle's blue ink, till all he would have sent us was a grass-green, earth-brown, beat-up old baseball. Beat-up old balls were all we'd ever had anyhow. They were all we'd ever needed. The dirtier they were, the more frayed the skin and stitching, the louder they'd hissed and the better they'd curved. And remembering this—recovering in an instant the knowledge of how little we'd needed in order to be happy—my grief for my brother became palpable, took on shape and weight, color and texture, even an odor: the measure of my loss was precisely the difference between one of the beat-up, earth-colored, grass-scented balls that had given us such happiness, and this antiseptic-smelling, sad-making icon ball on its bandage-box pedestal. And as I felt this—as I stood there palpating my grief, shifting it round like a throwing stone in my hand—I suddenly fell through a floor inside myself, landing in a deeper, brighter chamber just in time to feel something or someone tell me, *But who's to say we need even an old ball to be happy? Who's to say we couldn't do with less? Who's to say we couldn't* still *be happy—with no ball at all?*

And with that, the koan was solved.

I can't explain why this felt like a complete solution. Reading the bare words, two decades later, they don't look like much of a solution. But a koan answer is not a verbal or a literary or even a personal experience. It's a spiritual experience. And a boy, a man, a "me," does not have spiritual experiences: only the spirit has spiritual experiences. That's why churches so soon become bandage boxes propping up antiseptic icons that lost all value the instant they were removed from the greens and browns of grass and dirt and life. It's also why a good Zen monk always states a koan solution in the barest possible terms. "No ball at all!" is, perhaps, all I should have written about this thing—because then no one would have an inkling of what was meant, and so could form no misconceptions, and the immediacy and integrity and authority of the experience would be safely locked away. ("If you can't copy 'em, don't imitate 'em.") But it's a time-honored tradition, in baseball, to interview the bubbling, burbling athlete when the game is done. So I've bubbled and burbled.

This has gotten a bit iffy for a sports story. But jocks die, and then what? The brother I played a thousand games of catch with is dead, and so will I be, and unless you're one hell of an athlete, so will you be. In the face of this fact I find it more than a little consoling to recall my encounter, one October day, with an unspeakable spark in me that needs *nothing*—not even a dog-eared ball—to be happy. From that day forward the relic on the mantel lost its irksome overtones and became an autographed ball—nothing more, nothing less. It lives in my study now, beside an old beater ball my brother and I wore out, and it gives me a satisfaction I can't explain to sit back now and then and compare the two—though I'd still gladly trash the white one for a good game of catch.

As for the ticklish timing of its arrival, I only recently learned a couple of facts that shed some light. First I discovered—in a copy of the old letter my mother wrote to Mantle—that she'd made it clear that my brother was dying. So the Mick had signed the ball knowing perfectly well what the situation might be when it arrived. Second, I found out that my mother actually went ahead and showed the ball to my brother. True, he was embalmed when she did this. But what was embalmed, the koan taught me, wasn't all of him. And I've no reason to assume that the unembalmed part had changed much, so far. It should be remembered, then, that while he lived my brother was more than a little vain, that he'd been compelled by his death to leave a handsome head of auburn hair behind, and that when my mother and Mantle's baseball arrived at the funeral parlor, that hair was being prepared for an open-casket funeral by a couple of cadaverous-looking yahoos whose oily manners, hair and clothes made it plain they didn't know Kookie Kookson from Roger Maris or Solid Cool from Kool-Aid. What if this pair took it into their heads to spruce John up for the Hereafter with a Bible Camp cut? Worse yet, what if they tried to show what sensitive, accommodating artists they were and decked him out like a damned Elvis the Pelvis *greaser?* I'm not trying to be morbid here. I'm trying to state the facts. "The Bod" my brother had so delighted in grooming was about to be seen for the last time by all his buddies, his family and a girlfriend who was only 1.5 percent Crud, and the part of the whole ensemble he'd been most fastidious about—the coiffure—was completely out of his control! He *needed* "Best Wishes." He needed a "Pal." Preferably one with a comb.

Enter my mother—who took one look at what the two rouge-and-casket-wallahs were doing to the hair, said "No no no!" produced a snapshot, told them, "He wants it *exactly* like this," sat down to critique their efforts and kept on critiquing till in the end you'd have thought John had dropped in to groom himself.

Only then did she ask them to leave. Only then did she pull the autographed ball from her purse, share it with her son, read him the inscription.

As is always the case with arriving baseballs, timing is the key. Thanks to the timing that has made the Mick a legend, my brother, the last time we all saw him, looked completely himself.

I return those best wishes to my brother's pal.

David James Duncan
Born surrounded by water in Portland, Oregon in 1952, David James Duncan is the author of My Story as Told by Water, River Teeth, The River Why, *and* The Brothers K, *the latter two of which won the Pacific Northwest Booksellers Award. His essays, many concerned with the environment, have appeared in* Harper's, Orion, Northern Lights, Gray's Sporting Journal, Outside, *and numerous other publications. He lives in Montana beside a trout stream.*

The Measure of My Powers

M. F. K. Fisher

The first thing I remember tasting and then wanting to taste again is the grayish-pink fuzz my grandmother skimmed from a spitting kettle of strawberry jam. I suppose I was about four.

Women in those days made much more of a ritual of their household duties than they do now. Sometimes it was indistinguishable from a dogged if unconscious martyrdom. There were times for This, and other equally definite times for That. There was one set week a year for "the sewing woman." Of course, there was Spring Cleaning. And there were other periods, almost like festivals in that they disrupted normal life, which were observed no matter what the weather, finances, or health of the family.

Many of them seem odd or even foolish to me now, but probably the whole staid rhythm lent a kind of rich excitement to the housebound flight of time.

With us, for the first years of my life, there was a series, every summer, of short but violently active cannings. Crates and baskets and lug-boxes of fruits bought in their prime and at their cheapest would lie waiting with opulent fragrance on the screened porch, and a whole battery of enameled pots and ladles and wide-mouthed funnels would appear from some dark cupboard.

All I knew then about the actual procedure was that we had delightful picnic meals while Grandmother and Mother and the cook worked with a kind of drugged concentration in our big dark kitchen, and were tired and cross and at the same time oddly triumphant in their race against summer heat and the processes of rot.

Now I know that strawberries came first, mostly for jam. Sour red cherries for pies and darker ones for preserves were a little later, and then came the apricots. They were for jam if they were very ripe, and the solid ones were simply "put up." That, in my grandmother's language, meant cooking with little sugar, to eat for breakfast or dessert in the winter which she still thought of in terms of northern Iowa.

She was a grim woman, as if she had decided long ago that she could thus most safely get to Heaven. I have a feeling that my Father might have liked to help with the cannings, just as I longed to. But Grandmother, with that almost joyfully stern bowing to duty typical of religious women, made it clear that helping in the kitchen was a bitter heavy business forbidden certainly to men, and generally to children. Sometimes she let me pull stems off the cherries, and one year when I was almost nine I stirred the pots a little now and then, silent and making myself as small as possible.

But there was no nonsense anyway, no foolish chitchat. Mother was still young and often gay, and the cook too . . . and with Grandmother directing operations they all worked in a harried muteness . . . stir, sweat, hurry. It was a pity. Such a beautifully smelly task should be fun, I thought.

In spite of any Late Victorian asceticism, though, the hot kitchen sent out tantalizing clouds, and the fruit on the porch lay rotting in its crates, or readied for the pots and the wooden spoons, in fair glowing piles upon the juice-stained tables. Grandmother, saving always, stood like a sacrificial priestess in the steam, "skimming" into a thick white saucer, and I, sometimes permitted and more often not, put my finger into the cooling froth and licked it. Warm and sweet and odorous. I loved it, then.

M. F. K. Fisher
M. F. K. (Mary Frances Kennedy) Fisher was born on July 3, 1908 in Albion, Michigan, but divided most of her life between France and California. Fisher is known for writing about the art of dining, the pleasures of cooking and eating food with friends and family. Her books include Serve It Forth, How to Cook a Wolf, *and* The Gastronomical Me. *Five of her works on food have been compiled and published under one title,* The Art of Eating. *Fisher also wrote fiction, including* Sister Age, *a book of stories. She died in 1992.*

A Thing Shared

M. F. K. Fisher

Now you can drive from Los Angeles to my Great-Aunt Maggie's ranch on the other side of the mountains in a couple of hours or so, but the first time I went there it took most of a day.

Now the roads are worthy of even the All-Year-Round Club's boasts, but twenty-five years ago, in the September before people thought peace had come again, you could hardly call them roads at all. Down near the city they were oiled, all right, but as you went farther into the hills toward the wild desert around Palmdale, they turned into rough dirt. Finally they were two wheel-marks skittering every which way through the Joshua trees.

It was very exciting: the first time my little round brown sister Anne and I had ever been away from home. Father drove us up from home with Mother in the Ford, so that she could help some cousins can fruit.

We carried beer for the parents (it exploded in the heat), and water for the car and Anne and me. We had four blowouts, but that was lucky, Father said as he patched the tires philosophically in the hot sun; he'd expected twice as many on such a long hard trip.

The ranch was wonderful, with wartime crews of old men and loud-voiced boys picking the peaches and early pears all day, and singing and rowing at night in the bunkhouses. We couldn't go near them or near the pen in the middle of a green alfalfa field where a new prize bull, black as thunder, pawed at the pale sand.

We spent most of our time in a stream under the cottonwoods, or with Old Mary the cook, watching her make butter in a great churn between her mountainous knees. She slapped it into pats, and put them down in the stream where it ran hurriedly through the darkness of the butter-house.

She put stone jars of cream there, too, and wire baskets of eggs and lettuces, and when she drew them up, like netted fish, she would shake the cold water onto us and laugh almost as much as we did.

Then Father had to go back to work. It was decided that Mother would stay at the ranch and help put up more fruit, and Anne and I would go home with him. That was as exciting as leaving it had been, to be alone with Father for the first time.

298

He says now that he was scared daft at the thought of it, even though our grandmother was at home as always to watch over us. He says he actually shook as he drove away from the ranch, with us like two suddenly strange small monsters on the hot seat beside him.

Probably he made small talk. I don't remember. And he didn't drink any beer, sensing that it would be improper before two unchaperoned young ladies.

We were out of the desert and into deep winding canyons before the sun went down. The road was a little smoother, following streambeds under the live oaks that grow in all the gentle creases of the dry tawny hills of that part of California. We came to a shack where there was water for sale, and a table under the dark wide trees.

Father told me to take Anne down the dry streambed a little way. That made me feel delightfully grown-up. When we came back we held our hands under the water faucet and dried them on our panties, which Mother would never have let us do.

Then we sat on a rough bench at the table, the three of us in the deep green twilight, and had one of the nicest suppers I have ever eaten.

The strange thing about it is that all three of us have told other people that same thing, without ever talking of it among ourselves until lately. Father says that all his nervousness went away, and he saw us for the first time as two little brown humans who were fun. Anne and I both felt a subtle excitement at being alone for the first time with the only man in the world we loved.

(We loved Mother too, completely, but we were finding out, as Father was too, that it is good for parents and for children to be alone now and then with one another . . . the man alone or the woman, to sound new notes in the mysterious music of parenthood and childhood.)

That night I not only saw my Father for the first time as a person. I saw the golden hills and the live oaks as clearly as I have ever seen them since; and I saw the dimples in my little sister's fat hands in a way that still moves me because of that first time; and I saw food as something beautiful to be shared with people instead of as a thrice-daily necessity.

I forget what we ate, except for the end of the meal. It was a big round peach pie, still warm from Old Mary's oven and the ride over the desert. It was deep, with lots of juice, and bursting with ripe peaches picked that noon. Royal Albertas, Father said they were. The crust was the most perfect I have ever tasted, except perhaps once upstairs at Simpson's in London, on a hot plum tart.

And there was a quart Mason jar, the old-fashioned bluish kind like Mexican glass, full of cream. It was still cold, probably because we all knew the stream it had lain in, Old Mary's stream.

Father cut the pie in three pieces and put them on white soup plates in front of us, and then spooned out the thick cream. We ate with spoons too, blissful after the forks we were learning to use with Mother.

And we ate the whole pie, and all the cream . . . we can't remember if we gave any to the shadowy old man who sold water . . . and then drove on sleepily toward Los Angeles, and none of us said anything about it for many years, but it was one of the best meals we ever ate.

Perhaps that is because it was the first conscious one, for me at least; but the fact that we remember it with such queer clarity must mean that it had other reasons for being important. I suppose that happens at least once to every human. I hope so.

Now the hills are cut through with superhighways, and I can't say whether we sat that night in Mint Canyon or Bouquet, and the three of us are in some ways even more than twenty-five years older than we were then. And still the warm round peach pie and the cool yellow cream we ate together that August night live in our hearts' palates, succulent, secret, delicious.

After Yitzl

Albert Goldbarth

It is not for nothing that a Soviet historian once remarked that
the most difficult of a historian's tasks is to predict the past.

—Bernard Lewis, *History*

1.

This story begins in bed, in one of those sleepy troughs between the
crests of sex. I stroke the crests of you. The night is a gray permissive
color.

"Who do you think you were—do you think you were anyone, in
an earlier life?"

In an earlier life, I think, though chance and bombs and the salt-
grain teeth in ocean air have destroyed all documents, I farmed black
bent-backed turnips in the hardpan of a shtetl compound of equally
black-garbed bent-backed grandmama and rabbinic Jews.

My best friend there shoed horses. He had ribs like barrel staves,
his sweat was miniature glass pears. (I'm enjoying this now.) On Saturday nights, when the Sabbath was folded back with its pristine
linens into drawers for another week, this Yitzl played accordion at

301

the schnapps-house. He was in love with a woman, a counter girl, there. She kept to herself. She folded paper roses in between serving; she never looked up. But Yitzl could tell: she tapped her foot. One day the cousin from Milano, who sent the accordion, sent new music to play—a little sheaf with American writing on it. *Hot* polka. Yitzl took a break with me in the corner—I was sipping sweet wine as dark as my turnips and trying to write a poem—and when he returned to his little grocer's crate of a stand, there was an open paper rose on his accordion. So he knew, then.

In this story-*in*-my-story they say "I love you," and now I say it in the external story, too: I stroke you slightly rougher as I say it, as if underlining the words, or reaffirming you're here, and I'm here, since the gray in the air is darker, and sight insufficient. You murmur it back. We say it like anyone else—in part because our death is bonded into us meiotically, from before there was marrow or myelin, and we know it, even as infants our scream is for more than the teat. We understand the wood smoke in a tree is aching to rise from the tree in its shape, its green and nutritive damps are readying always for joining the ether around it—any affirming clench of the roots in soil, physical and deeper, is preventive for its partial inch of a while.

So: genealogy. The family tree. Its roots. Its urgent suckings among the cemeterial layers. The backsweep of teat under teat. The way, once known, it orders the Present. A chief on the island of Nios, off Sumatra, could stand in the kerosene light of his plank hut and (this is on tape) recite—in a chant, the names sung out between his betel-reddened teeth like ghosts still shackled by hazy responsibility to the living—his ancestral linkup, seventy generations deep; it took over an hour. The genealogical record banks of the Mormon Church contain the names and relationship data of 1½ to 2 billion of the planet's dead, "in a climate-controlled and nuclear-bomb-proof repository" called Granite Mountain Vault, and these have been processed through the Church's IBM computer system, the Genealogical Information and Names Tabulation, acronymed GIANT.

Where we come from. How we need to know.

If necessary, we'll steal it—those dinosaur tracks two men removed from the bed of Cub Creek in Hays County, using a masonry saw, a jackhammer, and a truck disguised as an ice cream vendor's.

If necessary (two years after Yitzl died, I married his schnapps-house sweetie: it was mourning him that initially drew us together; and later, the intimacy of hiding from the Secret Police in the burlap-draped back corner of a fishmonger's van. The guts were heaped to our ankles and our first true sex in there, as we rattled like bagged bones over the countryside, was lubricated—for fear kept her dry—with fishes' slime: and, after . . . but that's another story) we'll make it up.

2.

Which is what we did with love, you and I: invented it. We needed it, it wasn't here, and out of nothing in common we hammered a tree-house into the vee of a family tree, from zero, bogus planks, the bright but invisible nailheads of pure will. Some nights a passerby might spy us, while I was lazily flicking your nipple awake with my tongue, or you were fondling me into alertness, pleased in what we called bed, by the hue of an apricot moon, in what we called our life, by TV's dry-blue arctic light, two black silhouettes communing: and we were suspended in air. If the passerby yelled, we'd plummet.

Because each midnight the shears on the clock snip off another twenty-four hours. We're frightened, and rightfully so. Because glass is, we now know, a "slow liquid"; and we're slow dust. I've heard the universe howling—a conch from the beach is proof, but there are Ears Above for which the spiral nebulae must twist the same harrowing sound. Because pain, in even one cell, is an ant: it will bear a whole organ away. And a day is so huge—a Goliath; the tiny stones our eyes pick up in sleeping aren't enough to confront it. The marrow gives up. We have a spine, like a book's, and are also on loan with a due date. And the night is even more huge; what we call a day is only one struck match in an infinite darkness. This is knowledge we're born with, this is in the first cry. I've seen each friend I have, at one time or another, shake at thinking how susceptible and brief a person is: and whatever touching we do, whatever small narrative starring ourselves can bridge that unit of emptiness, is a triumph. "Tell me another story," you say with a yawn, "of life back then, with—what was her name?" "With Misheleh?" "Yes, with Misheleh." As if I can marry us backwards in time that way. As if it makes our own invented love more durable.

The Mormons marry backwards. "Sealing," they call it. In the sanctum of the temple, with permission called a "temple recommend," a Mormon of pious state may bind somebody long dead (perhaps an ancestor of his own, perhaps a name provided by chance from a list of cleared names in the computer)—bind that person to the Mormon faith, and to the flow of Mormon generations, in a retroactive conversion good "for time and all eternity." (Though the dead, they add, have "free agency" up in Heaven to accept this or not.) A husband and wife might be "celestially married" this way, from out of their graves and into the spun-sugar clouds of a Mormon Foreverness . . . from out of the Old World sod . . . from sand, from swampwater . . . Where does ancestry *stop?*

To pattern the present we'll fabricate the past from before there *was* fabric. Piltdown Man. On display in the British Museum. From 65 million years back—and later shown to be some forgery of human and orangutan lockings, the jawbone stained and abraded. Or, more openly and jubilant, the Civilization of Llhuros "from the recent excavations of Vanibo, Houndee, Draikum, and other sites"—in Ithaca, New York, Norman Daly, professor of art at Cornell and current "Director of Llhurosian Studies" has birthed an entire culture: its creatures (the Pruii bird, described in the article "Miticides of Coastal Llhuros"), its rites (". . . the Tokens of Holmeek are lowered into the Sacred Fires, and burned with the month-cloths of the Holy Whores"), its plaques and weapons and votive figurines, its myths and water clocks, its poems and urns and a "nasal flute." An elephant mask. An "early icon of Tal-Hax." Wall paintings. "Oxen bells." Maps. The catalogue I have is 48 pages—135 entries. Some of the Llhuros artifacts are paintings or sculpture. Some are anachronismed, a five-and-dime on-sale orange juicer becomes a *trallib,* an "oil container . . . Middle Period, found at Draikum." A clothes iron: "Late Archaic . . . that it may be a votive of the anchorite Ur Ur cannot be disregarded." Famous athletes. Textiles. "Fornicating gods."

Just open the mind, and the past it requires will surface. "Psychic archaeologists" have tranced themselves to the living worlds of the pyramids or the caves—one chipped flint scraper can be connection enough. When Edgar Cayce closed his eyes he opened them (inside his head, which had its eyes closed) in the undiluted afternoon light of dynastic Egypt: wind was playing a chafing song in the leaves of the palm and the persea, fishers were casting their nets. "His findings and methods tend to be dismissed by the orthodox scientific community," but Jeffrey Goodman meditates, and something—an invisible terraform diving bell of sorts—descends with his eyes to fully twenty feet below the sands of Flagstaff, Arizona, 100,000 B.C., his vision brailling happily as a mole's nose through the bones set in the darkness there like accent marks and commas.

Going back . . . The darkness . . . Closing your lids . . .

A wheel shocked into a pothole. Misheleh waking up, wild-eyed. Torches.

"We needed certain papers, proof that we were Jews, to be admitted to America. To pass the inspectors there. And yet if our van was stopped by the Secret Police and we were discovered in back, those papers would be our death warrant. Such a goat's dessert!—that's the expression we used then."

"And . . . ?"

"It comes from when two goats will fight for the same sweet morsel—each pulls a different direction."

"No, I mean that night, the escape—what *happened?*"

"The Secret Police stopped the van."

3.

Earlier, I said "in a trough between crests"—sea imagery. I mean in part that dark, as it grows deeper, takes the world away, and a sleepless body will float all night in horrible separation from what it knows and where it's nurtured. Freedom is sweet; but nobody wants to be flotsam.

Ruth Norman, the eighty-two-year-old widow of Ernest L. Norman, is Uriel, an Archangel, to her fellow Unarian members and is, in fact, the "Cosmic Generator," and head of all Unarius activities on Earth (which is an applicant for the "Intergalactic Confederation" of thirty-two other planets—but we need to pass a global test of "consciousness vibration"). In past lives, Uriel has been Socrates, Confucius, Henry VIII, and Benjamin Franklin—and has adventured on Vidus, Janus, Vulna, and other planets. All Unarians know their former lives. Vaughn Spaegel has been Charlemagne. And Ernest L. himself has been Jesus (as proved by a pamphlet, *The Little Red Box*) and currently is Alta; from his ankh-shaped chair on Mars he communicates psychically and through a bank of jeweled buttons with all the Confederation. Everyone works toward the day Earth can join. The 1981 Conclave of Light, at the Town and Country Convention Center in El Cajon, California, attracted over 400 Unarians, some from as far as New York and Toronto. Neosha Mandragos, formerly a nun for twenty-seven years, was there; and George, the shoe-store clerk, and Dan, assistant manager of an ice cream parlor.

Uriel makes her long-awaited entrance following the *Bolero*-backed procession of two girls dressed as peacocks, led by golden chains, then two nymphs scattering petals from cornucopias, someone wearing a feathered bird's head, and various sages. Four "Nubian slaves . . . wearing skin bronzer, headdresses, loincloths and gilded beach thongs" carry a palanquin adorned with enormous white swans, atop which . . . Uriel! In a black velvet gown falling eight feet wide at the hem, with a wired-up universe of painted rubber balls representing the thirty-two worlds and dangling out to her skirt's edge. According to Douglas Curran, "the gown, the painted golden 'vortex' headdress, and the translucent elbow-length gloves with rapier nails have tiny light bulbs snaked through the fabric. The bulbs explode into volleys of winking. Waves of light roll from bodice to fingertips, Infinite Mind to planets." People weep. Their rich remembered lives are a sudden brilliance over their nerves, like ambulance flashers on chicken wire, like . . . like fire approaching divinity. Nobody's worrying here over last week's sale of butter-pecan parfait.

We'll sham it. We need it. It's not that we lie. It's that we *make* the truth. The Japanese have a word especially for it: *nisekeizu,* false genealogies. Ruling-class Japan was obsessed with lineage and descent, and these connived links to the Sewangezi line of the Fujiwaras qualified one—were indeed the only qualification at the time—for holding office. "High birth." "Pedigree." It's no less likely in Europe. In the seventeenth century, Countess Alexandrine von Taxis "hired genealogists to fabricate a descent from the Torriani, a clan of warriors who ruled Lombardy until 1311."

European Jews, who by late in the 1700s needed to take on surnames in order to cross a national border, often invented family names that spoke of lush green woods and open fields—this from a people traipsing from one cramped dingy urban ghetto to another. Greenblatt. Tannenbaum. Now a child born choking on soot could be heir to a name saying miles of mild air across meadows. Flowers. Mossy knolls.

Misheleh's name was Rosenblum. I never asked but always imagined this explained the trail of paper roses she'd left through Yitzl's life. My name then was Schvartzeit, reference to my many-thousand-year heritage of black beets. The name on our papers, though, was Kaufman—"merchant." This is what you had to do, to survive.

I remember: they were rough with us, also with the driver of the van. But we pretended being offended, like any good citizens. It could have gone worse. This was luckily early in the times of the atrocities, and these officers—they were hounds set out to kill, but they went by the book. A hound is honest in his pursuit. The rat and the slippery eel—later on, more officers were like that.

They might have dragged us away just for being in back of the van at all. But we said we were workers. In this, the driver backed us up. And the papers that shouted out *Jew?* My Misheleh stuffed them up a salmon. Later, after the Secret Police were gone and we had clumped across the border, we were on our knees with a child's doll's knife slicing the bellies of maybe a hundred fish until we found it! Covered in pearly offal and roe. We had it framed when we came to America. Pretty. A little cherrywood frame with cherubim puffing a trump in each corner. We were happy, then. A very lovely frame around an ugliness.

"And you loved each other."

Every day, in our hearts. Some nights, in our bodies. I'll tell you this about sex: it's like genealogy. Yes. It takes you back, to the source. That's one small bit of why some people relish wallowing there. A burrowing, completely and beastly, back to where we came from. It tastes and smells "fishy" in every language I know. It takes us down to when the blood was the ocean, down the rivers of the live flesh to the ocean, to the original beating fecundity. It's as close as we'll ever get.

And this I'll tell you, about the smell of fish: For our earliest years, when I was starting the dry goods store and worrying every bolt of gabardine or every bucket of nails was eating another poem out of my soul—which I think is true—we lived over a fish store. Kipper, flounder, herring, the odors reached up like great gray leaves through our floorboards. And every night we lived there, Misheleh cried for a while. After the van, you see? She could never be around raw fish again, without panic.

But on the whole we were happy. There was security of a kind, and friends—even a social club in a patchy back room near the train tracks, that we decorated once a month with red and yellow crepe festoons and paper lanterns pouring out a buttery light.

Once every year she and I, we visited the cemetery. A private ritual: we pretended Yitzl was buried there. Because he'd brought us together, and we wanted him with us yet. For the hour it took, we always hired a street accordionist—it wasn't an uncommon instrument then. Like guitar now. Play a polka, we told him—*hot*. It drove the other cemetery visitors crazy! And always, Misheleh left a paper rose at the cemetery gates.

We heard that accordion music and a whole world came back, already better and worse than it was in its own time. Harsher. Gentler. Coarser. Little things—our shtetl dogs. Or big things too, the way we floated our sins away on toy-sized cork rafts once each spring, and everybody walking home singing . . . All of that world was keeping its shape but growing more and more transparent for us. Like the glass slipper in the fairy tale. The past was becoming a fairy tale. In it, the slipper predicates a certain foot and, so, a certain future.

At night I'd walk in my store. The moon like a dew on the barrel heaped with bolts, and the milky bodies of lamps, and the pen nibs, and shovels . . . Kaufman. Merchant.

4.

Within a year after death we have what Jewish tradition calls "the unveiling"—the gravestone dedication ceremony. September 14, 1986: I arrived in Chicago, joining my mother, sister, two aunts, and perhaps thirty others, including the rabbi, at the grave of my father Irving Goldbarth, his stone wrapped in a foolish square of cheesecloth. A stingy fringe of grass around the fresh mound. The burial had taken place in bitter city winter, the earth (in my memory) opening with the crack of axed oak. Now it was warmer, blurrier, everything soft. My mother's tears.

The rabbi spoke, his voice soft: to the Jews a cemetery is "a house of graves" . . . but also a "house of eternal life." The same in other faiths, I thought. There are as many dead now as alive. A kind of balance along the ground's two sides. That permeable membrane. Always new dead in the making, and always the long dead reappearing over our shoulders and in our dreams. Sometimes a face, like a coin rubbed nearly smooth, in a photo. We're supposed to be afraid of ghosts but every culture has them, conjures them, won't let go. Our smoky ropes of attachment to the past. Our anti-umbilici . . . My mind wandering. Then, the eldest and only son, I'm reciting the Kaddish. "Yisgadahl v'yisgadosh sh'may rahbbo . . ." In back, my father's father's grave, the man I'm named for. Staring hard and lost at the chiseling, ALBERT GOLDBARTH. My name. His dates.

In 1893 "Albert Goldbarth An Alien personally appeared in open Court and prayed to be admitted to become a Citizen of the United States . . ."—I have that paper, that and a sad, saved handful of others: September 15, 1904, he "attained the third degree" in the "Treue Bruder Lodge of the Independent Order of Odd Fellows." Five days after, J. B. Johnson, General Sales Agent of the Southern Cotton Oil Company, wrote a letter recommending "Mr. Goldbarth to whomsoever he may apply, as an honest and hardworking Salesman, leaving us of his own accord." That was 24 Broad Street, New York. In two years, in Cleveland, Ohio, John H. Silliman, Secretary, was signing a notice certifying Mr. Albert Goldbarth as an agent of The American Accident Insurance Company. And, from 1924, "$55 Dollars, in hand paid," purchasing Lot Number 703—this, from the envelope he labeled in pencil "Paid Deed from Semetery Lot from Hibrew Progresif Benefit Sociaty." I'm standing there now. I'm reading this stone that's the absolute last of his documents.

There aren't many stories. Just two photographs. And he was dead before I was born. A hundred times, I've tried inventing the callouses, small betrayals, tasseled mantle lamps, day-shaping waves of anger, flicked switches, impossible givings of love in the face of no love, dirty jokes, shirked burdens, flowerpots, loyalties, gold-shot silk page markers for the family Bible, violin strings, sweet body stinks from the creases, knickknacks, lees of tea, and morning-alchemized trolley tracks declaring themselves as bright script in the sooted-over paving bricks—everything that makes a life, which is his life, and buried.

And why am I busy repeating that fantastical list . . . ? We're "mountain gorillas" (this is from Alex Shoumatoff's wonderful study of kinship, *The Mountain of Names*) who "drag around moribund members of their troop and try to get them to stand, and after they have died" (above my grandfather's grave, imagining bouts of passion with imaginary Misheleh over my grandfather's grave now) "masturbate on them and try to get some reaction from them." An offering, maybe. A trying to read life backwards into that text of dead tongues. Give us any fabric scrap, we'll dream the prayer shawl it came from. Give us any worthless handful of excavated soil, we'll dream the scrap. The prayer. The loom the shawl took fragile shape on, in the setting shtetl hill-light. The immigrant ships they arrived in, the port, the year. We'll give that year whatever version of semen is appropriate, in homage and resuscitative ritual. We'll breathe into, rub, and luster that year.

1641: On a journey in Ecuador, a Portuguese Jew, Antonio de Montezinos, discovered—after a week-long, brush-clogged hell trek through the hinterlands—a hidden Jewish colony, and heard them wailing holy writ in Hebrew. Yes, there in the wild domain of ana-conda and peccary—or so he told the Jewish scholar and eminent friend of Rembrandt, Menasseh ben Israel. Or so Menasseh claimed, who had his own damn savvy purposes; and based on his claim that the Ten Lost Tribes of Israel were now found in the New World, and their global equi-dispersion near complete—as the Bible foretells will usher in an Age of Salvation—Britain's Puritan leaders readmitted their country's exiled Jews, the better to speed the whole world on its prophesied way to Redemption. (Maybe Rembrandt was an earlier body of Ernest L. Norman? Maybe the massed Confederation planets were holding their astro-collective breath even then, as destiny wound like spool thread on the windmills. And maybe, in the same Dutch-sunset oranges and mauves he let collect like puddled honey in his painted-dusk skies, Rembrandt helped Menasseh finagle this plot on behalf of a troubled people, tipped a flagon of burgundy in a room of laundered varnish rags, and plotted as the radio-telescope Monitor Maids of planet Vidus lounged about in their gold lamé uniforms, listening . . .)

Maybe. Always a maybe. Always someone forcing the scattered timbers of history into a sensible bridge. The Lost Tribes: China. The Lost Tribes: Egypt. The Lost Tribes: Africa. India. Japan. They formed a kingdom near "a terrible river of crashing stones" that roared six days a week "but on the Jewish Sabbath did cease." Lord Kingsbor-ough emptied the family fortune, won three stays in debtor's prison, "in order to publish a series of sumptuously illustrated volumes prov-ing the Mexican Indians . . ." Ethiopians. Eskimos. The Mormons have them reaching America's shores as early as "Tower of Babylon times" and later again, about 600 B.C., becoming tipi dwellers, hunters of lynx and buffalo, children of Fire and Water Spirits . . . Maybe. But today I think these caskets in Chicago soil are voyage enough. The moon's not that far.

We visit the other family graves: Auntie Regina (brain cancer) . . . Uncle Jake (drank; slipped me butterscotch candies) . . . Miles square and unguessably old, this cemetery's a city, districted, netted by streets and their side roads, overpopulated, undercared. Dead Jews dead Jews dead Jews. *Ruth Dale Noparstak * Age 2 Weeks * 1944*—death about the size of a cigar box.

My mother says to Aunt Sally (a stage whisper): "You'll see, Albert's going to write a poem about this." Later, trying to help that endeavor: "Albert, you see these stones on the graves? Jews leave stones on the graves to show they've visited." Not flowers? Why not flowers? . . . *I think I farmed black bent-backed turnips in the hardpan of a shtetl compound of equally black-garbed bent-backed grandmama and rabbinic Jews.*

My mother's parents are here in the Moghileff section, "Organized 1901." "You see the people here? They came from a town called Moghileff, in Russia—or it was a village. Sally, was Moghileff a town or a village?—you know, a little place where all the Jews lived. And those who came to Chicago, when they died, they were all buried here. Right next to your Grandma and Grandpa's graves, you see?— Dave and Natalie?—they were Grandma and Grandpa's neighbors in Moghileff, and they promised each other that they'd stay neighbors forever, here."

"Your Grandma Rosie belonged to the Moghileff Sisterhood. She was Chairlady of Relief. That meant, when somebody had a stillbirth, or was out of a job, or was beat in an alley, she'd go around to the members with an empty can and collect five dollars." Sobbing now. "Five dollars."

On our way out there's a lavish mausoleum lording it over this ghetto of small gray tenanted stones. My Uncle Lou says, still in his Yiddish-flecked English: "And *dis* one?" Pauses. "Gotta be a gengster."

5.

The Mormons marry backwards. "Sealing," they call it.
"Is that the end of your story of Misheleh and you?"
The story of marrying backwards never ends.

In Singapore not long ago, the parents of a Miss Cheeh, who had been stillborn twenty-seven years before, were troubled by ghosts in their dreams, and consulted a spirit medium. Independently, the parents of a Mr. Poon consulted her too—their son had been stillborn thirty-six years earlier and, recently, ghosts were waking them out of slumber. "And the medium, diagnosing the two ghosts' problem as loneliness, acted as their marriage broker." The Poons and the Cheehs were introduced, a traditional bride price paid, and dolls representing the couple were fashioned out of paper, along with a miniature one-story house with manservant, car, and chauffeur, a table with teacups and pot, and a bed with bolster and pillows. Presumably, on some plane of invisible, viable, ectoplasmic endeavor, connubial bliss was enabled. Who knows?—one day soon, they may wake in their version of that paper bed (his arm around her sex-dampened nape, a knock at the door . . .) and be given the chance to be Mormon, to have always been Mormon, and everlastingly Mormon. They'll laugh, but graciously. She'll rise and start the tea . . .

These ghosts. Our smoky ropes of attachment. And our reeling them in.

Eventually Misheleh and I prospered. The store did well, then there were two stores. We grew fat on pickled herring in cream, and love. I suppose we looked jolly. Though you could see in the eyes, up close, there was a sadness: where our families died in the camps, where I was never able to find time for the poetry—those things. Even so, the days and nights were good. The children never lacked a sweet after meals (but only if they cleaned their plates), or a little sailor suit, or kewpie blouse, or whatever silliness was in fashion. Before bed, I'd tell them a story. *Once, your mother and I, we lived in another country. A friend introduced us. He was a famous musician. Your mother danced to his songs and a thousand people applauded. I wrote poems about her, everyone read them. Gentlemen flung her roses . . .*

I died. It happens. I died and I entered the Kingdom of Worm and of God, and what happens then isn't part of this story, there aren't any words for it. And what I became on Earth—here, in the memory of the living . . . ?—it isn't over yet, it never ends, and now I'm me and I love you.

Because the ash is in this paper in which I'm writing (and in the page you're reading) and has been from the start. Because the blood is almost the chemical composition of the ocean, the heart is a swimmer, a very sturdy swimmer, but shore is never in sight. Because of entropy. Because of the nightly news. Because the stars care even less for us than we do for the stars. Because the only feeling a bone can send us is pain. Because the more years that we have, the less we have—the schools don't teach this Tragic Math but we know it; twiddling the fingers is how we count it off. Because because because. And so somebody wakes from an ether sleep: the surgeons have made him Elvis, he can play third-rate Las Vegas bars. And so someone revises the raven on top of the clan pole to a salmon-bearing eagle: now his people have a totem progenitor giving them certain territorial privileges that the spirits ordained on the First Day of Creation. So. Because.

In *He Done Her Wrong,* the "Great American Novel—in pictures—and not a word in it" that the brilliant cartoonist Milt Gross published in 1930, the stalwart square-jawed backwoods hero and his valiant corn-blonde sweetheart are torn from each other's arms by a dastardly mustachioed villain of oily glance and scowling brow, then seemingly endless deprivations begin: fistfights, impoverishment, unbearable loneliness, the crazed ride down a sawmill tied to one of its logs . . . And when they're reunited, as if that weren't enough, what cinches it as a happy ending is uncinched buckskin pants: the hero suddenly has a strawberry birthmark beaming from his tush, and is known for the billionaire sawmill owner's rightful heir . . .

Because it will save us.

The story-in-my-story is over: Misheleh and the children walk home from the cemetery. She's left a stone and a paper rose. We never would have understood it fifty years earlier, sweated with sex, but this is also love.

The story is over, too: the "I" is done talking, the "you" is nearly asleep, they lazily doodle each other's skin. We met them, it seems a long while ago, in what I called "a trough between crests." Let their bed be a raft, and let the currents of sleep be calm ones.

Outside of the story, I'm writing this sentence, and whether someone is a model for the "you" and waiting to see me put my pen down and toe to the bedroom—or even if I'm just lonely, between one "you" and the next—is none of your business. The "outside" is never the proper business between a writer and a reader, but this I'll tell you: tonight the rains strafed in, then quit, and the small symphonic saws of the crickets are swelling the night. This writing is almost over.

But nothing is ever over—or, if it is, then the impulse is wanting to *make* it over: "over" not as in "done," but "again." "Redo." Re-synapse. Re-nova.

I need to say "I love you" to someone and feel it flow down the root of her, through the raw minerals, over the lip of the falls, and back, without limit, into the pulse of the all-recombinant waters.

I meet Carolyn for lunch. She's with Edward, her old friend, who's been living in the heart of Mexico all of these years:

> Our maid, Rosalita, she must be over seventy. She had "female troubles," she said. She needed surgery. But listen: she's from the hills, some small collection of huts that doesn't even bear a name, so she hasn't any papers

at all—absolutely no identification. There isn't a single professional clinic that can accept you that way. There isn't any means for obtaining insurance or public aid.

So we went to a Records Division. I slipped the agent *dinero.* He knew what I was doing. It's everywhere. It's the way Mexico works. And when we left, Rosalita was somebody else. She had somebody else's birth certificate, working papers—everything.

She had somebody else's life from the beginning, and she could go on with her own.

Author's Note: In the writing of this essay I drew on many rich sources of information and inspiration, two of which deserve special mention: Douglas Curran's *In Advance of the Landing: Folk Concepts of Outer Space* (1986) and Alex Shoumatoff's *The Mountain of Names: An Informal History of Kinship* (1985).

Albert Goldbarth
A Chicago native, born there in 1948, Albert Goldbarth has made his mark as both essayist and poet. In 2002, he became the first poet to win the National Book Critics Circle Award twice; he took the prize for Saving Lives: Poems. *His essay collections are* Dark Waves and Light Matter, Great Topics of the World, *and* A Sympathy of Souls. *Recent books include* Pieces of Payne *and* Combinations of the Universe. *He lives in Wichita, Kansas.*

Still Life

Notes on Pierre Bonnard and My Mother's Ninetieth Birthday

Mary Gordon

In the year 1908, Pierre Bonnard painted *The Bathroom* and my mother was born. The posture of the young woman in the painting is that of someone enraptured by the miracle of light. The light is filtered through the lace curtains, and its patterning is reflected in the water that fills the tub into which she is about to step. Even the floral spread on the divan from which she has just risen is an emblem of prosperity and joy. Bonnard is famous for painting bathing women; in all her life my mother has never taken a bath. At three, she was stricken with polio, and she never had the agility to get in or out of a bathtub. She told me that once, after I was born, my father tried to lift her into a bath, but it made them both too nervous.

Ninety years after the painting of *The Bathroom,* ten days before my mother's ninetieth birthday, I am looking at the works of Bonnard at the Museum of Modern Art, a show I've been waiting for with the excitement of a teenager waiting for a rock concert. I was not brought to museums as a child; going to museums wasn't, as my mother would have said, "the kind of thing we went in for." It is very possible that my mother has never been inside a museum in her life. As a family we were pious, talkative, and fond of stories and the law. Our preference was for the invisible.

I can no longer remember how looking at art became such a source of solace and refreshment for me. Art history wasn't anything I studied formally. I think I must have begun going to museums as a place to meet friends. However and wherever it happened, a fully re- alized painterly vision that testifies in its fullness to the goodness of life has become for me a repository of faith and hope, two of the three theological virtues I was brought up to believe were at the center of things. It is no accident, I suppose, though at the time I might have said it was, that I've arranged to meet two friends at the Bonnard show at the same time that I'm meant to phone the recreation therapist at my mother's nursing home to plan her birthday party. Fifteen minutes after I arrive, I'll have to leave the show. The therapist will be available only for a specific half hour; after that, she's leaving for vacation.

Am I purposely creating difficulties for myself, a situation of false conflict, so that I can be tested and emerge a hero? There is the chance that I will not be able to leave the dazzle of the first room, to resist the intoxication of these paintings, so absorbing, so saturating, so suggestive of a world of intense color, of prosperous involvement, of the flow of good life and good fortune. There's the chance that I will forget to call the therapist. I do not forget, but my experience of the first paintings is poisoned by the fear that I will.

My mother has no idea that her ninetieth birthday is coming up. She has no notion of the time of day, the day of the week, the season of the year, the year of the century. No notion of the approaching mil- lennium. And no idea, any longer, who I am. Her forgetting of me happened just a few months ago, after I had been traveling for more than a month and hadn't been to see her. When I came back, she asked me if I were her niece. I said no, I was her daughter. "Does that mean I had you?" she asked, I said yes. "Where was I when I had you?" she asked me, I told her she was in a hospital in Far Rockaway, New York. "So much has happened to me in my life," she said. "You can't expect me to remember everything."

My mother has erased me from the book of the living. She is denying the significance of my birth. I do not take this personally. It is impossible for me to believe any longer that anything she says refers to me. As long as I remember this, I can still, sometimes, enjoy her company.

The day before I go to the Bonnard show, I visit my mother. It is not a good visit. It is one of her fearful days. I say I'll take her out to the roof garden for some air. She says, "But what if I fall off?" I bring her flowers, which I put in a vase near her bed. She says, "But what if they steal them or yell at me for having them?" She asks me thirty or more times if I know where I'm going as we wait for the elevator. When I say we'll go to the chapel in a little while, she asks if I think she'll get in trouble for going to the chapel outside the normal hours for Mass, and on a day that's not a Sunday or a holy day. She seems to believe me each time when I tell her that she won't fall off the roof, that no one will reprimand her or steal her flowers, that I know where I'm going, that she will not get in trouble for being in church and saying her prayers.

I have brought her a piece of banana cake and some cut-up watermelon. There are only three things to which my mother now responds: prayers, songs, and sweets. Usually, I sing to her as we eat cake and then I take her to the chapel, where we say a decade of the rosary. But today she is too cast down to sing, or pray, or even eat. There is no question of going out onto the roof. She just wants to go back to her room. She complains of being cold, though it is 95 degrees outside and the air conditioning is off. It is not a long visit. I bring her back to her floor after twenty minutes.

On my mother's floor in the nursing home, many people in wheelchairs spend most of their days in the hall. There is a man who is still attractive, though his face is sullen and his eyes are dull. Well, of course, I think, why wouldn't they be? He looks at me, and his dull eyes focus on my breasts in a way that is still predatory, despite his immobility. I take this as a sign of life. It's another thing I don't take personally. In fact, I want to encourage this sign of life. So I walk down the hall in an obviously sexual way. "*Putana!*" he screams out behind me. I believe that I deserve this; even though what I did was an error, a misreading, it was still, I understand now, wrong.

In front of the dayroom door sits a legless woman. Her hair is shoulder length, dyed a reddish color; her lips are painted red. The light blue and white nylon skirts of her dressing gown billow around her seat, and she looks like a doll sitting on a child's dresser or a child's crude drawing of a doll.

My mother was once a beautiful woman, but all her teeth are gone now. Toothless, no woman can be considered beautiful. Whenever I arrive, she is sitting at the table in the common dining room, her head in her hands, rocking. Medication has eased her anxiety, but nothing moves her from her stupor except occasional moments of fear, too deep for medication. This is a room that has no windows, that lets in no light, in which an overlarge TV is constantly blaring, sending images that no one looks at, where the floors are beige tiles, the walls cream-colored at the bottom, papered halfway up with a pattern of nearly invisible grayish leaves. Many of the residents sit staring, slack-jawed, open-mouthed. I find it impossible to imagine what they might be looking at.

It is difficult to meet the eyes of these people; it is difficult to look at their faces. I wonder if Bonnard could do anything with this light-less room. If he could enter it, see in these suffering people, including my mother, especially my mother, only a series of shapes and forms, concentrate on the colors of their clothing (a red sweater here, a blue shirt there), transform the blaring images on the TV screen to a series of vivid rectangles, and, failing to differentiate, insisting on the false-ness of distinctions, of an overly rigid individuality, saying that we must get over the idea that the features of the face are the important part—would he be able to create a scene of beauty from this scene, which is, to me, nearly unbearable? He once told friends that he had spent much of his life trying to understand the secret of white. How I envy him such a pure preoccupation, so removed from the inevitable degradations of human character and fate. So he could paint wilting flowers, overripe fruit, and make of them a richer kind of beauty, like the nearly deliquescing purple grapes, the visibly softening bananas, of *Bowl of Fruit,* 1933. "He let the flowers wilt and then he started painting; he said that way they would have more presence," his housekeeper once said.

The people in the dining room are wilting, they are decomposing, but I cannot perceive it as simply another form, simply another sub-ject or observation. I cannot say there are no differences between them and young, healthy people, no greater or lesser beauty, as one could say of buds or wilting flowers, unripe fruit or fruit on the verge of rotting. It is impossible for me to say that what has happened to these people is not a slow disaster.

And how important is it that when we read or look at a painting we do not use our sense of smell? The smells of age and misery hang over the common room. Overcooked food, aging flesh. My mother is kept clean, but when I bend over to kiss her hair, it smells like an old woman's. And there is the residual smell of her incontinence. My mother wears diapers. A residual smell that is unpleasant even in chil-dren but in the old is not only a bad smell but a sign of shame, of pun-ishment: a curse. I cannot experience it any other way. My mother's body is inexorably failing, but not fast enough. She is still more among the living than the dying, and I wonder, often, what might be the good of that.

I thought that the women in the Bonnard paintings would all be long dead. As it turns out, at least one is still alive.

It is the day of my mother's birthday. Two of my friends, Gary and Nola, have agreed to be with me for this day. They are both very good-looking people. They are both, in fact, beauties. Gary is a priest; in another age, he might be called my confessor, not that he has heard my confession in the sacramental sense but because he is someone to whom I could tell anything, with no shame. Nola was my prize student, then she worked as my assistant for four years. We are proud that we have transformed ourselves from teacher/student, employer/employee, into, simply, friends.

When I thank him for agreeing to come to my mother's party, Gary says, "This will be fun." "No it won't," I say, "it won't be fun at all." "Well, it will be something to be got through. Which is, in some ways, not so different from fun." "It is," I say, "it is." "No, not really. It isn't really," he says, and we both laugh.

Gary's mother is also in a nursing home, in St. Louis, Missouri, a city I have never visited. She accuses his father, who is devoted to her, who has been devoted for years, of the most flagrant infidelities. All he says in response is, "I didn't do that, I would never do that." When we speak about our mothers, of our mothers' fears and sadnesses, particularly about the shape his mother's rage has taken, Gary and I agree that if we could understand the mystery of sex and the mystery of our mothers' fates we would have penetrated to the heart of something quite essential. We very well know that we will not. This is very different from Bonnard's secret of white.

Gary's father visits his mother in the nursing home every day. The end of Marthe Bonnard's life was marked by a withdrawal into a depressed and increasingly phobic isolation, so that the shape of a large part of her husband's life was determined by her illness, finding places for her to take cures, and staying away from people whom she feared, who she thought were staring at her, laughing at her. In 1931, Bonnard wrote, "For quite some time now I have been living a very secluded life as Marthe has become completely antisocial [*Marthe étant devenue d'une sauvagerie complète*] and I am obliged to avoid all contact with other people. I have hopes though that this state of affairs will change for the better but it is rather painful."

Did this forced isolation, in fact, suit Bonnard very well; was it the excuse he could present to a sympathetic world so that he could have the solitude he needed for his work? What is the nature of the pain of which he spoke? What was the nature of her "*sauvagerie complète*"? In the painting in which he suggests Marthe's isolation, *The Vigil,* although she sits uncomfortably in her chair, in a room empty of people, alienated even from the furniture, unable to take comfort even from her dog, she appears still young, still attractive, still someone we want to look at. In fact, she was fifty-two, and someone whose misery, if we encountered it in person, might have caused us to avert our eyes.

I do not shape my life around my mother's needs or her condition. I try to visit her once a week, but sometimes I don't make it, sometimes it is two weeks, even three. If life is pressing on me, it is easy for me to put the visit off, because I don't know how much it means to her, and I know that she forgets I was there minutes after I have left, that she doesn't feel a difference between three hours and three weeks. If I believed that visiting my mother every day would give something important to my work, as the isolation required by Marthe Bonnard's illness gave something to her husband's, perhaps I would do it. But when I leave my mother, work is impossible for me; the rest of the afternoon is a struggle not to give in to a hopelessness that makes the creation of something made of words seem ridiculous, grotesque, a joke.

Two weeks before my mother's birthday, Gary celebrated the twenty-fifth anniversary of his ordination. His father couldn't be there; he wouldn't leave Gary's mother, even for a day. That was a grief for Gary, but most of the day was full of joy, a swelling of love, a church full of all the representatives of Gary's life—musicians, artists, dancers, writers, the bodybuilders he came to know at the gym where he works out, to whom he is an informal chaplain, as well as the parishioners he serves. The music was mostly provided by a gospel choir, who brought everyone to tears, and whose music blended perfectly with the parish choir's Gregorian chant, with which it alternated. It was a day of harmony, of perfect blending, but with high spots of color, like the paintings of Bonnard. I bought for the occasion a red silk dress with a fitted waist and an elaborate collar. I wore gold shoes. On the altar, flanked by red and white flowers in brass vases, I read the epistle of St. Paul to the Galatians, which assures that in Christ there is neither male nor female, slave nor free—a blurring of distinctions like the blurring of boundaries in Bonnard, where the edge of an arm melts into a tablecloth, a leg into the ceramic of a tub, flesh into water, the sun's light into the pink triangle of a crotch.

Nola has the long legs, slim hips, and small but feminine breasts of Marthe Bonnard. I know this because a certain part of our relationship centers around water. We swim together in the university pools; afterward we shower and take saunas. She has introduced me to a place where, three or four times a year, we treat ourselves to a day of luxury. A no-frills bath in the old style, a shvitz, a place where we sit in steam, in wet heat, in dry heat, in a room that sounds like something from the *Arabian Nights:* the Radiant Room. We spend hours naked among other naked women, women who walk unself-consciously, women of all ages and all ranges of beauty, in a place where wetness is the rule, where a mist hangs over things, as in the bathrooms of Bonnard. The preponderance of bathing women in Bonnard's work has been explained by Marthe Bonnard's compulsive bathing. She sometimes bathed several times a day. This may have been part of a hygienic treatment connected to her tuberculosis. But whatever the cause, her husband used it triumphantly.

Nola has just come from a friend's wedding in Maine. She was seated at the reception next to a German student, who became besotted with her. He grabbed her head and tried to put his own head on her shoulder. "You must come and have a drink with me at my inn," he said to her. She refused.

"You weren't tempted by all that ardor?" I ask her.

"No," she says. "I saw he had no lightness, that there was no lightness to him or anything that he did."

Bonnard's paintings are full of light, but they are not exactly about lightness, and his touch is not light, except in the sense that the paint is applied thinly and wetly. But he is always present in his paintings, and his hand is always visible. He has not tried to efface himself; he has not tried to disappear.

When I walk into the dining room on the day of my mother's birthday, I see that she has already been served lunch. The staff has forgotten to hold it back, though I told them a week ago that I would be providing lunch. She hasn't touched anything on her tray except a piece of carrot cake, which she holds in her hands. The icing is smeared on her hands and face. I don't want my friends to see her smeared with icing, so I wet a paper towel and wipe her. This fills me with a terrible tenderness, recalling, as it does, a gesture I have performed for my children. If I can see her as a child, it is easy to feel only tenderness for her. Bonnard paints children most frequently in his earlier period, in the darker Vuillard-like paintings, in which it is his natal family that is invoked. In the brighter pictures, children do not take their place as representatives of the goodness of the world. That place is taken up by dogs. In the painting *Marthe and Her Dog,* Marthe and a dachshund greet each other ecstatically in the foreground. In the far background, faceless, and having no communication with the woman and her dog, children run, leaving lime-colored shadows on the yellow grass.

As I wipe my mother's face, I see that her skin is still beautiful. I hold her chin in my hand and kiss her forehead. I tell her it's her birthday, that she's ninety years old. "How did that happen?" she asks. "I can't understand how that could happen."

I have brought her a bouquet of crimson, yellow, and salmon-pink snapdragons. She likes the flowers very much. She likes the name. "Snapdragons. It seems like an animal that's going to bite me. But it's not an animal, it's a plant. That's a funny thing."

One reason I bought the flowers is that the colors reminded me of Bonnard. I don't tell my mother that. Even if she still had her wits, I would not have mentioned it. Bonnard is not someone she would have heard of. She had no interest in painting.

I have bought food that I hope will please my mother, and that will be easy for her to eat: orzo salad with little pieces of crayfish cut into it, potato salad, small chunks of marinated tomatoes. I have bought paper plates with a rust-colored background, upon which are painted yellow and gold flowers and blue leaves. I deliberated over the color of the plastic knives, forks, and spoons and settled on dark blue, to match the leaves. I am trying to make an attractive arrangement of food and flowers, but it's not easy against the worn gray formica of the table. I think of Bonnard's beautiful food, which always looks as if it would be warm to the touch. It is most often fruit, fruit that seems to be another vessel of sunlight, as if pressing it to the roof of your mouth would release into your body a pure jet of sun. Bonnard's food is arranged with the generous, voluptuous propriety I associate with the south of France, though Bonnard moved often, dividing his time between the south and the north. He places his food in rooms or gardens that themselves contribute to a sense of colorful plentitude. Yet it is very rare in Bonnard that more than one person is with the food; none of the festal atmosphere of the Impressionists, none of Renoir's expansive party mood, enters the paintings of Bonnard in which food is an important component. The beautiful colors of the food are what is important, not that the food is part of an encounter with people who will eat it, speak of it, enjoy one another's company.

Nola and Gary and I enjoy one another's company; I do not know what my mother enjoys. Certainly, the colorful food—the pink crayfish in the saffron-colored orzo, the red tomatoes, the russet potatoes punctuated with the parsley's severe green—is not a source of joy for her. Joy, if it is in the room, comes from the love of friends, from human communion—usually absent in the paintings of Bonnard. I do not think, though, that my mother feels part of this communion.

I talk about the food a bit to my mother, but she isn't much interested in descriptions of food. She never has been. She always had contempt for people who talked about food, who recounted memorable meals. She doesn't join us in saying the Grace in which Gary leads us. Nor does she join us in singing the songs that, two weeks ago, she still was able to sing: "Sweet Rosie O'Grady," "Daisy Daisy," "When Irish Eyes Are Smiling." Nothing focuses her attention until the cake, a cheesecake, which she picks up in her hands and eats messily, greedily. I wonder if it is only the prospect of eating sweets that keeps my mother alive.

When we are about to leave, I tell my mother that I'm going on vacation, that I won't see her for three weeks, that I am going to the sea. "How will I stand that, how will I stand that?" she says, but I know that a minute after I'm gone she'll forget I was there.

I have bought the catalogue of the exhibition, and when I leave my mother I go home and look at it for quite a long time. I read that Bonnard once said that "he liked to construct a painting around an empty space." A critic named Patrick Heron says that Bonnard knew "how to make a virtue of emptiness." Illustrating Bonnard's affinities with Mallarmé, Sarah Whitfield, the curator of the show, quotes a description of a water lily in one of Mallarmé's prose poems. The lily encloses "in the hollow whiteness a nothing, made of intact dreams, of a happiness which will not take place."

Much of my mother's life is made up of emptiness. She does, literally, nothing most of the day. For many hours she sits with her head in her hands, her eyes closed, rocking. She is not sleeping. I have no idea what she thinks about or if she thinks, if she's making images. Are images the outgrowth of memory? If they are, I don't know how my mother can be making images in her mind, since she has no memory. And, if her eyes are mostly closed, can she be making images of what is in front of her? The beige walls and linoleum, her compatriots with their withered faces, thin hair, toothless mouths, distorted bodies? The nurses and caretakers, perhaps? No, I don't think so. I think that my mother's life is mostly a blank, perhaps an empty screen occasionally impressed upon by shadows.

Sarah Whitfield says that in the center of many of Bonnard's pictures is a hole or a hollow: a tub, a bath, a basket, or a bowl. A hole or hollow that makes a place for a beautiful emptiness. Nola once described her mother's life as having graceful emptiness so that a whole day could be shaped around one action. We both admired that, so different from the frantic buzz that often characterizes our lives. I am afraid that the emptiness at the center of my mother's life is neither beautiful nor graceful but a blankness that has become obdurate, no longer malleable enough even to contain sadness. An emptiness that, unlike Bonnard's or Mallarmé's or Nola's mother's, really contains nothing. And there is nothing I can do about it. Nothing.

I don't know what that emptiness once contained, if it once held Mallarmé's intact dreams; dreams of happiness, which, for my mother, will not now be realized. Perhaps she is experiencing the "emptying out" of which the mystics speak, an emptying of the self in order to make a place for God. I don't know, since my mother does not use language to describe her mental state. I try to allow for the possibility that within my mother's emptiness there is a richness beyond language and beyond visual expression, a truth so profound that my mother is kept alive by it, and that she lives for it. To believe that, I must reject all the evidence of my senses, all the ways of knowing the world represented by the paintings of Bonnard.

Bonnard's mistress, Renée Monchaty, killed herself. There are many stories that surround the suicide. One is that she killed herself in the bath, a punitive homage to her lover's iconography. Another is that she took pills and covered herself with a blanket of lilacs. I also have heard that Marthe, after the painter finally married her, insisted that Bonnard destroy all the paintings he had done of Renée. I don't know if any of these stories is true, and I no longer remember where I heard them.

   In one painting that survives, *Young Women in the Garden,* Renée is suffused in a yellow light that seems like a shower of undiluted sun; her blonde hair, the bowl of fruit, the undefined yet suggestively fecund floral background, are all saturated with a yellowness, the distilled essence of youthful hope. Renée sits, her head resting against one hand, a half smile on her face, her light eyes catlike and ambiguous; she sits in a light-filled universe, in front of a table with a striped cloth, a bowl of apples, a dish of pears. In the margins, seen from the rear and only in profile, Marthe peers, eclipsed but omnipresent. I am thinking of this painting as I stand in the corner of the dining room, watching my mother from the side, like Marthe, the future wife. How can it be, I wonder, that Renée—who inhabited a world of yellow light, striped tablecloths, red and russet-colored fruit, a world in which all that is good about the physical presented itself in abundance—chose to end her life? While these old people, sitting in a windowless room with nothing to look at but the hysterically colored TV screen, their bodies failing, aching, how can it be that they are fighting so desperately for the very life that this woman, enveloped in such a varied richness, threw away? I am angry at Renée; she seems ungrateful. At the same time I do not understand why these people whom my mother sits among do not allow themselves to die. Renée had so much to live for, to live in, and chose not to live. What do they have to live for? I often ask myself of my mother and her companions. And yet they choose, with a terrible animal avidity, to continue to live.

   In a 1941 letter to Bonnard, Matisse writes that "we must bless the luck that has allowed us, who are still here, to come this far. Rodin once said that a combination of extraordinary circumstances was needed for a man to live to seventy and to pursue with passion what he loves." And yet the last self-portraits painted by Bonnard in his seventies are as desolate as the monologues of Samuel Beckett. *Self-Portrait in the Bathroom Mirror* portrays a nearly featureless face, eyes that are more like sockets, a head that seems shamed by its own baldness, the defeatist's sloping shoulders, arms cut off before we can see hands. In the *Self-Portrait* of 1945, Bonnard's mouth is half open in a gesture of desolation; his eyes, miserable, are black holes, swallowing, rather than reflecting, light. At the end of his life, Bonnard was deeply dejected by the loss of Marthe, of his friends, by the hardship of the war, which he includes in one of his self-portraits by the presence of a blackout shade. Is it possible that, despite his portrayal of the joy and richness of the colors of this world, despite his mastery and his absorption in the process of seeing, despite his recognition and success, his last days were no more enviable than my mother's?

Mary Gordon

Mary Gordon has published a number of novels, memoirs, and short story collections. Her best-selling novels include Final Payments *and* The Company of Women, *and she is known for a memoir called* The Shadow Man, *about her father, and a book of essays,* Good Boys and Dead Girls. *Gordon has been awarded the Lila Acheson Wallace–Reader's Digest Award and received a Guggenheim fellowship. Born in 1949 in Long Island, New York, she lives in New York City and teaches at Barnard College, where she is the McIntosh Professor of English.*

Reading History to My Mother

Robin Hemley

Your silence will not protect you.

—Audre Lourde

"Everything's mixed up in those boxes, the past and the present," my mother tells me. "Those movers made a mess of everything." I'm visiting her at the Leopold late on a Monday night after reading to my kids and being read to by my eldest, Olivia, who at six is rightfully proud of her newfound reading ability. My mother and I have been readers for many years, but in some ways, she finds it more difficult than does Olivia. At eighty-two, my mother's eyesight has deteriorated. Glaucoma. Severe optic nerve damage to her left eye. Macular degeneration. Tomorrow, I'm taking her to the doctor for a second laser operation to "relieve the pressure." We have been told by the doctor that the surgery won't actually improve her eyesight, but, with luck, will stop it from deteriorating any more. After that there's another operation she'll probably undergo, eighty miles south in Seattle. Another operation that won't actually make her see any better.

"I always had such good eyesight," she tells me. And then, "I wish there was something that could improve my eyesight." And then, "When are we going to go shopping for that new computer?"

"Well, let's make sure you can see the screen first," I say, which sounds cruel, but she has complained to me tonight that she wasn't able to see any of the words on her screen, though I think this has less to do with her eyesight than the glasses she's wearing. Unnaturally thick and foggy. My mother looks foggy, too, almost drunk, disheveled in her dirty sweater, though she doesn't drink. It's probably the medicine she's been taking for her many conditions.

My mother owns at least half a dozen glasses, and I know I should have sorted through them all by now (we tried once) but so many things have gone wrong in the last five months since my mother moved to Bellingham that sorting through her glasses is a side issue. I get up from the couch in the cramped living room of her apartment, step over the coffee table—careful not to tip over the cup of peppermint tea I'm drinking out of a beer stein, careful not to bump into my mother—and cross to the bedroom crammed with wardrobe boxes and too much furniture, though much less than what she's used to. On her dresser there are parts of various eyeglasses: maimed glasses, the corpses of eyeglasses, a dark orphaned lens here, a frame there, an empty case, and one case with a pair that's whole. This is the one I grab and take out to my mother who is waiting patiently, always patient these days, or perhaps so unnerved and exhausted that it passes for patience. She takes the case from me and takes off the old glasses, places them beside her beer mug of licorice tea, and puts on the new pair.

She rubs an eye, says, "This seems to be helping. Maybe these are my reading glasses." I should know, of course. I should have had them color-coded by now, but I haven't yet.

She bends down to the photo from the newsletter on the coffee table, and says. "Yes, that's William Carlos Williams."

A little earlier she told me about the photo. "It's in one of those boxes," she told me. "I saw it the other day. I thought I'd told you about it before," but she hadn't, this photo of her with William Carlos Williams, Theodore Roethke, and other famous writers. So I spent fifteen minutes rifling through her boxes of bills and old papers mixed up on the kitchen counter (a Cascade Gas Company bill, final payment requested for service at the apartment she moved into in December, when we still thought she could live on her own; a letter from the superintendent of public schools of New York City, dated 1959, addressed to my grandmother, a teacher at the time, telling her how many sick days she was allowed), looking for the photo, until she explained that it was actually part of a newsletter from the artists' colony, Yaddo, in Saratoga Springs, New York: Armed with that crucial bit of information, I found it.

The photo is captioned "Class picture, 1950."

"Can you pick me out?" she says.

Not many of these people are smiling. Eugenic Gershoy, seated next to Jessamyn West, has a little smirk, and Mitsu Yashima, seated next to Flossie Williams, smiles broadly, and also Cid Corman in the back row, whom I met in 1975, when I was a high school exchange student in Japan. My mother visited me in Osaka and we traveled by train to Kyoto, to Cid Corman's ice-cream parlor where I ate a hamburger, had an ice-cream cone and listened to a poetry reading while my mother and Cid reminisced.

"Don't I look prim?" my mother says, and she does. Or maybe it's something else. Scared? Intimidated? Shocked? My mother was 34 then. This was a year or so before she met my father. My sister, Nola, was three, and my mother was an up-and-coming young writer, one novel published in 1947. John Crowe Ransom liked her work, publishing several of her stories in the *Kenyon Review*. I wasn't born until 1958.

She stands up straight, hands behind her back, a scarf tied loosely around her neck, draping down over a breast, a flower pinned to the scarf. Theodore Roethke stands, huge, imposing, dour. In an accompanying article Harvey Shapiro tells of how publicly Roethke liked to display his wounds, how he told Shapiro of his hurt that John Crowe Ransom had rejected "My Papa's Waltz," though Roethke was famous by then and the poem had been widely anthologized. What remained, still, was Roethke's pain, perhaps the pain of rejection meshed with the pain of the poem's subject matter—abuse at the hands of his drunken father. Shapiro also tells of Roethke's claim that he'd bummed his way to Yaddo after escaping in drag from a mental institution on the west coast earlier that summer. "He liked to romanticize his mental illness," Shapiro writes. Perhaps, but something honest still comes across in that picture, the despair clear for anyone to view head-on.

In the front row, William Carlos Williams sits cross-legged, dignified.

"He dreamed of my legs," my mother tells me.

"William Carlos Williams dreamed of your legs?" I ask.

"At breakfast one day he said he'd had a dream about my legs. 'That girl has nice legs,' he said."

We have to keep going back over histories, our own and the histories of others, constantly revising. There's no single truth . . . except that, perhaps. History is not always recorded and not always written by the victor. History is not always written. We carry our secret histories behind our words, in another room, in the eyeglass case on the dresser in the bedroom. Maybe someone comes along and finds the right pair. Maybe we have too many, unsorted.

My mother's former landlord, Loyce, wants to know the history of the "L." I was gone for the past week in Hawaii, and that's the only reason I haven't called before now. Loyce has left messages on my answering machine twice, ostensibly to see about getting my mother's deposit back to us: minus a charge for mowing, the ad for renting the apartment again, a reasonable charge for her time, and of course, for painting over the "L." She'd also like the keys back from us. But the "L" is the real reason she's called. My mother wrote an "L" on the wall of the apartment in indelible magic marker before she left. "I'm dying to know the story," Loyce says. "I know there's a good story behind it."

Loyce appreciates a good story, and this is one of the things I appreciate about Loyce, that and her compassion. She moved to Bellingham several years ago to take care of her ailing mother, and now lives in her mother's old house on top of a hill with a view of the bay and the San Juan Islands. So she understands our situation. She knows that my mother can't live alone anymore, that all of us were taken by surprise by her condition when she moved here five months ago. Until then, my mother had been living on her own in South Bend, Indiana, where she taught writing until ten years ago. She'd been living on her own since I moved out at the age of sixteen to go to boarding school, and had been taking care of herself since 1966 when my father died. But in the last several months things have fallen apart. Our first inkling was the mover, a man in his sixties who worked with his son. He took me aside on the first day and told me that in his thirty years of moving he'd never seen an apartment as messy as my mother's. When he and his son went to my mom's apartment in South Bend, they almost turned around. "You don't have to do this if you don't want," the mover told his son.

No, the first inkling was my brother's call from L.A., where my mother was visiting a few days prior to her big move. The van had loaded in South Bend and she'd flown off to L.A. to visit him and his family. The night before her flight from L.A. to Seattle he called me near midnight and said, "Mom's hallucinating."

I asked him what he meant, what she was seeing, and he told me that she was seeing all these people who didn't exist and making strange remarks. "When I picked her up at the airport, she said there was a group of Asians having a baby. She said they were a troupe of actors and they were doing a skit."

Still, the next day, he put her on the plane to me, and I picked her up and brought her to her new home. Since then, we have gone to three different doctors and my mother has had brain scans and blood tests and sonograms of her carotid arteries and been placed on a small dose of an anti-psychotic drug. One doctor says her cerebral cortex has shrunk and she's had a series of tiny strokes to individual arteries in her brain.

At three A.M. one morning, the police call me up and tell me that my mother thinks someone is trying to break into her apartment.

"Is there anyone living with her?" the policeman asks.

"No."

"She says a handicapped woman lives with her. You might want to see a doctor about this."

I take her to doctors and try to convince my mother that she needs to live where she can be safe, but she refuses to even consider it. "I should have stayed in New York," she tells me. "I never should have left." And then, "I should never have come here. Why can't you be on my side?" And then, "I'll move down to L.A. Your brother is much nicer than you are."

I spend a few nights at her apartment, and she tells me about the Middle Eastern couple who have taken over her bedroom and the children who are there, and the landlord comes over and puts a lock on the door from the kitchen to the garage, though we know no one was trying to break in. And homeless people are living on her back porch. And she keeps startling people in the garage who are removing her belongings.

But finally.

After my cousin David flies up from L.A. After visiting a dozen managed care facilities, after my brother says he thinks it's the medicine that's doing this and I talk to the doctors and the doctors talk to each other and they talk to my mother and she says, "The doctor says I'm fine," and I say "No, he doesn't," and she hangs up, turns off her hearing aid.

And coincidentally, a friend of my mother's in South Bend wins second place in a poetry competition run by the literary journal I edit. The poems were all anonymous, and I had nothing to do with the judging, but my mother's friend has won second prize for a poem about her delusional mother, called "My Mother and Dan Rather." I call her up to tell her the good news of her award, but she assumes, of course, I'm calling to talk about my mother. So that's what we do for half an hour. She tells me she's distanced herself over the last year from my mother because she seemed too much like her own mother, and she tells me that several of my mother's friends wondered if they should call me and let me know what was going on.

I almost forget to tell her about her prize.

No, the first inkling was two years ago. My wife, Beverly, wondered aloud about my mother's memory, her hold on reality. I told Beverly my mother had always been kind of scattered, messy, unfocused.

And finally. After I come into her apartment one day and feel the heat. I go to the stove and turn off the glowing burners. My mother has a blister on her hand the size of a walnut. Beverly tells me that it's insane for my mother to live alone, that somehow we have to force her to move. "What if she sets the apartment on fire? She might not only kill herself, but the people next door."

"I know," I tell her. "I'm trying," but I also know that short of a court order, short of being declared her legal guardian, I can't force her.

And finally. I convince my mother to come with me to the Leopold, an historic hotel in downtown Bellingham that has been converted into apartments for seniors, one wing assisted living, the other independent. We have lunch there one day. My mother likes the food.

And finally, she agrees to spend a couple of weeks there in a guest room.

Famous people stayed at the Leopold, I tell my mother. Rutherford B. Hayes, Jenny Lind, the Swedish Nightingale. This doesn't impress her, of course. She has known more famous people than can fit on a plaque. But she has a nice view of the bay, somewhat blocked by the Georgia Pacific Paper Mill. And she likes the food but the apartment is only two cramped rooms, and across the street at the Greek restaurant, people party until two each night and climb trees and conduct military rituals. And the Iraqi Army rolled through the streets one night. And a truck dumped two bodies, a man and a woman dressed in formal evening attire.

"They sometimes flood the parking lot," she tells me, "and use it as a waterway."

Or, "Look at that," pointing, reaching for nothing.

She keeps returning to the apartment, driven by the woman I've hired to clean it. My mother wants to drive again, and I tell her no, she can't possibly, and I read articles and watch programs that tell me not to reverse roles, not to become the parent, and I wonder how that's possible to avoid. One day, I walk into her apartment and find signs she's posted all around on the bed, in the guest room, on the kitchen counter. "Keep off." "Stay out." "Go away." I ask her about these signs and she tells me they're just a joke. She's become wary of me. I tell her she's safe, ask her why she feels so threatened. She tells me, "I've never felt safe in my life."

During this period, my mother writes her "L" on the wall of the kitchen.

And the weeks at the Leopold have turned to months, and now most of her belongings are stuffed into a heated mini-storage unit. More of her belongings are stuffed into the basement of The Leopold. Finally.

I almost don't want to tell Loyce the story of the "L" when she calls. I'd like to keep her in suspense, because sometimes that's stronger than the truth. She probably thinks it's about her, that the "L" stands for Loyce, but it doesn't. It stands for Leopold. One day my mother was at the apartment, after we finally convinced her she had to move, and I gave her a magic marker and asked her to mark the boxes she'd like taken to the Leopold. Apparently, she thought she was marking a box, but she was really marking the wall. This is what she really wanted. That was not lost on me. She loved that apartment. She wanted her independence, but this was just too much for me to move.

Loyce and I say goodbye after I assure her I'll return the keys and she assures me she'll return most of the deposit. It's already eight-thirty and I told my mother I'd be over around eight, but I had to read to my kids first. I haven't see them in a week. I've just returned from Hawaii.

In Hawaii, where I've been researching a new book, I probably had more fun than I should have. Not the kind of fun with life-bending consequences, but fun nonetheless, hanging out with a former student, eating out every night, smoking cigars, drinking. For ten dollars a day more, I was told at the airport, I could rent a convertible—a Ford Mustang, or a Caddie, and I'm not ready for that, so I take the Mustang. Stupid. The wife of the friend I'm staying with laughed when she saw it in her driveway. "Oh," she tells me. "I thought maybe Robbie was having a mid-life crisis." No, it's me probably, even though I hate to admit it. I refuse to believe such a thing could happen to me at this pre-ordained age, a month from forty, that I could be saddled with such a cliché crisis, such mediocre regrets.

Olivia wants to read to *me* tonight, all seven stories from an Arnold Lobel book. "They're short," she assures me. We compromise on three, her three favorites. One of these she read last week to her class while I was in Hawaii. Beverly, who sometimes works in Olivia's class as a volunteer, has already told me that the class was enthralled by Olivia. "She acted so confident. She took her time and showed them the pictures."

The one she read to her class, "The Journey," is about a mouse who wants to visit his mother, and in a sequence of transactions, acquires a car, roller skates, boots, sneakers and finally a new set of feet. When he reaches his mother she hugs him, kisses him and says, "Hello, my son, you are looking fine—and what nice new feet you have!" Olivia's whole class broke out in hysterical laughter, she assured me.

I've brought my mother a box of chocolate-covered macadamia nuts. She looks at it, bewildered. "Oh, I thought it was a book," she says.

I make tea for us, but she only has a few tea mugs and they're dirty, so we have to use beer steins. "I've ended up with such an odd assortment of things," she tells me, and she blames this on the movers.

A week before my trip to Hawaii, I visited her and she showed me a notebook in which she'd kept a journal during the mid-seventies. My mother has kept journals from the time she was sixteen, a series of secret histories written in any notebook she can find. But now, she cannot read these histories, and she asks me to read this one to her.

"I might use it in a story," she tells me. "It's about Moe and Helen." Moe is Moe Howard, of the Three Stooges. He was a cousin of ours by marriage, and whenever she visited California, she'd stop by to see them. Moe, who had such a violent on-screen persona: Think of him saying, "Wise guy, eh?" Poking the eyes of Larry, Curly, Shemp, or one of the later pseudo-Stooges, Curly Joe and Joe Besser. I met him once, a frail old man with white hair, too quiet to seem like Moe. Off-screen, he was a gentle family man, kind and grateful to his fans, never refusing to sign an autograph. What my mother wants me to read to her is an account of the last time she saw Moe and his wife Helen, when they were both dying.

> Seeing Moe and Helen was touching—a beautiful hill of purple flowers outside that Moe said was all theirs—a beautifully furnished, expensively comfortable house through which they glide, ghost-like. They don't kiss me because of the possibility of germs. Helen is in a loose purple nylon dressing gown. She has been recuperating from a breast operation and says in a slightly quaking voice that she will be going to the doctor soon and will probably have cobalt.
>
> Moe is red-faced and very thin. His thinness, wispiness, makes him look elfin—because he used to be heavier, he seemed bigger. His hair is white. He smiles proudly, talking about his appearances at colleges and his memoirs which comprise many books. Talk about the film I am supposed to have made with him. He reminds me that I acted in it (at the age of about 19) 8mm, I think, with his children. But it is packed somewhere with thousands of feet of other film.

As I'm reading this to my mother I feel odd, wondering if she notices the similarities between this passage and her own present life—

the things packed away, the memories, the frailty—but I say nothing about this, though it moves me. Instead, I ask her about this film she was in, and she tells me it was an impromptu home movie in which Moe was cast as the villain, of course, and she was the protector of his children. She has never seen it but it exists somewhere. Moe's daughter, Joan, once showed me the huge roll of home movies in her attic. Towards the end of his life, Moe took every home movie he made and spliced them all together onto one monstrous cumbersome roll that no one could ever possibly watch in its entirety. Somewhere on this roll exists a movie with my mother, age nineteen, circa 1935.

Silently, I flip through other pages in my mother's journal, as she sits near me, lost in her memories, needing no journal really.

> I am not in fantasy land. I am painfully living out my loneliness and nostalgia. I dream of my son every night and wish he were here. Those who have died are intolerably absent and I feel that all the love I need and want will not come because I had my chance and lost it, and what man will be responsible for or will react to my aging, my passion, my intolerable loneliness . . . ?

I am with her now, but not. We see each other through veils. We have battled for this moment, and neither sees the other as we would like.

William Carlos Williams dreamed of my mother's legs, as did other men that summer of 1950 at Yaddo.

As we bend over the class photo, circa 1950, she tells me the official history of that summer, how special it was for her, how it was so exciting to be around such vital intellects, such talented writers. "It was really something, going down to breakfast and having conversations with all these people. The talent was never quite the same after that."

I tell her I'd love to have a copy of this picture. "You could write to Yaddo," she says. "They use it for publicity." She tells me I could write to one of the writers pictured with her. "It's the least he could do," she says, with what seems like bitterness, and I let this remark wash over me because I think I know what's behind it.

Once, a number of years ago, Beverly and my mother and I were on a drive, and I was telling her about a friend of mine who'd done his dissertation on the poetry of one of the poets pictured in the photo. From the back seat my mother blurted, "You know, he raped me."

Beverly and I looked at one another. We didn't say anything. We didn't know what to say. The remark was so sudden, so unexpected, we hardly knew how to react. We were silent, all three of us. Neither Beverly nor I mentioned this to each other later.

My mother starts talking about him now, though I haven't asked. She says, "One time, he invited me to a private party, and innocent that I was, I went there." In memory, she's lucid. Only the present is slippery, tricky, untrustworthy.

"There were all these men there. They were all leches. Ted Roethke kept lunging for me, just making grabs. He really had problems," and she laughs. She mentions the name of the poet who was her friend, whom she trusted. He was younger than her, than all these other famous men. "I thought he'd protect me." She laughs again. This time, there's no mistaking the bitterness.

I think about asking her. What term to use? "He assaulted you?"

"Yes," she says.

"Did it happen at Yaddo?" I ask.

She nods.

"Did you ever confront him?"

"No," she says. "I don't want to talk about it."

But then she says, "There wasn't much I could do. In those days, there wasn't much to do. I just pretended it didn't happen. For a little while, he became my boyfriend."

I don't know what to say. I probably shouldn't say anything. I sigh. "He should have been locked up. How could he be your boyfriend after that?"

"He was drunk when it happened," and I want to say that's no excuse, but I keep my mouth shut and let her talk. "I left the party early and he followed me back to my room. I tried to lock the door, but the lock was broken.

"I turned things around. I had to. I was confused. In my mind, he became my protector from the other men there."

I study the picture again. My mother's expression and the expressions of the men. I wonder when this photo was taken, before or after the assault my mother describes. The photo has taken on the quality of a group mug shot to me, I think they look like jerks, most of them—except for Cid Corman, whom my mother says is a wonderful person, and maybe some others, too, maybe William Carlos Williams, who dreamed of my mother's legs and "had an eye for the ladies" as my mother says. Maybe even dour Theodore Roethke, though he lunged at her as though she was something being wheeled by on a dessert tray.

"They weren't famous for their personalities," she tells me.

I think about these people in the photo, how unfair it seems to me that someone can go on to have a career, hide behind his smirk, have dissertations written about him, how the actions of some people seem to have no visible consequences. I think of my mother's secret histories, her journals, her blurted comments, her assertion that she has never felt safe.

I flip the newsletter over to the section titled "Recent Works Produced by Yaddo Fellows," and see that the latest works reported are from 1987. For an absurd moment, I believe that none of the Fellows at Yaddo have been productive for over ten years, and this makes me happy, but then I realize the newsletter itself is ten years old.

My mother has taken to carrying a picture of me, Ideal Robin, I call it, skinny, sitting languorously, smiling beside a life-size cardboard cut-out of Rudolph Valentino. The son she longed for in her journal perhaps hardly exists anymore—I was away at boarding school that year, my choice, not hers, and I never returned.

I have come to visit her now. I've knocked lightly. I've used my key. She can barely see me when I walk into her apartment. I've told her I've returned from Hawaii, that she can expect me around eight, but I'm late and as I push open the door she's looking at me almost suspiciously, because really her eyesight is that bad, and until I speak she has no idea who's entering. The Iraqi army? A stranger who wants her belongings? A poet she thinks is her "protector" but means her harm? I half expect to see signs. "Keep Off," "Stay Out," "Go Away." I have brought a box of chocolate-covered macadamia nuts. I am wearing new feet, but she doesn't notice. Tomorrow she will have surgery on her eyes that will not improve anything, but keep things from getting worse. How much worse could things get for this woman who loves words, but can neither see nor write them anymore? Does her history go on inside her, on some gigantic roll of spliced-together home movies? Tell me the story of the "L." Tell me the story of the wall of your apartment. Tell me the story of those talented writers who publicly display their wounds and the writers who secretly wound others. Tell me which is worse. She kisses me lightly and I give her her gift. And she says, once, only once, though I keep hearing it, the disappointment, and strangely, even fear. "Oh, I thought it was a book."

Robin Hemley
Robin Hemley writes both nonfiction and fiction. His books include Invented Eden, Turning Life into Fiction, *and* The Big Ear. *He was awarded both the Independent Publisher's Book Award and Washington State's Governor's Award for* Nola: A Memoir of Faith, Art and Madness. *He has also received two Pushcart Prizes, a PEN Syndicated Fiction Award, the George Garrett Award, and the Nelson Algren Award from the* Chicago Tribune. *Hemley has been heard on NPR's "Selected Shorts" and "The Sound of Writing." Born in 1958 in New York City, he has taught at St. Lawrence University, the University of Utah, and Vermont College, where he currently chairs the MFA Writing Program.*

Where Worlds Collide

Pico Iyer

They come out, blinking, into the bleached, forgetful sunshine, in Dodgers caps and Rodeo Drive T-shirts, with the maps their cousins have drawn for them and the images they've brought over from *Cops* and *Terminator 2;* they come out, dazed, disoriented, heads still partly in the clouds, bodies still several time zones—or centuries—away, and they step into the Promised Land.

In front of them is a Van Stop, a Bus Stop, a Courtesy Tram Stop, and a Shuttle Bus Stop (the shuttles themselves tracing circuits A, B, and C). At the Shuttle Bus Stop, they see the All American Shuttle, the Apollo Shuttle, Celebrity Airport Livery, the Great American Stageline, the Movie Shuttle, the Transport, Ride-4-You, and forty-two other magic buses waiting to whisk them everywhere from Bakersfield to Disneyland. They see Koreans piling into the Taeguk Airport Shuttle and the Seoul Shuttle, which will take them to Koreatown without their ever feeling they've left home; they see newcomers from the Middle East disappearing under the Arabic script of the Sahara Shuttle. They see fast-talking, finger-snapping, palm-slapping jive artists straight from their TV screens shouting incomprehensible slogans about deals, destinations, and drugs. Over there is a block-long white limo, a Lincoln Continental, and, over there, a black Chevy Blazer with Mexican stickers all over its windows, being towed. They have arrived in the Land of Opportunity, and the opportunities are swirling dizzily, promiscuously, around them.

They have already braved the ranks of Asian officials, the criminal-looking security men in jackets that say "Elsinore Airport Services," the men shaking tins that say "Helping America's Hopeless." They have already seen the tilting mugs that say "California: a new slant on life" and the portable fruit machines in the gift shop. They have already, perhaps, visited the rest room where someone has written, "Yes on Proposition 187. Mexicans go home," the snack bar where a slice of pizza costs $3.19 (18 quetzals, they think in horror, or 35,000 dong), and the sign that urges them to try the Cockatoo Inn Grand Hotel. The latest arrivals at Los Angeles International Airport are ready now to claim their new lives.

Above them in the terminal, voices are repeating, over and over, in Japanese, Spanish, and unintelligible English, "Maintain visual contact with your personal property at all times." Out on the sidewalk, a man's voice and a woman's voice are alternating an unending refrain: "The white zone is for loading and unloading of passengers only. No parking." There are "Do Not Cross" yellow lines cordoning off parts of the sidewalk and "Wells Fargo Alarm Services" stickers on the windows; there are "Aviation Safeguard" signs on the baggage carts and "Beware of Solicitors" signs on the columns; there are even special phones "To Report Trouble." More male and female voices are intoning, continuously, "Do not leave your car unattended" and "Unattended cars are subject to immediate tow-away." There are no military planes on the tarmac here, the newcomers notice, no khaki soldiers in fatigues, no instructions not to take photographs, as at home; but there are civilian restrictions every bit as strict as in many a police state.

"This Terminal Is in a Medfly Quarantine Area," says the sign between the terminals. "Stop the Spread of Medfly!" If, by chance, the new Americans have to enter a parking lot on their way out, they will be faced with "Cars left over 30 days may be impounded at Owner's Expense" and "Do not enter without a ticket." It will cost them $16 if they lose their parking ticket, they read, and $56 if they park in the wrong zone. Around them is an unending cacophony of antitheft devices, sirens, beepers, and car-door openers; lights are flashing everywhere, and the man who fines them $16 for losing their parking ticket has the tribal scars of Tigre across his forehead.

The blue skies and palm trees they saw on TV are scarcely visible from here: just an undifferentiated smoggy haze, billboards advertising Nissan and Panasonic and Canon, and beyond those an endlessly receding mess of gray streets. Overhead, they can see the all-too-familiar signs of Hilton and Hyatt and Holiday Inn; in the distance, a sea of tract houses, mini-malls, and high-rises. The City of Angels awaits them.

It is a commonplace nowadays to say that cities look more and more like airports, cross-cultural spaces that are a gathering of tribes and races and variegated tongues; and it has always been true that airports are in many ways like miniature cities, whole, self-sufficient communities, with their own chapels and museums and gymnasiums. Not only have airports colored our speech (teaching us about being upgraded, bumped, and put on standby, coaching us in the ways of fly-by-night operations, holding patterns, and the Mile High Club); they have also taught us their own rules, their own codes, their own customs. We eat and sleep and shower in airports; we pray and weep and kiss there. Some people stay for days at a time in these perfectly convenient, hermetically sealed, climate-controlled duty-free zones, which offer a kind of caesura from the obligations of daily life.

Airports are also, of course, the new epicenters and paradigms of our dawning post-national age—not just the bus terminals of the global village but the prototypes, in some sense, for our polyglot, multicolored, user-friendly future. And in their very universality—like the mall, the motel, or the McDonald's outlet—they advance the notion of a future in which all the world's a multiculture. If you believe that more and more of the world is a kind of mongrel hybrid in which many cities (Sydney, Toronto, Singapore) are simply suburbs of a single universal order, then Los Angeles's LAX, London's Heathrow, and Hong Kong's Kai Tak are merely stages on some great global Circle Line, shuttling variations on a common global theme. Mass travel has made L.A. contiguous to Seoul and adjacent to São Paulo, and has made all of them now feel a little like bedroom communities for Tokyo.

And as with most social trends, especially the ones involving tomorrow, what is true of the world is doubly true of America, and what is doubly true of America is quadruply true of Los Angeles. L.A., legendarily, has more Thais than any city but Bangkok, more Koreans than any city but Seoul, more El Salvadorans than any city outside of San Salvador, more Druze than anywhere but Beirut; it is, at the very least, the easternmost outpost of Asia and the northernmost province of Mexico. When I stopped at a Traveler's Aid desk at LAX recently, I was told I could request help in Khamu, Mien, Tigrinya, Tajiki, Pashto, Dari, Pangasinan, Pampangan, Waray-Waray, Bambara, Twi, and Bicolano (as well, of course, as French, German, and eleven languages from India). LAX is as clear an image as exists today of the world we are about to enter, and of the world that's entering us.

For me, though, LAX has always had a more personal resonance: it was in LAX that I arrived myself as a new immigrant, in 1966; and from the time I was in the fourth grade, it was to LAX that I would go three times a year, as an "unaccompanied minor," to fly to school in London—and to LAX that I returned three times a year for my holidays. Sometimes it seems as if I have spent half my life in LAX. For me, it is the site of my liberation (from school, from the Old World, from home) and the place where I came to design my own new future.

Often when I have set off from L.A. to some distant place—Havana, say, or Hanoi, or Pyongyang—I have felt that the multicultural drama on display in LAX, the interaction of exoticism and familiarity, was just as bizarre as anything I would find when I arrived at my foreign destination. The airport is an Amy Tan novel, a short story by Bharati Mukherjee, a Henry James sketch set to an MTV beat; it is a cross-generational saga about Chang Hsieng meeting his daughter Cindy and finding that she's wearing a nose ring now and is shacked up with a surfer from Berlin. The very best kind of airport reading to be found in LAX these days is the triple-decker melodrama being played out all around one—a complex tragicomedy of love and war and exile, about people fleeing centuries-old rivalries and thirteenth-century mullahs and stepping out into a fresh, forgetful, born-again city that is rewriting its script every moment

Not long ago I went to spend a week in LAX. I haunted the airport by day and by night, I joined the gloomy drinkers listening to air-control-tower instructions on earphones at the Proud Bird bar. I listened each morning to Airport Radio (530 AM), and I slept each night at the Airport Sheraton or the Airport Hilton. I lived off cellophaned crackers and Styrofoam cups of tea, browsed for hours among Best Actor statuettes and Beverly Hills magnets, and tried to see what kinds of America the city presents to the new Americans, who are re-making America each day.

It is almost too easy to say that LAX is a perfect metaphor for L.A., a flat, spaced-out desert kind of place, highly automotive, not deeply hospitable, with little reading matter and no organizing principle. (There are eight satellites without a center here, many international arrivals are shunted out into the bleak basement of Terminal 2, and there is no airline that serves to dominate LAX as Pan Am once did JFK.) Whereas "SIN" is a famously ironical airline code for Singapore, cathedral of puritanical rectitude, "LAX" has always seemed perilously well chosen for a city whose main industries were traditionally thought to be laxity and relaxation. LAX is at once a vacuum waiting to be colonized and a joyless theme park—Tomorrowland, Adventureland, and Fantasyland all at once.

The postcards on sale here (made in Korea) dutifully call the airport "one of the busiest and most beautiful air facilities in the world," and it is certainly true that LAX, with thirty thousand international arrivals each day—roughly the same number of tourists that have visited the Himalayan country of Bhutan in its entire history—is not uncrowded. But bigger is less and less related to better: in a recent survey of travel facilities, *Business Traveller* placed LAX among the five worst airports in the world for customs, luggage retrieval, and passport processing.

LAX is, in fact, a surprisingly shabby and hollowed-out kind of place, certainly not adorned with the amenities one might expect of the world's strongest and richest power. When you come out into the Arrivals area in the International Terminal, you will find exactly one tiny snack bar, which serves nine items; of them, five are identified as Cheese Dog, Chili Dog, Chili Cheese Dog, Nachos with Cheese, and Chili Cheese Nachos. There is a large panel on the wall offering rental-car services and hotels, and the newly deplaned American dreamer can choose between the Cadillac Hotel, the Banana Bungalow (which offers a Basketball Court, "Free Toast," "Free Bed Sheets," and "Free Movies and Parties"), and the Backpacker's Paradise (with "Free Afternoon Tea and Crumpets" and "Free Evening Party Including Food and Champagne").

Around one in the terminal is a swirl of priests rattling cans, Iranians in suits brandishing pictures of torture victims, and Japanese girls in Goofy hats. "I'm looking for something called Clearasil," a distinguished-looking Indian man diffidently tells a cashier. "Clearasil?" shouts the girl. "For your face?"

Upstairs, in the Terrace Restaurant, passengers are gulping down "Dutch Chocolate" and "Japanese Coffee" while students translate back and forth between English and American, explaining that "soliciting" loses something of its cachet when you go across the Atlantic. A fat man is nuzzling the neck of his outrageously pretty Filipina companion, and a few Brits are staring doubtfully at the sign that assures them that seafood is "cheerfully served at your table!" Only in America, they are doubtless thinking. A man goes from table to table, plunking down on each one a key chain attached to a globe. As soon as an unsuspecting customer picks one up, touched by the largesse of the New World and convinced now that there is such a thing as a free lunch in America, the man appears again, flashes a sign that says "I Am a Deaf," and requests a dollar for the gift.

At a bank of phones, a saffron-robed monk gingerly inserts a credit card, while schoolkids page Jesse Jackson at the nearest "white courtesy telephone." One notable feature of the modern airport is that it is wired, with a vengeance: even in a tiny, two-urinal men's room, I found two telephones on offer; LAX bars rent out cellular phones; and in the Arrivals area, as you come out into the land of plenty, you face a bank of forty-six phones of every kind, with screens and buttons and translations, from which newcomers are calling direct to Bangalore or Baghdad. Airports are places for connections of all kinds and *loci classici,* perhaps, for a world ruled by IDD and MCI, DOS and JAL.

Yet for all these grounding reminders of the world outside, everywhere I went in the airport I felt myself in an odd kind of twilight zone of consciousness, that weightless limbo of a world in which people are between lives and between selves, almost sleepwalking, not really sure of who or where they are. Light-headed from the trips they've taken, ears popping and eyes about to do so, under a potent foreign influence, people are at the far edge of themselves in airports, ready to break down or through. You see strangers pouring out their life stories to strangers here, or making new life stories with other strangers. Everything is at once intensified and slightly unreal. One LA psychiatrist advises shy women to practice their flirting here, and religious groups circle in the hope of catching unattached souls.

Airports, which often have a kind of perpetual morning-after feeling (the end of the holiday, the end of the affair), are places where everyone is ruled by the clock, but all the clocks show different times. These days, after all, we fly not only into yesterday or this morning when we go across the world but into different decades, often, of the world's life and our own: in ten or fifteen hours, we are taken back into the twelfth century or into worlds we haven't seen since childhood. And in the process we are subjected to transitions more jolting than any imagined by Oscar Wilde or Sigmund Freud: if the average individual today sees as many images in a day as a Victorian saw in a lifetime, the average person today also has to negotiate switches between continents inconceivable only fifty years ago. Frequent fliers like Ted Turner have actually become ill from touching down and taking off so often; but, in less diagnosable ways, all of us are being asked to handle difficult suspensions of the laws of Nature and Society when moving between competing worlds.

This helps to compound the strange statelessness of airports, where all bets are off and all laws are annulled—modern equivalents, perhaps, to the hundred yards of no-man's-land between two frontier crossings. In airports we are often in dreamy, floating, out-of-body states, as ready to be claimed as that suitcase on Carousel C. Even I, not traveling, didn't know sometimes if I was awake or asleep in LAX, as I heard an announcer intone, "John Cheever, John Cheever, please contact a Northwest representative in the Baggage Claim area. John Cheever, please contact a service representative at the Northwest Baggage Claim area."

As I started to sink into this odd, amphibious, bipolar state, I could begin to see why a place like LAX is a particular zone of fear, more terrifying to many people than anywhere but the dentist's office.

Though dying in a plane is, notoriously, twenty times less likely than dying in a car, every single airline crash is front-page news and so dramatic—not a single death but three hundred—that airports are for many people killing grounds. Their runways are associated in the mind's (televisual) eye with hostages and hijackings; with bodies on the tarmac or antiterrorist squads storming the plane.

That general sense of unsettledness is doubtless intensified by all the people in uniform in LAX. There are ten different security agencies working the Tom Bradley Terminal alone, and the streets outside are jam-packed with Airport Police cars, FBI men, and black-clad airport policemen on bicycles. All of them do as much, I suspect, to instill fear as to still it. "People are scared here," a gloomy Pakistani security guard told me, "because undercover are working. Police are working. You could be undercover, I could be undercover. Who knows?"

And just as L.A. is a province of the future in part because so many people take it to be the future, so it is a danger zone precisely because it is imagined to be dangerous. In Osaka's new $16 billion airport recently, I cross-examined the Skynet computer (in the Departures area) about what to expect when arriving at LAX or any other foreign airport. "Guard against theft in the arrival hall," it told me (and, presumably, even warier Japanese). "A thief is waiting for a chance to take advantage of you." Elsewhere it added, "Do not dress too touristy," and, "Be on your guard when approached by a group of suspicious-looking children, such as girls wearing bright-colored shirts and scarves." True to such dark prognostications, the side doors of the Airport Sheraton at LAX are locked every day from 8:00 P.M. to 6:00 A.M., and you cannot even activate the elevators without a room key. "Be extra careful in parking garages and stairwells," the hotel advises visitors. "Always try to use the main entrance to your hotel, particularly late in the evening. Never answer your hotel room door without verifying who is there."

One reason airports enjoy such central status in our imaginations is that they play such a large part in forming our first (which is sometimes our last) impression of a place; this is the reason that poor countries often throw all their resources into making their airports sleek, with beautifully landscaped roads leading out of them into town. L.A., by contrast, has the bareness of arrogance, or simple inhospitability. Usually what you see as you approach the city is a grim penitential haze through which is visible nothing but rows of gray buildings, a few dun-hued warehouses, and ribbons of dirty freeway: a no-colored blur without even the comforting lapis ornaments of the swimming pools that dot New York or Johannesburg. (Ideally, in fact, one should enter L.A. by night, when the whole city pulses like an electric grid of lights—or the back of a transistor radio, in Thomas Pynchon's inspired metaphor. While I was staying in LAX, Jackie Collins actually told *Los Angeles* magazine that "Flying in [to LAX] at night is just an orgasmic thrill.") You land, with a bump, on a mess of gray runways with no signs of welcome, a hangar that says "T ans W rld Airlines," another broken sign that announces "Tom Bradl y International Ai port," and an air-control tower under scaffolding.

The first thing that greeted me on a recent arrival was a row of Asians sitting on the floor of the terminal, under a sign that told them of a $25,000 fine for bringing in the wrong kinds of food. As I passed through endless corridors, I was faced with almost nothing except long escalators (a surprisingly high percentage of the accidents recorded at airports comes from escalators, bewildering to newcomers) and bare hallways. The other surprise, for many of my fellow travelers, no doubt, was that almost no one we saw looked like Robert Redford or Julia Roberts or, indeed, like anyone belonging to the race we'd been celebrating in our in-flight movies. As we passed into the huge, bare assembly hall that is the Customs and Immigration Center here, I was directed into one of the chaotic lines by a Noriko and formally admitted to the country by a C. Chen. The man waiting to transfer my baggage (as a beagle sniffed around us in a coat that said "Agriculture's Beagle Brigade" on one side and "Protecting American Agriculture" on the other) was named Yoji Yosaka. And the first sign I saw, when I stepped into America, was a big board being waved by the "Executive Sedan Service" for one "Mr. T. Ego."

For many immigrants, in fact, LAX is quietly offering them a view of their own near futures: the woman at the Host Coffee Shop is themselves, in a sense, two years from now, and the man sweeping up the refuse is the American dream in practice. The staff at the airport seems to be made up almost entirely of recent immigrants: on my very first afternoon there, I was served by a Hoa, an Ephraim, and a Glinda; the wait-people at a coffee shop in Terminal 5 were called Ignacio, Ever, Aura, and Erick. Even at the Airport Sheraton (where the employees all wear nameplates), I was checked in by Viera (from "Bratislavia") and ran into Hasmik and Yovik (from Ethiopia), Faye (from Vietnam), Ingrid (from Guatemala City), Khrystyne (from Long Beach, by way of Phnom Penh, I think), and Moe (from West L.A., she said). Many of the bright-eyed dreamers who arrive at LAX so full of hope never actually leave the place.

The deeper drama of any airport is that it features a kind of interaction almost unique in our lives, wherein many of us do not know whom we are going to meet or whom others are going to meet in us. You see people standing at the barriers outside the Customs area looking into their pasts, while wide-open newcomers drift out, searching for their futures. Lovers do not know if they will see the same person who kissed them good-bye a month ago; grandparents wonder what the baby they last saw twenty years ago will look like now.

In L.A. all of this has an added charge, because unlike many cities, it is not a hub but a terminus: a place where people come to arrive. Thus many of the meetings you witness are between the haves and the hope-to-haves, between those who are affecting a new ease in their new home and those who are here in search of that ease. Both parties, especially if they are un-American by birth, are eager to stress their Americanness or their fitness for America; and both, as they look at each other's made-up self, see themselves either before or after a stay in L.A.'s theater of transformation. And so they stream in, wearing running shoes or cowboy hats or 49ers jackets, anxious to make a good first impression; and the people who wait for them, under a halfhearted mural of Desertland, are often American enough not to try to look the part. Juan and Esperanza both have ponytails now, and Kimmie is wearing a Harley-Davidson cap backwards and necking with a Japanese guy; the uncle from Delhi arrives to find that Rajiv not only has grown darker but has lost weight, so that he looks more like a peasant from back home than ever.

And the newcomers pour in in astonishing numbers. A typical Sunday evening, in a single hour, sees flights arriving from England, Taiwan, the Philippines, Indonesia, Mexico, Austria, Germany, Spain, Costa Rica, and Guatemala; and each new group colors and transforms the airport: an explosion of tropical shades from Hawaiian Air, a rash of blue blazers and white shirts around the early flight from Tokyo. Red-haired Thais bearing pirated Schwarzenegger videos, lonely Africans in Aerial Assault sneakers, farmers from changeless Confucian cultures peering into the smiles of a Prozac city, children whose parents can't pronounce their names. Many of them are returning, like Odysseus, with the spoils of war: young brides from Luzon, business cards from Shanghai, boxes of macadamia nuts from Oahu. And for many of them the whole wild carnival will feature sights they have never seen before: Japanese look anxiously at the first El Salvadorans they've ever seen, and El Salvadorans ogle sleek girls from Bangkok in thigh-high boots. All of them, moreover, may not be pleased to realize that the America they've dreamed of is, in fact, a land of tacos and pita and pad thai—full, indeed, of the very Third World cultures that other Third Worlders look down upon.

One day over lunch I asked my Ethiopian waitress about her life here. She liked it well enough, she said, but still she missed her home. And yet, she added, she couldn't go back. "Why not?" I asked, still smiling. "Because they killed my family," she said. "Two years back.

They killed my father. They killed my brother." "They," I realized, referred to the Tigreans—many of them working just down the corridor in other parts of the hotel. So, too, Tibetans who have finally managed to flee their Chinese-occupied homeland arrive at LAX to find Chinese faces everywhere; those who fled the Sandinistas find themselves standing next to Sandinistas fleeing their successors. And all these people from ancient cultures find themselves in a country as amnesiac as the morning, where World War II is just a rumor and the Gulf War a distant memory. Their pasts are escaped, yes, but by the same token they are unlikely to be honored.

It is dangerously tempting to start formulating socioeconomic principles in the midst of LAX: people from rich countries (Germany and Japan, say) travel light, if only because they are sure that they can return any time; those from poor countries come with their whole lives in cardboard boxes imperfectly tied with string. People from poor countries are often met by huge crowds—for them each arrival is a special occasion—and stagger through customs with string bags and Gold Digger apple crates, their addresses handwritten on them in pencil; the Okinawan honeymooners, by contrast, in the color-coordinated outfits they will change every day, somehow have packed all their needs into a tiny case.

If airports have some of the excitement of bars, because so many people are composing (and decomposing) selves there, they also have some of the sadness of bars, the poignancy of people sitting unclaimed while everyone around them has paired off. A pretty girl dressed in next to nothing sits alone in an empty Baggage Claim area, waiting for a date who never comes; a Vietnamese man, lost, tells an official that he has friends in Orange County who can help him, but when the friends are contacted, they say they know no one from Vietnam. I hear of a woman who got off and asked for "San Mateo," only to learn that she was meant to disembark in San Francisco; and a woman from Nigeria who came out expecting to see her husband in Monroe, Louisiana, only to learn that someone in Lagos had mistaken "La." on her itinerary for "L.A."

The greetings I saw in the Arrivals area were much more tentative than I had expected, less passionate—as ritualized in their way as the kisses placed on Bob Barker's cheek—and much of that maybe because so many people are meeting strangers, even if they are meeting people they once knew. Places like LAX—places like L.A.—perpetuate the sense that everyone is a stranger in our new floating world. I spent one afternoon in the airport with a Californian blonde, and I saw her complimented on her English by a sweet Korean woman and asked by an Iranian if she was Indian. Airports have some of the unsteady brashness of singles bars, where no one knows quite what is expected of them. "Mike, is that you?" "Oh, I didn't recognize you." "I'd have known you anywhere." "It's so kind of you to come and pick me up." And already at a loss, a young Japanese girl and a broad, lonely-looking man head off toward the parking lot, not knowing, in any sense, who is going to be in the driver's seat.

The driving takes place, of course, in what many of the newcomers, primed by video screenings of *L.A. Law* and *Speed,* regard as the ultimate heart of darkness, a place at least as forbidding and dangerous as Africa must have seemed to the Victorians. They have heard about how America is the murder capital of the world; they have seen Rodney King get pummeled by L.A.'s finest; they know of the city as the site of drive-by shootings and freeway snipers, of riots and celebrity murders. The "homeless" and the "tempest-tost" that the Statue of Liberty invites are arriving, increasingly, in a city that is itself famous for its homeless population and its fires, floods, and earthquakes.

In that context, the ideal symbol of LAX is, perhaps, the great object that for thirty years has been the distinctive image of the place: the ugly white quadruped that sits in the middle of the airport like a beached white whale or a jet-age beetle, featuring a 360-degree circular restaurant that does not revolve and an observation deck from which the main view is of twenty-three thousand parking places. The Theme Building, at 201 World Way, is a sad image of a future that never arrived, a monument to Kennedy-era idealism and the thrusting modernity of the American empire when it was in its prime; it now has the poignancy of an abandoned present with its price tag stuck to it. When you go there (and almost nobody does) you are greeted by photos of Saturn's rings and Jupiter and its moons, by a plaque laid down by L.B.J. and a whole set of symbols from the time when NASA was shooting for the heavens. Now the "landmark" building, with its "gourmet-type restaurant," looks like a relic from a time long past, when it must have looked like the face of the future.

Upstairs, a few desperately merry waiters are serving nonalcoholic drinks and cheeseburgers to sallow diners who look as if they've arrived at the end of the world; on the tarmac outside, speedbirds inch ahead like cars in a traffic jam. "Hello All the New People of LAX—Welcome," says the graffiti on the elevator.

The Theme Restaurant comes to us from an era when L.A. was leading the world. Nowadays, of course, L.A. is being formed and reformed and led by the world around it. And as I got ready to leave LAX, I could not help but feel that the Theme Building stands, more and more, for a city left behind by our accelerating planet. LAX, I was coming to realize, was a good deal scruffier than the airports even of Bangkok or Jakarta, more chaotic, more suggestive of Third World lawlessness. And the city around it is no more golden than Seoul, no more sunny than Taipei, and no more laid-back than Moscow. Beverly Hills, after all, is largely speaking Farsi now. Hollywood Boulevard is sleazier than 42nd Street. And Malibu is falling into the sea.

Yet just as I was about to give up on L.A. as yesterday's piece of modernity, I got on the shuttle bus that moves between the terminals in a never-ending loop. The seats next to me were taken by two tough-looking dudes from nearby South Central, who were riding the free buses and helping people on and off with their cases (acting, I presumed, on the safe assumption that the Japanese, say, new to the country and bewildered, had been warned beforehand to tip often and handsomely for every service they received). In between terminals, as a terrified-looking Miss Kudo and her friend guarded their luggage, en route from Nagoya to Las Vegas, the two gold-plated sharks talked about the Raiders' last game and the Lakers' next season. Then one of them, without warning, announced, "The bottom line is the spirit is with you. When you work out, you chill out and, like, you meditate in your spirit. You know what I mean? Meditation is recreation. Learn math, follow your path. That's all I do, man, that's all I live for: learnin' about God, learnin' about Jesus. I am *possessed* by that spirit. You know, I used to have all these problems, with the flute and all, but when I heard about God, I learned about the body, the mind, and the flesh. People forget, they don't know, that the Bible isn't talkin' about the flesh, it's talkin' about the spirit. And I was re-born again in the spirit."

His friend nodded. "When you recreate, you meditate. Recreation is a spiritually uplifting experience."

"Yeah. When you do that, you allow the spirit to breathe."

"Because you're gettin' into the physical world. You're lettin' the spirit flow. You're helpin' the secretion of the endorphins in the brain."

Nearby, the Soldiers of the Cross of Christ Church stood by the escalators, taking donations, and a man in a dog collar approached another stranger.

I watched the hustlers allowing the spirit to breathe, I heard the Hare Krishna devotees plying their wares, I spotted some Farrakhan flunkies collecting a dollar for a copy of their newspaper, *The Final Call*—redemption and corruption all around us in the air—and I thought: welcome to America, Miss Kudo, welcome to L.A.

Pico Iyer
Born in England to Indian parents in 1957, Pico Iyer grew up in California and now divides his time between California and Japan. Known as the "poet laureate of wanderlust," Iyer is one of the most well-known travel writers of our day. He has authored six books, including Falling Off the Map, Video Night in Kathmandu, *and* The Global Soul. *He has written for* Time *since the early eighties, and he also frequently contributes essays to* Sports Illustrated, *the* Condé Nast Traveler, Harper's, *the* New York Review of Books, *and the* New York Times.

No Name Woman

Maxine Hong Kingston

"You must not tell anyone," my mother said, "what I am about to tell you. In China your father had a sister who killed herself. She jumped into the family well. We say that your father has all brothers because it is as if she had never been born.

"In 1924 just a few days after our village celebrated seventeen hurry-up weddings—to make sure that every young man who went 'out on the road' would responsibly come home—your father and his brothers and your grandfather and his brothers and your aunt's new husband sailed for America, the Gold Mountain. It was your grandfather's last trip. Those lucky enough to get contracts waved good-bye from the decks. They fed and guarded the stowaways and helped them off in Cuba, New York, Bali, Hawaii. 'We'll meet in California next year,' they said. All of them sent money home.

"I remember looking at your aunt one day when she and I were dressing; I had not noticed before that she had such a protruding melon of a stomach. But I did not think, 'She's pregnant,' until she began to look like other pregnant women, her shirt pulling and the white tops of her black pants showing. She could not have been pregnant, you see, because her husband had been gone for years. No one said anything. We did not discuss it. In early summer she was ready to have the child, long after the time when it could have been possible.

"The village had also been counting. On the night the baby was to be born the villagers raided our house. Some were crying. Like a great saw, teeth strung with lights, files of people walked zigzag across our land, tearing the rice. Their lanterns doubled in the disturbed black water, which drained away through the broken bunds. As the villagers closed in, we could see that some of them, probably men and women we knew well, wore white masks. The people with long hair hung it over their faces. Women with short hair made it stand up on end. Some had tied white bands around their foreheads, arms, and legs.

"At first they threw mud and rocks at the house. Then they threw eggs and began slaughtering our stock. We could hear the animals scream their deaths—the roosters, the pigs, a last great roar from the ox. Familiar wild heads flared in our night windows; the villagers encircled us. Some of the faces stopped to peer at us, their eyes rushing like searchlights. The hands flattened against the panes, framed heads, and left red prints.

"The villagers broke in the front and the back doors at the same time, even though we had not locked the doors against them. Their knives dripped with the blood of our animals. They smeared blood on the doors and walls. One woman swung a chicken, whose throat she had slit, splattering blood in red arcs about her. We stood together in the middle of our house, in the family hall with the pictures and tables of the ancestors around us, and looked straight ahead.

"At that time the house had only two wings. When the men came back, we would build two more to enclose our courtyard and a third one to begin a second courtyard. The villagers pushed through both wings, even your grandparents' rooms, to find your aunt's, which was also mine until the men returned. From this room a new wing for one of the younger families would grow. They ripped up her clothes and shoes and broke her combs, grinding them underfoot. They tore her work from the loom. They scattered the cooking fire and rolled the new weaving in it. We could hear them in the kitchen breaking our bowls and banging the pots. They overturned the great waist-high earthenware jugs; duck eggs, pickled fruits, vegetables burst out and mixed in acrid torrents. The old woman from the next field swept a broom through the air and loosed the spirits-of-the-broom over our heads. 'Pig.' 'Ghost.' 'Pig,' they sobbed and scolded while they ruined our house.

"When they left, they took sugar and oranges to bless themselves. They cut pieces from the dead animals. Some of them took bowls that were not broken and clothes that were not torn. Afterward we swept up the rice and sewed it back up into sacks. But the smells from the spilled preserves lasted. Your aunt gave birth in the pigsty that night. The next morning when I went for the water, I found her and the baby plugging up the family well.

"Don't let your father know that I told you. He denies her. Now that you have started to menstruate, what happened to her could happen to you. Don't humiliate us. You wouldn't like to be forgotten as if you had never been born. The villagers are watchful."

Whenever she had to warn us about life, my mother told stories that ran like this one, a story to grow up on. She tested our strength to establish realities. Those in the emigrant generations who could not reassert brute survival died young and far from home. Those of us in the first American generations have had to figure out how the invisible world the emigrants built around our childhoods fits in solid America.

The emigrants confused the gods by diverting their curses, misleading them with crooked streets and false names. They must try to confuse their offspring as well, who, I suppose, threaten them in similar ways—always trying to get things straight, always trying to name the unspeakable. The Chinese I know hide their names; sojourners take new names when their lives change and guard their real names with silence.

Chinese-Americans, when you try to understand what things in you are Chinese, how do you separate what is peculiar to childhood, to poverty, insanities, one family, your mother who marked your growing with stories, from what is Chinese? What is Chinese tradition and what is the movies?

If I want to learn what clothes my aunt wore, whether flashy or ordinary, I would have to begin, "Remember Father's drowned-in-the-well sister?" I cannot ask that. My mother has told me once and for all the useful parts. She will add nothing unless powered by Necessity, a riverbank that guides her life. She plants vegetable gardens rather than lawns; she carries the odd-shaped tomatoes home from the fields and eats food left for the gods.

Whenever we did frivolous things, we used up energy; we flew high kites. We children came up off the ground over the melting cones our parents brought home from work and the American movie on New Year's Day—*Oh, You Beautiful Doll* with Betty Grable one year, and *She Wore a Yellow Ribbon* with John Wayne another year. After the one carnival ride each, we paid in guilt; our tired father counted his change on the dark walk home.

Adultery is extravagance. Could people who hatch their own chicks and eat the embryos and the heads for delicacies and boil the feet in vinegar for party food, leaving only the gravel, eating even the gizzard lining—could such people engender a prodigal aunt? To be a woman, to have a daughter in starvation time was a waste enough. My aunt could not have been the lone romantic who gave up everything for sex. Women in the old China did not choose. Some man had commanded her to lie with him and be his secret evil. I wonder whether he masked himself when he joined the raid on her family.

Perhaps she had encountered him in the fields or on the mountain where the daughters-in-law collected fuel. Or perhaps he first noticed her in the marketplace. He was not a stranger because the village housed no strangers. She had to have dealings with him other than sex. Perhaps he worked an adjoining field, or he sold her the cloth for the dress she sewed and wore. His demand must have surprised, then terrified her. She obeyed him; she always did as she was told.

When the family found a young man in the next village to be her husband, she had stood tractably beside the best rooster, his proxy, and promised before they met that she would be his forever. She was lucky that he was her age and she would be the first wife, an advantage secure now. The night she first saw him, he had sex with her. Then he left for America. She had almost forgotten what he looked like. When she tried to envision him, she only saw the black and white face in the group photograph the men had had taken before leaving.

The other man was not, after all, much different from her husband. They both gave orders: she followed. "If you tell your family, I'll beat you. I'll kill you. Be here again next week." No one talked sex, ever. And she might have separated the rapes from the rest of living if only she did not have to buy her oil from him or gather wood in the same forest. I want her fear to have lasted just as long as rape lasted so that the fear could have been contained. No drawn-out fear. But women at sex hazarded birth and hence lifetimes. The fear did not stop but permeated everywhere. She told the man, "I think I'm pregnant." He organized the raid against her.

On nights when my mother and father talked about their life back home, sometimes they mentioned an "outcast table" whose business they still seemed to be settling, their voices tight. In a commensal tradition, where food is precious, the powerful older people made wrongdoers eat alone. Instead of letting them start separate new lives like the Japanese, who could become samurais and geishas, the Chinese family, faces averted but eyes glowering sideways, hung on to the offenders and fed them leftovers. My aunt must have lived in the same house as my parents and eaten at an outcast table. My mother spoke about the raid as if she had seen it, when she and my aunt, a daughter-in-law to a different household, should not have been living together at all. Daughters-in-law lived with their husbands' parents, not their own; a synonym for marriage in Chinese is "taking a daughter-in-law." Her husband's parents could have sold her, mortgaged her, stoned her. But they had sent her back to her own mother and father, a mysterious act hinting at disgraces not told me. Perhaps they had thrown her out to deflect the avengers.

She was the only daughter; her four brothers went with her father, husband, and uncles "out on the road" and for some years became western men. When the goods were divided among the family, three of the brothers took land, and the youngest, my father, chose an education. After my grandparents gave their daughter away to her husband's family, they had dispensed all the adventure and all the property. They expected her alone to keep the traditional ways, which her brothers, now among the barbarians, could fumble without detection. The heavy, deep-rooted women were to maintain the past against the flood, safe for returning. But the rare urge west had fixed upon our family, and so my aunt crossed boundaries not delineated in space.

The work of preservation demands that the feelings playing about in one's guts not be turned into action. Just watch their passing like cherry blossoms. But perhaps my aunt, my forerunner, caught in a slow life, let dreams grow and fade and after some months or years went toward what persisted. Fear at the enormities of the forbidden kept her desires delicate, wire and bone. She looked at a man because she liked the way the hair was tucked behind his ears, or she liked the question-mark line of a long torso curving at the shoulder and straight at the hip. For warm eyes or a soft voice or a slow walk—that's all— a few hairs, a line, a brightness, a sound, a pace, she gave up family. She offered us up for a charm that vanished with tiredness, a pigtail that didn't toss when the wind died. Why, the wrong lighting could erase the dearest thing about him.

It could very well have been, however, that my aunt did not take subtle enjoyment of her friend, but, a wild woman, kept rollicking company. Imagining her free with sex doesn't fit, though. I don't know any women like that, or men either. Unless I see her life branching into mine, she gives me no ancestral help.

To sustain her being in love, she often worked at herself in the mirror, guessing at the colors and shapes that would interest him, changing them frequently in order to hit on the right combination. She wanted him to look back.

On a farm near the sea, a woman who tended her appearance reaped a reputation for eccentricity. All the married women blunt-cut their hair in flaps about their ears or pulled it back in tight buns. No nonsense. Neither style blew easily into heart-catching tangles. And at their weddings they displayed themselves in their long hair for the last time. "It brushed the backs of my knees," my mother tells me. "It was braided, and even so, it brushed the backs of my knees."

At the mirror my aunt combed individuality into her bob. A bun could have been contrived to escape into black streamers blowing in the wind or in quiet wisps about her face, but only the older women in our picture album wear buns. She brushed her hair back from her forehead, tucking the flaps behind her ears. She looped a piece of thread, knotted into a circle between her index fingers and thumbs, and ran the double strand across her forehead. When she closed her fingers as if she were making a pair of shadow geese bite, the string twisted together catching the little hairs. Then she pulled the thread away from her skin, ripping the hairs out neatly, her eyes watering from the needles of pain. Opening her fingers, she cleaned the thread, then rolled it along her hairline and the tops of her eyebrows. My mother did the same to me and my sisters and herself. I used to believe that the expression "caught by the short hairs" meant a captive held with a depilatory string. It especially hurt at the temples, but my mother said we were lucky we didn't have to have our feet bound when we were seven. Sisters used to sit on their beds and cry together, she said, as their mothers or their slave removed the bandages for a few minutes each night and let the blood gush back into their veins. I hope that the man my aunt loved appreciated a smooth brow, that he wasn't just a tits-and-ass man.

Once my aunt found a freckle on her chin, at a spot that the almanac said predestined her for unhappiness. She dug it out with a hot needle and washed her wound with peroxide.

More attention to her looks than these pullings of hairs and pickings at spots would have caused gossip among the villagers. They owned work clothes and good clothes, and they wore good clothes for feasting the new seasons. But since a woman combing her hair hexes beginnings, my aunt rarely found an occasion to look her best. Women looked like great sea snails—the corded wood, babies, and laundry they carried were the whorls on their backs. The Chinese did not admire a bent back; goddesses and warriors stood straight. Still there must have been a marvelous freeing of beauty when a worker laid down her burden and stretched and arched.

Such commonplace loveliness, however, was not enough for my aunt. She dreamed of a lover for the fifteen days of New Year's, the time for families to exchange visits, money, and food. She plied her secret comb. And sure enough she cursed the year, the family, the village, and herself.

Even as her hair lured her imminent lover, many other men looked at her. Uncles, cousins, nephews, brothers would have looked, too, had they been home between journeys. Perhaps they had already been restraining their curiosity, and they left, fearful that their glances, like a field of nesting birds, might be startled and caught. Poverty hurt, and that was their first reason for leaving. But another, final reason for leaving the crowded house was the never-said.

She may have been unusually beloved, the precious only daughter, spoiled and mirror gazing because of the affection the family lavished on her. When her husband left, they welcomed the chance to take her back from the in-laws; she could live like the little daughter for just a while longer. There are stories that my grandfather was different from other people, "crazy ever since the little Jap bayoneted him in the head." He used to put his naked penis on the dinner table, laughing. And one day he brought home a baby girl, wrapped up inside his brown western-style greatcoat. He had traded one of his sons, probably my father, the youngest, for her. My grandmother made him trade back. When he finally got a daughter of his own, he doted on her. They must have all loved her, except perhaps my father, the only brother who never went back to China, having once been traded for a girl.

Brothers and sisters, newly men and women, had to efface their sexual color and present plain miens. Disturbing hair and eyes, a smile like no other, threatened the ideal of five generations living under one roof. To focus blurs, people shouted face to face and yelled from room to room. The immigrants I know have loud voices, unmodulated to American tones even after years away from the village where they called their friendships out across the fields. I have not been able to stop my mother's screams in public libraries or over telephones. Walking erect (knees straight, toes pointed forward, not pigeon-toed, which is Chinese-feminine) and speaking in an inaudible voice, I have tried to turn myself American-feminine. Chinese communication was loud, public. Only sick people had to whisper. But at the dinner table, where the family members came nearest one another, no one could talk, not the outcasts nor any eaters. Every word that falls from the mouth is a coin lost. Silently they gave and accepted food with both hands. A preoccupied child who took his bowl with one hand got a sideways glare. A complete moment of total attention is due everyone alike. Children and lovers have no singularity here, but my aunt used a secret voice, a separate attentiveness.

She kept the man's name to herself throughout her labor and dying; she did not accuse him that he be punished with her. To save her inseminator's name she gave silent birth.

He may have been somebody in her own household, but intercourse with a man outside the family would have been no less abhorrent. All the village were kinsmen, and the titles shouted in loud country voices never let kinship be forgotten. Any man within visiting distance would have been neutralized as a lover—"brother," "younger brother," "older brother"—one hundred and fifteen relationship titles.

Parents researched birth charts probably not so much to assure good fortune as to circumvent incest in a population that has but one hundred surnames. Everybody has eight million relatives. How useless then sexual mannerisms, how dangerous.

As if it came from an atavism deeper than fear, I used to add "brother" silently to boys' names. It hexed the boys, who would or would not ask me to dance, and made them less scary and as familiar and deserving of benevolence as girls.

But, of course, I hexed myself also—no dates. I should have stood up, both arms waving, and shouted out across libraries, "Hey, you! Love me back." I had no idea, though, how to make attraction selective, how to control its direction and magnitude. If I made myself American-pretty so that the five or six Chinese boys in the class fell in love with me, everyone else—the Caucasian, Negro, and Japanese boys—would too. Sisterliness, dignified and honorable, made much more sense.

Attraction eludes control so stubbornly that whole societies designed to organize relationships among people cannot keep order, not even when they bind people to one another from childhood and raise them together. Among the very poor and the wealthy, brothers married their adopted sisters, like doves. Our family allowed some romance, paying adult brides' prices and providing dowries so that their sons and daughters could marry strangers. Marriage promises to turn strangers into friendly relatives—a nation of siblings.

In the village structure, spirits shimmered among the live creatures, balanced and held in equilibrium by time and land. But one human being flaring up into violence could open up a black hole, a maelstrom that pulled in the sky. The frightened villagers, who depended on one another to maintain the real, went to my aunt to show her a personal, physical representation of the break she had made in the "roundness." Misallying couples snapped off the future, which was to be embodied in true offspring. The villagers punished her for acting as if she could have a private life, secret and apart from them.

If my aunt had betrayed the family at a time of large grain yields and peace, when many boys were born, and wings were being built on many houses, perhaps she might have escaped such severe punishment. But the men—hungry, greedy, tired of planting in dry soil— and had been forced to leave the village in order to send food-money home. There were ghost plagues, bandit plagues, wars with the Japanese, floods. My Chinese brother and sister had died of an unknown sickness. Adultery, perhaps only a mistake during good times, became a crime when the village needed food.

The round moon cakes and round doorways, the round tables of graduated size that fit one roundness inside another, round windows and rice bowls—these talismans had lost their power to warn this family of the law: a family must be whole, faithfully keeping the descent line by having sons to feed the old and the dead, who in turn look after the family. The villagers came to show my aunt and her lover-in-hiding a broken house. The villagers were speeding up the circling of events because she was too shortsighted to see that her infidelity had already harmed the village, that waves of consequences would return unpredictably, sometimes in disguise, as now, to hurt her. This roundness had to be made coin-sized so that she would see its circumference: punish her at the birth of her baby. Awaken her to the inexorable. People who refused fatalism because they could invent small resources insisted on culpability. Deny accidents and wrest fault from the stars.

After the villagers left, their lanterns now scattering in various directions toward home, the family broke their silence and cursed her. "Aiaa, we're going to die. Death is coming. Death is coming. Look what you've done. You've killed us. Ghost! Dead ghost! Ghost! You've never been born." She ran out into the fields, far enough from the house so that she could no longer hear their voices, and pressed herself against the earth, her own land no more. When she felt the birth coming, she thought that she had been hurt. Her body seized together. "They've hurt me too much," she thought. "This is gall, and it will kill me." With forehead and knees against the earth, her body convulsed and then relaxed. She turned on her back, lay on the ground. The black well of sky and stars went out and out and out forever; her body and her complexity seemed to disappear. She was one of the stars, a bright dot in blackness, without home, without a companion, in eternal cold and silence. An agoraphobia rose in her, speeding higher and higher, bigger and bigger; she would not be able to contain it; there would be no end to fear.

Flayed, unprotected against space, she felt pain return, focusing her body. This pain chilled her—a cold, steady kind of surface pain. Inside, spasmodically, the other pain, the pain of the child, heated her. For hours she lay on the ground, alternately body and space. Sometimes a vision of normal comfort obliterated reality: she saw the family in the evening gambling at the dinner table, the young people massaging their elders' backs. She saw them congratulating one another, high joy on the mornings the rice shoots came up. When these pictures burst, the stars drew yet further apart. Black space opened.

She got to her feet to fight better and remembered that old-fashioned women gave birth in their pigsties to fool the jealous, pain-dealing gods, who do not snatch piglets. Before the next spasms could stop her, she ran to the pigsty, each step a rushing out into emptiness. She climbed over the fence and knelt in the dirt. It was good to have a fence enclosing her, a tribal person alone.

Laboring, this woman who had carried her child as a foreign growth that sickened her every day, expelled it at last. She reached down to touch the hot, wet, moving mass, surely smaller than anything human, and could feel that it was human after all—fingers, toes, nails, nose. She pulled it up on to her belly, and it lay curled there, butt in the air, feet precisely tucked one under the other. She opened her loose shirt and buttoned the child inside. After resting, it squirmed and thrashed and she pushed it up to her breast. It turned its head this way and that until it found her nipple. There, it made little snuffling noises. She clenched her teeth at its preciousness, lovely as a young calf, a piglet, a little dog.

She may have gone to the pigsty as a last act of responsibility: she would protect this child as she had protected its father. It would look after her soul, leaving supplies on her grave. But how would this tiny child without family find her grave when there would be no marker for her anywhere, neither in the earth nor the family hall? No one would give her a family hall name. She had taken the child with her into the wastes. At its birth the two of them had felt the same raw pain of separation, a wound that only the family pressing tight could close. A child with no descent line would not soften her life but only trail after her, ghostlike, begging her to give it purpose. At dawn the villagers on their way to the fields would stand around the fence and look.

Full of milk, the little ghost slept. When it awoke, she hardened her breasts against the milk that crying loosens. Toward morning she picked up the baby and walked to the well.

Carrying the baby to the well shows loving. Otherwise abandon it. Turn its face into the mud. Mothers who love their children take them along. It was probably a girl; there is some hope of forgiveness for boys.

"Don't tell anyone you had an aunt. Your father does not want to hear her name. She has never been born." I have believed that sex was unspeakable and words so strong and fathers so frail that "aunt" would do my father mysterious harm. I have thought that my family, having settled among immigrants who had also been their neighbors in the ancestral land, needed to clean their name, and a wrong word would incite the kinspeople even here. But there is more to this silence: they want me to participate in her punishment. And I have.

In the twenty years since I heard this story I have not asked for details nor said my aunt's name; I do not know it. People who can comfort the dead can also chase after them to hurt them further—a reverse ancestor worship. The real punishment was not the raid swiftly inflicted by the villagers, but the family's deliberately forgetting her. Her betrayal so maddened them, they saw to it that she would suffer forever, even after death. Always hungry, always needing, she would have to beg food from other ghosts, snatch and steal it from those whose living descendants give them gifts. She would have to fight the ghosts massed at crossroads for the buns a few thoughtful citizens leave to decoy her away from village and home so that the ancestral spirits could feast unharassed. At peace, they could act like gods, not ghosts, their descent lines providing them with paper suits and dresses, spirit money, paper houses, paper automobiles, chicken, meat, and rice into eternity—essences delivered up in smoke and flames, steam and incense rising from each rice bowl. In an attempt to make the Chinese care for people outside the family, Chairman Mao encourages us now to give our paper replicas to the spirits of out-standing soldiers and workers, no matter whose ancestors they may be. My aunt remains forever hungry. Goods are not distributed evenly among the dead.

My aunt haunts me—her ghost drawn to me because now, after fifty years of neglect, I alone devote pages of paper to her, though not origamied into houses and clothes. I do not think she always means me well. I am telling on her, and she was a spite suicide, drowning herself in the drinking water. The Chinese are always very frightened of the drowned one, whose weeping ghost, wet hair hanging and skin bloated, waits silently by the water to pull down a substitute.

Maxine Hong Kingston
Maxine Hong Kingston was born in 1940 in Stockton, California to Chinese immi-grants who operated a gambling house. In 1967, she moved with her actor hus-band to Hawaii, where she taught high school for over a decade. In 1976, she published her debut novel, The Woman Warrior, *which became a critically ac-claimed best-seller and received the National Book Critic's Circle Award. This and most of her other works, including* China Men *and* Tripmaster Monkey: His Fake Book, *explore the Chinese-American experience.*

Why I Don't Meditate

Anne Lamott

I have been reading books on meditation with great enthusiasm since 1975, but have not quite gotten around to becoming a person who meditates. The only times I remember practicing with any regularity were during my drug days when I'd find myself awake at 4 or 5 A.M., which are the hours of the black dogs even under the best of circumstances. I remember lying in bed many nights after all the cocaine was gone, feeling and maybe looking like Bobcat Goldthwaithe, grinding away at my teeth like a horse, lockjawed, weepy, considering the wooden bedpost as a possible teething device, idly wondering what it would feel like to close my hands, slowly, around the sleeping boyfriend's throat. But all of a sudden I would start saying Hail Marys or a mantra, thousands of times in a row, to quiet my feral mind. It always worked, maybe not as effectively as a little something from the Schedule III column, but usually, at some point, I would be able to sleep.

Perhaps a purist would not consider this true meditation. At any rate, right around the time I got sober, I discovered the books of Jack Kornfield, who writes about meditation and compassion. And they were so wonderfully written and wise that I became utterly committed to meditating. To the idea of meditating. Now, while my commitment remains firm, I cannot actually report any real—what is the word?—progress. I still don't meditate. I still just pray like a mother, in the mo-fo sense of the word. My mind remains a bad neighborhood that I try not to go into alone.

But the last few times I've gone out on a book tour, Jack Kornfield has been waiting for me in various cities when I arrived. Maybe not exactly in the flesh, maybe a little bit more like the face of Jesus in a tortilla, but any port in a storm, right? And he's been a reliable birth coach who keeps showing up even when I am at my most narcissistic and mentally ill.

In a month or so, Sam and I will travel around from city to city by plane, and I will try to get people to like me and buy my books. I'll do readings and Sam will lie on his stomach in bookstores and draw. I'll talk about writing and Jesus and the new book, and discuss my personal problems at length, secretly trying to con my audience into having some sort of awakening—spiritual, creative—so that we can all save the world together, and Sam can grow up and have children and provide me with grandchildren. (Or Sam can grow and be as gay as a box of birds and provide me with someone who laughs at all my jokes and makes me nice snacks.) Sounds like fun, right?

But the problem, the reason I rely so on Jack, is that I do not travel well. Sam does, he thrives. He loves bookstores and hotels, which all have nice floors for drawing, and he loves Spectra-vision, and snacks from the mini-bar. He even likes flying. I, on the other hand, do not believe in flying, or at any rate, am deeply unclear on the concept. I believe that every plane I get on is doomed, and this is why I like to travel with Sam—so that if and when the plane goes down, we will at least be together, and almost certainly get adjoining seats in heaven—ideally, near the desserts.

Then when we do arrive safely at a bookstore, there are either hardly any people in the audience, at which point my thoughts naturally turn to suicide, or there are so many people, so expectant and so full of love, that it fills me with self-loathing, makes me just anxious as a cat. I start to see myself as a performer or a product, or a performer pitching a product, as if I'm up there at the podium trying to get people to buy a Veg-O-Matic. It's like the Martin Buber line from *I and Thou:* "This is the exalted melancholy of our age, that every Thou in our world must become an it." I become an it, with really, really bad nerves. I seek refuge in shutting down, in trying to hide behind my false self like it's some psychic Guard-All shield.

So this is where Jack has helped me more times than he can possibly be aware. When I first show up at each bookstore, I've usually either stopped breathing or am wheezing away like a dying asthmatic pug. But a number of times, something has nudged me over toward a copy or stash of Jack's books, and they whisper this subversive message to me: Breathe. Pay attention. Be kind. Stop grabbing. And I always end up feeling like I've somehow gotten a grip, or a little grippage, as the French say.

I was in St. Louis once in a bookstore where only ten people had shown up, and of course I was just a little bit disappointed. I peeked around a stack of books at those ten people and imagined mowing them down with an AK-47. I know that makes me sound a little angry, but I had jet lag, the self esteem of a prawn, and to top it off, I had stopped breathing. I sounded just like the English Patient. But it turned out I was standing in front of a shelf full of Jack's books. I opened one and read one sentence, words to the effect that life is so hard, how can we be anything but kind. It was as if God had reached down with God's magic wand, because I looked out at the crowd, which by then had swelled to twelve people—a third of them guilty, beaming employees of the bookstore—and I gave one of the most joyful talks of my life.

I have walked into tables while trying to hide from crowds and rows of empty seats, and knocked over stacks of his books. I was once handed one of his books to use as a tiny desk while autographing something for someone in Seattle. He keeps showing up when I need the message most, when I feel most like Mr. Magoo at the top of an unfinished high-rise, about to step into empty space but finding instead a girder rising up beneath my feet. I show up in crowded bookstores so stoned on myself and adrenaline that I could chase down an airplane, and I read about quietness, peace. I show up to a sea of empty metal chairs, and I read about the fullness of an open heart, and I'm suddenly a sea anemone unfurling her tendrils again, after the danger has passed.

Maybe what I like best about Jack's message is that it's so subversive. The usual message is that there are all kinds of ways for you to fill up, so you'll be strong and nourished and no one can get you; but when you're fortified, fortification by its very nature is braced, and can break. So you're still vulnerable, but now you're anxious and shamed too. You're going to be vulnerable anyway, because you're a small soft little human animal—so the only choice is whether you are most going to resemble Richard Nixon, with his neck jammed down into his shoulders, trying to figure out who to blame, or the sea anemone, tentative and brave, trying to connect, the formless fleshy blob out of which grows the frills, the petals.

It's pretty obvious stuff. And it's wonderful chutzpah not to be afraid of the obvious, to know it instead as a great teacher, to know that right behind the cliché is the original message. So many other people trick it out with draperies and garments and piercing glances;

while Jack, in his simplicity and kindness, returns you to yourself; and maybe that's all we have. To know that the simple truth, of love, and the moment, is here to be passed around and around, like a polished stone from the sea, only because it is of itself, and for no other reason. You don't hang words onto it, and you don't need to, because it's got the great beauty and smoothness of having been whacked around for eons. It's beautiful in a muted way, beautiful through feeling, the way it's been smoothed and roughed up and relaxed on the shore, and you pick it up and feel the stasis, the beauty of something lifted out of its ordinary flow, that's gotten its beauty by being tossed about.

I got to meet him finally, just last month, introduced him at one of his readings. He had actually asked the bookstore if it could get me to introduce him, because he cares for me. I couldn't believe it. My heart soared like an eagle. But I showed up feeling self-conscious and anxious anyway. There was a huge crowd. Sam immediately lay on the floor in the back of the bookstore and began to draw. He's simple people. But I went up to the front of the bookstore and in this sort of gritchy, obsequious mood, introduced myself to Jack. You'd have to use the word luminous to describe him. One has the impression also of sandalwood, so smooth and brown, giving off a light, delicious spicy ancient smell. He looked at me with such affection that I might have been a child of his, one he hadn't seen in a while. I thought about all those times in other bookstores, when I was out there trying to get people to buy my book, and out of all that tension and lumpiness something graceful and baroque appeared. And this amazing thing happened: I felt lovely all of a sudden, in a goofy sort of way, exuberant and shy. Clingy scared old me made beautiful, made much more elegant than what's going on—all that self-consciousness and grasping—and I moved from Richard Nixon to a sea anemone, which is something I love. They're so funny and clownish, absurd and lovely, like a roomful of very young girls learning to ballet dance, all those long legs in white tights, or a boy lying on his stomach, drawing on the floor.

Anne Lamott
Anne Lamott has written a number of novels, including Blue Shoe, Hard Laughter, *and* Rosie, *but she is even better known for her best-selling works of nonfiction, which include* Bird by Bird: Some Instructions on Writing and Life, Operating Instructions, *and* Traveling Mercies. *A single mother, she has taught at University of California at Davis and a number of writing conferences. She was awarded a Guggenheim Fellowship, and her popular online diary* Word by Word *was voted Best of the Web by* Time. *She was born in San Francisco in 1954.*

File & Sandpaper

Fabio Morabito

The file is a blood relative of beheading instruments, cousin to the guillotine, kin to instruments that raze, amputate and cleave in half. But unlike the ice pick, the chisel or the machete, all of which concentrate their energies on a single point, the file spreads its impact over a network of points, an impact of apparent modesty and minimal caprices that a backward glance exposes as inexorable. A file works by persuasion; it reduces the force of its assault instead of intensifying it. In place of one strong jab, it resorts to a host of weak prods, one after the other, which attack in an orderly fashion like an army of ants, with more monotony than passion, but with no chance of a mistake. In its movements we can spy the action of waves as they crash deafeningly on the beach. Any projection that has to be eliminated from the surface of an object will suffer under the sea-like assault of the file. It will never have time to recover from a blow, because the blows that follow will already be coming down on it, submerging it. This is what a file does; it submerges whatever protrudes, anything that is over and above, it drowns it out thanks to the perseverance of its serried troops. That impression of massive numbers is so acute that at first glance it seems that a file is boiling. And this isn't to be wondered at. It is a tool stuffed with fire. Its livelihood depends on swearing oaths of loyalty. This characteristic need to swear oaths derives from the reticular design of its grating surface. A file is a succession of nodules. That's what those oaths are, its nodules. We already know only too well how those bumps squash the world into shape. "I swear I'll never love anybody but you," is the thing lovers tell each other, and their world is reduced to the room they currently occupy. That's what a file is like: it is pure narrowness, accumulation, asphyxia. Its grooves cluster into a labyrinth. Anything that gets bunched up too tight turns wrinkly; it becomes a file. There's a second reason a file swears oaths: it is blind. It has a thousand eyes, and that's what turns it blind, the way its thousand mouths render it mute. They swear away to the point of exhaustion. It's enough to glimpse at a file in action, to observe how it soldiers on and on, getting hotter and hotter, to know it never quits muttering its oaths and vows. It never leaves off spitting out a drizzle of chips, sawdust, splinters, or granules, exactly the way certain groups of men do when they swear, spitting on the ground to rid the body of its moisture, striving to become fiery and dry. A guy with water inside him is hardly one to be trusted. Water masks, it muddies, it effeminizes. A man who wants people to believe him when he takes a vow has to spit first and get tense and in order to confer tension and orneriness on his words. A file's the same. It has everything spitten out of it, its throat gets bone-dry, it is all scar and cauterizing flame. You can't touch it after it's been used. The grooves are so hot they're almost buzzing. They have been swearing away like women possessed. A file moves in when the other beheading tools can't get the foothold they need to do the job. It makes its appearance when the bump you want eliminated is too modest to merit a frontal attack, because files specialize in oblique offensives. A file gets cracking when its amputating kindred begin to slip and slide for want of a firm place to grip onto, when they lose their footing and start to look frivolous. A file never drifts off topic; it's a model of earnestness. It is incapable of being distracted. It is the diametrical opposite of oil and dampness. A culture without files is threatened by esoteric and erotic dangers, by slither and skid; it's a culture where everything's come close to rolling away and skipping about, of taking wing, of blasting to smithereens the decencies of proportion and distance. In contrast, a file doesn't permit itself the slightest lapse, the most minimal break in its concentration. It suffices just to see how it functions to know that. Two opposing forces are exercised on it: one presses down on the surface you want filed and makes the file stick like glue to it, as if it wanted to reduce the file to immobility; the other, a longitudinal thrust, drives the file forward and represents that portion of the file's material that hasn't forgotten the pleasure of sliding along and that makes a constant effort to ensure that something happens. Out of this conflict arises the file, with its network of points, its crisscrossed ridges. There the primordial, urbane smoothness, which is a thing of water and loquaciousness, gets disciplined into a sort of virility, while the rustic interior, a thing of stone and gruff taciturnity, gets transformed into something slenderer and more docile that allows the speech to speak, the song to sing. The result is the file's perfect pronunciation— clear, rigorous, virtually human. A file speaks by using every one of its teeth, without swallowing a single vowel or consonant, doing justice to the whole alphabet, a paragon of good diction. Human beings who are subject to the same conflicting pressures, from the urbane and the rustic, from water and stone, are nothing other than files, ridged and wrinkled animals. That's why they possess the gift of speech. Unlike the file, sandpaper isn't constituted of grooves but of a horde of granules which sweeten its impact. Here, instead of a job of persuasion, we get what we might call the work of prayer, even of supplication. What must have inspired the invention of sandpaper, as well of the file itself, is the beach. The sea keeps itself clean by rubbing itself on beaches, and in return, as a poet put it, it puts the beaches to sleep. But beaches not only polish and cleanse; they also soak up water and get sodden. The file with its grooves easily gets rid of any liquid; it's a perfect example of a drainage system. Sandpaper, however, is pure pulverization. This makes it more flexible and able to sneak into corners impossible for a file, but it brings it closer to chaos and dampness. But both of them, file and sandpaper alike, whether they are dry or moist, swearing oaths or abjectly begging, get the same type of pleasure: that of abrasion, erosion, abstraction. Thanks to them, all materials can, with a bit of patience, get to the bottom of their true nature, can reach their   innermost   noontide.

Fabio Morabito
Born to Italian parents in Egypt in 1955, Fabio Morabito spent most of his life in Mexico. Morabito always writes in Spanish, even though it is his second language. He writes fiction, poetry, and essays, and he has been awarded the White Raven Prize for Children's Fiction in Munich. The English translation of Toolbox *was published in 1998.*

Screw

Fabio Morabito

Oil is water equipped with hips, an impure sort of water that is on close terms with desire, time and death. Instead of advancing fluidly and unproblematically like water, oil insinuates itself and minces along. Where water, frank and anarchic, simpleminded and monotonous, liberates the world from its secrets, oil is a water that piles on secrets, water that lost its mission in some cranny and ever after forfeited its innocence. It is water with bad nerves.

Exactly the same distinction exists between a nail and a screw. A screw is morose and circumspect, like oil. It is like a lubricated nail, manufactured to be mindful of other materials and to get along with them, careful not to impose its laws on them. In a screw the tough monologue of the nail has been transmuted into dialogue and negotiation. Hence the joints made by a screw are more durable. In place of a brusque conquest, there is piecemeal infiltration. The thing that a nail doesn't have a clue about, namely the action of grazing, reaches its highest temperature in a screw. As a result of a continual, uniform grazing action that resembles a smoldering fire, a screw lulls the material to rest, softening it up; it takes it without taking it, almost with disinterest, without appetite.

A nail is much more heroic and exciting. It moves in an epic world. A screw is ugly, torpid, asthmatic, short of initial impact, betraying no eagerness, no feeling whatever. But there lies its strength. How is it possible to resist something that never looks you full in the face but offers you only its perpetual profile? How can you argue with it? The threads of a screw are a profile in its purest form; they are simply the absence of all face and all intention. How can you tell when you see that spiral in motion whether it's going in or coming out? Whether it's addressing us or ignoring us? It's the great opportunist; it launches into a longwinded, winding discourse that doesn't allow us the slightest chance to interrupt it or to say no. There's no way into it. Rather than penetrate, it insinuates; it sneaks inside, totally impersonally, without showing its face. If it could, it would become invisible.

Its strength resides in its longwindedness. As a talker, it is unbeatable. It's never lacking for an argument. It waits for its opportunity and then never shuts up. But the talkativeness of a screw relies more on suggestion and a wealth of examples than on the profundity of its reasoning. Reasons, like faces, are the children of pauses. A screw, which has never heard of a pause, is a superlative handler of examples. Each one of its turns is the equivalent of exclaiming "for example"; each turn of the screw is a different example of a nail, of the point that penetrates. A screw is a deluge of questions, but it never gives an answer. That's why, by sacrificing the excitement of entering its material with a blunt incisiveness, it secures every millimeter it gains as it advances. Like the delicate slime of a snail, it leaves behind, as it moves ahead, a winding track that guarantees it will find its way back cleanly,   without   obstacles. And since its route is composed of questions, a hypothetical route in other words, a second screw can use it in the future. We can go as far as to say that one screw is always another, that it starts over at every turn, inexhaustible and   replete   with   arguments. Hence it's careful never to go against the grain. It advances via the most timid of associations and the slenderest of similarities, without the slightest stumbling, like a hand that caresses us without ever detaching itself from our skin so that we don't awaken. Perhaps the spiral edges of a screw, in which continuity and rootedness, progression and permanence, have found a common solution, may shelter the   mysterious   secret   of   language. It's precisely this compromise solution, this innate caution in its conduct, that gives a screw its melancholic, almost tubercular appearance. It envies the impetus of a nail, its   gleeful   versatility,   its   Dionysian   merriment, its   uncompromised   purity. By wanting to be a nail, a screw displays a yearning for a lost, pristine world where everything was transparent, effusive, ready to be discovered, obvious at first glance, where deals were violent but without subterfuge, without profiles, full in the face, with no sign of a frown, and where everything could be used as something else. That profound longing for a more fiery world is clearly visible in the head of a screw, a head always split painfully into two, like the face of frustration or a heart that's been deeply wounded.

A Four-Hundred-Year-Old Woman

Bharati Mukherjee

I was born into a class that did not live in its native language. I was born into a city that feared its future, and trained me for emigration. I attended a school run by Irish nuns, who regarded our walled-off school compound in Calcutta as a corner (forever green and tropical) of England. My "country"—called in Bengali *desh,* and suggesting more a homeland than a nation of which one is a citizen—I have never seen. It is the ancestral home of my father and is now in Bangladesh. Nevertheless, I speak his dialect of Bengali, and think of myself as "belonging" to Faridpur, the tiny green-gold village that was his birthplace. I was born into a religion that placed me, a Brahmin, at the top of its hierarchy while condemning me, as a woman, to a role of subservience. The larger political entity to which I gave my first allegiance—India—was not even a sovereign nation when I was born.

My horoscope, cast by a neighborhood astrologer when I was a week-old infant, predicted that I would be a writer, that I would win some prizes, that I would cross "the black waters" of oceans and make my home among aliens. Brought up in a culture that places its faith in horoscopes, it never occurred to me to doubt it. The astrologer meant to offer me a melancholy future; to be destined to leave India was to be banished from the sources of true culture. The nuns at school, on the other hand, insinuated that India had long outlived its glories, and that if we wanted to be educated, modern women and make something of our lives, we'd better hit the trail westward. All my girlhood, I straddled the seesaw of contradictions. *Bilayat,* meaning the scary, unknown "abroad," was both boom time and desperate loss.

I have found my way to the United States after many transit stops. The unglimpsed phantom Faridpur and the all too real Manhattan have merged as "desh." I am an American. I am an American writer, in the American mainstream, trying to extend it. This is a vitally important statement for me—I am not an Indian writer, not an exile, not an expatriate. I am an immigrant; my investment is in the American reality, not the Indian. I look on ghettoization—whether as a Bengali in India or as a hyphenated Indo-American in North America—as a temptation to be surmounted.

It took me ten painful years, from the early seventies to the early eighties, to overthrow the smothering tyranny of nostalgia. The remaining struggle for me is to make the American readership, meaning the editorial and publishing industries as well, acknowledge the same fact. (As the reception of such films as *Gandhi* and *A Passage to India* as well as *The Far Pavillions* and *The Jewel in the Crown* shows, nostalgia is a two-way street. Americans can feel nostalgic for a world they never knew.) The foreign-born, the exotically raised Third World immigrant with non-Western religions and non-European languages and appearance, can be as American as any steerage passenger from Ireland, Italy, or the Russian Pale. As I have written in another context (a review article in *The Nation* on books by Studs Terkel and Al Santoli), we are probably only a few years away from a Korean *What Makes Choon-li Run?* or a Hmong *Call It Sleep.* In other words, my literary agenda begins by acknowledging that America has transformed *me.* It does not end until I show how I (and the hundreds of thousands like me) have transformed America.

The agenda is simply stated, but in the long run revolutionary. Make the familiar exotic; the exotic familiar.

I have had to create an audience. I cannot rely on shorthand references to my community, my religion, my class, my region, or my old school tie. I've had to sensitize editors as well as readers to the richness of the lives I'm writing about. The most moving form of praise I receive from readers can be summed up in three words: *I never knew.* Meaning, I see these people (call them Indians, Filipinos, Koreans, Chinese) around me all the time and I never knew they had an inner life. I never knew they schemed and cheated, suffered, felt so strongly, cared so passionately. When even the forms of praise are so rudimentary, the writer knows she has an inexhaustible fictional population to enumerate. Perhaps even a mission, to appropriate a good colonial word.

I have been blessed with an enormity of material. I can be Chekhovian and Tolstoyan—with melancholy and philosophical perspectives on the breaking of hearts as well as the fall of civilizations—and I can be a brash and raucous homesteader, Huck Finn and Woman Warrior, on the unclaimed plains of American literature. My material, reduced to jacket-flap copy, is the rapid and dramatic transformation of the United States since the early 1970s. Within that perceived perimeter, however, I hope to wring surprises.

Yet (I am a writer much given to "yet") my imaginative home is also in the tales told by my mother and grandmother, the world of the Hindu epics. For all the hope and energy I have placed in the process of immigration and accommodation—I'm a person who couldn't ride a public bus when she first arrived, and now I'm someone who watches tractor pulls on obscure cable channels—there are parts of me that remain Indian, parts that slide against the masks of newer selves. The form that my stories and novels take inevitably reflects the resources of Indian mythology—shape-changing, miracles, godly perspectives. My characters can, I hope, transcend the straitjacket of simple psychologizing. The people I write about are culturally and politically several hundred years old: consider the history they have witnessed (colonialism, technology, education, liberation, civil war, uprooting). They have shed old identities, taken on new ones, and learned to hide the scars. They may sell you newspapers, or clean your offices at night.

Writers (especially American writers, weaned on the luxury of affluence and freedom) often disavow the notion of a "literary duty" or "political consciousness," citing the all-too-frequent examples of writers ruined by their shrill commitments. Glibness abounds on both sides of the argument, but finally I have to side with my "Third World" compatriots: I do have a duty, beyond telling a good story or drawing a convincing character. My duty is to give voice to continents, but also to redefine the nature of *American* and what makes an American. In the process, work like mine and dozens like it will open up the canon of American literature.

It has not been an easy transition, from graduate student to citizen, from natural-born expatriate to the hurly-burly of immigration. My husband (Clark Blaise) and I spent fifteen years in his *desh* of Canada, and Canada was a country that discouraged the very process of assimilation. Eventually, it also discouraged the very presence of "Pakis" in its midst, and in 1980, a low point in our lives, we left, gave up our tenured, full-professor lives for the free-lancing life in the United States.

We were living in Iowa City in 1983 when Emory University called me to be writer-in-residence for the winter semester. My name, apparently, had been suggested to them by an old friend. I hadn't published a book in six years (two earlier novels, *The Tiger's Daughter* and *Wife,* as well as our joint nonfiction study, *Days and Nights in Calcutta,* were out of print) but somehow Emory didn't hold it against me.

Atlanta turned out to be the luckiest writing break of my life. For one of those mysterious reasons, stories that had been gathering in me suddenly exploded. I wrote nearly all the stories in *Darkness* (Penguin, 1985) in those three months. I finally had a glimpse of my true material, and that is immigration. In other words, transformation—not preservation. I saw myself and my own experience refracted through a dozen separate lives. Clark, who remained in Iowa City until our younger son finished high school, sent me newspaper accounts, and I turned them into stories. Indian friends in Atlanta took me to dinners and table gossip became stories. Suddenly, I had begun appropriating the American language. My stories were about the hurly-burly of the unsettled magma between two worlds.

Eventually—inevitably—we made our way to New York. My next batch of stories (*The Middleman and Other Stories,* Grove, 1988) appropriate the American language in ways that are personally most satisfying to me (one Chicago reviewer likened it to Nabokov's *Lolita*), and my characters are now as likely to be American as immigrant, and Chinese, Filipino, or Middle Eastern as much as Indian. That book has enjoyed widespread support both critically and commercially, and empowered me to write a new novel, *Jasmine,* and to contract for a major work, historical in nature, that nevertheless incorporates a much earlier version of my basic theme, due for completion in the next three years. *Days and Nights in Calcutta* is being made into a feature film.

My theme is the making of new Americans. Wherever I travel in the (very) Old World, I find "Americans" in the making, whether or not they ever make it to these shores. I see them as dreamers and conquerors, not afraid of transforming themselves, not afraid of abandoning some of their principles along the way. In *Jasmine,* my "American" is born in a Punjabi village, marries at fourteen, and is widowed at sixteen. Nevertheless, she is an American and will enter the book as an Iowa banker's wife.

Ancestral habits of mind can be constricting; they also confer one's individuality. I know I can appropriate the American language, but I can never be a minimalist. I have too many stories to tell. I am aware of myself as a four-hundred-year-old woman, born in the captivity of a colonial, pre-industrial oral culture and living now as a contemporary New Yorker.

My image of artistic structure and artistic excellence is the Moghul miniature painting with its crazy foreshortening of vanishing point, its insistence that everything happens simultaneously, bound only by shape and color. In the miniature paintings of India, there are a dozen separate foci, the most complicated stories can be rendered on a grain of rice, the corners are as elaborated as the centers. There is a sense of the interpenetration of all things. In the Moghul miniature of my life, there would be women investigating their bodies with mirrors, but they would be doing it on a distant balcony under fans wielded by bored serving girls; there would be a small girl listening to a bent old woman; there would be a white man eating popcorn and watching a baseball game; there would be cocktail parties and cornfields and a village set among rice paddies and skyscrapers. In a sense, I wrote that story, "Courtly Vision," at the end of *Darkness*. And in a dozen other ways I'm writing it today, and I will be writing, in the Moghul style, till I get it right.

Bharati Mukherjee
Born in India in 1940, Bharati Mukherjee spent part of her childhood in London and then lived in both the United States and Canada. She taught at McGill University in Montreal for a decade, then journeyed to India with her Canadian husband. These travels and her conflicted feelings about returning to India inspired a now published diary co-authored with her husband, Days and Nights in Calcutta, *and several novels, including* The Tiger's Daughter. *Mukherjee earned the National Book Critics' Award for her collection* The Middleman and Other Stories. *She now lives in New York and teaches at City University of New York, Queens College.*

Excerpts from A Brief Natural History of the Plastic Pink Flamingo

Jennifer Price

The plastic pink flamingo? What can a lawn ornament that sells for $7.95 (for a pair) at K-Mart really mean? "Nothing," had always been my own answer—but the pink creature turns out to be packed with surprising resonance and revelations for what *nature* has meant to Americans in the twentieth century. The bird's history speaks beautifully to my own generation of well-to-do baby boomers in particular—about our own meaningful, post-World War II exploits, and our specific failures of connection. It's especially eloquent about big, broad definitions of Nature. And yet, the pink flamingo? As the environmentalist and nature writer Terry Tempest Williams has branded it, "our unnatural link to the natural world?"

My faith in the meaningfulness of the plastic birds dates back to a day in 1992, when after I had made disparaging comments about the flock of birds in the yard of our rented house, my housemate Kathy responded that she had moved in because she liked them. An avid outdoorswoman, Kathy told me she had traveled with a friend who had a pink flamingo named Eudora and who had taken the bird backpacking, mountain-biking and cross-country skiing across the Sierras and Alaska. Our houseguest Phil chimed in that he had taken a pink flamingo on spring skiing trips in Colorado. I began to ask around. Another friend had stolen pink flamingos off lawns on drunken late-night outings in high school. A literary agent told me about a *New Yorker* editor with a well-known collection. My thesis advisor remembered an NPR story on a kidnapped pair that had sent back postcards from the Eiffel Tower. Between two commentators for a 1992 paper I presented at an American history conference, the geographer had kept a flamingo that a scholar of landscape architecture had brandished at the start of a lecture (as the nadir of poor taste) and handed to him in the front row; and the British historian loved them. My neighbor had created a pink flamingo installation for an art show at college. A friend's family gave the birds as joke gifts to each other at Christmas. Everyone seemed to have a pink flamingo story to tell. Eudora herself had gotten left behind accidentally one summer in a cabin at Donner Pass. In memoriam, Kathy took one of ours on a winter kayaking trip to the Baja; and in the spring, she drafted all the birds as croquet wickets for her bring-your-own-Jell-O lawn party.

The plastic flamingo has been a compelling and pervasive object in American post-World War II culture. A cheap polyethylene replica of a real bird species that no longer even inhabits the United States, it has achieved fame and notoriety as a popular lawn ornament, the symbolic excrescence of bad taste, a travel companion, and even an objet d'art. The human stories around the plastic creatures have raged wildly and abundantly. Why put them on lawns? Why steal them *off* lawns? Why take a fake pink bird up a ski lift? And why put it in a backpack, where the allotment of every square inch is so remarkably careful? The deepest meanings of each of these flamingos, I've become convinced, owe their logic and fervor to deep meanings and big definitions of nature. The story of the pink lawn bird is the tale of how Americans converted a plastic object into the very symbol of what is artificial. It is a story of the meanings of Artifice. And that is a history, at the same tune, of the meanings of Nature. In the 1990s, Nature has never seemed so urgent a place to turn for meaning, and the plastic flamingo has never sold as well. The two developments—and Nature and Artifice—are locked together absolutely in the same history.

The flamingo splashed into the market in the fifties as an especially bold and emphatic statement. The bird staked two major claims to boldness. First, it was a flamingo. Since the 1930s, Americans had been flocking south to Florida for vacations and traveling back home with flamingo souvenirs. In the 1910s and 1920s, entrepreneurs had dredged Miami Beach out of the swamps as a winter resort for the rich and had made the first grand hotel, the Flamingo, synonymous with the wealth and pizazz of south Florida. After a 1926 hurricane leveled Millionaire's Row, developers built hundreds of more modest resort hotels, in an anomalous building boom in the heart of the Depression, to cater to new train lines and an eager middle class. In South Beach, especially, architects built in the playful Art Deco style, replete with pinks, bright colors and flamingo motifs. The flamingo also symbolized Hialeah Park, the elegant and sophisticated racetrack that boasted private boxes for the Vanderbilts and Kennedys and had a stately landscape of lakes, palms and tropical gardens. In 1932, for opening day, the owners imported a flock of real flamingos, which promptly flew back to Cuba. The next season, a new flock with clipped wings made the infield lake at the site of the prestigious Flamingo Stakes their permanent habitat.

All of which was a little ironic, since flamingos had been hunted to extinction in south Florida in the late 1800s, for plumes and meat. But no matter. In the 1950s, the new interstates also drew working-class tourists to south Florida—and back in New Jersey, flamingo postcards, mugs, lamps and shower curtains testified to these vacations. The plastic bird from Union Products inscribed a suburban lawn emphatically with the same cachet of leisure, wealth and extravagance. The flamingo acquired an extra fillip of boldness, too, from the direction of Las Vegas, the flamboyant oasis of instant riches that the gangster Benjamin "Bugsy" Siegel had conjured from the desert in 1946. Siegel had launched his resort with a grand Flamingo Hotel, which boasted a neon flamingo sign, and imported live flamingos for opening day. His garish creation (he came from working-class Brooklyn) looks like a parody of extravagance. Anyone who has seen Las Vegas knows that a flamingo stands out in a desert far more boldly even than on a suburban green lawn. In the 1950s, namesake Flamingo hotels, restaurants and lounges cropped up across the country like semiotic sprouts.

And the pink flamingo was pink—a second and commensurate claim to boldness. In the 1950s the plastics industries marketed a vast array of consumer items in flashy colors, with pinks in the vanguard. The popular bright new colors, as Tom Wolfe described them, were "the new electrochemical pastels of the Florida littoral: tangerine, broiling magenta, livid pink, incarnadine, fuschia demure, Congo ruby, methyl green." The hues were forward-looking and not old-fashioned: they were for a generation raised in the Depression who were ready boldly to celebrate their new affluence. The new plastics seemed boldest, and most futuristic and high-tech, in colors you didn't often see in nature. The plastics and bright colors were not-Nature in a *good* way. Washing machines, cars and kitchen counters proliferated in passion pink, sunset pink, and Bermuda pink. As the historian Karal Ann Marling has written, the "sassy pinks" were "the hottest color of the decade." Even many middle-class suburbanites who stayed faithful to aesthetics of Taste and Nature on their lawns indulged a flashier style in their kitchens—as *Life* and *House Beautiful* droned on about the dangers of tasteless excess. Yet according to 1959 surveys in Vance Packard's *The Status Seekers,* working-class consumers on average favored brighter colors. Bugsy Siegel filled the Flamingo's hotel rooms in Vegas with bright-pink leather furniture. Elvis, as Marling has written, bought his first pink Cadillac after he signed his first recording contract in 1956: the working-class singer "was bound for glory in a fleet of Cadillacs and wanted the whole world to sit up and take notice." After all, why call the birds "pink flamingos"—as if they could be blue or green? The pink flamingo is a hotter pink than a real flamingo. On a green lawn, it is bold. Among even the pinkest of real pink flowers and real pink birds it is emphatic. It sticks out. Having put two of them in my mother's English shade garden, I can tell you this is true.

Historically, flamingos have always stood out. There are five species of real flamingos, which gather and feed in large flocks on algae and invertebrates in saline and alkaline shallow lakes and lagoons, in a range of mostly warm and generally inhospitable habitats around the world. The people who have lived near and around these places have without exception singled out the bright, big birds as special. Early Christians associated the flamingo with the red Phoenix. In ancient Egypt, it symbolized the sun god Ra. In Mexico and the Caribbean, the bird remains a major motif in art, dance and literature. Like other obvious and unusual creatures—such as lions, grizzly bears and passenger pigeons—flamingos have taken on heavy doses of human myth and symbol. But in the 1950s, people made the American flamingo meaningful for the very fact that it stood out. As with pigeon ballotines and terns on hats, the meanings of the plastic birds said a little about real flamingos—which latitudes they lived in and what color they were—but not much. Americans reproduced the likeness of a subtropical flamingo species in New England, and set the birds out across temperate latitudes onto an inland sea of grass.

Jennifer Price

Environmental historian and cultural theorist Jennifer Price received her Ph.D. in History from Yale University. She is the author of Flight Maps: Adventures with Nature in Modern America, *and her essays have appeared in the collections* Uncommon Ground: Rethinking the Human Place in Nature *and* The Nature of Nature: New Essays from America's Finest Writers on Nature. *She lives in Los Angeles, California.*

The Night My Mother Met Bruce Lee

Paisley Rekdal

Age sixteen, my mother loads up red tubs of noodles, teacups chipped and white-gray as teeth, rice clumps that glue themselves to the plastic tub sides or dissolve and turn papery in the weak tea sloshing around the bottom. She's at Diamond Chan's restaurant, where most of her cousins work after school and during summer vacations some of her friends, too. There's Suzy at the cash register, totaling up bills and giving back change, a little dish of toothpicks beside her and a basket of mints that taste like powdered cream. A couple of my mother's cousins are washing dishes behind the swinging kitchen door, and some woman called Auntie #2 (at her age, everyone is Auntie and each must take a number) takes orders at a table of women that look like Po Po's mah-jongg club. They don't play anymore. They go to the racetrack.

The interior of Diamond Chan's restaurant is red: red napkins, red walls, red carp in the tank and in signature seals on the cheap wall hangings. Luck or no luck, it's like the inside of an esophagus. My mother's nails are cracked, kept short by clipping or gnawing, glisten only when varnished with the grease of someone else's leftovers. Still, she enjoys working here, its repetitive actions, the chores that keep her from thinking. The money my mother earns will soon get sucked into the price of a pink cashmere sweater for Po Po's birthday, along with a graduation photo of herself, also in a pink sweater, pearls, her face airbrushed fog-rose at the cheeks and mouth.

Graduation? Unlike her brothers, she knows she's going to college. Smith, to be exact, though without the approval of the school counselor. "Smith is . . . expensive," the school counselor told my mother only yesterday, which is why my mother is slightly irritated now, clomping around under the weight of full tubs of used dishes. "Smith is not for girls like you." What does she plan to be when she grows up? "A doctor?" my mother suggests. Um, no. "Nursing. Or teaching, perhaps, which is even more practical. Don't you think?"

My mother, who is practical above all things, agreed.

So it's the University of Washington in two years with a degree in education. Fine. She slams down full vials of soy sauce onto each table, makes sure the nozzle heads are screwed on exactly. Someone the other week stuck chewing gum up under the lid of one, and my mother had to dig it out with an old chopstick and then forgot to fully tighten the lid. Black, sweet-smelling pool on the white tablecloth. Seeing it, she could feel the back of her throat fill up with salt. Smith is not for girls like her.

"Cindy!" someone shouts. The kitchen door swings open. A momentary view: white chef shirts stained with red and brown grease. A woman wiping her brow with the back of her hand.

It is not, my mother would argue, the fact she could be denied the dream of Smith so much that someone should *tell* her she could be denied it. My mother knows the counselor was hinting at some limitation my mother would prefer to ignore. Still, she is whiter than white, should intelligence be considered a pale attribute. Deep down she understands she has a special capacity for work; she likes it, she's good at it, she excels at school and its predictable problems. Hers is a discipline entirely lacking in the spirits of whatever *loh fan* may sneer or wonder at her in study hall; to be told by a fat, dyed-blond guidance counselor she may be inferior? The monkey calling the man animal.

Now out of the kitchen erupts the newcomer, a smatter of duck fat and ash. Like everyone here, he's someone's cousin's cousin, though he talks like he's got marbles piled in his mouth.

"I come from Hong Kong," he told my mother on break in the alley. "From *real* Chinese." Is there a substitute? He leers at Suzy, waves his hand dismissively over the carved dragon beams, the waitresses gossiping in English. He's two years older than my mother, lean, high-cheekboned, shaggy-headed. He has big plans for himself. He likes to whip his arms and legs around in the kitchen, threaten the other busboy. Already he's dropped a dish, insulted the cook, cut his thumb on a knife blade. He smells funny.

"Mr. B. O. Jangles," Suzy calls him. "Kung Fooey."

"What the hell the matter with him?" growls Auntie #2. "I never seen nobody act like that before."

"It's all the rage in China," my mother says. She is repeating what he told her in a tone of voice that is meant to seem sarcastic but comes out another way. All the rage. In China.

She stacks more dishes in her tub. From the kitchen comes a high-pitched human squawk and the sound of something clattering to the floor. He's going to get fired soon and my mother is never going to Smith. A waitress scurries out of the kitchen, bearing more food, a panicked look on her face. My mother stands and watches the kitchen door swing in place behind her. Back and forth, back and forth, back and forth.

Around age thirteen, for summer vacation I come down with laziness heretofore unheard of in a child. I doze in bed till noon at least, stay up every night watching bad movies or reading. Sometimes, if it's a bad enough movie and she is not teaching the next morning, my mother wakes and joins me.

Tonight is *Enter the Dragon*. I remember it because a year or two ago when it came out, all the boys on the block bought numchucks. We smacked our backs with the sticks on chains, left thumb-thick bruise prints on our rib cages. Jeff down the street still has the movie poster, still tells people he has a black belt in karate.

My mother and I watch Bruce Lee set foot on the island, followed closely by the playboy and the black man who will die after the banquet and all his women. Bruce Lee narrows his eyes, ripples his chest muscles underneath his white turtleneck.

"I knew him," my mother tells me. "I worked with him in a restaurant when I was in high school."

"Really?" This is now officially the only cool thing about her. "What was he like?"

"I don't remember. No one liked him, though. All that kung fu stuff, it looked ridiculous. Like a parody."

We watch in the dark as Bruce Lee confronts himself, over and over. In the hall of mirrors, his bloody chest and face seem outlined in silver. He is handsome and wiry; he caws at his opponents like an ethereal avenger. I peek at my mother beside me on the sofa. In the television light, her broad face twists into an expression I do not recognize. Then the light flickers, changes, makes her ordinary again.

Paisley Rekdal

Poet and essayist Paisley Rekdal's books include The Night My Mother Met Bruce Lee, A Crash of Rhinos, *and* Six Girls Without Pants. *Her poems, essays, and articles have appeared in numerous publications, including* the New York Times Sunday Magazine, Nerve, the Village Voice Literary Supplement, Michigan Quarterly Review, Indiana Review, Humor Me: An Anthology of Humor by Writers of Color, *and* The New Asian American Poets. *Also, she's been heard on NPR's "Along for the Ride." Born in 1970 in Seattle, Rekdal was a Fulbright Fellow and teacher in South Korea, and she currently teaches creative writing at the University of Utah.*

Three Voices

Bhanu Kapil Rider

I

The bath heated by pans of water from the stove, the man's glistening mouth when he pours the water over my belly, the oil in my hair, the ice snapping in the tree outside my room, and then, after the green and brown night, I drink hoji-cha, eat toast with black cherry jam, eat a banana, and answer the man's questions. There are phones ringing beyond Beethoven. It is eleven in the morning, and already the day has backed up farther and farther inside me. Today, I cannot shake the lump of coal out of my body. The man wants to go to the supermarket to buy fresh fruit, and some milk. Okay, okay.

A bowl of avocado meat, softened and pressed by the back of a spoon is my pleasure. Beneath the pleasure, the hunger that's made of eggshells, and pieces of cloth. Perhaps it is simply a matter of studying and exercising. Okay, okay. But I am not in the mood to read novels, or spend time with friends, or sing. No. I think I want to sing. But what's this? My voice is a stone in my chest. It doesn't stream. I am filled with music! But I can't swallow.

I am not writing about myself as a rational human being. I'm writing about the substances of an animal and female life: magic, pain, the cracked nails of four feet, and the days like this one, when it is difficult to speak to a good-looking man. He returns with sesame seeds, unleavened bread, ginger and coriander powders, coffee, chives, chocolate, yoghurt, onions, cucumbers, potatoes, and a quart of milk. He thinks I am a woman, because he bathes me, and puts his hands on the sides of my face, and tells me I am beautiful. Yes. Okay. But there is something hard between my lungs. It is the size of a blood orange from northern California.

II

And then, one woman, she cannot breathe from her stomach, tells the man: "I am not in love with you. Next year, I will be twenty-five years old, and perhaps I will panic, and perhaps I will not tell you the truth about my heart. And listen, don't ask me about it unless you want to hear about the piece of stale bread I ate one day, when you were sleeping in my bed. I don't know how this happened. Enough!"

The man is not stupid. He's noticed how, in her own sleep, she rubs her palm between her breasts. He replies: "What the hell do you want from me?"

And the woman starts to speak. There is an orange-colored wave rising up her spine.

III

I am blessed. Even in this loneliness, I am blessed. I open the Spanish dictionary at random to "algun" (someday), and "marriage" (matrimonio). I open a book of symbols to "crane," which is connected to pine trees and the sun. And Neruda, in his memoirs, writes: "She gave up her husband, and she also gave up the soft lighting and the excellent armchairs, for an acrobat in a Russian circus that passed through Santiago."

There are not many Russian acrobats in upstate New York. But here is an orange on the kitchen table. I will learn to juggle it on the tips of my fingers. No. I think I'll place it on the front step. A stranger passing by will, perhaps, noticing it, come into my rooms. He is the coming power of the future.

Anhelo: longing. My life: joven. Joven: young woman. Stranger: Angel. Naranjo: orange. Wonder: milagro. My life: sagrado. Sagrado: sacred.

Bhanu Kapil Rider
Bhanu Kapil Rider, poet and essayist, is a British citizen of Indian origin; she is currently in the process of becoming an American citizen. The author of The Vertical Interrogation of Strangers, *her first published work was* Autobiography of a Cyborg, *a handbound chapbook published by Renee Gladman's Leroy Press in 2000. She lives in Colorado with her husband and child.*

Buckeye

Scott Russell Sanders

Years after my father's heart quit, I keep in a wooden box on my desk the two buckeyes that were in his pocket when he died. Once the size of plums, the brown seeds are shriveled now, hollow, hard as pebbles, yet they still gleam from the polish of his hands. He used to reach for them in his overalls or suit pants and click them together, or he would draw them out, cupped in his palm, and twirl them with his blunt carpenter's fingers, all the while humming snatches of old tunes.

"Do you really believe buckeyes keep off arthritis?" I asked him more than once.

He would flex his hands and say, "I do so far."

My father never paid much heed to pain. Near the end, when his worn knee often slipped out of joint, he would pound it back in place with a rubber mallet. If a splinter worked into his flesh beyond the reach of tweezers, he would heat the blade of his knife over a cigarette lighter and slice through the skin. He sought to ward off arthritis not because he feared pain but because he lived through his hands, and he dreaded the swelling of knuckles, the stiffening of fingers. What use would he be if he could no longer hold a hammer or guide a plow? When he was a boy he had known farmers not yet forty years old whose hands had curled into claws, men so crippled up they could not tie their own shoes, could not sign their names. "I mean to tickle my grandchildren when they come along," he told me, "and I mean to build doll houses and turn spindles for tiny chairs on my lathe."

So he fondled those buckeyes as if they were charms, carrying them with him when our family moved from Ohio at the end of my childhood, bearing them to new homes in Louisiana, then Oklahoma, Ontario, and Mississippi, carrying them still on his final day when pain a thousand times fiercer than arthritis gripped his heart.

The box where I keep the buckeyes also comes from Ohio, made by my father from a walnut plank he bought at a farm auction. I remember the auction, remember the sagging face of the widow whose home was being sold, remember my father telling her he would prize that walnut as if he had watched the tree grow from a sapling on his own land. He did not care for pewter or silver or gold, but he cherished wood. On the rare occasions when my mother coaxed him into a museum, he ignored the paintings or porcelain and studied the exhibit cases, the banisters, the moldings, the parquet floors.

I remember him planing that walnut board, sawing it, sanding it, joining piece to piece to make foot stools, picture frames, jewelry boxes. My own box, a bit larger than a soap dish, lined with red corduroy, was meant to hold earrings and pins, not buckeyes. The top is inlaid with pieces fitted so as to bring out the grain, four diagonal joints converging from the corners toward the center. If I stare long enough at those converging lines, they float free of the box and point to a center deeper than wood.

I learned to recognize buckeyes and beeches, sugar maples and shagbark hickories, wild cherries, walnuts, and dozens of other trees while tramping through the Ohio woods with my father. To his eyes, their shapes, their leaves, their bark, their winter buds were as distinctive as the set of a friend's shoulders. As with friends, he was partial to some, craving their company, so he would go out of his way to visit particular trees, walking in a circle around the splayed roots of a sycamore, laying his hand against the trunk of a white oak, ruffling the feathery green boughs of a cedar. "Trees breathe," he told me. "Listen."

I listened, and heard the stir of breath.

He was no botanist; the names and uses he taught me were those he had learned from country folks, not from books. Latin never crossed his lips. Only much later would I discover that the tree he called ironwood, its branches like muscular arms, good for ax handles, is known in books as hop hornbeam; what he called tuliptree or canoewood, ideal for log cabins, is officially the yellow poplar; what he called hoop ash, good for barrels and fence posts, appears in books as hackberry.

When he introduced me to the buckeye, he broke off a chunk of the gray bark and held it to my nose. I gagged.

"That's why the old-timers called it stinking buckeye," he told me. "They used it for cradles and feed troughs and peg legs."

"Why for peg legs?" I asked.

"Because it's light and hard to split, so it won't shatter when you're clumping around."

He showed me this tree in late summer, when the fruits had fallen and the ground was littered with prickly brown pods. He picked up one, as fat as a lemon, and peeled away the husk to reveal the shiny seed. He laid it in my palm and closed my fist around it so the seed peeped out from the circle formed by my index finger and thumb. "You see where it got the name?" he asked.

I saw: what gleamed in my hand was the bright eye of a deer. "It's beautiful," I said.

"It's beautiful," my father agreed, "but also poisonous. Nobody eats buckeyes, except maybe a fool squirrel."

I knew the gaze of deer from living in the Ravenna Arsenal, in Portage County, up in the northeastern corner of Ohio. After supper we often drove the Arsenal's gravel roads, past the munitions bunkers, past acres of rusting tanks and wrecked bombers, into the far fields where we counted deer. One June evening, while mist rose from the ponds, we counted 311, our family record. We found deer in herds, in bunches, in amorous pairs. We came upon lone bucks, their antlers lifted against the sky like the bare branches of dogwood. If you were quiet, if your hands were empty, if you moved slowly, you could leave the car and steal to within a few paces of a grazing deer, close enough to see the delicate lips, the twitching nostrils, the glossy, fathomless eyes.

Scott Russell Sanders
Scott Russell Sanders has published numerous novels (including The Invisible Company *and* Terrarium*), collections of fiction (*Wilderness Plots *and* Fetching the Dead*), and works of creative nonfiction (including* Writing from the Center, The Paradise of Bombs, Secrets of the Universe, *and* In Limestome Country*). He also writes children's books, which include* The Floating House *and* Here Comes the Mystery Man. *Sanders' most recent books are* Hunting for Hope, The Country of Language, *and* The Force of Spirit. *His writing appears regularly in* The Georgia Review, Orion, Audubon, *and in a number of anthologies, including four editions of* The Best American Essays. *He has been awarded the Lannan Literary Award, the AWP Award in Creative Nonfiction, the Kenyon Review Award for Literary Excellence, the Great Lakes Book Award, and the Ohioana Book Award. Sanders is a Distinguished Professor at Indiana University. He was born in 1945 in Memphis, Tennessee.*

The Drama Bug

David Sedaris

The man was sent to our class to inspire us, and personally speaking, I thought he did an excellent job. After introducing himself in a relaxed and genial manner, he started toward the back of the room, only to be stopped midway by what we came to know as "the invisible wall," that transparent barrier realized only by psychotics, drug fiends, and other members of the show business community.

I sat enthralled as he righted himself and investigated the imaginary wall with his open palms, running his hands over the seemingly hard surface in hopes of finding a way out. Moments later he was tugging at an invisible rope, then struggling in the face of a violent, fantastic wind.

You know you're living in a small town when you can reach the ninth grade without ever having seen a mime. As far as I was concerned, this man was a prophet, a genius, a pioneer in the field of entertainment—and here he was in Raleigh, North Carolina! It was a riot, the way he imitated the teacher, turning down the corners of his mouth and riffling through his imaginary purse in search of gum and aspirin. Was this guy funny or what!

I went home and demonstrated the invisible wall for my two-year-old brother, who pounded on the very real wall beside his playpen, shrieking and wailing in disgust. When my mother asked what I'd done to provoke him, I threw up my hands in mock innocence before lowering them to retrieve the imaginary baby that lay fussing at my feet. I patted the back of my little ghost to induce gas and was investigating its soiled diaper when I noticed my mother's face assume an expression she reserved for unspeakable horror. I had seen this look only twice before: once when she was caught in the path of a charging, rabid pig and then again when I told her I wanted a peach-colored velveteen blazer with matching slacks.

"I don't know who put you up to this," she said, "but I'll kill you myself before I watch you grow up to be a clown. If you want to paint your face and prance around on street corners, then you'll have to find some other place to live because I sure as hell won't have it in my house." She turned to leave. "*Or in my yard,*" she added.

Fearful of her retribution, I did as I was told, ending my career in mime with a whimper rather than the silent bang I had hoped for.

The visiting actor returned to our classroom a few months later, removing his topcoat to reveal a black body stocking worn with a putty-colored neck brace, the result of a recent automobile accident. This afternoon's task was to introduce us to the works of William Shakespeare, and once again I was completely captivated by his charm and skill. When the words became confusing, you needed only to pay attention to the actor's face and hands to understand that this particular character was not just angry, but vengeful. I loved the undercurrent of hostility that lay beneath the surface of this deceptively beautiful language. It seemed a shame that people no longer spoke this way, and I undertook a campaign to reintroduce Elizabethan English to the citizens of North Carolina.

"Perchance, fair lady, thou dost think me unduly vexed by the sorrowful state of thine quarters," I said to my mother as I ran the vacuum cleaner over the living-room carpet she was inherently too lazy to bother with. "These foul specks, the evidence of life itself, have sullied not only thine shag-tempered mat but also thine character. Be ye mad, woman? Were it a punishable crime to neglect thine dwellings, you, my feeble-spirited mistress, would hang from the tallest tree in penitence for your shameful ways. Be there not garments to launder and iron free of turbulence? See ye not the porcelain plates and hearty mugs waiting to be washed clean of evidence? Get thee to thine work, damnable lady, and quickly, before the products of thine very loins raise their collected fists in a spirit born both of rage and indignation, forcibly coaxing the last breath from the foul chamber of thine vain and upright throat. Go now, wastrel, and get to it!"

My mother reacted as if I had whipped her with a short length of yarn. The intent was there, but the weapon was strange and inadequate. I could tell by the state of my room that she spent the next day searching my dresser for drugs. The clothes I took pride in neatly folding were crammed tight into their drawers with no regard for color or category. I smelled the evidence of cigarettes and noticed the coffee rings on my desk. My mother had been granted forgiveness on several previous occasions, but mess with mine drawers and ye have just made thyself an enemy for life. Tying a feather to the shaft of my ballpoint pen, I quilled her a letter. "The thing that ye search for so desperately," I wrote, "resideth not in mine well-ordered chamber, but in the questionable content of thine own character." I slipped the note into her purse, folded twice and sealed with wax from the candles I now used to light my room. I took to brooding, refusing to let up until I received a copy of Shakespeare's collected plays. Once they were acquired, I discovered them dense and difficult to follow. Reading the words made me feel dull and stupid, but speaking them made me feel powerful. I found it best to simply carry the book from room to room, occasionally skimming for fun words I might toss into my ever fragrant vocabulary. The dinner hour became either unbearable or excruciating, depending on my mood.

"Methinks, kind sir, most gentle lady, fellow siblings all, that this barnyard fowl be most tasty and succulent, having simmered in its own sweet juices for such a time as it might take the sun to pass, rosy and full-fingered, across the plum-colored sky for the course of a twilight hour. 'Tis crisp yet juicy, this plump bird, satisfied in the company of such finely roasted neighbors. Hear me out, fine relations, and heed my words, for methinks it adventurous, and fanciful, too, to saddle mine fork with both fowl *and* carrot at the exact same time, the twin juices blending together in a delicate harmony which doth cajole and enliven mine tongue in a spirit of unbridled merriment! What say ye, fine father, sisters, and infant brother, too, that we raise our flagons high in celebration of this hearty feast, prepared lovingly and with utmost grace by this dutiful woman we have the good fortune to address as wife, wench, or mother!"

My enthusiasm knew no limits. Soon my mother was literally begging me to wait in the car while she stepped into the bank or grocery store.

I was at the orthodontist's office, placing a pox upon the practice of dentistry, when the visiting actor returned to our classroom.

"You missed it," my friend Lois said. "The man was so indescribably powerful that I was practically crying, that's how brilliant he was." She positioned her hands as if she were supporting a tray. "I don't know what more I can say. The words, they just don't exist. I could try to explain his realness, but you'd never be able to understand it. Never," she repeated. "Never, never, never."

Lois and I had been friends for six months when our relationship suddenly assumed a competitive edge. I'd never cared who made better grades or had more spending money. We each had our strengths; the important thing was to honor each other for the thing that person did best. Lois held her Chablis better than I, and I respected her for that. Her frightening excess of self-confidence allowed her to march into school wearing a rust-colored Afro wig, and I stood behind her one hundred percent. She owned more records than I did, and because she was nine months older, also knew how to drive a car and did so as if she were rushing to put out a fire. *Fine,* I thought, *good for her.* My superior wisdom and innate generosity allowed me to be truly happy for Lois up until the day she questioned my ability to understand the visiting actor. The first few times he visited, she'd been just like the rest of them, laughing at his neck brace and rolling her eyes at the tangerine-sized lump in his tights. *I* was the one who first identified his brilliance, and now she was saying I couldn't understand him? Methinks not.

"Honestly, woman," I said to my mother on our way to the dry cleaner, "to think that this low-lying worm might speak to me of greatness as though it were a thing invisible to mine eyes is more than I can bear. Her words doth strike mine heart with the force of a punishing blow, leaving me both stunned and highly vexed, too. Hear me, though, for I shall bide my time, quietly, and with cunning, striking back at the very hour she doth least expect it. Such an affront shall not go unchallenged, of that you may rest assured, gentle lady. My vengeance will hold the sweet taste of the ripest berry; and I shall savor it slowly."

"You'll get over it," my mother said. "Give it a week or two and I'm sure everything will be back to normal. I'm going in now to get your father's shirts and I want you to wait here, *in the car.* Trust me, this whole thing will be forgotten about in no time."

This had become her answer to everything. She'd done some asking around and concluded I'd been bitten by what her sister referred to as "the drama bug." My mother was convinced that this was a phase, just like all the others. A few weeks of fanfare and I'd drop show business, just like I had the guitar and my private detective agency. I hated having my life's ambition reduced to the level of a common cold. This wasn't a bug, but a full-fledged virus. It might lay low for a year or two, but this little germ would never go away. It had nothing to do with talent or initiative. Rejection couldn't weaken it, and no amount of success would ever satisfy it. Once diagnosed, the prognosis was terminal.

The drama bug seemed to strike hardest with Jews, homosexuals, and portly girls, whose faces were caked with acne medication. These were individuals who, for one reason or another, desperately craved attention. I would later discover it was a bad idea to gather more than two of these people in an enclosed area for any length of time. The stage was not only a physical place but also a state of mind, and the word *audience* was defined as anyone forced to suffer your company. We young actors were a string of lightbulbs left burning twenty-four hours a day, exhausting ourselves and others with our self-proclaimed brilliance.

I had the drama bug and Lois had a car. Weighing the depth of her momentary transgression against the rich rewards of her private chariot, I found it within my bosom to forgive my wayward friend. I called her the moment I learned the visiting actor had scheduled a production of *Hamlet* set to take place in the amphitheater of the Raleigh Rose Garden. He himself would direct and play the title role, but the other parts were up for grabs. We auditioned, and because we were the youngest and least experienced, Lois and I were assigned the roles of the traveling players Hamlet uses to bait his uncle Claudius. It wasn't the part I was hoping for, but I accepted my role with quiet dignity. I had a few decent speeches and planned to work them to the best of my ability.

Our fellow cast members were in their twenties and thirties and had wet their feet in such long-running outdoor dramas as *The Lost Colony* and *Tender Is the Lamb.* These were professionals, and I hoped to benefit from their experience, sitting literally at their feet as the director paced the lip of the stage addressing his clenched fist as "poor Yorick."

I worshiped these people. Lois slept with them. By the second week of rehearsal, she had abandoned Fortinbras in favor of Laertes, who, she claimed, had a "real way with the sword." Unlike me, she was embraced by the older crowd, attending late-night keg parties with Polonius and Ophelia and driving to the lake with the director while Gertrude and Rosencrantz made out in the backseat. The killer was that Lois was nowhere near as committed as I was. Her drama bug was the equivalent of a twenty-four-hour flu, yet there she was, playing bumper pool with Hamlet himself while I practiced lines alone in my room, dreaming up little ways to steal the show.

It was decided that as traveling players, Lois and I would make our entrance tumbling onto the outdoor stage. When she complained that the grass was irritating her skin, the director examined the wee pimples on her back and decided that, from this point on, the players would en-ter skipping. I had rehearsed my tumble until my brain lost its mooring and could be heard rattling inside my skull, and now, on the basis of one complaint, we were skipping? He'd already cut all my speeches, leaving me with the one line "Aye, my lord." That was it, three lousy syllables. A person could wrench more emotion out of a sneeze than all my dialogue put together. While the other actors strolled the Rose Garden memorizing their vengeful soliloquies, I skipped back and forth across the parking lot repeating, "Aye, my lord," in a voice that increasingly sounded like that of a trained parrot. Lois felt silly skipping and spoke to the director, who praised her instincts and announced that, henceforth, the players would enter walking.

The less I had to do, the more my fellow actors used me as a personal slave. I would have been happy to help them run lines, but instead, they wanted me to polish their crowns or trot over to a car, searching the backseat for a misplaced dagger.

"Looking for something to do? You can help Doogan glow-tape the props," the director said. "You can chase the spiders out of the dressing room, or better yet, why don't you run down to the store and get us some drinks."

For the most part, Lois sat in the shade doing nothing. Not only did she refuse to help out, but she was always the first one to hand me a large bill when placing an order for a thirty-cent diet soda. She'd search through her purse, bypassing the singles in favor of a ten or a twenty. "I need to break this anyway," she'd say. "If they charge you extra for a cup of ice, tell them to fuck themselves." During the rehearsal breaks she huddled in the stands, gossiping with the other actors while I was off anchoring ladders for the technicians.

When it came time for our big scene, Lois recited her lines as if she were reading the words from the surface of some distant billboard. She squinted and paused between syllables, punctuating each word with a question mark. "Who this? Has seen with tongue? In venom steeped?"

If the director had a problem with her performance, he kept it to himself. I, on the other hand, was instructed to remove the sweater from around my neck, walk slower, and drop the accent. It might have been easier to accept the criticism had he spread it around a little, but that seemed unlikely. She could enter the scene wearing sunglasses and eating pizza and that was "fine, Lois. Great work, babe."

By this time I was finding my own way home from rehearsal. Lois couldn't give me a ride, as she was always running off to some party or restaurant with what she referred to as "the gang from Elsinore."

"I can't go," I'd say, pretending I had been invited. "I really need to get home and concentrate on my line. You go ahead, though. I'll just call my mother. She'll pick me up."

"Are we vexed?" my mother would ask, pulling her station wagon into the parking lot.

"We are indeed," I answered. "And highly so."

"Let it go," she said. "Ten years from now I guarantee you won't remember any of these people. Time passes, you'll see." She frowned, studying her face in the rearview mirror. "Enough liquor, and people can forget anything. Don't let it get to you. If nothing else, this has taught you to skim money while buying their drinks."

I didn't appreciate her flippant attitude, but the business with the change was insightful.

"Round everything off to the nearest dollar," she said. "Hand them their change along with their drinks so they'll be less likely to count it—and never fold the bills, keep the money in a wad."

My mother had the vengeful part down. It was the craft of acting I thought she knew nothing about.

We were in dress rehearsal when the director approached Lois regarding a new production he hoped to stage that coming fall. It was to be a musical based on the lives of roving Gypsies. "And you," he said, "shall be my lusty bandit queen."

Lois couldn't sing; everyone knew that. Neither could she act or play the tambourine. "Yours is the heart of a Gypsy," he said, kneeling in the grass. "The vibrant soul of a nomad."

When I expressed an interest, he suggested I might enjoy working behind the scenes. He meant for me to hang lights or lug scenery, to become one of those guys with the low-riding pants, their tool belts burdened with heavy wrenches and thick rolls of gaffer tape. Anyone thinking I might be trusted with electrical wiring had to be a complete idiot, and that's what this man was. I looked at him clearly then, noticing the way his tights made a mockery of his slack calves and dumpy little basket. Vibrant soul of a nomad, indeed. If he were such a big stinking deal, what was he doing in Raleigh? His blow-dried hair, the cheap Cuban-heeled shoes, and rainbow-striped suspenders—it was all a sham. Why wear tights with suspenders when their only redeeming feature was that they stayed up on their own—that's how they got their name, tights. And acting? The man performed as if the audience were deaf. He shouted his lines, grinning like a jack-o'-lantern and flailing his arms as if his sleeves were on fire. His was a form of acting that never fails to embarrass me. Watching him was like opening the door to a singing telegram: you know it's supposed to be entertaining, but you can't get beyond the sad fact that this person actually thinks he's bringing some joy into your life. Somewhere he had a mother who sifted through a shoe box of mimeographed playbills, pouring herself another drink and wondering when her son would come to his senses and swallow some drain cleaner.

I finally saw Hamlet for who he really was and recognized myself as the witless Yorick who had blindly followed along behind him.

My mother attended the opening-night performance. Following my leaden "Aye, my lord," I lay upon the grassy stage as Lois poured a false vial of poison into my ear. As I lay dying, I opened my eyes just a crack, catching sight of my mother stretched out on her hard, stone pew, fighting off the moths that, along with a few dozen seniors, had been attracted by the light.

There was a cast party afterward, but I didn't go. I changed my clothes in the dressing room, where the actors stood congratulating one another, repeating the words "brilliant" and "intense" as if they were describing the footlights. Horatio asked me to run to the store for cigarettes, and I pocketed his money, promising to return "with lightning speed, my lord."

"You were the best in the whole show," my mother said, stopping for frozen pizza on our way home. "I mean it, you walked onto that stage and all eyes went right to you."

It occurred to me then that my mother was a better actor than I could ever hope to be. Acting is different than posing or pretending. When done with precision, it bears a striking resemblance to lying. Stripped of the costumes and grand gestures, it presents itself as an unquestionable truth. I didn't envy my mother's skill, neither did I contradict her. That's how convincing she was. It seemed best, sitting beside her with a frozen pizza thawing on my lap, to simply sit back and learn.

David Sedaris
NPR commentator and best-selling author David Sedaris has been called "the funniest man alive" by Time Out New York, *and* Time *magazine named him Humorist of the Year in 2001. Sedaris is the author of* Barrel Fever, Naked, Holidays on Ice, *and* Me Talk Pretty One Day. *He is known for his commentaries on National Public Radio's* Morning Edition *and his essays appear regularly in* Esquire. *He is the recipient of the Thurber Prize for American Humor. David and his sister, Amy Sedaris, have written several plays together, including* Stump the Host, Stitches, One Woman Shoe, Incident at Cobbler's Knob, *and* The Book of Liz. *Born in 1957 in Raleigh, North Carolina, a former apartment cleaner and Macy's Christmas elf, Sedaris now lives with his partner in Paris.*

The Knife

Richard Selzer

One holds the knife as one holds the bow of a cello or a tulip—by the stem. Not palmed nor gripped nor grasped, but lightly, with the tips of the fingers. The knife is not for pressing. It is for drawing across the field of skin. Like a slender fish, it waits, at the ready, then, go! It darts, followed by a fine wake of red. The flesh parts, falling away to yellow globules of fat. Even now, after so many times, I still marvel at its power—cold, gleaming, silent. More, I am still struck with a kind of dread that it is I in whose hand the blade travels, that my hand is its vehicle, that yet again this terrible steel-bellied thing and I have conspired for a most unnatural purpose, the laying open of the body of a human being.

A stillness settles in my heart and is carried to my hand. It is the quietude of resolve layered over fear. And it is this resolve that lowers us, my knife and me, deeper and deeper into the person beneath. It is an entry into the body that is nothing like a caress; still, it is among the gentlest of acts. Then stroke and stroke again, and we are joined by other instruments, hemostats and forceps, until the wound blooms with strange flowers whose looped handles fall to the sides in steely array.

There is sound, the tight click of clamps fixing teeth into severed blood vessels, the snuffle and gargle of the suction machine clearing the field of blood for the next stroke, the litany of monosyllables with which one prays his way down and in: *clamp, sponge, suture, tie, cut.* And there is color. The green of the cloth, the white of the sponges, the red and yellow of the body. Beneath the fat lies the fascia, the tough fibrous sheet encasing the muscles. It must be sliced and the red beef of the muscles separated. Now there are retractors to hold apart the wound. Hands move together, part, weave. We are fully engaged, like children absorbed in a game or the craftsmen of some place like Damascus.

Deeper still. The peritoneum, pink and gleaming and membranous, bulges into the wound. It is grasped with forceps, and opened. For the first time we can see into the cavity of the abdomen. Such a primitive place. One expects to find drawings of buffalo on the walls. The sense of trespassing is keener now, heightened by the world's light illuminating the organs, their secret colors revealed—maroon and salmon and yellow. The vista is sweetly vulnerable at this moment, a kind of welcoming. An arc of the liver shines high and on the right, like a dark sun. It laps over the pink sweep of the stomach, from whose lower border the gauzy omentum is draped, and through which veil one sees, sinuous, slow as just-fed snakes, the indolent coils of the intestine.

You turn aside to wash your gloves. It is a ritual cleansing. One enters this temple doubly washed. Here is man as microcosm, representing in all his parts the earth, perhaps the universe.

I must confess that the priestliness of my profession has ever been impressed on me. In the beginning there are vows, taken with all solemnity. Then there is the endless harsh novitiate of training, much fatigue, much sacrifice. At last one emerges as celebrant, standing close to the truth lying curtained in the Ark of the body. Not surplice and cassock but mask and gown are your regalia. You hold no chalice, but a knife. There is no wine, no wafer. There are only the facts of blood and flesh.

And if the surgeon is like a poet, then the scars you have made on countless bodies are like verses into the fashioning of which you have poured your soul. I think that if years later I were to see the trace from an old incision of mine, I should know it at once, as one recognizes his pet expressions.

But mostly you are a traveler in a dangerous country, advancing into the moist and jungly cleft your hands have made. Eyes and ears are shuttered from the land you left behind; mind empties itself of all other thought. You are the root of groping fingers. It is a fine hour for the fingers, their sense of touch so enhanced. The blind must know this feeling. Oh, there is risk everywhere. One goes lightly. The spleen. No! No! Do not touch the spleen that lurks below the left leaf of the diaphragm, a manta ray in a coral cave, its bloody tongue protruding. One poke and it might rupture, exploding with sudden hemorrhage. The filmy omentum must not be torn, the intestine scraped or denuded. The hand finds the liver, palms it, fingers running along its sharp lower edge, admiring. Here are the twin mounds of the kidneys, the apron of the omentum hanging in front of the intestinal coils. One lifts it aside and the fingers dip among the loops, searching, mapping territory, establishing boundaries. Deeper still, and the womb is touched, then held like a small muscular bottle—the womb and its earlike appendages, the ovaries. How they do nestle in the cup of a man's hand, their power all dormant. They are frailty itself.

There is a hush in the room. Speech stops. The hands of the others, assistants and nurses, are still. Only the voice of the patient's respiration remains. It is the rhythm of a quiet sea, the sound of waiting. Then you speak, slowly, the terse entries of a Himalayan climber reporting back.

"The stomach is okay. Greater curvature clean. No sign of ulcer. Pylorus, duodenum fine. Now comes the gall-bladder. No stones. Right kidney, left, all right. Liver . . . uh-oh."

Your speech lowers to a whisper, falters, stops for a long, long moment, then picks up again at the end of a sigh that comes through your mask like a last exhalation.

"Three big hard ones in the left lobe, one on the right. Metastatic deposits. Bad, bad. Where's the primary? Got to be coming from somewhere."

The arm shifts direction and the fingers drop lower and lower into the pelvis—the body impaled now upon the arm of the surgeon to the hilt of the elbow.

"Here it is."

The voice goes flat, all business now.

"Tumor in the sigmoid colon, wrapped all around it, pretty tight. We'll take out a sleeve of the bowel. No colostomy. Not that, anyway. But, God, there's a lot of it down there. Here, you take a feel."

You step back from the table, and lean into a sterile basin of water, resting on stiff arms, while the others locate the cancer.

When I was a small boy, I was taken by my father, a general practitioner in Troy, New York, to St. Mary's Hospital, to wait while he made his rounds. The solarium where I sat was all sunlight and large plants. It smelled of soap and starch and clean linen. In the spring, clouds of lilac billowed from the vases; and in the fall, chrysanthemums crowded the magazine tables. At one end of the great high-ceilinged, glass-walled room was a huge cage where colored finches streaked and sang. Even from the first, I sensed the nearness of that other place, the Operating Room, knew that somewhere on these premises was that secret dreadful enclosure where *surgery* was at that moment happening. I sat among the cut flowers, half drunk on the scent, listening to the robes of the nuns brush the walls of the corridor, and felt the awful presence of *surgery*.

Oh, the pageantry! I longed to go there. I feared to go there. I imagined surgeons bent like storks over the body of the patient, a circle of red painted across the abdomen. Silence and dignity and awe enveloped them, these surgeons; it was the bubble in which they bent and straightened. Ah, it was a place I would never see, a place from whose walls the hung and suffering Christ turned his affliction to highest purpose. It is thirty years since I yearned for that old Surgery. And now I merely break the beam of an electric eye, and double doors swing open to let me enter, and as I enter, always, I feel the surging of a force that I feel in no other place. It is as though I am suddenly stronger and larger, heroic. Yes, that's it!

The operating room is called a theatre. One walks onto a set where the cupboards hold tanks of oxygen and other gases. The cabinets store steel cutlery of unimagined versatility, and the refrigerators are filled with bags of blood. Bodies are stroked and penetrated here, but no love is made. Nor is it ever allowed to grow dark, but must always gleam with a grotesque brightness. For the special congress into which patient and surgeon enter, the one must have his senses deadened, the other his sensibilities restrained. One lies naked, blind, offering; the other stands masked and gloved. One yields; the other does his will.

I said no love is made here, but love happens. I have stood aside with lowered gaze while a priest, wearing the purple scarf of office, administers Last Rites to the man I shall operate upon. I try not to listen to those terrible last questions, the answers, but hear, with scorching clarity, the words that formalize the expectation of death. For a moment my resolve falters before the resignation, the *attentiveness,* of the other two. I am like an executioner who hears the cleric comforting the prisoner. For the moment I am excluded from the centrality of the event, a mere technician standing by. But it is only for the moment.

The priest leaves, and we are ready. Let it begin.

Later, I am repairing the strangulated hernia of an old man. Because of his age and frailty, I am using local anesthesia. He is awake. His name is Abe Kaufman, and he is a Russian Jew. A nurse sits by his head, murmuring to him. She wipes his forehead. I know her very well. Her name is Alexandria, and she is the daughter of Ukrainian peasants. She has a flat steppe of a face and slanting eyes. Nurse and patient are speaking of blintzes, borscht, piroshki—Russian food that they both love. I listen, and think that it may have been her grandfather who raided the shtetl where the old man lived long ago, and in his high boots and his blouse and his fury this grandfather pulled Abe by his side curls to the ground and stomped his face and kicked his groin. Perhaps it was that ancient kick that caused the hernia I am fixing. I listen to them whispering behind the screen at the head of the table. I listen with breath held before the prism of history.

"Tovarich," she says, her head bent close to his.

He smiles up at her, and forgets that his body is being laid open.

"You are an angel," the old man says.

One can count on absurdity. There, in the midst of our solemnities, appears, small and black and crawling, an insect: The Ant of the Absurd. The belly is open; one has seen and felt the catastrophe within. It seems the patient is already vaporizing into angelhood in the heat escaping therefrom. One could warm one's hands in that fever. All at once that ant is there, emerging from beneath one of the sterile towels that border the operating field. For a moment one does not really see it, or else denies the sight, so impossible it is, marching precisely, heading briskly toward the open wound.

Drawn from its linen lair, where it snuggled in the steam of the great sterilizer, and survived, it comes. Closer and closer, it hurries toward the incision. Ant, art thou in the grip of some fatal *ivresse?* Wouldst hurtle over these scarlet cliffs into the very boil of the guts? Art mad for the reek we handle? Or in some secret act of formication engaged?

The alarm is sounded. An ant! An ant! And we are unnerved. Our fear of defilement is near to frenzy. It is not the mere physical contamination that we loathe. It is the evil of the interloper, that he scurries across our holy place, and filthies our altar. He *is* disease—that for whose destruction we have gathered. Powerless to destroy the sickness before us, we turn to its incarnation with a vengeance, and pluck it from the lip of the incision in the nick of time. Who would have thought an ant could move so fast?

Between thumb and forefinger, the intruder is crushed. It dies as quietly as it lived. Ah, but now there is death in the room. It is a perversion of our purpose. Albert Schweitzer would have spared it, scooped it tenderly into his hand, and lowered it to the ground.

The corpselet is flicked into the specimen basin. The gloves are changed. New towels and sheets are placed where it walked. We are pleased to have done something, if only a small killing. The operation resumes, and we draw upon ourselves once more the sleeves of office and rank. Is our reverence for life in question?

In the room the instruments lie on trays and tables. They are arranged precisely by the scrub nurse, in an order that never changes, so that you can reach blindly for a forceps or hemostat without looking away from the operating field. The instruments lie *thus!* Even at the beginning, when all is clean and tidy and no blood has been spilled, it is the scalpel that dominates. It has a figure the others do not have, the retractors and the scissors. The scalpel is all grace and line, a fierceness. It grins. It is like a cat—to be respected, deferred to, but which returns no amiability. To hold it above a belly is to know the knife's force—as though were you to give it slightest rein, it would pursue an intent of its own, driving into the flesh, a wild energy.

In a story by Borges, a deadly knife fight between two rivals is depicted. It is not, however, the men who are fighting. It is the knives themselves that are settling their own old score. The men who hold the knives are mere adjuncts to the weapons. The unguarded knife is like the unbridled war-horse that not only carries its helpless rider to his death, but tramples all beneath its hooves. The hand of the surgeon must tame this savage thing. He is a rider reining to capture a pace.

So close is the joining of knife and surgeon that they are like the Centaur—the knife, below, all equine energy, the surgeon, above, with his delicate art. One holds the knife back as much as advances it to purpose. One is master of the scissors. One is partner, sometimes rival, to the knife. In a moment it is like the long red fingernail of the Dragon Lady. Thus does the surgeon curb in order to create, restraining the scalpel, governing it shrewdly, setting the action of the operation into a pattern, giving it form and purpose.

It is the nature of creatures to live within a tight cuirass that is both their constriction and their protection. The carapace of the turtle is his fortress and retreat, yet keeps him writhing on his back in the sand. So is the surgeon rendered impotent by his own empathy and compassion. The surgeon cannot weep. When he cuts the flesh, his own must not bleed. Here it is all work. Like an asthmatic hungering for air, longing to take just one deep breath, the surgeon struggles not to feel. It is suffocating to press the feeling out. It would be easier to weep or mourn—for you know that the lovely precise world of proportion contains, just beneath, *there,* all disaster, all disorder. In a surgical operation, a risk may flash into reality: the patient dies . . . of *complication.* The patient knows this too, in a more direct and personal way, and he is afraid.

And what of that *other,* the patient, you, who are brought to the operating room on a stretcher, having been washed and purged and dressed in a white gown? Fluid drips from a bottle into your arm, diluting you, leaching your body of its personal brine. As you wait in the corridor, you hear from behind the closed door the angry clang of steel upon steel, as though a battle were being waged. There is the odor of antiseptic and ether, and masked women hurry up and down the halls, in and out of rooms. There is the watery sound of strange machinery, the tinny beeping that is the transmitted heartbeat of yet another *human being*. And all the while the dreadful knowledge that soon you will be taken, laid beneath great lamps that will reveal the secret linings of your body. In the very act of lying down, you have made a declaration of surrender. One lies down gladly for sleep or for love. But to give over one's body and will for surgery, to *lie down* for it, is a yielding of more than we can bear.

Soon a man will stand over you, gowned and hooded. In time the man will take up a knife and crack open your flesh like a ripe melon. Fingers will rummage among your viscera. Parts of you will be cut out. Blood will run free. Your blood. All the night before you have turned with the presentiment of death upon you. You have attended your funeral, wept with your mourners. You think, "I should never have had surgery in the springtime." It is too cruel. Or on a Thursday. It is an unlucky day.

Now it is time. You are wheeled in and moved to the table. An injection is given. "Let yourself go," I say. "It's a pleasant sensation," I say. "Give in," I say.

Let go? Give in? When you know that you are being tricked into the hereafter, that you will end when consciousness ends? As the monstrous silence of anesthesia falls discourteously across your brain, you watch your soul drift off.

Later, in the recovery room, you awaken and gaze through the thickness of drugs at the world returning, and you guess, at first dimly, then surely, that you have not died. In pain and nausea you will know the exultation of death averted, of life restored.

What is it, then, this thing, the knife, whose shape is virtually the same as it was three thousand years ago, but now with its head grown detachable? Before steel, it was bronze. Before bronze, stone—then back into unremembered time. Did man invent it or did the knife precede him here, hidden under ages of vegetation and hoofprints, lying in wait to be discovered, picked up, used?

The scalpel is in two parts, the handle and the blade. Joined, it is six inches from tip to tip. At one end of the handle is a narrow notched prong upon which the blade is slid, then snapped into place. Without the blade, the handle has a blind, decapitated look. It is helpless as a trussed maniac. But slide on the blade, click it home, and the knife springs instantly to life. It is headed now, edgy, leaping to mount the fingers for the gallop to its feast.

Now is the moment from which you have turned aside, from which you have averted your gaze, yet toward which you have been hastened. Now the scalpel sings along the flesh again, its brute run unimpeded by germs or other frictions. It is a slick slide home, a barracuda spurt, a rip of embedded talon. One listens, and almost hears the whine—nasal, high, delivered through that gleaming metallic snout. The flesh splits with its own kind of moan. It is like the penetration of rape.

The breasts of women are cut off, arms and legs sliced to the bone to make ready for the saw, eyes freed from sockets, intestines lopped. The hand of the surgeon rebels. Tension boils through his pores, like sweat. The flesh of the patient retaliates with hemorrhage, and the blood chases the knife wherever it is withdrawn.

Within the belly a tumor squats, toadish, fungoid. A gray mother and her brood. The only thing it does not do is croak. It too is hacked from its bed as the carnivore knife lips the blood, turning in it in a kind of ecstasy of plenty, a gluttony after the long fast. It is just for this that the knife was created, tempered, heated, its violence beaten into paper-thin force.

At last a little thread is passed into the wound and tied. The monstrous booming fury is stilled by a tiny thread. The tempest is silenced. The operation is over. On the table, the knife lies spent; on its side, the bloody meal smear-dried upon its flanks. The knife rests.

And waits.

Richard Selzer

In addition to being a writer, Richard Selzer is a surgeon. Born in 1928 in Troy, New York, Dr. Selzer was Assistant Clinical Professor of Surgery at Yale until 1985, and he also maintained a private practice. His experiences in the field of medicine are often the focus of his writing. In 1973, he published Rituals of Surgery, *a collection of short stories. He went on to publish* Mortal Lessons: Notes on the Art of Surgery, Confessions of a Knife *(a collection of 24 essays)*, Letters to a Young Doctor, Taking in the World for Repairs, Imagine a Woman *(five novellas)*, and A Mile and a Half of Ink *(a diary)*. His articles have appeared in numerous periodicals, including* Esquire *and* Harper's. *He is the recipient of many awards, including a National Magazine Award, an American Medical Writers Award, and a Guggenheim fellowship.*

Three Fragments

Charles Simic

I didn't tell you how I got lice wearing a German helmet. This used to be a famous story in our family. I remember those winter evenings just after the war with everybody huddled around the stove, talking and worrying late into the night. Sooner or later, somebody would bring up my German helmet full of lice. They thought it was the funniest thing they ever heard. Old people had tears of laughter in their eyes. A kid dumb enough to walk around with a German helmet full of lice. They were crawling all over it. Any fool could see them!

I sat there saying nothing, pretending to be equally amused, nodding my head while thinking to myself, what a bunch of idiots! All of them! They had no idea how I got the helmet, and I wasn't about to tell them.

It was in those first days just after the liberation of Belgrade, I was up in the old cemetery with a few friends, kind of snooping around. Then, all of a sudden, we saw them! A couple of German soldiers, obviously dead, stretched out on the ground. We drew closer to take a better look. They had no weapons. Their boots were gone, but there was a helmet that had fallen to the side of one of them. I don't remember what the others got, but I went for the helmet. I tiptoed so as not to wake the dead man. I also kept my eyes averted. I never saw his face, even if sometimes I think I did. Everything else about that moment is still intensely clear to me.

That's the story of the helmet full of lice.

Beneath the swarm of high-flying planes we were eating watermelon. While we ate the bombs fell on Belgrade. We watched the smoke rise in the distance. We were hot in the garden and asked to take our shirts off. The watermelon made a ripe, cracking noise as my mother cut it with a big knife. We also heard what we thought was thunder, but when we looked up, the sky was cloudless and blue.

My mother heard a man plead for his life once. She remembers the stars, the dark shapes of trees along the road on which they were fleeing the Austrian army in a slow-moving ox-cart. "That man sounded terribly frightened out there in the woods," she says. The cart went on. No one said anything. Soon they could hear the river they were supposed to cross.

Charles Simic

Charles Simic was born in Yugoslavia in 1938, and he moved to the United States with his family when he was 15. Just two years after getting his first poems published, he was drafted into the U.S. Army in 1961. He went on to publish What the Grass Says, *his first poetry collection, in 1967. Simic has now published over sixty books, including* Jackstraws *(a* New York Times *Notable Book of the Year),* Walking the Black Cat *(a National Book Award in Poetry finalist), and* The World Doesn't End: Prose Poems *(for which he received the Pulitzer Prize for Poetry). In 1998, he published* Orphan Factory, *his most recent book of essays. Simic's awards include fellowships from the Guggenheim Foundation, the MacArthur Foundation, and the National Endowment for the Arts. Today he is an English Professor at the University of New Hampshire.*

The Coroner's Photographs

Brent Staples

My brother's body lies dead and naked on a stainless steel slab. At his head stands a tall arched spigot that, with tap handles mimicking wings, easily suggests a swan in mourning. His head is squarish and overlarge. (This, when he was a toddler, made him seem top-heavy and unsteady on his feet.) His widow's peak is common among the men in my family, though this one is more dramatic than most. An inverted pyramid, it begins high above the temples and falls steeply to an apex in the boxy forehead, over the heart-shaped face. A triangle into a box over a heart. His eyes (closed here) were big and dark and glittery; they drew you into his sadness when he cried. The lips are ajar as always, but the picture is taken from such an angle that it misses a crucial detail: the left front tooth tucked partly beyond the right one. I need this detail to see my brother full. I paint it in from memory.

A horrendous wound runs the length of the abdomen, from the sternum all the way to the pubic mound. The wound resembles a mouth whose lips are pouting and bloody. Massive staplelike clamps are gouged into these lips at regular intervals along the abdomen. This is a surgeon's incision. The surgeon was presented with a patient shot six times with a large-caliber handgun. Sensing the carnage that lay

within, he achieved the largest possible opening and worked franti-
cally trying to save my brother's life. He tied off shattered vessels, re-
sectioned the small intestine, repaired a bullet track on the liver, then
backed out. The closing would have required two pairs of hands. An
assistant would have gripped the two sides of the wound and drawn
them together while a second person cut in the clamps. The pulling
together has made my brother's skin into a corset that crushes in on
the abdomen from all sides. The pelvic bones jut up through the skin.
The back is abnormally arched from the tension. The wound strains at
the clamps, threatening to rip itself open. The surgeon worked all
night and emerged from surgery gaunt, his greens darkened with
sweat. "I tied off everything I could," he said, and then he wept at the
savagery and the waste.

   This is the body of Blake Melvin Staples, the seventh of my family's nine children, the third of my four brothers, born ten years after
me. I know his contours well. I bathed and diapered him when he
was a baby and studied his features as he grew. He is the smallest of
the brothers, but is built in the same manner: short torso but long
arms and legs; a more than ample behind set high on the back;
knocking knees; big feet that tend to flat. The second toe is also a signature. It curls softly in an extended arc and rises above the others in
a way that's unique to us. His feelings are mine as well. Cold: The
sensation moves from my eyes to my shoulder blades to my bare ass
as I feel him naked on the steel. I envision the reflex that would run
through his body, hear the sharp breath he would draw when steel
met his skin. Below the familiar feet a drain awaits the blood that will
flow from this autopsy.

   The medical examiner took this picture and several on February
13, 1984, at 9:45 A.M. The camera's flash is visible everywhere: on the
pale-green tiles of the surrounding walls, on the gleaming neck of the
spigot, on the stainless steel of the slab, on the bloody lips of the
wound.

The coroner's report begins with a terse narrative summary: "The deceased, twenty-two-year-old Negro male, was allegedly shot by another person on the premises of a night club as a result of a 'long
standing quarrel.' He sustained multiple gunshot wounds of the abdomen and legs and expired during surgery."

Blake was a drug dealer; he was known for carrying guns and for using them. His killer, Mark McGeorge, was a former customer and cocaine addict. At the trial Mark's lawyer described the shooting as a
gunfight in which Blake was beaten to the draw. This was doubtful.
Blake was shot six times: three times in the back. No weapon was
found on or near his body. Blake's gunbearer testified that my brother

was unarmed when Mark ambushed and gunned him down. But a gunbearer is not a plausible witness. A drug dealer known for shooting a rival in plain public view gets no sympathy from a jury. The jury turned back the prosecution's request for a conviction of murder in the first degree. Mark was found guilty of second-degree murder and sentenced to seven years in jail. Five years for the murder. Two years for using the gun.

Blake is said to have cried out for his life as he lay on the ground. "Please don't shoot me no more. I don't want to die." *"Please don't shoot me no more. I don't want to die."* His voice had a touch of that dullness one hears from the deaf, a result of ear infections he suffered as a child. The ear openings had narrowed to the size of pinholes. He tilted his head woefully from side to side trying to pour out the pain. His vowels were locked high in his throat, behind his nose. This voice kept him a baby to me. This is the voice in which he would have pleaded for his life.

The coroner dissects the body, organ by organ:

HEART:	300 grams. No valve or chamber lesions. Coronary arteries show no pathologic changes.
LUNGS:	900 grams combined. Moderate congestion. Tracheobronchial and arterial systems are not remarkable.
LIVER:	1950 grams. There is a sutured bullet track at the interlobar sulcus and anterior portion of the right hepatic lobe. There has been moderate subcapsular and intraparenchymal hemorrhage.
SPLEEN:	150 grams. No pathologic changes.
KIDNEYS:	300 grams combined. No pathologic changes.
ADRENALS:	No pathologic changes.
PANCREAS:	No pathologic changes.
GI TRACT:	The stomach is empty. Portions of the small bowel have been resected, along with portions of the omentum. The bowel surface is dusky reddish-brown, but does not appear gangrenous.
URINARY BLADDER:	Empty.
NECK ORGANS:	Intact. No airway obstructions.
BRAIN:	1490 grams. Sagittal and serial coronal sections show no discrete lesions or evidence of injury.

SKULL:	Intact.
VERTEBRAE:	Intact.
RIBS:	Intact.
PELVIS:	There is a chip fracture of the left pubic ramus, and there is also fracturing of the right pubic ramus. There is extensive fracturing of the left femur, and there is a through-and-through bullet wound of the right femur just below the hip joint.

The coroner describes the wounds in detail. The surgical incision and its grisly clamps are dismissed in a single sentence. The six bullet holes receive one full paragraph each. The coroner records the angle that each bullet traveled through the body, the organs it passed through along the way, and where it finally came to rest. With all this to occupy him, the coroner fails to note the scar on Blake's left hand. The scar lies in the webbing between the thumb and index finger and is the result of a gun accident. A shotgun recoiled when Blake fired it and drove the hammer deep into the web, opening a wound that took several stitches to close.

I saw the wound when it was fresh, six weeks before Blake was murdered. I was visiting Roanoke from Chicago, where I then lived. I sought Blake out to tell him that it was time to get out of the business and leave Roanoke. The signs of death were everywhere; his name was hot in the street. Blake and I were making small talk when we slapped each other five. Blake clutched his hand at the wrist and cried out in pain. Then he showed me the stitches. This ended the small talk. I told him that he was in danger of being killed if he didn't leave town.

Staples men have been monolinguists for generations. We love our own voices too much. Blake responded to my alarm by telling me stories. He told me about the awesome power of the shotgun that had injured him. He told me about making asses of the police when they raided his apartment looking for drugs. The door of his apartment was steel, he said; they'd sent for a tow truck to pull it from its frame. Inside they found him twiddling his thumbs in the bathroom. He'd flushed the cocaine down the toilet. The night he told me these stories was the last time I saw him alive.

Six weeks later my brother Bruce called me with the news "Brent, Blake is dead," he said. "Some guy pulled up in a car and emptied out on him with a magnum. Blake is dead." I told myself to feel nothing. I had already mourned Blake and buried him and was determined not to suffer his death a second time. I skipped the funeral and avoided Roanoke for the next three years. The next time I visited my family I went to see the Roanoke Commonwealth Attorney and questioned him about the case. He was polite and impatient. For him, everything about the killing had been said. This, after all, had been an ordinary death.

I asked to see the files. A secretary brought a manila pouch and handed it to the Commonwealth Attorney, who handed it to me and excused himself from the room. The pouch contained a summary of the trial, the medical examiner's report, and a separate inner pouch wrapped in twine and shaped like photographs. I opened the pouch; there was Blake dead and on the slab, photographed from several angles. The floor gave way, and I fell down and down for miles.

Brent Staples

Born in the economically depressed factory town of Chester, Pennsylvania in 1951, Brent Staples earned a PhD in psychology from the University of Chicago on a scholarship, and went on to pursue a career in journalism. He became the assistant metropolitan editor for the New York Times, *and he also served as editor of the* New York Times Book Review *and as a reporter for the* Chicago Sun Times. *Although Staples writes lyrically and insightfully about many topics, the one he always returns to is education, and his own success is convincing testimony of education's ability to change lives. His memoir,* Parallel Time: Growing Up in Black and White, *recalls his escape from life in a town where the culture of violence claimed his brother's life. The book was a finalist for the* Los Angeles Times *Book Award and won the Annisfield-Wolff Book Award.*

A Postcard Memoir

Lawrence Sutin

"Jeune Mère"

I was born to a strong and tender and frightened woman. My mother lost her parents and her sisters in the Holocaust. She was gang-raped by Russian partisans in the Polish woods after escaping from the Nazi ghetto established in her hometown of Stolpce. In marrying my father—a Jewish partisan leader who gave her shelter in an underground bunker—she was staking her soul on creating a new family. Her first baby, a boy, died shortly after his premature birth in the fall of 1945. Dread brought on that early delivery. My mother had learned of a pogrom carried out by Poles against those surviving Jews trying to return to their homes in the nearby town of Katowice. "Even after the Germans surrendered, the Poles continued to kill us," my mother told me. She told me everything from the time I was old enough to follow the basic sense, at six or so. I was the third child, after my unnamed dead brother and after my sister, who entered life in a displaced persons camp in Germany in 1947. As to bearing children, my mother knew an old Yiddish saying: "Three is two and two is one." My sister and I were both treated as if we were each the only one, the precious one, the one who could be lost at any time. I came out of my mother's womb on time and healthy in October 1951, the first member of the family born in America. But I was not born into an American home. There was herring, butter, and pumpernickel bread on our breakfast table, along with strong sweet tea. We spoke Yiddish a lot. As a young boy, I would ask Mother what we were having for dinner and she would tell me, "*drek mit leber,*" "shit with liver," meaning don't ask what there will be to eat, be thankful there will be something. When I was born, she remembered, I know, the emaciated lost one laid on the windowsill to die by a small-town Polish physician who had no way to treat him. Mother never wanted to give him a name. I never asked why but I knew that naming him would have made it worse. I was named after her father Lazar, in Hebrew Eliezer, in English Larry. I was one, living for two, and my mother was living for me, but fiercely, tending me like a bruise.

"Man and Boy"

Fathers more easily love their daughters. Sons are the continuation of us in an obvious sense, so obvious that it is unbearable. In the case of my father and myself, I had the fullness of his face and his desire to write, which had been abandoned when he came to America with a family to raise. What he wanted to see in me were the practical choices he had made confirmed. At times in my youth he justly found me clumsy, cowardly, callous, and he let it be known. His anger had, then, the finality of a curse. The great task in the life of a son is to realize that his father is right and then to proceed to be wrong. It's your only chance to become someone you haven't already met. My father also let his love be known. Once he cried because he feared I did not love him back. Lay down on his bed fully dressed in the middle of the day and cried. My mother found me and pulled me by my scruff to the doorway of their bedroom to see. She was hating me so I lay down beside him and hugged him. That was hard. He was a middle-aged man who was sobbing and sweaty and his body was heavy and so soft I imagined his ribs giving way like a snowman's on the first warm winter day. I could hear his heart and it sounded as if it was working harder than it could take. I hugged him until he stopped crying. I whispered in his ear that I loved him.

"The Fairchild Rambler" which makes tour of the garden. Fairchild Tropical Garden.

"Fairchild Tropical Garden"

My fifth-grade teacher took our class on a tour of a potato-chip factory. Her uncle was a manager there and made sure we got the best treatment—a free bag of Red Dot Chips for each of us, along with a red Red Dot baseball cap, a red Red Dot balloon, and a red round Red Dot plastic change purse you squeezed to open and close. We saw crates of potatoes poured into machines that washed, peeled, sliced, and sent the glistening discs on conveyor belts to boiling vats of oil. We saw fried chips draining and drying. The men and women who worked there were so covered with grease—it misted the air—that they seemed ready for frying themselves. Not doing what they had dreamed of doing as children, they took no pleasure in being observed by us. They understood that we kids were hoping we would never be them. Our teacher had arranged the tour to get herself out of the classroom in which her own dream was dying. She had always wanted to be beloved by her students. But none of us did love her—her gestures were stiff, her voice failed in the afternoons, her eyes wandered out the windows as often as ours did. Now, in the chip factory, as our cheeks swelled and reddened from humidity and oil, she nibbled at a new strategy, displaying the consequences of indifference to teachers and their lessons. You grew up and took readings on grease vats while kids watched.

"Father Holding Baby"

I say to you that I have been a good father. The one and only time I slipped hard came when Sarah was just a few months old. My wife Mab had gone off one evening to a meeting. Did the young suckling baby miss her mama? Yes, she did. Was Daddy confident with baby alone with him in the house? No. Shortly after Mama left, baby cried and Daddy fed her a bottle and some soft blended apricots from a glass jar. It was quiet for a while and baby played with colored rings on a blanket spread on the living-room carpet. Then baby started to cry again and Daddy picked her up and held her and walked with her and cooed to her and kissed her lightly on the top of her head and sang to her in the fleeciest voice he could some Grateful Dead ballads that had always sounded to him like lullabies. He had wanted to be a father someday and had thought he would be a good one because he wanted to be. Baby kept crying. Daddy kept walking and rocking baby in his arms and cooing and singing and trying to keep a smile on his face when it came close to hers. Baby kept crying. Baby kept crying. It was nearly an hour and the crying only stopped when baby sobbed, running out of breath. Sleep, baby. No. Baby kept crying. Crying. The sound of a cry is designed by nature to make you unable to stand it and determined to get it to stop. I couldn't. That's why I screamed at her to stop. Thank God at least I did not shake her. Then, shaking all over myself, I laid her on the sofa and sat across the room watching, but saying and doing no more as baby cried and gasped and caught her breath and cried until Mama finally came home. I was yellow and the baby was yellow and we glowed in the dimness of the house from our strain. I have failed to do a good many things in my life. All of those things bother me still, but none so much as that evening alone with a baby for whom a father did and was nothing.

Lawrence Sutin

Lawrence Sutin, memoirist and biographer, is the recipient of many awards for his writing. His published books include Jack and Rochelle: a Holocaust Story of Love and Resistance, Divine Invasions, A Life of Phillip K. Dick, *and the forthcoming* Do What Thou Wilt: A Life of Aleister Crowley. *He teaches in the MFA program at Hamline University in Saint Paul, Minnesota, the city in which he was born in 1951.*

Becoming What We're Called

Alice Walker

"Boy, Man, Fellow, Chap"

Last night before I could stop myself I put my arms around a dear friend who'd just said she'd see us later, "you guys!" and told her I don't like being called "guy." In fact, I told her, noting her puzzled expression, I detest it.

I remember once, many years ago, attending a spring festival in the seaside village of this same friend. The air was scented with early flowers, the sun was shining brightly off the ocean. My friend found a table for us not far from the grill on which hot dogs and tofu burgers were being flipped. Within minutes, unbeckoned, three teenage maidens brought us overflowing platters of food, freshly prepared, lovingly arranged, a feast. One was brown-haired, one blond, and one as red-headed as the daughter of my next-hill-over neighbors, who was named after the Irish Goddess Bridget. I suppose it was partly this that caused me to think of the three young women, so solicitous, so gracefully nurturing, as Goddesses. Thanking them, I was just about to comment on the Goddess nature of their behavior when my friend said cheerfully, "Thank you, you guys!" I felt they had not been seen, that their essential nature had been devalued, but I said nothing, not wanting to offend my friend.

Sometimes I think these struggles about identity will never end; this one reminds me of nothing so much as of the battle black people seem to have lost a decade ago against the word "nigger." Seeking to redeem it, to render it harmless, many people deliberately kept it alive among themselves. Now, because of rap, it is commonplace to hear it bouncing through the air, no matter where you are, and if you are not fond of it, you feel all the assault such a negative description brings. (*Nigger:* a vulgar, offensive term of hostility and contempt, as used by Negrophobes.) Recently, for instance, two other friends and I were walking through the San Francisco Botanical Garden, the only black people there, the only black women. It is crucial, living in the city, to have access to nature: a place where you can relax, be yourself, and relate to the magnificence of the earth without thinking every moment of life in a racist, violent society. We stood by a pond on which there were hundreds of birds and marveled at the way the fluttering of their wings stirred the air. It was a beautiful day. The sun was warm, the sky blue, the Asian magnolias in full expression. Suddenly, out of nowhere, it seemed, we heard, very loud, "black nigger black . . . dah, dah, dah." We looked about for the racist white man who had dared shatter our peace. He was not there. Instead, the retreating back of a young black man, bopping in tune to music from his Walkman, told the story. He was singing along with someone whose refrain, "black nigger black," he echoed. We watched as he swung along, oblivious to the beauty all around him, his attention solely on this song. He went the length of the garden, seeing nothing; only thinking of how he was black and a nigger and this was all the identity he had. It was like watching him throw mud, or worse, all over himself.

I have asked people, both men and women, why they like "you guys." Some admit they picked it up from a television commercial that seemed cute to them. Others add, incredibly, that they felt it was an all-inclusive term for males and females; they considered it gender free. Some recalled the expression "guys and gals" and said, laughing, nobody wanted to be "gals." I tried to imagine everyone in American calling themselves and each other "you gals." How many men would accept it? Personally, for gender-free inclusivity, I prefer the Southern expression "you all."

After the completion of *Warrior Marks,* a film we made about female genital mutilation, Pratibha Parmar and I premiered it in ten European and American cities, an exhausting but at times exhilarating tour. But after about the third city, we realized that the most exhausting thing was neither the travel nor the stress we experienced as we anticipated each audience's response to the film; it was having, at every theater, to endure the following questions: How long did it take "you guys" to do this? What was it like for "you guys" to travel and film in Africa? The women asking us these questions seemed blind to us, and in their blindness we felt our uniqueness as female creators disappear. We had recently been in societies where some or all of a woman's genitalia were forcibly cut from her by other women who collaborated—wholeheartedly, by now—with men. To us, the refusal to acknowledge us as women seemed a verbal expression of this same idea. It made us quite ill. After all, it would have been impossible for "guys" to make the film we had made. No women would have talked to them, for one thing. Each night, over and over, we told the women greeting us: We are not "guys." We are women. Many failed to get it. Others were amused. One woman amused *us,* she had so much difficulty not saying "you guys," every two minutes, even after we'd complained!

It would seem from the dictionary that the verb "guy" is another word for "guide," or "control": bearing a very real resemblance to "husband." It means "to steady, stay, or direct by means of a guy, from the French *guying.*" The noun means "a boy or man; fellow; chap." It means "a person whose appearance or dress is odd." Again, as a verb, "guy" can mean "to tease; to ridicule." And this last is how I feel it when the word is used by men referring to women, and by women referring to themselves. I see in its use some women's obsequious need to be accepted at any cost, even at the cost of erasing their own femaleness, and that of other women. Isn't it at least ironic that after so many years of struggle for women's liberation, women should end up calling themselves this?

I think my friend is probably exasperated with me because of what I said to her last night. After all, "you guys" is a habitual expression in conversation around the world; I am asking her not to call me something that comes easily, apparently, to her. I think perhaps I am a trying friend to have; one who wonders, as I can't help but do, why this should be so. The magic of naming is that people often become what they are called. What in me evokes this word from her? I will call her up in a day or two and suggest we go for a walk and discuss this issue in the open arena of nature, where the larkspur is not called delphinium and the hummingbird is not labeled dove. Grass is not called tree and rocks are not called bears. When I look at her I see a black woman daily overcoming incredible odds to live a decent, honest, even merry life. Someone who actively nurtures community wherever she goes. Someone who has raised a strong daughter and now showers affection and attention on a beautiful grandchild. I see someone who dances like a Nubian and cooks like a Creole. I don't respect "guys" enough to obliterate the woman that I see by calling her by their name.

Alice Walker

Alice Walker was born in 1944 in Georgia to sharecropper parents. She was active in the 1960s civil rights movement, and most of her work focuses on sexual and racial realities within African American communities as well as the connections between family and society. She is best known for her novel The Color Purple, *and she has published numerous other works of fiction, including* Meridian *and* By the Light of My Father's Smile; *books of poetry, including* Sent by Earth: A Message from the Grandmother Spirit after the Attacks on the World Trade Center and the Pentagon *and* Horses Make a Landscape Look More Beautiful; *and collections of essays including* Living by the Word: Selected Writings *and* In Search of Our Mother's Gardens.

Afternoon of an American Boy

E. B. White

When I was in my teens, I lived in Mount Vernon, in the same block with J. Parnell Thomas, who grew up to become chairman of the House Committee on Un-American Activities. I lived on the corner of Summit and East Sidney, at No. 101 Summit Avenue, and Parnell lived four or five doors north of us on the same side of the avenue, in the house the Diefendorfs used to live in.

Parnell was not a playmate of mine, as he was a few years older, but I used to greet him as he walked by our house on his way to and from the depot. He was a good-looking young man, rather quiet and shy. Seeing him, I would call "Hello, Parnell!" and he would smile and say "Hello, Elwyn!" and walk on. Once I remember dashing out of our yard on roller skates and executing a rink turn in front of Parnell, to show off, and he said, "Well! Quite an artist, aren't you?" I remember the words. I was delighted at praise from an older man and sped away along the flagstone sidewalk, dodging the cracks I knew so well.

The thing that made Parnell a special man in my eyes in those days was not his handsome appearance and friendly manner but his sister. Her name was Eileen. She was my age and she was a quiet, nice-looking girl. She never came over to my yard to play, and I never went over there, and, considering that we lived so near each other, we were remarkably uncommunicative; nevertheless, she was the girl I singled out, at one point, to be of special interest to me. Being of special interest to me involved practically nothing on a girl's part—it simply meant that she was under constant surveillance. On my own part, it meant that I suffered an astonishing disintegration when I walked by her house, from embarrassment, fright, and the knowledge that I was in enchanted territory.

In the matter of girls, I was different from most boys of my age. I admired girls a lot, but they terrified me. I did not feel that I possessed the peculiar gifts or accomplishments that girls liked in their male companions—the ability to dance, to play football, to cut up a bit in public, to smoke, and to make small talk. I couldn't do any of these things successfully, and seldom tried. Instead, I stuck with the accomplishments I was sure of: I rode my bicycle sitting backward on the handle bars, I made up poems, I played selections from *Aïda* on the piano. In winter, I tended goal in the hockey games on the frozen pond in the dell. None of these tricks counted much with girls. In the four years I was in the Mount Vernon High School, I never went to a school dance and I never took a girl to a drugstore for a soda or to the Westchester Playhouse or to Proctor's. I wanted to do these things but did not have the nerve. What I finally did manage to do, however, and what is the subject of this memoir, was far brassier, far gaudier. As an exhibit of teen-age courage and ineptitude, it never fails to amaze me in retrospect. I am not even sure it wasn't un-American.

My bashfulness and backwardness annoyed my older sister very much, and at about the period of which I am writing she began making strong efforts to stir me up. She was convinced that I was in a rut, socially, and she found me a drag in her own social life, which was brisk. She kept trying to throw me with girls, but I always bounced. And whenever she saw a chance she would start the phonograph and grab me, and we would go charging around the parlor in the toils of the one-step, she gripping me as in a death struggle, and I hurling her finally away from me through greater strength. I was a skinny kid but my muscles were hard, and it would have taken an unusually powerful woman to have held me long in the attitude of the dance.

One day, through a set of circumstances I have forgotten, my sister managed to work me into an afternoon engagement she had with some others in New York. To me, at that time, New York was a wonderland largely unexplored. I had been to the Hippodrome a couple of times with my father, and to the Hudson-Fulton Celebration, and to a few matinées; but New York, except as a setting for extravaganzas, was unknown. My sister had heard tales of tea-dancing at the Plaza Hotel. She and a girl friend of hers and another fellow and myself went there to give it a try. The expedition struck me as a slick piece of arrangement on her part. I was the junior member of the group and had been roped in, I imagine, to give symmetry to the occasion. Or perhaps Mother had forbidden my sister to go at all unless another member of the family was along. Whether I was there for symmetry or for decency I can't really remember, but I was there.

The spectacle was a revelation to me. However repulsive the idea of dancing was, I was filled with amazement at the setup. Here were tables where a fellow could sit so close to the dance floor that he was practically on it. And you could order cinnamon toast and from the safety of your chair observe girls and men in close embrace, swinging along, the music playing while you ate the toast, and the dancers so near to you that they almost brushed the things off your table as they jogged by. I was impressed. Dancing or no dancing, this was certainly high life, and I knew I was witnessing a scene miles and miles ahead of anything that took place in Mount Vernon. I had never seen anything like it, and a ferment must have begun working in me that afternoon.

Incredible as it seems to me now, I formed the idea of asking Parnell's sister Eileen to accompany me to a tea dance at the Plaza. The plan shaped up in my mind as an expedition of unparalleled worldliness, calculated to stun even the most blasé girl. The fact that I didn't know how to dance must have been a powerful deterrent, but not powerful enough to stop me. As I look back on the affair, it's hard to credit my own memory, and I sometimes wonder if, in fact, the whole business isn't some dream that has gradually gained the status of actuality. A boy with any sense, wishing to become better acquainted with a girl who was "of special interest," would have cut out for himself a more modest assignment to start with—a soda date or a movie date—something within reasonable limits. Not me. I apparently became obsessed with the notion of taking Eileen to the Plaza and not to any darned old drugstore. I had learned the location of the Plaza, and just knowing how to get to it gave me a feeling of confidence. I had learned about cinnamon toast, so I felt able to cope with the waiter when he came along. And I banked heavily on the general splendor of the surroundings and the extreme sophistication of the function to carry the day, I guess.

I was three days getting up nerve to make the phone call. Meantime, I worked out everything in the greatest detail. I heeled myself with a safe amount of money. I looked up trains. I overhauled my clothes and assembled an outfit I believed would meet the test. Then, one night at six o'clock, when Mother and Father went downstairs to dinner, I lingered upstairs and entered the big closet off my bedroom where the wall phone was. There I stood for several minutes, trembling, my hand on the receiver, which hung upside down on the hook. (In our family, the receiver always hung upside down, with the big end up.)

I had rehearsed my first line and my second line. I planned to say, "Hello, can I please speak to Eileen?" Then, when she came to the phone, I planned to say, "Hello, Eileen, this is Elwyn White." From there on, I figured I could ad-lib it.

At last, I picked up the receiver and gave the number. As I had suspected, Eileen's mother answered.

"Can I please speak to Eileen?" I asked, in a low, troubled voice.

"Just a minute," said her mother. Then, on second thought, she asked, "Who is it, please?"

"It's Elwyn," I said.

She left the phone, and after quite a while Eileen's voice said, "Hello, Elwyn." This threw my second line out of whack, but I stuck to it doggedly.

"Hello, Eileen, this is Elwyn White," I said.

In no time at all I laid the proposition before her. She seemed dazed and asked me to wait a minute. I assume she went into a huddle with her mother. Finally, she said yes, she would like to go tea-dancing with me at the Plaza, and I said fine, I would call for her at quarter past three on Thursday afternoon, or whatever afternoon it was—I've forgotten.

I do not know now, and of course did not know then, just how great was the mental and physical torture Eileen went through that day, but the incident stacks up as a sort of unintentional un-American activity, for which I was solely responsible. It all went off as scheduled: the stately walk to the depot; the solemn train ride, during which we sat staring shyly into the seat in front of us; the difficult walk from Grand Central across Forty-second to Fifth, with pedestrians clipping us and cutting in between us; the bus ride to Fifty-ninth Street; then the Plaza itself, and the cinnamon toast, and the music, and the excitement. The thundering quality of the occasion must have delivered a mental shock to me, deadening my recollection, for I have only the dimmest memory of leading Eileen onto the dance floor to execute two or three unspeakable rounds, in which I vainly tried to adapt my violent sister-and-brother wrestling act into something graceful and appropriate. It must have been awful. And at six o'clock, emerging, I gave no thought to any further entertainment, such as dinner in town. I simply herded Eileen back all the long, dreary way to

Mount Vernon and deposited her, a few minutes after seven, on an empty stomach, at her home. Even if I had attempted to dine her, I don't believe it would have been possible; the emotional strain of the afternoon had caused me to perspire uninterruptedly, and any restaurant would have been justified in rejecting me solely on the ground that I was too moist.

Over the intervening years, I've often felt guilty about my afternoon at the Plaza, and many years ago, during Parnell's investigation of writers, my feeling sometimes took the form of a guilt sequence in which I imagined myself on the stand, in the committee room, being questioned. It went something like this:

PARNELL: Have you ever written for the screen, Mr. White?

ME: No, sir.

PARNELL: Have you ever been, or are you now, a member of the Screen Writers' Guild?

ME: No, sir.

PARNELL: Have you ever been, or are you now, a member of the Communist Party?

ME: No, sir.

Then, in this imaginary guilt sequence of mine, Parnell digs deep and comes up with the big question, calculated to throw me.

PARNELL: Do you recall an afternoon, along about the middle of the second decade of this century, when you took my sister to the Plaza Hotel for tea under the grossly misleading and false pretext that you knew how to dance?

And as my reply comes weakly, "Yes, sir," I hear the murmur run through the committee room and see reporters bending over their notebooks, scribbling hard. In my dream, I am again seated with Eileen at the edge of the dance floor, frightened, stunned, and happy—in my ears the intoxicating drumbeat of the dance, in my throat the dry, bittersweet taste of cinnamon.

I don't know about the guilt, really. I guess a good many girls might say that an excursion such as the one I conducted Eileen on belongs in the un-American category. But there must be millions of aging males, now slipping into their anecdotage, who recall their Willie Baxter period with affection, and who remember some similar journey into ineptitude, in that precious, brief moment in life before love's pages, through constant reference, had become dog-eared, and before its narrative, through sheer competence, had lost the first, wild sense of derring-do.

E. B. White

Although Elwyn Brooks White is best known for children's classics like Stuart Little, Charlotte's Web, *and* The Trumpet of the Swan, *he began his career as a journalist and essayist. He was one of the early staff writers for the* New Yorker *magazine, and his first published book—*Is Sex Necessary—*was a collaborative effort with fellow* New Yorker *writer James Thurber. His essay collections include* One Man's Meat, The Second Tree from the Corner, *and a final collection of his life's work,* The Essays of E. B. White. *He worked to bring out a posthumous edition of his teacher William Strunk's precepts on good writing, the now-classic* Elements of Style. *White received numerous awards, including the Presidential Medal for Freedom (awarded by John F. Kennedy), the National Institute of Arts and Letters' Gold Medal for Essays and Criticism, the National Medal for Literature, and the Pulitzer Prize. Born in Mt. Vernon, New York in 1899, White died on October 1, 1985.*

The Clan of One-Breasted Women

Terry Tempest Williams

I belong to a Clan of One-Breasted Women. My mother, my grand-mothers, and six aunts have all had mastectomies. Seven are dead. The two who survive have just completed rounds of chemotherapy and radiation.

I've had my own problems: two biopsies for breast cancer and a small tumor between my ribs diagnosed as a "borderline malignancy."

This is my family history.

Most statistics tell us breast cancer is genetic, hereditary, with rising percentages attached to fatty diets, childlessness, or becoming pregnant after thirty. What they don't say is living in Utah may be the greatest hazard of all.

We are a Mormon family with roots in Utah since 1847. The "word of wisdom" in my family aligned us with good foods—no coffee, no tea, tobacco, or alcohol. For the most part, our women were finished having their babies by the time they were thirty. And only one faced breast cancer prior to 1960. Traditionally, as a group of people, Mormons have a low rate of cancer.

Is our family a cultural anomaly? The truth is, we didn't think about it. Those who did, usually the men, simply said, "bad genes." The women's attitude was stoic. Cancer was part of life. On February 16, 1971, the eve of my mother's surgery, I accidently picked up the telephone and overheard her ask my grandmother what she could expect.

"Diane, it is one of the most spiritual experiences you will ever encounter."

I quietly put down the receiver.

Two days later, my father took my brothers and me to the hospital to visit her. She met us in the lobby in a wheelchair. No bandages were visible. I'll never forget her radiance, the way she held herself in a purple velvet robe and how she gathered us around her.

"Children, I am fine. I want you to know I felt the arms of God around me."

We believed her. My father cried. Our mother, his wife, was thirty-eight years old.

A little over a year after Mother's death, Dad and I were having dinner together. He had just returned from St. George, where the Tempest Company was completing the gas lines that would service southern Utah. He spoke of his love for the country, the sandstoned landscape, bare-boned and beautiful. He had just finished hiking the Kolob trail in Zion National Park. We got caught up in reminiscing, recalling with fondness our walk up Angel's Landing on his fiftieth birthday and the years our family had vacationed there.

Over dessert, I shared a recurring dream of mine. I told my father that for years, as long as I could remember, I saw this flash of light in the night in the desert—that this image had so permeated my being that I could not venture south without seeing it again, on the horizon, illuminating buttes and mesas.

"You did see it," he said.

"Saw what?"

"The bomb. The cloud. We were driving home from Riverside, California. You were sitting on Diane's lap. She was pregnant. In fact, I remember the day, September 7, 1957. We had just gotten out of the Service. We were driving north, past Las Vegas. It was an hour or so before dawn, when this explosion went off. We not only heard it, but felt it. I thought the oil tanker in front of us had blown up. We pulled over and suddenly, rising from the desert floor, we saw it, clearly, this golden-stemmed cloud, the mushroom. The sky seemed to vibrate with an eerie pink glow. Within a few minutes, a light ash was raining on the car."

I stared at my father.

"I thought you knew that," he said. "It was a common occurrence in the fifties."

It was at this moment that I realized the deceit I had been living under. Children growing up in the American Southwest, drinking contaminated milk from contaminated cows, even from the contaminated breasts of their mothers, my mother—members, years later, of the Clan of One-Breasted Women.

It is a well-known story in the Desert West, "The Day We Bombed Utah," or more accurately, the years we bombed Utah: above ground atomic testing in Nevada took place from January 27, 1951 through July 11, 1962. Not only were the winds blowing north covering "low-use segments of the population" with fallout and leaving sheep dead in their tracks, but the climate was right. The United States of the 1950s was red, white, and blue. The Korean War was raging. McCarthyism was rampant. Ike was it, and the cold war was hot. If you were against nuclear testing, you were for a communist regime.

Much has been written about this "American nuclear tragedy." Public health was secondary to national security. The Atomic Energy Commissioner, Thomas Murray, said, "Gentlemen, we must not let anything interfere with the series of tests, nothing."

Again and again, the American public was told by its government, in spite of burns, blisters, and nausea, "It has been found that the tests may be conducted with adequate assurance of safety under conditions prevailing at the bombing reservations." Assuaging public fears was simply a matter of public relations. "Your best action," an Atomic Energy Commission booklet read, "is not to be worried about fallout." A news release typical of the times stated, "We find no basis for concluding that harm to any individual has resulted from radioactive fallout."

On August 30, 1979, during Jimmy Carter's presidency, a suit was filed, *Irene Allen v. The United States of America.* Mrs. Allen's case was the first on an alphabetical list of twenty-four test cases, representative of nearly twelve hundred plaintiffs seeking compensation from the United States government for cancers caused by nuclear testing in Nevada.

Irene Allen lived in Hurricane, Utah. She was the mother of five children and had been widowed twice. Her first husband, with their two oldest boys, had watched the tests from the roof of the local high school. He died of leukemia in 1956. Her second husband died of pancreatic cancer in 1978.

In a town meeting conducted by Utah Senator Orrin Hatch, shortly before the suit was filed, Mrs. Allen said, "I am not blaming the government, I want you to know that, Senator Hatch. But I thought if my testimony could help in any way so this wouldn't happen again to any of the generations coming up after us . . . I am happy to be here this day to bear testimony of this."

God-fearing people. This is just one story in an anthology of thousands.

On May 10, 1984, Judge Bruce S. Jenkins handed down his opinion. Ten of the plaintiffs were awarded damages. It was the first time a federal court had determined that nuclear tests had been the cause of cancers. For the remaining fourteen test cases, the proof of causation was not sufficient. In spite of the split decision, it was considered a landmark ruling. It was not to remain so for long.

In April 1987, the Tenth Circuit Court of Appeals overturned Judge Jenkins's ruling on the ground that the United States was protected from suit by the legal doctrine of sovereign immunity, a centuries-old idea from England in the days of absolute monarchs.

In January 1988, the Supreme Court refused to review the Appeals Court decision. To our court system it does not matter whether the United States government was irresponsible, whether it lied to its citizens, or even that citizens died from the fallout of nuclear testing. What matters is that our government is immune: "The King can do no wrong."

In Mormon culture, authority is respected, obedience is revered, and independent thinking is not. I was taught as a young girl not to "make waves" or "rock the boat."

"Just let it go," Mother would say. "You know how you feel, that's what counts."

For many years, I have done just that—listened, observed, and quietly formed my own opinions, in a culture that rarely asks questions because it has all the answers. But one by one, I have watched the women in my family die common, heroic deaths. We sat in waiting rooms hoping for good news, but always receiving the bad. I cared for them, bathed their scarred bodies, and kept their secrets. I watched beautiful women become bald as Cytoxan, cisplatin, and Adriamycin were injected into their veins. I held their foreheads as they vomited green-black bile, and I shot them with morphine when the pain became inhuman. In the end, I witnessed their last peaceful breaths, becoming a midwife to the rebirth of their souls.

The price of obedience has become too high.

The fear and inability to question authority that ultimately killed rural communities in Utah during atmospheric testing of atomic weapons is the same fear I saw in my mother's body. Sheep. Dead sheep. The evidence is buried.

I cannot prove that my mother, Diane Dixon Tempest, or my grandmothers, Lettie Romney Dixon and Kathryn Blackett Tempest, along with my aunts developed cancer from nuclear fallout in Utah. But I can't prove they didn't.

My father's memory was correct. The September blast we drove through in 1957 was part of Operation Plumbbob, one of the most intensive series of bomb tests to be initiated. The flash of light in the night in the desert, which I had always thought was a dream, developed into a family nightmare. It took fourteen years, from 1957 to 1971, for cancer to manifest in my mother—the same time, Howard L. Andrews, an authority in radioactive fallout at the National Institutes of Health, says radiation cancer requires to become evident. The more I learn about what it means to be a "downwinder," the more questions I drown in.

What I do know, however, is that as a Mormon woman of the fifth generation of Latter-day Saints, I must question everything, even if it means losing my faith, even if it means becoming a member of a border tribe among my own people. Tolerating blind obedience in the name of patriotism or religion ultimately takes our lives.

When the Atomic Energy Commission described the country north of the Nevada Test Site as "virtually uninhabited desert terrain," my family and the birds at Great Salt Lake were some of the "virtual uninhabitants."

One night, I dreamed women from all over the world circled a blazing fire in the desert. They spoke of change, how they hold the moon in their bellies and wax and wane with its phases. They mocked the presumption of even-tempered beings and made promises that they would never fear the witch inside themselves. The women danced wildly as sparks broke away from the flames and entered the night sky as stars.

And they sang a song given to them by Shoshone grandmothers:

Ah ne nah, nah	Consider the rabbits
nin nah nah—	How gently they walk on the earth—
ah ne nah, nah	Consider the rabbits
nin nah nah—	How gently they walk on the earth—
Nyaga mutzi	We remember them
oh ne nay—	We can walk gently also—
Nyaga mutzi	We remember them
oh ne nay—	We can walk gently also—

The women danced and drummed and sang for weeks, preparing themselves for what was to come. They would reclaim the desert for the sake of their children, for the sake of the land.

A few miles downwind from the fire circle, bombs were being tested. Rabbits felt the tremors. Their soft leather pads on paws and feet recognized the shaking sands, while the roots of mesquite and sage were smoldering. Rocks were hot from the inside out and dust devils hummed unnaturally. And each time there was another nuclear test, ravens watched the desert heave. Stretch marks appeared. The land was losing its muscle.

The women couldn't bear it any longer. They were mothers. They had suffered labor pains but always under the promise of birth. The red hot pains beneath the desert promised death only, as each bomb became a stillborn. A contract had been made and broken between human beings and the land. A new contract was being drawn by the women, who understood the fate of the earth as their own.

Under the cover of darkness, ten women slipped under a barbed-wire fence and entered the contaminated country. They were trespassing. They walked toward the town of Mercury, in moonlight, taking their cues from coyote, kit fox, antelope squirrel, and quail. They moved quietly and deliberately through the maze of Joshua trees. When a hint of daylight appeared they rested, drinking tea and sharing their rations of food. The women closed their eyes. The time had come to protest with the heart, that to deny one's genealogy with the earth was to commit treason against one's soul.

At dawn, the women draped themselves in mylar, wrapping long streamers of silver plastic around their arms to blow in the breeze. They wore clear masks, that became the faces of humanity. And when they arrived at edge of Mercury, they carried all the butterflies of a summer day in their wombs. They paused to allow their courage to settle.

The town that forbids pregnant women and children to enter because of radiation risks was asleep. The women moved through the streets as winged messengers, twirling around each other in slow motion, peeking inside homes and watching the easy sleep of men and women. They were astonished by such stillness and periodically would utter a shrill note or low cry just to verify life.

The residents finally awoke to these strange apparitions. Some simply stared. Others called authorities, and in time, the women were apprehended by wary soldiers dressed in desert fatigues. They were taken to a white, square building on the other edge of Mercury. When asked who they were and why they were there, the women replied, "We are mothers and we have come to reclaim the desert for our children."

The soldiers arrested them. As the ten women were blindfolded and handcuffed, they began singing:

You can't forbid us everything
You can't forbid us to think—
You can't forbid our tears to flow
And you can't stop the songs that we sing.

The women continued to sing louder and louder, until they heard the voices of their sisters moving across the mesa:

Ah ne nah, nah
nin nah nah—
Ah ne nah, nah
nin nah nah—
Nyaga mutzi
oh ne nay—
Nyaga mutzi
oh ne nay—

"Call for reinforcements," one soldier said.

"We have," interrupted one woman, "we have—and you have no idea of our numbers."

I crossed the line at the Nevada Test Site and was arrested with nine other Utahns for trespassing on military lands. They are still conducting nuclear tests in the desert. Ours was an act of civil disobedience. But as I walked toward the town of Mercury, it was more than a gesture of peace. It was a gesture on behalf of the clan of One-Breasted Women.

As one officer cinched the handcuffs around my wrists, another frisked my body. She found a pen and a pad of paper tucked inside my left boot.

"And these?" she asked sternly.

"Weapons," I replied.

Our eyes met. I smiled. She pulled the leg of my trousers back over my boot.

"Step forward, please," she said as she took my arm.

We were booked under an afternoon sun and bused to Tonopah, Nevada. It was a two-hour ride. This was familiar country. The Joshua trees standing their ground had been named by my ancestors, who believed they looked like prophets pointing west to the Promised Land. These were the same trees that bloomed each spring, flowers appearing like white flames in the Mojave. And I recalled a full moon in May, when Mother and I had walked among them, flushing out mourning doves and owls.

The bus stopped short of town. We were released.

The officials thought it was a cruel joke to leave us stranded in the desert with no way to get home. What they didn't realize was that we were home, soul-centered and strong, women who recognized the sweet smell of sage as fuel for our spirits.

Terry Tempest Williams

Much of Terry Tempest Williams' writing explores how the natural landscape affects us, both politically and personally. She is best known for her book Refuge: An Unnatural History of Family and Place. *Her other books include a collection of essays,* An Unspoken Hunger, Desert Quartet: An Erotic Landscape, Leap, *and* Red: Patience and Passion in the Desert. *She has also written two children's books,* The Secret Language of Snow *and* Between Cattails. *Her essays have appeared in numerous publications, including the* New Yorker, *the* Nation, Outside, Orion, *the* Iowa Review, *and* Audubon, *and she edited the book* Testimony: Writers Speak on Behalf of Utah Wilderness. *She has served on the Governing Council of the Wilderness Society and as naturalist-in-residence at the Utah Museum of Natural History, and today she serves on the advisory board of the National Parks and Conservation Association, The Nature Conservatory, and the Southern Utah Wilderness Alliance. Williams has received many awards, among them induction to the Rachel Carson Honor Roll and the National Wildlife Federation's Conservation Award for Special Achievement. Born in Corona, California in 1955, she lives in Castle Valley, Utah.*

The Death of the Moth

Virginia Woolf

Moths that fly by day are not properly to be called moths; they do not
excite that pleasant sense of dark autumn nights and ivy-blossom
which the commonest yellow-underwing asleep in the shadow of the
curtain never fails to rouse in us. They are hybrid creatures, neither
gay like butterflies nor sombre like their own species. Nevertheless
the present specimen, with his narrow hay-coloured wings, fringed
with a tassel of the same colour, seemed to be content with life. It was
a pleasant morning, mid-September, mild, benignant, yet with a
keener breath than that of the summer months. The plough was already scoring the field opposite the window, and where the share had
been, the earth was pressed flat and gleamed with moisture. Such
vigour came rolling in from the fields and the down beyond that it
was difficult to keep the eyes strictly turned upon the book. The rooks
too were keeping one of their annual festivities; soaring round the
tree tops until it looked as if a vast net with thousands of black knots
in it had been cast up into the air; which, after a few moments sank
slowly down upon the trees until every twig seemed to have a knot at
the end of it. Then, suddenly, the net would be thrown into the air
again in a wider circle this time, with the utmost clamour and vocifer-
ation, as though to be thrown into the air and settle slowly down
upon the tree tops were a tremendously exciting experience.

The same energy which inspired the rooks, the ploughmen, the horses, and even, it seemed, the lean bare-backed downs, sent the moth fluttering from side to side of his square of the window-pane. One could not help watching him. One was, indeed, conscious of a queer feeling of pity for him. The possibilities of pleasure seemed that morning so enormous and so various that to have only a moth's part in life, and a day moth's at that, appeared a hard fate, and his zest in enjoying his meagre opportunities to the full, pathetic. He flew vigorously to one corner of his compartment, and, after waiting there a second, flew across to the other. What remained for him but to fly to a third corner and then to a fourth? That was all he could do, in spite of the size of the downs, the width of the sky, the far-off smoke of houses, and the romantic voice, now and then, of a steamer out at sea. What he could do he did. Watching him, it seemed as if a fibre, very thin but pure, of the enormous energy of the world had been thrust into his frail and diminutive body. As often as he crossed the pane, I could fancy that a thread of vital light became visible. He was little or nothing but life.

Yet, because he was so small, and so simple a form of the energy that was rolling in at the open window and driving its way through so many narrow and intricate corridors in my own brain and in those of other human beings, there was something marvellous as well as pathetic about him. It was as if someone had taken a tiny bead of pure life and decking it as lightly as possible with down and feathers, had set it dancing and zigzagging to show us the true nature of life. Thus displayed one could not get over the strangeness of it. One is apt to forget all about life, seeing it humped and bossed and garnished and cumbered so that it has to move with the greatest circumspection and dignity. Again, the thought of all that life might have been had he been born in any other shape caused one to view his simple activities with a kind of pity.

After a time, tired by his dancing apparently, he settled on the window ledge in the sun, and, the queer spectacle being at an end, I forgot about him. Then, looking up, my eye was caught by him. He was trying to resume his dancing, but seemed either so stiff or so awkward that he could only flutter to the bottom of the window-pane; and when he tried to fly across it he failed. Being intent on other matters I watched these futile attempts for a time without thinking, unconsciously waiting for him to resume his flight, as one waits for a machine, that has stopped momentarily, to start again without considering the reason of its failure. After perhaps a seventh attempt he slipped from the wooden ledge and fell, fluttering his wings, on to his back on the window sill. The helplessness of his attitude roused me. It flashed upon me that he was in difficulties; he could no longer raise himself; his legs struggled vainly. But, as I stretched out a pencil, meaning to help him to right himself, it came over me that the failure and awkwardness were the approach of death. I laid the pencil down again.

The legs agitated themselves once more. I looked as if for the enemy against which he struggled. I looked out of doors. What had happened there? Presumably it was mid-day, and work in the fields had stopped. Stillness and quiet had replaced the previous animation. The birds had taken themselves off to feed in the brooks. The horses stood still. Yet the power was there all the same, massed outside indifferent, impersonal, not attending to anything in particular. Somehow it was opposed to the little hay-coloured moth. It was useless to try to do anything. One could only watch the extraordinary efforts made by those tiny legs against an oncoming doom which could, had it chosen, have submerged an entire city, not merely a city, but masses of human beings; nothing, I knew had any chance against death. Nevertheless after a pause of exhaustion the legs fluttered again. It was superb this last protest, and so frantic that he succeeded at last in righting himself. One's sympathies, of course, were all on the side of life. Also, when there was nobody to care or to know, this gigantic effort on the part of an insignificant little moth, against a power of such magnitude, to retain what no one else valued or desired to keep, moved one strangely. Again, somehow, one saw life, a pure bead. I lifted the pencil again, useless though I knew it to be. But even as I did so, the unmistakable tokens of death showed themselves. The body relaxed, and instantly grew stiff. The struggle was over. The insignificant little creature now knew death. As I looked at the dead moth, this minute wayside triumph of so great a force over so mean an antagonist filled me with wonder. Just as life had been strange a few minutes before, so death was now as strange. The moth having righted himself now lay most decently and uncomplainingly composed. O yes, he seemed to say, death is stronger than I am.

Virginia Woolf

Virginia Woolf was born in 1882 in London. One of the most influential and experimental authors of the twentieth century, she revolutionized the conventions of narrative structure and form in the British novel. A member of the Bloomsbury Group, she also co-founded the Hogarth Press with her husband Leonard; they published many groundbreaking Modernist works, including the first edition of T. S. Eliot's The Waste Land. *Woolf herself is the author of nine novels, including* To the Lighthouse, Orlando, *and* The Waves. *She is also well-known for her extended essay* A Room of One's Own, *based on her lectures at a woman's college at Cambridge, wherein she discusses "the question of women and fiction." Woolf began writing reviews and articles for the* Times Literary Supplement *and other periodicals in 1906 and earned a steady income from this throughout her life. Her essays were collected in two volumes,* The Common Reader, *Vols. 1 and 2. Woolf struggled with depression throughout her life, and in 1941 she died, a suicide by drowning.*

Credits

Text Credits

Atwood, Margaret, "Nine Beginnings." Copyright © 1990 by Margaret Atwood. Reprinted with permission from Phoebe Larmore Literary Agency.

Baker, Will, "My Children Explain the Big Issues," *Whole Earth Review, #79,* Summer 1993. Copyright © 1993 Will Baker. Used with permission.

Baldwin, James, from *Notes of a Native Son.* Copyright © 1949, 1951, 1953, 1954, 1955 by James Baldwin. Reprinted by permission of Beacon Press, Inc.

Bausch, Richard, "So Long Ago." Copyright © 1999 by Richard Bausch. Reprinted from *Graywolf Forum 3: The Business of Memory* with the permission of Graywolf Press, Saint Paul, Minnesota.

Beard, Jo Ann, "The Fourth State of Matter" from *The Boys of My Youth.* Copyright © 1998 by Jo Ann Beard. By permission of Little, Brown and Company, Inc.

Berry, Wendell, "An Entrance to the Woods," from *Recollected Essays,* 1965–1980. Copyright © 1981 Wendell Berry. Reprinted by permission of the author.

Cooper, Bernard, "The Fine Art of Sighing" from *Truth Serum.* Copyright © 1996 by Bernard Cooper. Reprinted by permission of International Creative Management, Inc.

Dickinson, Emily, poem 1129, "Tell It Slant." Reprinted by permission of the publishers and the Trustees of Amherst College from *The Poems of Emily Dickinson,* Thomas H. Johnson. Ed., Cambridge, Mass.: The Belknap Press of Harvard University Press. Copyright 1951, 1955, © 1979 by the President and Fellows of Harvard College.

Didion, Joan, "Goodbye to All That," from *Slouching Towards Bethlehem.* Copyright © 1966, 1968, renewed 1996 by Joan Didion. Reprinted by permission of Farrar, Straus and Giroux, LLC.

Dillard, Annie, "Total Eclipse" from *Teaching a Stone to Talk: Expeditions and Encounters* by Annie Dillard. Copyright © 1982 by Annie Dillard. Reprinted by permission of HarperCollins Publishers Inc.

Duncan, David James, "The Mickey Mantle Koan" from *River Teeth: Stories and Writings* by David James Duncan. Copyright © 1995 by David James Duncan. Used by permission of Doubleday, a division of Random House, Inc.

Dunn, Stephen, "Little Essay on Form" from *Walking Light: Essays & Memoirs,* New and Expanded Edition. Copyright © 1993, 2001 by Stephen Dunn. Reprinted with the permission of BOA Editions, Ltd.

Fisher, M.F.K., "The Measure of My Powers" and "A Thing Shared" from

A Life Through Meals and *The Art of Eating*. Copyright © M.F.K. Fisher. Reprinted by permission of Hungry Minds, Inc.

Geisel, Ted, from *One Fish, Two Fish, Red Fish, Blue Fish* by Dr. Seuss®, and copyright © 1960 by Dr. Seuss Enterprises, L.P., renewed 1988. Used by permission of Random House Children's Books, a division of Random House, Inc.

Goldbarth, Albert, "After Yitzl" from *A Sympathy of Souls*. Copyright © 1990 by Albert Goldbarth. Reprinted with the permission of Coffee House Press, Minneapolis.

Gordon, Mary, "Notes on Pierre Bonnard and My Mother's Ninetieth Birthday," *Harper's,* December 1998. Copyright © 1998 Mary Gordon. Reprinted by permission of Sterling Lord Literistic.

Hemley, Robin, "Reading History to My Mother" from *The Fourth Genre*. Copyright © 1999, 2003 Robin Hemley. Used by permission of the author.

Iyer, Pico, "Where Worlds Collide," *Harper's,* August 1995. Copyright © 1995 by Harper's Magazine. All rights reserved. Reproduced from the August issue by special permission.

Kingston, Maxine Hong, "No Name Woman" from *The Woman Warrior* by Maxine Hong Kingston. Copyright © 1975, 1976 by Maxine Hong Kingston. Used by permission of Alfred A. Knopf, a division of Random House, Inc.

Lamott, Anne, "Why I Don't Meditate" from *Yoga Journal*. Copyright © 1998 by Anne Lamott. Reprinted with permission of The Wylie Agency, Inc.

Miller, Brenda, Sections of the Writing the Arts chapter appeared previously, in slightly different form, in "Prologue to a Sad Spring" by Brenda Miller in *Season of the Body,* Sarabande Books, 2002; Sections of the Lyric Essay chapter appeared previously, in slightly different form, in "A Braided Heart: Shaping the Lyric Essay" by Brenda Miller in *Writing Creative Nonfiction,* edited by Philip Gerard and Carolyn Forche, Story Press, 2001.

Morabito, Fabio, "File and Sandpaper" and "Screws" from *Toolbox*. Copyright © Bloomsbury Publishing. Used with permission.

Mukherjee, Bharati, "The Four-Hundred-Year-Old Woman." Copyright © Bharati Mukherjee. Reprinted by permission of Janklow & Nesbit.

Price, Jennifer, "A Brief Natural History of the Plastic Pink Flamingo" from *Flight Maps*. Copyright © 1999 by Jennifer Price. Reprinted by permission of Basic Books, a member of Perseus Books, L.L.C.

Rekdal, Paisley, "The Night My Mother Met Bruce Lee," from *The Night My Mother Met Bruce Lee* by Paisley Rekdal. Copyright © 2000 by Paisley Rekdal. Used by permission of Pantheon Books, a division of Random House, Inc.

Rider, Bhanu Kapil, "Three Voices" from *The Vertical Interrogation of Strangers*. Copyright © Bhanu Kapil. Published by Kelsey St. Press.

Sanders, Scott Russell, "Buckeye." Copyright © 1995 by Scott Russell Sanders. First published in *Orion,* collected in the author's *Writing from the Center,* Indiana University Press, 1995. Reprinted by permission of the author.

Sedaris, David, "The Drama Bug" from *Naked*. Copyright © 1997 by David Sedaris. By permission of Little, Brown and Company, Inc.

Photo Credits

Index